CONTEMPORARY BUSINESS REPORT WRITING

CONTEMPORARY BUSINESS REPORT WRITING

Second Edition

IRIS I. VARNER

Illinois State University

The Dryden Press
Harcourt Brace Jovanovich College Publishers
Fort Worth   Philadelphia   San Diego
New York   Orlando   Austin   San Antonio
Toronto   Montreal   London   Sydney   Tokyo

Acquisitions Editor: Robert Gemin
Project Editor: Karen Hill
Design Manager: Alan Wendt
Production Manager: Barb Bahnsen
Permissions Editor: Cindy Lombardo
Director of Editing, Design, and Production: Jane Perkins
Text and Cover Designer: Stuart Paterson, Image House Inc.
Copy Editor: Jean Berry
Indexer: Leoni McVey
Compositor: Trade Composition Systems, Inc.
Text Type: 10/12 ITC Garamond Light

Library of Congress Cataloging-in-Publication Data

Varner, Iris I.
    Contemporary business report writing/Iris I. Varner.—2nd ed.
      p.   cm.
    Includes bibliographical references.
    ISBN 0-03-033289-3
    1. Business report writing.   I. Title.
    HF5719.V37   1991
    808'.06665—dc20   90-2808

Printed in the United States of America
  2-040-98765432
Copyright © 1991, 1987 by The Dryden Press

Requests for permission to make copies of any part of the work
should be mailed to: Permissions Department, Harcourt Brace
Jovanovich, Publishers, 8th Floor, Orlando, Florida 32887.

Address orders:
The Dryden Press
Orlando, FL 32887

4 5 6 7 8 9 - 040 - 9876543

The Dryden Press
Holt, Rinehart and Winston
Saunders College Publishing

To Carson

PREFACE

In survey after survey business people indicate the increasing importance of effective written communication. Technological developments in the workplace have given managers the ability to generate more and more written communications and distribute this information to ever larger audiences. Anyone who wants a successful career in business must be able to communicate effectively.

Well-written reports are essential in disseminating the information needed to make sound and timely business decisions. In a good report the format draws the reader's attention to important points, headings provide a framework for the text, and visuals clarify information and support key concepts. The text is clear, precise, and accurate. Conclusions and recommendations are valid and follow logically from the analysis of the data presented in the report.

Contemporary Business Report Writing leads students through the process of preparing effective business reports. Numerous examples illustrate the principles of good report writing applicable to an array of business professions, from marketing analysts and accountants to financial consultants and managers. This text will help students to become better communicators—to solve problems, to present ideas persuasively, and to evaluate alternatives.

ORGANIZATION

The chapters in this edition are divided into parts that reflect the major steps in the writing of business reports. In the first part, "Fundamentals of Business Reports," students study the influence of business organizations on the writing of reports. Students also examine the communication process as it relates to report writing.

To be effective, a report must reflect the audience for which it is intended. The second part, "The Language of Business Reports," presents the principles of effective writing, the writing process, and ethical dimensions of business report writing.

Good writers plan their reports thoroughly. Part III, "The Preparation of Business Reports," presents classification and format systems. It introduces students to the planning process and outlining systems. The part ends by focusing on short reports and their myriad uses.

Before managers can write reports, they must collect and analyze data. Part IV, "Research for Business Reports," presents the fundamentals for secondary and primary research, emphasizing the aspects of research and documentation of sources the business writer must consider.

To be useful, data must be meaningful. Statistics can be helpful in analyzing data, but the writers cannot rely solely on numbers. They must examine quantitative and qualitative aspects of the available information. Part V, "Evaluation of Data," discusses how to interpret information, draw conclusions, and make recommendations.

The final part, "Presentation of Business Reports," discusses the visual presentation of information, the format for the long formal report, and the oral presentation of business reports.

CHANGES IN THE SECOND EDITION

In its first edition, *Contemporary Business Report Writing* was one of the first textbooks to include extensive coverage of writing with a computer, the international dimensions of business communications, and the ethical aspects of report writing. These topics remain strengths of the second edition.

Computers are an integral part of business writing today. They have changed the way managers write, revise, and present documents. To reflect the importance of word processing on all aspects of report writing, the chapter on computers has been integrated throughout the text. The discussion of planning, writing, and editing with the computer has been integrated in Part II, largely in Chapter 4, "The Writing Process." Coverage of computer software for graphics and secondary research has been increased to reflect new developments.

With the international dimension of American business increasing—the major changes to Western Europe that will occur in 1992, the recent dramatic changes in Eastern European countries, and increasing investment in the United States by Japan and other countries—business writers must know how to communicate with business people from other cultures. International coverage has been integrated throughout the text to indicate the importance of international adaptation in constructing effective reports. International coverage is highlighted through the use of a logo, which draws attention to this important area.

The ethical aspects of writing have been moved earlier in the text, to Chapter 5, so these principles can be considered and applied throughout the report-writing process described in the text.

TEXT FEATURES

Each chapter begins with a list of learning objectives. These learning objectives are reviewed and expanded upon in the summaries at the end of the chapter to give students an excellent study tool for the key concepts presented. Key terms are highlighted in bold in the body of the text and also defined in the margins to reinforce all definitions. New to the second edition are separate "Questions and Discussion Points" and "Exercises" sections. Many new problems have been added to give students an opportunity to apply chapter concepts. Finally, end-of-text cases help integrate the material for the course. This section provides a number of cases that include all the data and information needed to write a report, as well as cases that require the student to perform secondary research, primary research, or both to complete the assignment.

To help professors plan for teaching this course, the *Instructor's Manual* that accompanies this textbook provides sample syllabi, suggestions for approaching each chapter, a complete set of test questions, and transparency masters.

ACKNOWLEDGMENTS

The second edition of *Contemporary Business Report Writing* would not have been possible without the help and support of my family, friends, and colleagues. A special thanks to Paula Pomerenke, who gave invaluable advice and tested the new edition in her classes. I am indebted to my graduate assistants, Eric Hoss and Eileen Ni, who proofed the text and did much of the detailed background checking. I want to thank my many friends from business and industry who provided examples and advice on actual business practice.

I particularly appreciate the support of my students, who were willing to try the new edition and give feedback.

A special thanks to the reviewers of the manuscript. They worked very hard and made many suggestions that I incorporated into the second edition.

Doris L. Cost, Metropolitan State College
Robert F. Litro, Mahatuck Community College
Oscar H. Schuette, Metropolitan State College

Last, but not least, I want to thank the people at The Dryden Press: Robert Gemin, Karen Hill, Alan Wendt, Jean Berry, Barb Bahnsen, and Cindy Lombardo. When things got rough, the enthusiasm and support of Robert Gemin helped me continue with the task.

Iris I. Varner
Illinois State University
September 1990

ABOUT THE AUTHOR

Iris I. Varner, Ph.D. from the University of Oklahoma, is Professor of Business Communication at Illinois State University. She has published numerous articles in the field of business communication. She is very active in the areas of writing with the computer, business ethics, and international dimensions of business communication. Varner is an active member of the Association of Business Communication, with past service on numerous committees and the board of directors. She consults for a variety of national and international firms.

CONTENTS

PART I

FUNDAMENTALS OF BUSINESS REPORTS

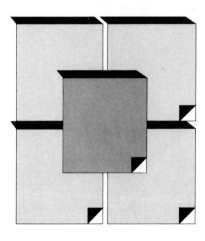

ORIENTATION TO BUSINESS REPORTS

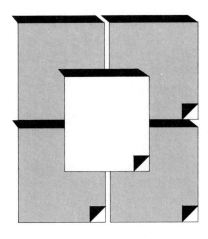

Learning Objectives

- To understand the role of reports in modern business organizations.
- To understand the influence of global expansion on report writing.
- To examine and define the basic characteristics of business reports.
- To become aware of the differences between business reports and term papers.
- To recognize the importance of good report-writing skills in career development.

THE ROLE OF REPORTS IN ORGANIZATIONS

Why Do Businesses Need Reports?

Report writing has been important to business since writing began. During the 1970s archaeologists unearthed clay tablets in Syria that are among the oldest written documents discovered so far. Most of these tablets are tax records, inventory accounts, and records of business transactions. Similarly, many reports today, such as balance sheets and income statements, provide historical data and records; but, increasingly, modern reports also help in planning and decision making.

Every year American businesses, government agencies, and nonprofit organizations produce thousands of reports. Although these reports are expensive to write, duplicate, and file, their number is increasing. This growth is a direct result of changes in the size and organization of businesses, global expansion, government requirements, technology, and legal considerations.

Business Size and Organization.   In a small business much less need exists for written reports than in a large business. Let us assume Greta Hillstrom has a small tailoring business in Pleasant Hills, Illinois. She employs five women as seamstresses. Greta herself keeps the books, distributes the work, and meets with customers. When necessary, she will also help with the sewing.

In this environment Greta will communicate directly with her employees. If Mrs. Perry brings in material for a new suit, Greta will discuss the project with her. She may take Mrs. Perry to a particular seamstress for details, or she may jot down basic instructions, but most communication in this environment is oral. If Susan starts the work on Mrs. Perry's suit and later Natasha finishes it, Susan will most likely give oral instructions to Natasha. The environment is informal, and the owner-manager is easily accessible.

Business Expansion
Managers in large businesses write more reports than managers in small businesses.

As the small **business expands** into a factory, the personal contact between the owner and the workers changes. To guarantee a smooth and efficient production process, Greta must hire supervisors and managers for finance, personnel, marketing, and production. The factory is divided into smaller manageable units. Now Greta will communicate directly with the heads of the various areas, and her direct contact with the seamstresses will decrease. Much of the communication will be indirect, and much of it will be in written form.

As Exhibits 1.1 and 1.2 illustrate, the need for written reports increases as the company grows. As layers are added to the organizational structure, the direct contact between upper management and workers diminishes. The workers know their supervisors, and they may occasionally talk to the department head, but they will rarely see the person above that level.

If a company has operations in several locations, written reports save time. If the officers of a steel company need information on the production process in the foundry, they could go directly to the foundry, but that would be time consuming, especially if the foundry is in another part of town. Requesting a written report from the foundry might be much more efficient.

Exhibit 1.1   Direct Communication

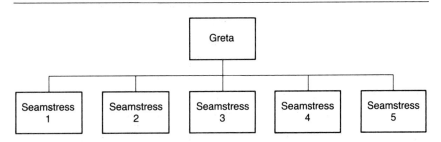

Reports help to improve company performance. Let us assume upper management has decided that improving competitiveness is a major goal for the coming year. Before it can be improved, management must have current information on competitors, equipment, price of raw materials, production costs, and customer satisfaction. Obtaining this information would involve visiting a number of areas in the company and talking to many people. Although a personal visit may eventually be necessary, the time such a visit would require might not be spent effectively on a preliminary report. At the beginning management can request a report from the production department. The production manager, in turn, can contact the other appropriate departments. Each department can ask the people who are most knowledgeable to prepare a report.

Good reports contribute to efficiency. They provide management with the information necessary to make appropriate decisions.

Exhibit 1.2   Communication in a Large Organization

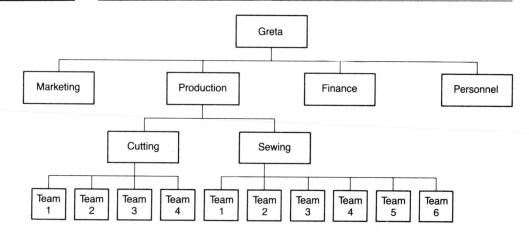

Global Expansion. *The Influence of Distance on Business Reporting.* As companies grow, they frequently maintain branches in many different locations. As divisions and subsidiaries spread around the globe, management faces new communication challenges. With the advances in satellite technology and fiber optics, people take instant communication for granted. Until recently, however, global communication was slow and often dangerous. For example, Columbus took 70 days to make the trip from Spain to the Americas. Nobody in Spain knew what happened to the expedition until the Niña and the Pinta returned to Spain almost eight months after Columbus had left. All this has changed.

Today a letter from New York takes no longer to reach Frankfurt, Germany, than Austin, Texas. A manager from Chicago can call a partner in Tokyo or Sydney to discuss business opportunities. Telex and facsimile make even instant written communication possible. Contact with foreign business is faster, cheaper, and more frequent than at any other time in history.

The personal visit and the face-to-face exchange of ideas are very important in international business. These personal meetings can become even more productive if the meeting partners have prepared themselves by reading proposals, position statements, and expansion plans ahead of time.

Written reports are also important because geographic distance, spanning many time zones, often makes telephone conversations impractical. For example, the time difference between Chicago and Tokyo allows for no overlapping business hours. If business partners in these cities want to communicate, they must arrange for telephone calls, send reports via fax or telex, or travel.

The Influence of Organizational Structure on Reporting. Report writers must be aware of the **organizational structures** of many international companies and their influence on report writing and general communication practices. Traditionally, companies have had an international division in charge of all international activities including marketing, finance, accounting, and management. This organizational structure has sometimes interfered with important and necessary communication.

Organizational Structure
Many international businesses are changing their structures to facilitate international operations.

As an example, Laura Bozich has worked in marketing at her company's headquarters in Chicago for five years. She knows the marketing people well and is familiar with the company's overall marketing strategy, marketing philosophy, and advertising practices. Laura, who speaks Portuguese, is assigned to work in Brazil. She reports to the manager in charge of South American operations in São Paulo. He, in turn, is responsible to the vice president of the international division in Chicago. As Laura considers a marketing problem in Brazil, should she go through channels or directly contact her friends in Chicago? From Chicago she may receive a quick answer; at least she can discuss the problem with the marketing people she knows. Going through channels may require waiting for an answer. However, the manager in charge of Latin America has experience with solving Latin American problems, and, in any case, Laura needs to keep him informed of what she does so that he can develop a unified approach to marketing in Latin America.

Because of problems in choosing the appropriate channel for communication, many multinational companies are reorganizing. They are internationalizing all areas of the company by abolishing their international divisions. With the new arrangement, marketing people from the subsidiary contact marketing people at headquarters; finance people contact finance people rather than someone in an international division. As a result, more people will write reports in an increasingly international environment and must be familiar with the international dimensions.

Business will in all likelihood be even more international in the next 40 years than it is now, and you may work in international business whether you choose to or not. Some experts predict that all business will someday be international. Even today an increasing number of medium and small companies engage in importing and exporting. To work in international business, you do not have to work overseas. With the revolution in transportation and communications, you can do business with any business person in the world without leaving your desk.

Many banks are involved in international loans to help finance projects of foreign companies in this country or to provide money to American companies wishing to expand overseas. Even the investment departments of insurance companies look at overseas opportunities because, at present, one half of all equity investments are overseas.

International communication concerns transcend the areas of international relations, advertising, and marketing. If you plan a career in banking or insurance, you may communicate with people from other countries and cultures. Your success will depend not only on your technical expertise but also your ability to communicate successfully with these people in writing.

Even domestic business in the United States is becoming more and more international. As more Asians and Hispanics enter the United States, the cultural mix in the country is changing. As a result, companies must address an increasing cultural variety in the workforce and in the market. A major American insurance company, for example, has started to conduct seminars for its employees to deal with the cultural mix of employees and policyholders.

Values and Attitudes
Values and attitudes influence the number and the organization of reports.

The Influence of Attitudes and Cultural Practices on Reporting.   American **values and attitudes** have also led to an increase in written reports. Americans are number oriented. They want to know where they stand and want to have records of decisions and recommendations. Not all cultures share this desire for detailed records and multiple copies. People in Japan and the Middle East, for example, regard business as a personal relationship. To request or provide detailed specifications or detailed records of all transactions might be seen as cold and impersonal and could hinder the development of trust. American business people, in order to be successful in the international environment, may have to change their report-writing practices.

Oriental Cultures
Business people in cultures with complex languages and writing systems write fewer reports.

Another reason why **Oriental cultures** do not emphasize written reports is that in Japan and China the writing of reports is much more time consuming and cumbersome than in the United States. Written Chinese uses characters that stand for complete words, expressions, or even short sentences. Chinese, which does not have an alphabet and is written from top to bottom and right to left, does not lend itself to the use of typewriters.

A Chinese typewriter needs 4,000 to 5,000 characters to be of any practical use in business. Such a typewriter takes up much space and is difficult to use. For example, Taiwan Normal University in Taipei, Taiwan, has only one Chinese typewriter, which is used for important and official occasions. One secretary in the university knows how to operate it. All memos within the university and most reports and correspondence to the outside are written by hand. Writing by hand is faster and more economical, although it takes much longer than typing a memo in English. Computers, even though they simplify the process, are still complex.

As in China, writing in Japan has traditionally been very slow and cumbersome. The Japanese use three different writing systems: *Kanji,* the Chinese-based characters; *Katakana,* a syllabary used for loan words from abroad; and *Hiragana,* a syllabary for Japanese words. Japanese computers are designed to use *Hiragana* for keyboarding. The computer can then convert the data from *Hiragana* to *Kanji.* The syllabary has undoubtedly facilitated the development and use of Japanese computers, but whether it will increase the number of written reports prepared by Japanese companies remains to be seen.

Filing Practices

Traditional filing systems in some countries make it difficult to retrieve reports.

The number of reports produced is also influenced by the **filing practices** in use. Horizontal filing systems, which are used in America and most industrial countries, encourage written reports, because they are easy to store and retrieve. Modern American filing systems go back about 100 years. In the Middle East files are traditionally stored vertically. Folders are simply stacked on top of one another. When I visited a government office in Baghdad, for example, all the files containing visa applications and records were in piles about three feet high on the floor. When a foreign traveler applied for a visa extension, the official checked the passport to see when the visa was granted. A clerk then checked one of the piles to locate the file. After the official prepared the necessary documents for the extension, the clerk returned the folder to the pile. It is hardly surprising that files are not checked often and that only the most necessary documents are kept.

Lack of an alphabet as in Japan and China also complicates filing systems and cuts down on report writing and report storage.

The approach to filing also differs from culture to culture. In the United States documents remain in the department that receives them. If Cheryl Huenink, for example, is transferred from production to personnel, the production reports that she wrote or received, while she worked in production, stay in the production department. This is not true in traditional Indian companies. In India, Cheryl would take the reports with her to her new position. Anyone who later needed to refer to a production report from that period would first have to determine that Cheryl was the production manager.

Americans use reports in planning and making business decisions. Americans are goal oriented, accustomed to looking ahead and shaping the future in their favor. In Islamic countries planning is frowned upon because the future is in Allah's hands. To plan is considered presumptuous and equated to playing God. Any planning documents must take Islamic attitudes toward planning into consideration. The American business person must be aware of these cultural influences on report writing.

Government Requirements
The government requires companies to submit reports in many areas.

Government Requirements. The **government requires** reports in order to make certain that businesses obey the law. Business people file numerous reports with the Occupational Safety and Health Administration (OSHA), the Internal Revenue Service, the Environmental Protection Agency, the Equal Employment Opportunity Commission, the Security and Exchange Commission, and many other agencies. Government reports require much detail and supporting information.

Charles Cecil, the president of a medium-sized canning factory, complains frequently about all the reporting he has to do. In his opinion he could cut down the number of clerks and accountants he employs if he did not have to file so many reports. The types of reports he must submit include tax and income reports to the IRS. He also has to make certain that his company keeps detailed records on the hiring and promotion of employees to prove that the company follows affirmative action guidelines. OSHA representatives come regularly for plant inspections, and he must have reports ready to show that the plant meets safety regulations. For workmen's compensation he has to prepare additional reports.

When the plant was expanded a few years ago, Cecil had to furnish an environmental impact study to show that the plant did not disturb a wildlife refuge close by. At this point he is thinking of using a new canning process. The process will have to be approved by authorities and thus will involve more reports. In addition, the company has to file reports with local and state authorities. Charles Cecil's grandfather, who founded the company, would be surprised to see the amount of paperwork involved in running a canning factory today.

Technology
Technology has had a tremendous impact on the writing of reports.

Technology. **Technology** is a modern ally in the communication process. When the Egyptians prepared business reports, clerks wrote on papyrus rolls. Reports were handwritten until Gutenberg developed the modern printing press in the middle of the 15th century, revolutionizing written communication. The 19th century gave us modern record systems and the typewriter. Our century has given us the ability to transmit messages, not only by pen and paper and the U.S. postal service, but also by telephone, telegraph, satellite, modem, and computer. The table in Exhibit 1.3 shows when new types of equipment and supplies were introduced into offices.

Today, word-processing equipment and microcomputers are changing the work of the secretary, but the influence of the technology does not stop there. New equipment is beginning to influence the structure of the organization and to change the role of both the manager and the secretary.

Traditionally a business person wrote reports in longhand and gave them to a secretary. At the beginning of his career he might share a secretary with several other people, but as he advanced in the corporation, he might ultimately have his own private secretary. The private secretary's many functions

Exhibit 1.3   Office Innovations

Carbon paper	1806
Typewriters	1872
Mimeograph machines	1875
Telephones	1877
Ballpoint pens	1938
Electric computers	1946
Dry-duplicating machines	1950
Mass-produced computers	1951
Word-processing equipment	1976
Local area networks	1979
Integrated office automation	1982

Source: Rothman, S., & Mosman, C. (1985). *Computer uses and issues,* p. 243. Chicago: Science Research Association.

included typing, editing, and proofreading. In other instances secretaries wrote reports from rough notes. It was generally understood that a manager's time was too valuable to be spent typing. A manager did not need keyboarding skills. If the manager decided to make any changes in the final copy, the secretary retyped the entire report.

Self-correcting cartridges and memory typewriters brought significant changes and made life easier for the secretary. Now the secretary did not have to retype an entire page because of a typographical error, although even a memory typewriter did not permit the rearrangement of material once it had been typed. The new typewriters did improve the appearance of reports and letters and saved some time. They did not, however, change the roles of the manager and the secretary in any significant way.

The traditional division of work was not questioned until the arrival of microcomputers, which are beginning to have a significant impact on many business organizations. As an example, Jeff Johnson, a manager in a large insurance company, no longer has a private secretary. He abolished that position shortly after he began using a microcomputer. He decided that the time of his former secretary, now an administrative assistant, was too valuable to be spent typing reports from longhand drafts. He now keys in his own reports, which a secretary will later finish and proofread. The report is typed only once.

The time that was formerly spent on retyping an entire report can now be used to make corrections and improvements. Of course, to write efficiently on the computer, the manager needs computer and keyboarding skills. In the future more and more businesses will probably look for good keyboarding skills in the people they hire. Research indicates that managers with poor keyboarding skills are reluctant to use the computer, and a computer assigned to a manager who does not use it is a waste of money. If you think that keyboarding wastes a manager's valuable time, consider that reports composed on the microcomputer require less time than those written out in longhand.

Writing with a microcomputer requires an understanding of word processing, which can be done on either a free-standing word processor or on a microcomputer with a word-processing software package. If the equipment is to be used strictly for typing and editing texts, a word processor may be the best choice because it is faster. If it will also be used for statistical calculations, graphs and tables, then a microcomputer is the best choice.

Free-standing, or dedicated, word processors are mostly used in word-processing centers. The word-processing center in that sense has replaced the typing pool. The report writer may bring the rough copy to the word-processing center, where secretaries type it and then return it for revision. The writer may also dictate the report into the word-processing center. The difference between this and the old typing pool is that corrections are easier to make. The report does not need to be retyped when the manager decides to rearrange paragraphs, change a phrase, or change a word. A word-processing center increases productivity, but it does not change the roles of people in the organization.

The effect of technology on the writing process is discussed in detail in Chapter 4.

Legal Aspects
Business reports must conform to the law.

Legal Considerations.   The report writer must be aware of the **legal aspects** of business reports. Although the company lawyer issues guidelines and instructions to ensure that no laws are violated, the lawyer cannot read every report an employee writes. All business people must, therefore, be familiar with the basics of business law.

As a manager you will be involved in hiring and promotion decisions, and you will periodically write evaluations of employees. You must be able to present the facts fairly and be aware of the legal and ethical implications of what you say in your reports. A careless report may lead to complaints or even legal action, upset your career, and damage the company's reputation. If you become a marketing specialist, you must know the laws regulating advertising and product claims to avoid costly litigation. The choice of words becomes crucial. Can you prove that your product is the best? Are your claims against the competition fair and justifiable? International marketing reports are even more complex because marketing and advertising laws are different from country to country. If you become an accountant, you must represent the financial performance of your company fairly and according to legal requirements.

When Marla Kelly negotiates a contract with another business, she must know that in the United States it is not enough to say, "I called in an order on the 15th." Marla should see to it that she has a written record of the order signed by both parties. Price, terms, and method of payment must be in writing. A handshake agreement will not be sufficient if she has trouble with the delivery.

Marla should know, however, that attitudes toward contracts vary from culture to culture. In the Middle East, for example, contracts are often verbal.

Even if the contract is in writing, it may not be considered binding. As the business climate changes, managers in some countries assume that the terms of the contract will also change. If Marla's firm submits a proposal for a joint venture or a production facility, she may find that, even after the proposal has been formally accepted, the terms are subject to renegotiation. If Marla refuses to discuss new terms, she shows that she does not understand business as practiced by the other party to the contract. She must learn to balance local customs with business practices and contract laws in the United States.

The ethical and legal aspects of writing are discussed in detail in Chapter 5.

Who Writes Reports?

Everyone writes reports. The typical business person spends 9 percent of the business day writing, 16 percent reading, 30 percent speaking, and 45 percent listening. Although these figures seem to indicate that writing is of no great importance, writing comprises a permanent record. Writing may provide the background for discussions, serve as the only source of information for other managers, or become the foundation for major decisions. Writing must be effective.

The types of reports a manager writes will change with career level and experience. For example, at the beginning of his career, a business person may write mostly short reports, and most of these reports will deal with aspects of his immediate department. As an example, John Grawe, who is the newly hired supervisor of a production line for dog food, will prepare reports relating to operations in his area, including production reports, personnel reports, and accident reports. At this stage in his career, John Grawe will not be asked to write reports that analyze broad company issues and policies. His contribution to those reports will be limited to factual information about his area of work.

For less complex situations people in beginning management positions may analyze information. If the production area for dog food wants to rearrange the office space, production can gather the information, analyze it, and make recommendations. John Grawe, for example, may be asked to examine such possibilities and recommend a solution.

As John Grawe advances to middle management, his reports will change. He will be fitting together pieces of information that he collects from lower level management and supervisors. He will then synthesize the information into one report and make recommendations. He can examine the productivity of the entire dog-food production area and work on coordination with sales and marketing.

As John Grawe reaches upper management, he increasingly will find that he is a user of reports written by others. He will base complex and far-reaching production decisions on the information he receives. Sometimes he may ask for recommendations; sometimes he may want only the analysis. At this stage in his career he does not collect information himself; he uses information.

As managers' jobs widen and their responsibilities grow, their reporting functions grow also.

Who Requests Reports?

Most report requests come from superiors because they need information to make decisions. The finished reports in that case go up in the organization.

Not all reports, however, are written because of a specific request. Policies, instructions, and announcements are usually sent down in the organization. These reports, which are often distributed in pamphlets, in handbooks, and on bulletin boards, are to inform employees of decisions made at higher levels.

Some unrequested reports may go up in the organization. For example, if you have noticed that the production process is not set up very efficiently and that with a few changes production could be improved, you may want to write a report. Because nobody asked for that report, you have to take great pains to sell your idea. You must support your recommendation with facts. You must provide figures on what it costs the company to keep the old process and how much the company could save by adopting your suggestion. Because others have not recognized the problem, you must describe the problem in great detail. This type of report is called a justification report. It is discussed in detail in Chapter 8.

Sometimes reports are requested by a person who is at the same level in the organization as the sender. For example, the marketing department and the collection department may exchange reports on a regular basis. If marketing would like to expand the number of credit card holders in order to increase sales, the collection area should be informed. As the number of credit card holders increases, the number of people who do not pay or pay late will probably increase also. Marketing and collections must cooperate by sharing plans and decisions through reports.

DEFINITION OF BUSINESS REPORTS

All good business reports share certain characteristics. They must be:

Do it necessary.

1. **Functional.** Many of the points we discuss in this text also apply to reports in science and the humanities, but the focus of this book is on the writing of useful business reports.

   A business report should help business people to make good decisions. It may simply provide the information for decisions, or it can analyze the information, draw conclusions, and make recommendations. In each case the report should help the company to become more productive and efficient.

Always Present Facts

2. **Factual.** Business decisions are based on facts, not on feelings. You must be able to substantiate your conclusions and recommendations. You may find the facts in company records; you may talk to fellow employees; you may do a survey or conduct an experiment. Your assumptions must be supported by correct and complete facts. If the facts are accurate and you have experience, you can make intelligent decisions and judgments. If you provide incorrect information, on the other hand, your company may lose thousands of dollars.

For example, if you are asked to recommend the purchase of new equipment, you will compare the cost of equipment. Based on your research, you may find that Machine A costs $10,500, Machine B costs $15,000, and Machine C costs $16,000. Based on just those figures, you may lean toward Machine A. But let us assume that the price for Machine A does not include installation costs, delivery costs, and first-year maintenance. Those items are, however, included in the price for Machines B and C. Once you add those costs to Machine A, the price may be higher than that for Machines B and C. The facts as first presented are not complete and, therefore, not correct.

3. **Objective.** A report must be objective in its presentation. Bias can creep in at many stages of the report-writing process. Before even starting the report the writer may have decided what the outcome should be. Such gross bias may be rare; more frequent are subtler biases. The writer may read research data selectively and subconsciously block out information that does not fit his bias. The writer may use vague or emotional words that will change the climate of the text. For example, the writer may use words such as *tremendous, great, fast, inferior,* and *superior* to describe products or business actions without substantiating the terms. Those words create a frame of reference in the mind of the reader that in some cases may not match the actual figures. A report that says "production increased by one percent in June" will create a different impression from one that says "production increased by a tremendous one percent in only one month."

4. **Precise.** "The cost is fairly high." "The new machinery will be needed soon." "The production quality improved quite a bit during last month." All of these are examples of vague writing or lack of precision. The reader does not know the meaning of *fairly high, soon,* or *quite a bit.* The writer should give specific numbers and dates. For example, the writer might say: "Machine X costs $25,000. This is $3,000 higher than was estimated six months ago." "The new machine will be needed by the end of March. The mechanics estimate that the current equipment will not last longer than two more months. Any repairs to the current machine are no longer cost effective. In addition, the machinery is outdated." "During the last month the rejection rate of products from Department B dropped from five percent to three percent." The specific examples not only provide numbers but also put them in perspective.

5. **Well Organized.** Good organization helps in reading. Logical presentation and development of material will help the reader to understand the report and to use the information in it. The organization you choose will depend on the purpose of your report and the needs of the reader.

6. **Clear.** The reader must understand a report after one reading. A writer can achieve clarity by using concrete words and correct sentence structure. A report that is not clear does not get its message across effectively and may cause the reader to simply give up before finishing it.

7. **Concise.** Business people are busy. They do not want to waste valuable time reading useless information. Reports should give the necessary information in as few words as possible. Conciseness and brevity are not necessarily the same, of course. For example, the preceding illustrations of precise writing are all longer than the vague ones. What many managers refuse to read is rambling reports.

8. **Adapted to Cultural Environment.** The modern report writer must be aware of different attitudes and practices around the globe. Gone are the days when the American approach to problem solving and communication was considered appropriate everywhere. The report writer must be knowledgeable about the various communication channels that can be helpful in effective worldwide communication.

9. **Attractive in Appearance.** Before the reader reads the report, he sees the report. A report that is visually appealing will give the impression of being well done. Although the reader may later decide that, despite the good appearance, the clear print, and the visual aids, the report is not well done, the reader initially approaches it with a positive attitude and reads at least part of it. A sloppy looking report may not generate the same goodwill at the beginning. In extreme cases it may not be read at all. Appearance is important, and modern office technology will help to set up reports, draw clear visual aids, and organize page layout.

A specific definition of business reports can be synthesized from these nine characteristics.

> A business report is an organized and objective presentation of facts needed to make effective business decisions in an increasingly global environment.

COMPARISON OF BUSINESS REPORTS AND TERM PAPERS

During your years in school and college, you have probably written a number of term papers.

Different Purposes
Term papers and business reports have different purposes.

Although the skills necessary to write a good term paper are prerequisites for writing a good business report, the two have **different purposes.** In traditional term papers the student writes to demonstrate what he has learned. The term paper shows that the student understands the material, that he can use and/or apply it. The student strives to demonstrate an ability to analyze information, to think critically, to collect and organize data, and to express ideas. In short, a term paper is a testimony to the student's knowledge and abilities.

A business report has a different objective. It has a practical purpose and is to help business in the decision-making process by providing pertinent data. The emphasis is on the usefulness of the message and not on the learning experience of the writer. The reader of the report, unlike the reader of the term paper, does not primarily use the report to judge the writer; he uses the information in the report to make business decisions. This purpose influences the presentation of the report. Business reports use headings, illustrations, and itemization to help the reader understand and remember the content.

IMPORTANCE OF REPORTS IN CAREER SUCCESS

The reports you write are important to the company you work for, the advancement of fellow employees, and your own career. The most important consideration is the usefulness of your reports to the company, of course. If the information and the analysis of material are clear, correct, and convincing, management can make appropriate decisions and, as a result, the company may prosper.

As you advance in your career, you may be asked to prepare personnel reports, recommendation reports, and evaluations of employees you know and have worked with. Your reports can influence the advancement of subordinates. If your recommendation is written well, your opinion will carry more weight. A well-organized and knowledgeable evaluation of the employee will be credible. A disorganized and poorly written report may not.

Well-written reports will not only benefit subordinates but will also reflect favorably on you. Even though the purpose of a report is not to demonstrate your writing ability, good reports will "silently" work for you. They may tell more about you than any verbal statements could. It pays to write good business reports. You receive satisfaction from doing a good job, and you may also obtain direct personal benefits.

The following examples illustrate how well-written business reports can help a corporation and advance the career of an individual.

Alfred Sloan

Alfred P. Sloan's great contribution to management was the concept of running a large, diversified company, such as General Motors, through decentralization. What is often overlooked is that in 1919, early in his career at GM, Sloan wrote down his ideas in a memorandum. This memorandum, called "The Organization Study," clearly and concisely laid out the concept of decentralization. After much discussion, the board of directors asked him to implement his ideas. Sloan was enormously successful in his more than 20 years as chief executive officer at GM. No matter how good his ideas were, they would never have attracted the directors' attention without that memo.

Harry B. Cunningham

Harry B. Cunningham took two years away from his operating responsibilities at S.S. Kresge Company (now K mart Corporation) in 1957 and 1958 to see what could be done to reverse the downward trend in Kresge's profitability. Kresge stores were historically located in downtown areas. They sold low-priced, low-margin items. Cunningham recommended in a comprehensive report that S.S. Kresge take advantage of the affluent suburban areas that had developed after World War II by shifting its strategy from the downtown stores to large, self-service discount department stores called K marts. After much deliberation by the board of directors, Cunningham's report won support for his plans. Like Sloan, Cunningham was entrusted with the job of implementing his profit-generating K mart strategy.

An essential ingredient in the extraordinary business success of both Sloan and Cunningham was their ability to express complex ideas well in writing.

SUMMARY OF LEARNING OBJECTIVES

To understand the role of reports in modern business organizations:

How do the Size and Organization of the Company Relate to the Number of Business Reports Written?   Reports help in planning and decision making. They also provide records of transactions and agreements. The number of reports increases as the business expands or diversifies. As layers of organization are added in a company, the personal contact between upper and lower management decreases. Reports are needed for communication between the various levels in an organization. Reports also play an important role in a company's efforts to coordinate domestic and international branches and subsidiaries. The business person of the future must be aware of the communication implications of international business.

How Does Career Advancement Affect Report Writing?   The types of reports will change as the writer advances in the company. At the beginning, reports will provide mostly information for upper managers; later, as a middle manager the writer will synthesize information and analyze it; finally, as an executive the writer will become mostly a user of reports.

Who Requests Reports? Who Writes Reports?   Report requests tend to travel down in the organization, while most reports travel up. All business persons write reports.

To understand the influence of global expansion on report writing.

The growth in international business directly affects business communication and report writing. The report writer must be aware of cultural differences and communication practices. What is considered a good and effective report in the United States may not be effective in Japan or France. The organization of reports changes from culture to culture. To be successful in international business, the report writer must be sensitive and willing to adapt the principles of good writing to a different environment.

To examine and define the basic characteristics of business reports.

A business report should be clear, precise, concise, well organized, factual, objective, attractive in appearance, and business oriented.

To become aware of the differences between business reports and term papers.

In a term paper the writer's goal is to show the reader that he has mastered the material of the course. In the business report the emphasis is on the content and usefulness of the report rather than on the achievements of the writer.

To recognize the importance of good report writing skills in career development.

Business reports benefit the business for which they are written. Recommendations made by the writer can influence the advancement of fellow employees. Good business reports work "silently" for the writer, bringing direct personal benefits.

KEY TERMS

Business Expansion	Government Requirements
Organizational Structure	Technology
Values and Attitudes	Legal Aspects
Oriental Cultures	Different Purposes
Filing Practices	

QUESTIONS AND DISCUSSION POINTS

1. Discuss how the growth of business has influenced business reports.
2. Discuss some of the possible reasons why improvements in technology have led to an increase rather than a decrease in the number of reports businesses produce.
3. What types of reports can you expect to write at various levels in your career?
4. What are the characteristics of a good business report?
5. What are some of the major differences between business reports and term papers?
6. What roles do reports play in business careers?
7. Who requests business reports?
8. Discuss the direction of reports. Which kinds of reports go up, down, or laterally in an organization?

EXERCISES

1. Obtain a copy of a business report from a local company and analyze it according to the characteristics of good reports.
2. Examine *The Wall Street Journal, Business Week,* and *Time* for one week and note the number of articles on international business. Compare this with the number of international articles and the international topics covered 10 and 20 years ago.
3. Check telephone rates, postage rates, and facsimile costs to Germany, Great Britain, France, Saudi Arabia, Singapore, Australia, Japan, and Brazil. Find out how long a letter would take to reach each of those countries. Determine by how many hours the business day in each country overlaps with the business day in your time zone. Which channel of communication do you consider most effective for each of the countries? Explain your decisions.

REPORTS AND THE COMMUNICATION PROCESS

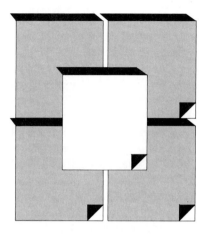

Learning Objectives

- To explore the communication process and understand the importance of reader adaptation in effective communication.
- To understand the influence of cultural differences on business communication.
- To be aware of barriers to effective communication.

THE COMMUNICATION PROCESS

Communication
Communication transfers meaning.

Effective **communication** achieves transfer of meaning. Effective and ineffective communication, communication problems, communication improvements, and miscommunication are popular terms today. For example, if a manager and a secretary do not work well together, someone may say, "They sure have communication problems." A recruiter may say after an employment interview, "Well, a good academic record, but poor communication skills."

Often we interpret problems in human interaction as communication problems. This viewpoint is not always correct. People may communicate quite well; however, they may simply disagree. Two political candidates from opposing parties, for example, may understand each other very well, but they may never agree on foreign policy, domestic issues, or the role of the government in the economy.

Communication in its broadest sense does not require agreement, but in business communication that is often the goal. The business writer has a special goal: the understanding and the acceptance of the report by the reader. The purpose of the report is to transfer meaning to the reader and to elicit agreement. For example, when assigned the task of analyzing the company's personnel policies, Beth Stone expects her superior to accept her conclusions and recommendations. If Beth and her boss have similar philosophies and if both know the personnel goals of the company, the likelihood of agreement increases. Any changes in personnel policy would need to be communicated to all employees, who may view policies from different perspectives and reach different conclusions. This is particularly likely if they are not familiar with the facts and the long-range goals of the company.

Employees at different levels of the organization are not equally aware of the organizational goals and financial situation. A study by the Opinion Research Corporation revealed that information generated at the top of organizations did not filter down to workers. In a large metal industry plant, 91 percent of top-level management knew about the company's declining profit margin, but only 5 percent of front-line supervisors did.

Another study estimates the information loss from the board of directors to the workers at 80 percent (see Exhibit 2.1). Research in the area of downward communication indicates that management usually believes that lower level employees know more than they actually do.

Examinations of upward communication expose a related problem. Higher levels of management generally believe that they understand the concerns of lower levels. However, lower levels do not share this perception. If, as Exhibit 2.2 illustrates, 73 percent of the foremen in a company believe they understand the ideas of subordinates but only 16 percent of the subordinates believe the foremen understand them, then something is wrong in the communication process.

A number of factors may account for the problem. Apparently organization members prefer to communicate with those whom they perceive as having higher status than themselves. They may not communicate readily with those

Exhibit 2.1

Dilution of Information in Downward Communication

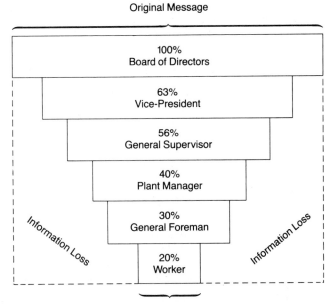

Source: Fisher, D. (1981). *Communication in organizations.* St. Paul, MN: West Publishing Co.

Exhibit 2.2

Disagreements between Superiors and Subordinates Concerning Upward Communication

	Workers Say about the Foremen	Foremen Say about Themselves	Foremen Say about Higher Managers	Higher Managers Say about Themselves
1. Always or almost always gets subordinates' ideas	16%	73%	52%	70%
2. Is someone with whom subordinates can feel free to discuss important things about the job	51%	85%	67%	90%
3. Understands subordinates' problems well	34%	95%	51%	90%

Source: Fisher, D. (1981). *Communication in organizations.* St. Paul, MN: West Publishing Co.

whom they perceive to be of lower status. Yet effective communication requires that all employees have access to data relating to the organization.

In order to understand the relationship between people who communicate, let us examine how communication works.

Encoding and Decoding of Messages

Communication theorists have developed various models to depict the communication process. Communication models are excellent vehicles for the discussion of the process, but they can never present the total reality because they cannot account for all of the variables affecting communication.

Often the communication process is presented in a diagram similar to the one in Exhibit 2.3.

A sender (writer or speaker) sends a message to a receiver (reader or listener). The receiver then provides **feedback** to the sender. Feedback is the response to the message. Feedback can be positive, negative, or neutral. Feedback does not necessarily mean agreement with the sender.

In Exhibit 2.3 the communication process is depicted as a **cycle,** a two-way process in which both the sender and receiver are involved. In written communication the sender of a message often waits for a response before sending another message. When the original sender receives the feedback, a communication cycle has been completed. The feedback to a report or a speech can be oral, written, or nonverbal in form. Not to answer a question may provide feedback. This "silent" feedback can have a variety of meanings, such as "I did not hear the message"; "I don't know what to say"; "I agree with you"; "I disagree with you"; "I am undecided." Nonverbal clues may help to decipher the feedback, but the important point is that a refusal to answer is a message in itself.

In all communication the sender has an idea he wants to share with someone. Before he can communicate this idea, he has to transform the idea into words; he has to **encode** the message. Let us assume a manager must explain a new inventory ordering and maintenance system to the inventory clerks. He and other managers have worked together on complicated formulas to keep stockouts at a minimum while at the same time cutting down on

Feedback
The receiver's answer to the sender is called feedback.

Cycle
Sending a message and receiving an answer form a cycle.

Encode
The sender transforms an idea into words.

Exhibit 2.3   **Basic Communication Model**

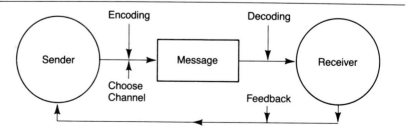

[handwritten margin annotations: experience, impression, knowledge, Decoding Message]

inventory-carrying cost. The manager who wrote the proposal for upper management spent hours poring over old records, research material on inventory control, and computer printouts. The proposal was accepted by upper management; now, in order to communicate the decision to the clerks, the manager must encode the message so that they will understand it.

Decode
The receiver gives meanings to words.

The inventory clerks, upon receiving the message, must **decode** it. They have to figure out what the new system is and how it will function. In order to work with the new system, they must understand how it differs from the old one. They can ask the manager questions. The feedback they provide will help the manager to determine whether he has communicated effectively. Ideally, the manager will explain the system, and the clerks will be ready to use it without difficulty. In reality, the manager may have to explain it several times before the system functions well.

Audience Adaptation

How can a painless switch to the new inventory system be achieved? The manager encoding the message has to think, How much do the inventory clerks have to know? What is their background? He then **adapts** the message to his audience.

Adapt
The sender encodes the message with the reader in mind.

The manager understands the formulas and intricate calculations underlying the new system and might be tempted to simply send the clerks a copy of the proposal prepared for upper management. This approach would save time. However, if he uses the document that he prepared to persuade upper management, the clerks might not understand the information. In that case they might simply put the document aside and continue with the old system. If they do not understand the message, they cannot decode it.

*[handwritten margin note: * always use the "YOU" approach. - know your audience - what they need to know. - what is work background.]*

To communicate successfully, the manager must be able to answer the following questions:

> What do the clerks know?
>
> What do they *need* to know?
>
> What is the work background of the clerks?

The clerks probably have never worked with inventory models and inventory formulas, and they may not be interested. There is no need for them to understand the mathematical foundation of the new system. All they need to know is what they are expected to do. The manager must explain to them when and how to order products. They need to know which forms to fill out, how to fill them out, and how to enter receipts. The manager may want to tell the clerks why the system was changed, but rather than go into great detail, it may be enough to point out how much money the new system will save the company every year or how much easier their jobs will be.

Audience adaptation requires the sender to encode the message with the background and experiences of the reader in mind. The receiver, on the other hand, must decode the message while keeping in mind the background and experiences of the sender. In the inventory example, the clerks must understand what the manager wants them to do. The decoding and interpretation of the message depend not only on the facts but also on the receiver's perceptions. Communication researchers estimate that 80 percent of what is communicated is influenced by personal perception of the receiver.

Communication is never perfect, because it is the transfer of meaning. Meaning is influenced by perception. Perception is influenced by experience, education, emotions, and mood.

People give different meanings to messages because they do not all use words in the same way. Although dictionaries provide definitions, words have many more meanings than those given. An example is the word *make:*

> Chevy is my favorite *make* of car. (**Make** in this context means *brand.*)
>
> I hate to get up and *make* breakfast. (*Make* here means *prepare.*)
>
> What do you *make* of her attitude? (*Make* is used in the sense of *think.*)
>
> How did you *make* out on the exam? (In this context *make* stands for *score.*)

A person who is not familiar with the various meanings of *make* may wonder at the use of the verb. Foreigners, because they rely more on the dictionary meanings, may not understand at all.

Many foreigners have difficulty understanding American sports idioms. Americans probably use more sports metaphors than people in any other country. Even Americans who have never excelled in sports understand and may use such phrases and expressions as *home run, the bases are loaded, third down and seven to go, Monday-morning quarterbacking,* and *touchdown.* A person from Germany, Saudi Arabia, or Korea may understand the separate words but not the idea expressed. To avoid problems, American business people should stay away from sports terminology in their communication with people for whom English is a second language.

Americans should also avoid slang and buzzwords in international business communication. These change frequently, and, as a result, foreigners are usually not familiar with the latest expressions. In most cases foreigners learn formal English; therefore, reports should be written in standard and more formal English.

Problems in the encoding and decoding process include the following:

1. The sender may not have the idea clearly in his own mind. He may, therefore, have difficulty putting his idea into words.
2. The sender may have difficulty in adapting the message to the receiver because he does not know anything about the receiver or is not familiar with the technical vocabulary that the receiver uses.
3. The receiver may not understand the special vocabulary the sender uses.
4. The receiver may not know the sender very well and thus misinterpret the message.
5. Communication may be hindered because sender and receiver are not aware that they use common words differently. Each may give a very personal meaning to certain words or connect certain associations with words.

Exhibit 2.4   **Oral Communication Process**

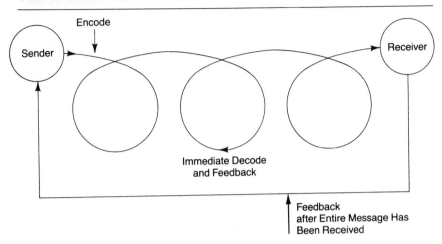

Comparison of Written and Oral Communication

The problems discussed so far apply to both oral and written communications, but there are differences between the two. The sender must be aware of these differences in order to choose the most effective means for communicating a particular message.

In written communication the process is linear. The sender sends the message; the receiver then reads the message and provides feedback. The communication cycle is completed before the next one is started. Written communication offers a special challenge because the sender does not have any immediate feedback in the form of eye contact, facial expression, or body language, but must wait for another message.

In oral communication the process resembles a spiral (see Exhibit 2.4). The sender, in this case the speaker, encodes the message. From the beginning, the listener provides immediate feedback either verbally or nonverbally. The speaker can immediately change the message by reencoding it. This process continues until the end of the discussion, presentation, or conversation.

Telephone communication introduces additional challenges to the communication process. The sender has less time to plan the message than in written communication and has little nonverbal feedback. Because much business is conducted over the telephone, many businesses are training their employees to become effective telephone communicators.

Communication Climates

The more the sender and the receiver know about each other, the more successful they will be in communicating effectively. Exhibit 2.5 illustrates the communication process when communication takes place in an area of common experiences.

Exhibit 2.5

Communication between People of Common Backgrounds

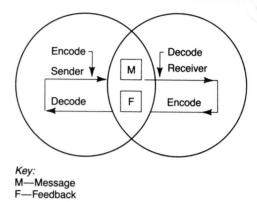

Key:
M—Message
F—Feedback

Two people who discuss a project they have been working on for some time may be able to cut misunderstandings to a minimum in that particular area. They have a common experience, which increases the chance of effective communication. The same two people may have more difficulty discussing subjects that are not related to their project.

Larry Reed and Chip Stuart, for example, have worked together on a production evaluation project for several weeks. They meet regularly to discuss the project, write reports, and present their findings to upper management. They work well together.

Their personal interests are entirely different, however. Larry loves college football. He follows the ratings closely and watches every game shown on television. Chip, on the other hand, has no interest in sports or the outdoors. He likes theater and concerts. These two men have a lot in common as long as they talk about their work, but they may have a hard time communicating about anything not work related. In fact, they may be so different that they just give up talking about anything outside work.

A perfect overlap of experiences would be possible only with cloning. In reality, there are always differences in backgrounds, experiences, preferences, and outlook on life, resulting in the constant danger of miscommunication. The less two people have in common, the more likely it is that communication problems will arise.

COMMUNICATIONS PROBLEMS IN INTERNATIONAL BUSINESS

The Larry Reed–Chip Stuart example involves communication between two people who work for the same company and who come from the same cultural background. You can imagine that communication problems mushroom when participants enter the field of international business.

The Influence of Cultural Attitudes on Communication

Americans of European descent and Europeans share a common Western heritage. Their histories are related, and they have common ancestors. They look to Greece and Rome as the cradles of their civilization. The American of European descent has much less in common with Asians. Their languages, their histories, and their outlooks on life are very different. They show their emotions in different ways.

Suppose, for example, that Paul Craig from the United States and Kyofumi Katsuki from Japan are negotiating a business deal. Their negotiation styles are different, and contracts have different meanings in the two cultures. Mr. Craig is a goal-oriented and efficient American manager who hates to waste time. Mr. Katsuki has the patience associated with the Orient: he wants to do business with a friend, and he is willing to invest the time it takes to develop a personal relationship. Because Mr. Craig speaks only English and Mr. Katsuki speaks only Japanese, they need an interpreter.

The communication process in this situation is illustrated in Exhibit 2.6. The only overlap, which is their interest in doing business with each other, is overshadowed by cultural differences and linguistic hurdles. The interpreter functions as middleman. This means that Mr. Craig encodes the message, the interpreter decodes Mr. Craig's message and then encodes it for Mr. Katsuki, and finally Mr. Katsuki decodes the message.

Interpreters
Translations are influenced by the culture of the interpreter.

All international companies employ **interpreters,** and competent interpreters try to be objective and can solve most of the language problems international business partners face. However, a Japanese interpreter always brings his Japanese background to the translation, just as an American interpreter always brings his American background to the translation. The danger of bias and error are ever present.

Not every American is impatient and boisterous, and not every Japanese is quiet and patient. Individuals have their own characteristics. Yet careful generalizations help in communicating with people from other cultures because generalizations bring out some of the major differences.

Exhibit 2.6   **Communicating through an Interpreter**

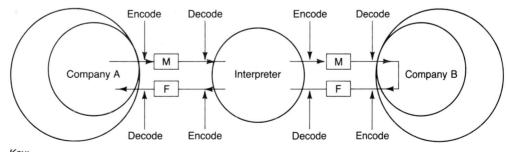

Key:
M—Message
F—Feedback

Some people emphasize that everyone is a human being and an individual. They resent the discussion of differences and prefer to concentrate on similarities. Although the orientation toward similarities may be very well meant, it can lead to a false sense of security and cultural understanding. Superficial similarities between cultures can be deceptive and lead to serious misunderstandings.

A number of business managers, apprehensive about expanding to other cultures, begin their international ventures in Great Britain. They feel more comfortable doing business in Great Britain than in France because the language is the same and many customs are similar. They feel secure and are, therefore, surprised when plans do not always work out. They would be well advised to remember Churchill's comment that we are two people divided by a common language.

As an example, assume that representatives of British and American firms have met to negotiate a contract. The Americans would like to drop one point from the discussion or, at least, postpone discussion on this point until a later time. They suggest to the British tabling that particular point, and the British accept the request without hesitation. As the negotiations begin, however, the Americans are astonished that the British bring up that very point. To the Americans *tabling* means postponing or dropping a point, whereas to the British it means bringing a point to the table for discussion. Both sides understand the words, but they do not share a common meaning.

To experience cultural problems in communications, you do not have to go to Japan or China. Many different cultural groups exist in the United States. To communicate effectively with Mexican-Americans, Italian-Americans, Blacks, Native American Indians, Japanese-Americans, or Chinese-Americans, an understanding of their particular cultural backgrounds is helpful.

Language Considerations in International Communication

Statements such as "Everyone speaks English" or "English is the language of international business" or "One can always go to Berlitz and pick up a language in a few weeks" do not contribute to effective international business communication.

English is an **international language.** Neither the English nor Americans have ever been particularly protective of their language, which has, therefore, absorbed words from many other languages. At the same time, English business terms have been absorbed into other languages. Business managers in many countries, for example, speak of *marketing, stress, management, and training.* Computer terminology used around the globe is almost exclusively in English. The language in airport control towers is English. Given that so many people speak and understand English, it seems reasonable to ask, Why should Americans bother to learn a foreign language? But *is* it a reasonable question?

Students in many countries do learn English; in some, such as Germany, the study of English is compulsory. Many Japanese, Chinese, Indians, and Koreans study English. However, having studied English does not mean that the

International Language
Even though it is an international language, English is not spoken and understood by everyone.

speaker understands it perfectly. The knowledge of business terminology may be rudimentary and insufficient for contract negotiations. Furthermore, cultural pride is a factor. Many business people in other countries resent always having to accommodate Americans. By speaking only English, Americans convey the message that other languages, and therefore other people, are not important. Finally, monolinguism is an expensive way of doing business. As a buyer you may be able to conduct business entirely in English because the other person is eager to sell. If you are the seller, however, you must adapt. The Japanese say that the most important language in international business is the language of the customer.

A French businessman in the wool industry, for example, refused to see an English salesman who was unable to speak enough French to request the appointment. The salesman did not even have the chance to present his products. Another French businessman refused to do business with an American manufacturer of components for printing equipment, even though he was interested in the product, because he believed that business is too personal a relationship to be conducted entirely through interpreters. He himself spoke English but was not willing to accommodate the American by always speaking and writing in English.

Cultural Knowledge
Effective international communication requires a knowledge of language and culture.

The mastery of a language goes beyond the mastery of mechanics; it includes a **cultural knowledge**—particularly business conventions and practices. Americans tend to be informal. Moreover, the English language lacks the distinction between familiar and polite forms of the personal pronoun *you*. Whether addressing friends, a customer, a colleague, or the president of a company, the speaker uses the same word, *you*. Most other languages have a familiar and a polite form—in German *Du* and *Sie,* in French *tu* and *vous,* and in Spanish *tu* and *usted.*

If Eric Vanderveer, an American, greets Kurt Miller, a German business person, by saying "Hallo, Kurt, Wie geht es Dir?" he may have lost a business deal. The greeting, "Hello, Kurt. How are you?" is correct grammatically but incorrect culturally. Until they know each other well and have specifically agreed to say *Du* and to use first names, Eric Vanderveer should never call Mr. Miller by his first name or address him as *Du*. Even close friends in Europe are often on a last-name basis. Almost all cultures are more formal than the American. Wanting to be friendly, Americans may alienate people who come from more formal backgrounds. What is appropriate in Denver may not be good business in Frankfurt or Singapore.

Monolingual business people have difficulties communicating with foreign subsidiaries and foreign governments. In most countries correspondence with the government and reports for the government must be prepared in the language of the country. In Saudi Arabia correspondence with the tax department must be in Arabic, for example. The French government expects reports in French; the Germans want them in German; the Chinese want them in Chinese. Some countries will accept material relating to international business in the local language or in English. India, for example, will accept documents in Hindi and English. As a result, even Japanese business people will write in English when they transact business in India. Multinational companies also designate which language to use as the official company language. For American companies that language is English; for companies headquartered in France, the language is typically French. In Dutch companies the corporate language may very well be English because very few people around the globe speak Dutch.

Americans should check the language policies of a country and individual companies before submitting documents.

BARRIERS TO EFFECTIVE COMMUNICATION

Barriers
Barriers are hindrances to effective communication.

Each time business people communicate, they face **barriers** that can affect the communication process negatively. The barriers can be of a personal, organizational, technical, environmental, or cultural nature. The following list summarizes some of the major barriers discussed in the chapter.

1. The sender and the receiver view the purpose of the message differently.
2. The sender and the receiver have different areas of expertise and interests.
3. The sender and the receiver may not like each other. Their relationship may be strained.
4. The channel chosen for sending the message may be inappropriate. For example, a letter may arrive after a deadline. The phone call from Chicago may come after the office in Tokyo has closed for the day.
5. The sender may send too much information or not enough information.
6. Because of different cultural backgrounds, the sender and the receiver may have different perceptions and may interpret a message on the basis of their cultural experiences.
7. The sender and the receiver may interpret words and meaning differently.
8. The organization of the company may inhibit open and frank communication.
9. Outsiders may interfere and influence the communication process.

[handwritten marginalia]
• Break down barriers •
① Use "you" format•
② Relationship stranded•
③ Remove barriers (see 4)
④ Keep it short & simple
⑤ Cultural differences
⑥ interpret
⑦ open & frank commun.
⑧ communication process•
⑨

SUMMARY OF LEARNING OBJECTIVES

To explore the communication process and understand the importance of reader adaptation in effective communication.

The sender of a message must encode the message; the receiver must decode it. The receiver gives feedback to the originator of the message. The encoding and decoding of the message depend on the complexity of the message as well as the educational background, the needs, and the experience of both the sender and the receiver.

The more the communicators have in common, the better they can communicate with each other.

To understand the influence of cultural differences on business communication.

The growth in international business directly affects business communication and report writing. The report writer must be aware of cultural differences and communication practices. What is considered a good and effective report in America may not be effective in Japan or France.

To be successful in international business, a report writer must be sensitive and willing to adapt the principles of good writing to different environments.

To be aware of barriers to effective communication.

An awareness of communication barriers is necessary to become an effective communicator. Some barriers arise out of personal attitudes while others grow out of organizational and technical differences.

KEY TERMS

Communication	Adapt
Feedback	Interpreters
Cycle	International Language
Encode	Cultural Knowledge
Decode	Barriers

QUESTIONS AND DISCUSSION POINTS

1. Discuss and compare the different communication models presented in this chapter.
2. Define the term *feedback*.
3. Compare written and oral communication processes.
4. What role does perception play in the communication process?
5. Define the terms *encoding* and *decoding*.

EXERCISES

1. Interview at least two foreign students on your campus and find out how to start a telephone conversation in their countries. What do people say at the beginning? How do they introduce themselves? How do those practices differ from what Americans do?
2. Rewrite the following paragraph for an international reader whose English is limited and who is not familiar with American culture.

   John did not reach the sales goal for the last quarter, but he was at least in the ballpark. In contrast, some of the other sales people were far off the target. John had hit the goal the first two quarters and was convinced that with three down and one to go, he could have positive results for the year. At the Monday morning sales meeting, the sales manager was very strong on reaching the set targets. He made it quite clear that everybody was expected to score and make the quotas. John was somewhat uncomfortable because the manager seemed to indicate that the sales force should have foreseen some of the problems that had kept sales down. John was tired of this Monday-morning quarterbacking. How was he supposed to know what was going to happen? In his opinion that was the job of the manager.

3. Examine the distortions of translation in oral communication. Give an oral message to a foreign student in class. Have the foreign student then translate the message into his own language and pass it on to another student from his country. The second foreign student translates the message back into English and reports it back to the originator of the message. Examine any changes in the content, emphasis of facts, and tone.

4. Examine the distortions of translation in written communication. Ask either a foreign student to translate an American business report into her own language or an American student to translate it into a language she has studied. Give the written translation to another student and have that student translate the report back into English. Examine the differences between the original and the translated version.

II

THE LANGUAGE OF BUSINESS REPORTS

■

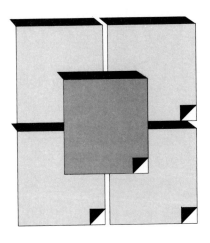

■

CHAPTER 3

PRINCIPLES OF EFFECTIVE WRITING

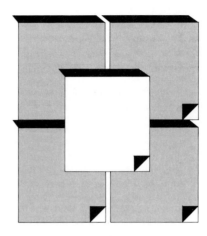

Learning Objectives

- To write with clarity and precision.
- To examine the use of business jargon.
- To use action verbs to make writing more interesting and lively.
- To master correct sentence structure.
- To review the rules of punctuation.
- To write concisely.
- To organize material logically.

Writers impress readers, either positively or negatively, by writing correctly or incorrectly. A positive impression results not only from writing with clarity and using good grammar, but also from meeting the reader's expectations. The calculation of readability formulas, presented in Chapter 4, allows for a quick measure of overall reader adaptation, but there are additional factors that have to be considered in good writing. In this chapter we will examine these factors.

CLARITY AND PRECISION

tools for having your reader understand the

Clear Terms and Phrases

"This tax measure will be good for the middle income family, but it will hurt the poor," a candidate for political office may argue. "The new subsidiary of Company X will bring many new jobs to town and result in a sizable boost to the local economy," you may read in the newspaper. Both of these sentences are vague. What is the definition of a middle-income family? What is poor, well off, rich? The government has an official definition of these terms, but most people do not know it. That problem becomes apparent as soon as you ask people to define (1) the income necessary for a family of four to be above the poverty level, (2) the income for a family of four to qualify as middle income, and (3) the income for a family of four to qualify as rich. You will find that there is little agreement on the categories. What some may consider as middle income, others may consider as poor or even rich.

If you use words such as *poor, middle income,* or *rich* in a report, you must define the terms so that the reader knows exactly what you are talking about. The reader need not absolutely agree with your definition, but it is important that the reader know what your definition is.

The two examples would be more meaningful if they read:

> This tax measure will help the family of four in the $20,000 to $30,000 income range, but it will definitely hurt families with incomes below $9,000.

> The new subsidiary of Company X will bring 500 jobs to town and add $1,000,000 to the local economy.

The following examples further illustrate how you can add clarity to your writing by substituting a precise expression for a vague one:

Vague	Precise
A sizable profit	A profit of $500,000 last year compared with $200,000 the year before
The equipment will be needed very soon.	The equipment will be needed by April 1, 19XX.
He was the leading salesman.	He sold $300,000 worth of merchandise in one month, $50,000 more than the second best salesman.
This is a work-saving machine.	This machine will do the work of ten people.
The new production process will result in significant savings.	The new production process will save the company $20,000 over a period of three months.

Keep It Short Simple
Keep "KISS"

Clear Writing
The definition of clear
writing depends on cultural
norms.

① *Is report needed*
② *Simple & concrete words*
③ *Paragraph short & simple*

All the rewritten versions are longer than the original ones, but they are also more precise and descriptive. The business manager who must decide whether to buy the new equipment wants to know how much money the new machine will save and when the old equipment will be worn out and have to be replaced. Terms such as *work saving* and *soon* will not help in the decision-making process.

The international business writer may face some unique obstacles to **clear writing.** For example, texts for business communication in both Germany and the United States emphasize clarity, conciseness, and simple and direct language. A closer examination, however, will show that what a German considers a direct and straightforward opening may strike an American as stilted and unnatural. Perceptions of what is simple, concrete, direct, formal, and informal vary from culture to culture. Therefore, allowances for cultural differences must be made when either writing a report for a person in another country or reading one written by a foreign business person.

The following guidelines should help you in writing clear and effective reports in international business:

1. Carefully examine whether the report is actually needed. This should be done for any report but is especially important for international business. You do not want to burden someone with reading or writing an unnecessary report in a foreign language.

2. Use even more simple and concrete English words than when writing to an American. Do not try to impress the foreign business person with your vocabulary. You want to get your message across. However, an exception to this rule might be when you write to a French person, because many difficult English words are derived from French and Latin. A Frenchman might more easily understand *ascend* and *descend* than *going up* and *going down.*

3. Keep paragraphs short and simple.

4. Stick to the truth and avoid superlatives. Use words you can justify. Do not describe your product as the best unless you can prove that it is. You will need to be familiar with local laws as they apply to superlatives and comparisons of products. Germany, for example, does not allow the comparison of specific products.

5. Know the technology. Your report must show that you understand the technical aspects of your subject. Chinese buyers, for example, are not interested in advertising slogans and the public relations aspects of a product. They want to know the technical features of the product. They want numbers, graphs, and detailed technical descriptions.

6. Use figures, pictures, graphs, and tables to make your point. The foreign reader who has trouble with the text may still be able to understand the visual presentation.

7. Use plenty of white space. Wide margins make reading easier and, in addition, can be used for notations and translations.

8. Be courteous and prompt. Observe the conventions of formality. Write your letters and reports with the cultural background of the reader in mind.

Simple and Difficult Words

Difficult Words
The perception of difficulty
depends on the
background of the reader.

Reports that use **difficult words** will be more difficult to read. Moreover, a word that may be easy for one person may be difficult for another. For example, *consolidated income statements, cost accounting, depreciation,* and *goodwill* may be easy words for accountants but difficult for the layperson. A marketing person knows what *advertising copy* is, but a chemist may never have heard the words. Theory X and Theory Y are common terms in management, but how many assembly-line workers could define them? We are familiar with the technical vocabulary in our area and may, therefore, assume that those words are simple.

The origin of words also influences the difficulty level. In English many words of Latin and French origin are considered difficult. Think of the language part of the SAT test. Most of the word definitions you had trouble with were probably of Latin and French origin.

The Gunning Fog Index, which uses the number of syllables as the criterion of word difficulty as discussed in detail in Chapter 4, does not take into account familiarity and frequency of usage. In business, for example, much of the technical vocabulary—management, assembly, depreciation—has three or more syllables. Even though the words are long, the business person who uses them frequently does not necessarily consider them difficult.

In your business reports you should strive to use words that are easy to understand. In many cases a simpler word can be substituted for a more difficult one:

Difficult	Simple
alleviate	solve
commence	begin
ameliorate	improve
finalize	end
incorporate	include
utilize	use
promulgate	publish
ascertain	find out
endeavor	try
exacerbate	make worse
interrogate	ask
capable of	can

Although the simple word can often replace the difficult one, word pairs are not interchangeable in all contexts. For example, the verb *interrogate* is not only stronger than the verb *ask,* but it is also more negative. (You are welcome to ask me, but please don't interrogate me.) People trying to *find out* something might be judged snoopy; *ascertain* is a word with fewer negative connotations. To *alleviate* a problem is to relieve it in some way, which is not the same as *solving* it. *Promulgate* has a broader meaning than *publish.* Before you substitute any words, you should make certain that the new word clearly communicates the meaning you intend it to communicate.

Difficulty is not determined by word choice alone. The concept and the subject matter of a discipline may be difficult to grasp for people from outside the discipline; therefore, audience analysis and audience adaptation are crucial. For example, if your field is production, then a report on quality-control problems in production is easier for you to understand than for someone whose expertise is music. If, on the other hand, you are a cost accounting specialist and are asked to read a report on the application of rhetorical principles to business communication, you may not feel very motivated to go ahead with the reading.

The perception of difficulty, interest, and boredom will influence whether the report will be easy or difficult to understand. Writers must consider the needs and the fears of the reader and adapt the material to the reader as much as possible. A marine biologist, for example, may be lost if asked to read an article in a professional journal on econometrics. This same biologist may have no problem reading an article on econometrics in *Time* or *Newsweek* because these magazines adapt the material to a more general audience.

Correct Usage of Words

The English language has a very rich vocabulary. Because English has readily incorporated words from many foreign languages, the writer has many different ways of expressing ideas. At the same time this wealth of words and possibilities can lead to confusion. Many words that appear to be similar may have entirely different meanings. The good writer uses words correctly. Some of the words many people have difficulty with are given below.

Accept/Except

Accept: To take something that is offered.
I accepted the reward with great pride.

Except: Something left out or excluded.
All employees except John Jones went to the picnic.

Adapt/Adept/Adopt

Adapt: To make suitable.
He adapted his speech to the audience.

Adept: Highly trained, very good, proficient.
She was adept at explaining new processes to workers.

Adopt: To take into possession, to take into a loose relationship.
The company adopted the new strategy without much discussion.

Affect/Effect

Affect: To have an impact on, to influence.
The storm affected the delivery schedule.

Effect: As verb: to result in, to bring about.
The committee effected a change in the procedures.

As noun: result.
The new procedures had a positive effect on production.

Appraise/Apprise

Appraise: To estimate.
The realtor appraised the property.

Apprise: To inform.
The manager apprised him of the new policy.

As/As if/Like

As: As conjunction.
As he predicted, the meeting was very long.

As if: As conjunction.
He acted as if he had not understood the instructions.

Like: As preposition.
The company needs people like you.

Assure/Ensure/Insure

Assure: To promise.
He assured her that the goods had been shipped yesterday.

Ensure: To make certain.
By adding personnel he ensured that the crowded train could leave on time.

Insure: To protect against loss.
The company was insured against theft.

Biannual/Biennial

Biannual: Twice a year.
The report is issued on a biannual basis, January and July.

Biennial: Every two years.
The production plans are examined on a biennial basis.

Cite/Site/Sight

Cite: To quote.
He cited seven sources in his report.

Site: Location.
They visited the new construction site.

Sight: Vision.
His sight was deteriorating.

Complement/Compliment

Complement: To go well with.
The team members complemented each other.

Compliment: As verb: to praise.
She complimented him on his good presentation.

As noun: a word of praise.
She paid him a compliment.

Continual/Continuous

Continual: Regular but interrupted.
She studied continually for the exam.

Continuous: Uninterrupted.
The continuous noise from the street below made him nervous.

Council/Counsel

Council: A group of people who give advice.
The Board appointed a special council.

Counsel: As verb: to give advice.
The professor counsels the student.

As noun: advice.
The professor's counsel was to go to summer school.

As noun: lawyer.
He was represented by counsel.

Precede/Proceed

Precede: To come before something else.
The dinner will precede the address of the guest speaker.

Proceed: To continue, to go on.
After a brief explanation the speaker proceeded to the next point.

Principal/Principle

Principal: As adjective: the most important.
His principal task was to edit reports.

As noun: the chief administrator of a school.
Mr. Stuart was appointed principal of Green Bay High School.

As noun: a capital sum invested at interest or due as a debt.
Alex Green used the interest income to pay for his vacation; he did not touch the principal.

Principle: Basic truth, belief.
His actions were based on sound ethical principles.

Stationary/Stationery

Stationary: Not moving, fixed.
He bought a stationary bike.

Stationery: Writing paper.
The company ordered new stationery.

BUSINESS JARGON

Almost every profession has words, terms, and phrases that are peculiar to it. Business people talk about computers, the economy, production, management techniques, and marketing. The technical language that a business person uses is not necessarily easy to understand for an outsider.

Jargon
Jargon is the technical language of a field.

Every field has its **jargon.** Jargon is acceptable as long as both the sender and the receiver of the communication understand it. If the receiver does not understand it, then the sender will miscommunicate using jargon.

Computer experts are known for the use of such jargon as *access a program* and *input material.* Many other people have begun to use *access* and *input* as verbs because they want to appear up-to-date. Computer jargon is fairly new but spreading rapidly.

A different kind of jargon consists of old-fashioned business clichés. Many business people still use them in letters and reports. Some people believe that these clichés are more courteous and polite than the direct style, which they interpret as being pushy. Some people copy the clichés from old reports when writing their own reports, without thinking of what they actually mean. The clichés that follow lack conciseness and directness; the revisions are much more to the point and, therefore, clearer.

Poor: *It has been brought to my attention . . .*
Better: *I have noticed . . .*

Poor: *Per your request . . .*
Better: *As you requested . . .*

Poor: *Enclosed herewith please find the following material.*
Better: *The enclosed material further demonstrates the benefits of the program.*

Poor: *Kindly be advised that the bill is due by the end of the month.*
Better: *The bill is due at the end of the month.*

Poor: *I thank you in advance for your efforts.*
Better: *I appreciate your efforts.*

Poor: *Attached herewith is the pamphlet you requested.*
Better: *The attached pamphlet answers your questions.*

USE OF NUMBERS

Business people use many numbers, and you, as a business writer, will have to know how to communicate numbers clearly. The following rules for writing numbers are general guidelines. In your reports you may have to modify them to meet special needs.

1. Spell out numbers from one to ten. If a sentence has several numbers, spell them out if the majority of numbers is under ten and use numerals if the majority is above ten.
   Mr. Fernandez has been with the company for 15 years. Ms. Alvarez sold three cars in one day.
2. When a sentence has two sets of numbers, spell out the set with the smaller numbers.
   Ten students had scores of 93; five students had scores of 85.
3. Write out numbers in legal documents. The figure can follow or precede the word.
   The finished product will be delivered at a price of $5,000 (five thousand dollars).
   The finished product will be delivered at a price of five thousand dollars ($5,000).
4. Spell out numbers at the beginning of a sentence. If possible, you should avoid numbers at the beginning of sentences.
   Five hundred employees took advantage of the investment plan.

Communication Conventions
In order to avoid miscommunication, the international business writer must know how other cultures write dates and numbers.

For writing numbers **communication conventions** vary. Americans separate decimal fractions from whole numbers with a period. To facilitate reading large numbers, Americans use commas to set off thousands. In most other countries, the decimal fractions are set off by commas and the thousands by periods, if at all. The sum thirty-three thousand dollars and sixty-six cents could be written as follows:

American	European
$333,000.66	333.000,66$.

Business partners must be aware of different conventions. If necessary, large numbers should be spelled out.

Measurements for weights and distances vary also. Most countries now follow the metric system, and a number of business people argue that the traditional English system of ounces, gallons, pints, inches, feet, yards, miles, and bushels puts the United States at a competitive disadvantage in foreign markets. Therefore, many businesses in the United States have already converted to the metric system. The way measurements are communicated can differ also. For example, Americans measure fuel efficiency in miles per gallon. Germans, on the other hand, measure it in terms of gasoline consumption per 100 kilometers. The conversion of miles per gallon into kilometers per liter is meaningless to Germans.

The American report writer must consider international conventions when writing dates. Europeans write dates in this sequence: day, month, year. Americans use the sequence: month, day, year. A new international sequence might give the year first:

American	European	International
7/4/19XX	4.7.19XX	19XX, 7, 4

Until all countries adopt the same format for dates, the month should always be spelled out.

Times are also written differently. Europeans use the 24-hour clock. A meeting at 4:30 p.m. takes place at 16:30 hours. Timetables for buses, planes, and trains are written on the 24-hour basis.

Americans doing business with countries in the Far East must also take into account the international dateline. The 24 time zones around the world were established by Europeans when most international traffic and commerce were across the Atlantic Ocean. The dateline where the first and twenty-fourth zones meet was therefore put in the middle of the Pacific.

With increasing business among Pacific Rim countries, the dateline is an inconvenience. For example, when it is March 3 in San Francisco, it is already March 4 in Tokyo. Contracts must stipulate exactly when they are to be fulfilled. The parties must agree on whether goods are to be delivered when it is March 3 in San Francisco or March 3 in Tokyo. When scheduling a meeting in Seoul, Korea, the manager from headquarters in Los Angeles must take into consideration the day that will be lost on the trip to Seoul. On the other hand, a business person traveling from Tokyo to San Francisco gains a day and may, if not careful, arrive one day earlier than necessary.

USE OF VERBS

Verbs denote action; they describe what the subject of the sentence does. Each of the following sentences has a slightly different meaning.

> He went to the office.
>
> He strolled to the office.
>
> He ran to the office.
>
> He walked to the office.
>
> He jogged to the office.
>
> He rushed to the office.

The careful choice of verbs adds precision to the sentence. Verbs create a certain mood. Unfortunately, in everyday language we have a tendency to overuse weak or nondescriptive verbs such as forms of *to get, to have,* and *to be.* Look at the verbs in the following paragraph:

> Because the material did not get in until yesterday afternoon, we couldn't get started on the project till this morning. This delay will be a problem in getting the work finished on time.

Changing the verbs makes the writing more lively.

> Because the material did not arrive until yesterday afternoon, we could not start the project earlier. This delay will postpone the completion of the work.

ACTIVE VERSUS PASSIVE VOICE

Active Voice
The verb carries the action.

Passive Voice
The verb is deemphasized.

In the **active voice** the action is in the verb, whereas in the **passive voice** the action is in a form of *to be* and a past participle. As a result, the action is weaker as the following example illustrates:

Passive: The business use of personal computers shall be approved by the regional executive officers and corporate department heads. All hardware will be purchased by the Computer Products Administration Unit of General Administrative Services. A list of tested and approved items will be made available from that source, and all requisitions should be channeled through them. Centralized purchasing is important so that volume discounts can be taken and new programs and developments in the computer field can be disseminated.

Active: Regional executive officers and corporate department heads shall approve the business use of personal computers. The Computer Products Administration Unit of General Administrative Services will purchase all hardware and software. That unit will send a list of tested and approved items to all offices. Centralized purchasing will ensure us of volume discounts; it will also help in the dissemination of new programs and developments in the computer field.

The first example uses mainly passive voice, the second one active voice. The active voice has several advantages over the passive voice:

1. The active voice is more concise. In the example the active paragraph has 68 words; the passive paragraph has 78 words.
2. In the active sentence the subject is the actor, performing the action that the verb designates. In the passive sentence the subject is acted upon. In the active example the officers approve the use of computers. In the passive example the use is approved by the officers.
3. Active writing is more direct, more interesting, and easier to read.

The following examples further illustrate the differences between the active and passive voices:

Passive: *After the report was finished by the secretary, it was sent to the customer.*

Active: *After the secretary had finished the report, she mailed it to the customer.*

Passive: *The office was informed by the insurance company of the change in policy.*

Active: *The insurance company informed the office of the change in policy.*

Passive: *A copy of the results will be sent to all offices by Mr. James.*

Active: *Mr. James will send a copy of the results to all offices.*

Even though the active voice is preferable, in some cases the passive voice is more appropriate. If you do not want to emphasize the actor or if you want to keep the sentence vague on purpose, you may prefer the passive voice.

Let us assume that one of your customers bought a waffle iron. The instructions clearly said not to put the iron into water. The waffle iron fails to heat, and the unhappy customer demands a replacement. As you examine the iron, you find that it was submerged in water. If you say, "You put the iron into water even though the instructions clearly said not to . . ." you will probably alienate the customer. You might prefer to say, "A careful examination of the iron shows that it was put in water . . . ." This sentence does not directly accuse the customer of doing something wrong; the damage simply "occurred."

In some cases you may not want the emphasis on the actor. For example, the sentence, "Mr. Smith wrote this report," puts the emphasis on Mr. Smith. You may want to emphasize that *this* report was written by Mr. Smith, whereas *that* report was written by Mr. James. In such a case the passive voice may be more appropriate.

In your writing you must weigh whether the active or the passive voice is more effective. The goal is not to eliminate the passive voice completely but to use the most appropriate form and to avoid slipping routinely or accidentally into the passive voice.

The computer, with the help of style-evaluation software, can help determine the number of passive phrases used in a report. The software will not change the sentence from passive to active for you; it simply flags the passive constructions. As the cursor stops at each passive construction, you can decide which voice to use.

Camouflaged Verbs

Because verbs indicate action more effectively than any other sentence element can, they should carry the action. If the action is hidden in another word, usually a noun, the verb then used in the sentence tends to be a weak one.

Hidden Verb: *It was Cathy's decision to sign up for the new training course.*

Cathy's action is hidden in the noun *decision.* The verb *was,* a form of *to be,* is much weaker than the verb *to decide.* The sentence can easily be rewritten as follows:

Action Verb: *Cathy decided to sign up for the training course.*

In the rewritten version the actor and the verb are close together. The sentence is more concise, clear, and lively.

Camouflaged Verbs
The active verb is changed into a noun.

When action is hidden in a noun, the verb is **camouflaged.** Bureaucratic styles tend to emphasize nouns because nouns are perceived to carry more authority than verbs. A text with many camouflaged verbs may seem more impressive but is less action oriented and less interesting. Camouflaged verbs may have their place if you want to deemphasize an idea or the action, but you should use them sparingly. The following examples further illustrate how camouflaged verbs weaken the action:

Camouflaged Verb: *It is my understanding that the meeting was cancelled.*

Action Verb: *I understand the meeting was cancelled.*

Camouflaged Verb: *Mr. Hurtado can be of great help to the organization.*

Action Verb: *Mr. Hurtado may help the organization greatly.*

Camouflaged Verb: *Completion of the project should be accomplished by May 1.*

Action Verb: *You should complete the project by May 1.*

Camouflaged Verb: *The department is undergoing a reorganization.*

Action Verb: *The department is reorganizing.*

The action-oriented sentences are more direct and thus easier to read and understand.

SENTENCE CONSTRUCTION

Sentence Length

Short sentences are easier to read than long ones. As a general rule, the average sentence in a business report should be about 16 to 20 words long. Some sentences will be much shorter and some much longer than this average. Of course, the sentence difficulty is measured not only by length but also by the complexity of the sentence structure. A sentence with many relative clauses and appositives is more difficult to understand than a simple sentence or series of simple sentences.

This sentence with complex relationship between parts:

> Kathy Wood, a personnel manager, who had been with Smith Robertson, an accounting firm, for three years, was very concerned about her future with the company—that was not surprising because the office had been full of takeover rumors for weeks—and she decided to look for another job.

can be written as more than one sentence to clarify the relationships:

> Kathy Wood, a personnel manager, had been with the accounting firm Smith Robertson for three years. She was very concerned about her future with the company because of strong takeover rumors. Finally she decided to look for another job.

On the other hand, a series of short sentences can be more difficult to understand than long ones if the short sentences are not clearly related. When subordination or coordination is needed to show relationships between ideas, the resulting sentences may be longer, but the message may be clearer. A series of short sentences, such as these:

> The personal robot came on the market in 1982. Optimists predicted tremendous sales. Consumers soon realized the limitations of the robot. Sales fell short of predictions. Consultants still think there is much potential. Right now manufacturers are cautious.

can be written to show the connection between the ideas and thus improve clarity:

> When the personal robot came on the market in 1982, optimists predicted tremendous sales. Consumers, however, soon realized the limitations of the robots, and as a result sales fell short of predictions. Today manufacturers are cautious even though consultants still think there is much potential.

In the second example the writer used *when, however, as a result,* and *even though* to relate the ideas in the paragraph to each other. As a result, ideas are not isolated and are easier to comprehend.

Parallelism

When a sentence contains a list of items or a series, the items or the series must be grammatically and logically parallel. If one part in a series is an adjective, the other parts must be adjectives. If one is a noun phrase, the others must be noun phrases. Contrasting ideas must also be expressed in parallel phrasing.

The following examples illustrate parallel structure:

Wrong: *He is either a capable programmer or someone whose program designs are lucky.*
The parts following *either* and *or* must be parallel.

Correct: *He is either a capable or a lucky programmer.*

Wrong: *Not only has he been promoted, but also a cash award was given to him.*

Correct: *Not only has he been promoted, but he was also given a cash award.*

Wrong: *He decided that dictating a letter was better than to call the customer.*

Correct: *He decided that to dictate a letter was better than to call the customer.*
or
He decided that dictating a letter was better than calling the customer.

Wrong: *Executives living abroad need bodyguards, security devices for their homes, and to follow carefully common-sense rules for living abroad.*

Correct: *Executives living abroad need bodyguards, security devices for their homes, and sensible rules for everyday life in a strange environment.*

Wrong: *The company's new office building was modern, functional, and incorporated the latest technology on energy use.*

Correct: *The company's new office building was modern, functional, and energy efficient.*

Subject-Verb Agreement

If the subject is singular, the verb must be singular; if the subject is plural, the verb must also be plural.

> *Mary writes* the weekly sales report.
>
> *Mary and John write* the weekly sales report.
>
> *A series* of problems *is* slowing the production line.
>
> *Each manager needs* training on the new computer.

In most cases it is easy to determine whether the subject is singular or plural, but some words can be used as either:

> The faculty have worked hard.

or

> The faculty has worked hard.

In the first sentence the writer thinks of the faculty as a collection of individuals; in the second sentence the writer considers the faculty as a single unit. Other nouns that can be used as both plural and singular include

Board	Class
Army	Group
Committee	Team

Once you have decided to use one of these nouns as either singular or plural, you have to be consistent within the sentence. It is incorrect to say:

> The committee publishes their report.

You may say:

> The committee publishes its report.

or

> The committee publish their report.

To avoid awkward expressions, writers sometimes add *members* to collective nouns so as to use them as plurals. For example, the writer may say:

> The committee has ranked job applicants.

or

> The committee members have ranked job applicants.

> The Board meets every month.

or

> The Board members meet every month.

> The team gets along well.

or

> The team members get along well.

Many writers have difficulty maintaining correct subject-verb agreement when the subject is separated from the verb by intervening modifiers.

Wrong: *The problem with having too many workers are that our sales cannot cover their pay.*

Correct: *The problem with having too many workers is that our sales cannot cover their pay.*

Wrong: *There is far too many details to cover in one meeting.*

Correct: *There are far too many details to cover in one meeting.*

Pronoun-Antecedent Agreement

A personal pronoun must refer to a specific noun or pronoun. If the reference is not clear, a sentence becomes more difficult to understand. The reference to a particular person, as in the following sentences, usually presents no problem:

> Mary finished her report.
>
> John finished his work early.
>
> John and Mary finished their report.

Pronouns are more difficult to keep in agreement when the nouns to which they refer are not specific persons:

Wrong: *Each* of the workers cleaned *their* work area.

Correct: *Each* of the workers cleaned *his* or *her* work area.
               or
               All workers cleaned *their* work areas.

Wrong: *Everyone* has to do *their* duty.

Correct: *Everyone* has to do *her* or *his* duty.
               or
               All employees have to do *their* duty.

In order to avoid sexist language and the awkward *his* or *her,* some writers use the pronoun *their* with a singular noun. Often, the problem is overcome by substituting the plural noun, as in the preceding examples. Although *they* is sometimes used as a singular pronoun in spoken English, its use is not acceptable in written English.

Dangling Modifiers

A dangling modifier does not logically modify a word or words and is therefore unclear. In the following example, *walking through the factory* seems to modify *changes.* This connection does not make sense. In the corrected version a logical subject has been added to the sentence:

Wrong: *Walking through the factory, all the changes were clearly visible.*

Correct: *Walking through the factory, the manager could observe all the changes.*

Literally, the following sentence means that the wind read the report:

Wrong: *While reading the weekly sales report, the wind slammed the door shut.*

The sentence can be corrected in this way:

Correct: *As John was reading the report, the wind slammed the door shut.*

In these examples the reader may understand what the writer means even though the dangling modifier is confusing. In some cases the reader may have to reread the sentence in order to grasp the intended meaning.

Shift in Construction

The writer must be consistent in the use of person, number, pronoun, voice, and tense. Shifts in construction are confusing because they change perspective in the middle of the sentence. To avoid a shift in construction, the writer should use pronouns that clearly refer to a logical antecedent.

Wrong:	*He discussed one's report.*
Correct:	*He discussed his (her, their, our) report.*
Wrong:	*One should proofread his report carefully.*
Correct:	*He should proofread his report carefully.*
Correct but Awkward:	*One should proofread one's report carefully.*
Better:	*Writers should proofread their reports carefully.*

USE OF PUNCTUATION

Punctuation aids clarity. Proper punctuation tells the reader which parts of a sentence are related and how they are related. Because it is beyond the scope of this text to discuss and illustrate all of the rules for punctuation, only the most important ones follow.

Apostrophe

Use the apostrophe to indicate possession.

The manager's office

The student's report

The company's retirement plan

The companies' retirement plans

A year's experience

Two years' experience

The employees' lunch breaks

The employee's lunch break

Use an apostrophe in contractions.

It's	It is
There's	There is
Don't	Do not
Mustn't	Must not
Couldn't	Could not
Shouldn't	Should not
You're	You are

In formal writing you should avoid contractions.

Commas

Coordinating Conjunctions. Use a comma to separate two independent sentences connected by a coordinating conjunction. *And, but, or, nor, for* are coordinating conjunctions.

> He finished his report, and then he went to the meeting.
>
> Susan wanted to move to Chicago, but she could not find a job there.

Introductory Subordinate Clauses. Use a comma to set off an introductory subordinate clause at the beginning of a sentence from the independent clause that follows. *If, when, before, because, since, although,* or *unless* often introduces the subordinate clause.

> If he can borrow the money, he will start his own business.
>
> Although he was very tired, he had to stay to finish the job.

Appositive. Set an appositive off with commas. An appositive is a noun or noun phrase that describes another noun.

> Mr. Baker, the president of Compact Disk Company, will be the speaker at the conference.
>
> Arthur Andersen, one of the Big Six accounting firms, is looking for a manager for the London office.

Nonrestrictive and Restrictive Modifiers. Set nonrestrictive modifiers off with commas. A nonrestrictive modifier can be omitted without changing the meaning of the sentence. Restrictive modifiers are not set off by commas.

> **Nonrestrictive**
> John Smith, who was the best production worker, received a special bonus. (If the modifier is left out, the meaning of the sentence remains the same.)
>
> **Restrictive**
> The worker who has the best production record will get a special bonus. (If the modifier is left out, the meaning of the sentence changes.)

Introductory Phrases. Use a comma after introductory phrases.

> To get the material for class, go to the reserve room in the library.
>
> To analyze the data, review the necessary statistical techniques.
>
> Excited over her success in sales, she began to think about her career options.
>
> Thinking that everyone knew about the company takeover offer, he openly talked about it in the office.

Items in a Series. Use a comma to set off items in a series. Business writers prefer to use a serial comma preceding the word *and.*

> During the afternoon she called clients, discussed the next meeting with her boss, ordered the new equipment, and finished the evaluation of her employees.
>
> Sam Irwin demanded a higher salary, better hours, and a larger office.

Adjectives of Equal Rank.   Use a comma to separate adjectives of equal rank.

> She was an efficient, conscientious worker.
>
> The beautiful, modern office arrangement was chosen to improve productivity.

Parenthetical Phrases.   Use commas to set off parenthetical words or phrases such as *however, therefore, in fact, of course, for example, consequently, nevertheless, moreover, on the other hand.* They interrupt the normal sentence pattern by providing supplementary information.

> The company will, however, start a new training program next month.
>
> We will, therefore, add Roberson to the list of suppliers.
>
> For example, most of the employees participate in the company's wellness program.

Semicolon

Independent Clauses.   Use a semicolon to separate two independent clauses that are not connected by a coordinating conjunction. To join two independent clauses by comma is called a *comma splice;* it is a serious punctuation error.

> Prairie State University has a distinct mission; it wants to attract the nontraditional student.

Independent Clauses Joined by a Parenthetical Word.   When a parenthetical word or phrase joins two independent sentences, it is preceded by a semicolon and followed by a comma.

> Our regular supplier has had difficulty meeting our growing needs; therefore, we will add Roberson to our list of suppliers.
>
> Porter Plumbing submitted the lowest construction bid; however, management decided to postpone the project.

Items in a Complex Series.   Use a semicolon to separate items in a series with internal punctuation.

> For his report he interviewed Dr. Hallam, his accounting professor; Dr. Locker, his report writing professor; and Ms. Reed, the personnel director for a local company

Colon

Use a colon to introduce a series.

> The professor considered four criteria in the evaluation of the report: correct use of the English language, reader adaptation, content, and organization.

Use a colon or a comma to introduce a direct quotation.

> At the end of the interview the recruiter said: "Mr. Jones, I am impressed with your resume. I will talk things over with personnel, and you will hear from me within a week."

Do not use a colon to separate the verb from the direct object.

Correct: The most important aspects in evaluating performance are quality of work, attitude, compatibility with other workers, and motivation.

Wrong: The most important aspects in evaluating performance are: quality of work, attitude, compatibility with other workers, and motivation.

Quotation Marks

Use quotation marks to enclose direct quotations.

> The recruiter said, "Our company is dedicated to the welfare of the employees."

Use quotation marks to enclose the title of an article or of a chapter in a book.

> He found the article by Keith Davis, "The Care and Cultivation of the Corporate Grapevine," helpful in planning his communication strategy.

Always place commas and periods inside quotation marks, colons and semicolons outside. Place question marks and exclamation marks inside quotation marks if they punctuate the quoted material, outside if they punctuate the entire sentence.

CONCISENESS

A writer who writes a report with the reader in mind, a writer who wants to assure that his report will be read, will strive for conciseness. Conciseness does not necessarily mean brevity. In a concise report every word counts in conveying the intended meaning. Sentences and paragraphs move forward, and the ideas are logically organized.

Concise writing requires practice and careful editing. If you weigh conciseness against precision, you should decide in favor of precision. A concise report will not serve its purpose if it is not clear and precise.

When editing for conciseness, you should follow these guidelines:

1. Look for words that restate what is already clearly written and eliminate them.

   Weak: *The new uniforms are red in color.*

   Better: *The new uniforms are red. (The word* red *implies color.)*

2. Find ways to eliminate "there is/are."

   Weak: *There are 30 people interested in attending the conference on speed writing.*

   Better: *Thirty people want to attend the conference on speed writing.*

3. Avoid camouflaged verbs.

   Weak: *He came to the conclusion that the training program was too expensive.*

   Better: *He concluded that the training program was too expensive.*

4. Omit *who, whom,* and *that* when possible.

Weak: *The customer was told that the goods had been ordered.*

Better: *The customer was told the goods had been ordered.*

Weak: *The factory workers whom the company had laid off in March were called back to work.*

Better: *The factory workers the company had laid off in March were called back to work.*

Weak: *Tom's broker, who is an expert in the computer field, makes a lot of money.*

Better: *Tom's broker, an expert in the computer field, makes a lot of money.*

Weak: *The cars that were sold in February had to be recalled.*

Better: *The cars sold in February had to be recalled.*

5. Replace wordy expressions with less wordy ones.

Wordy	Concise
In the month of June	In June
In the county of McLean	In McLean County
In the near future	Soon, next month
In the distant past	Three hundred years ago
For the reason that	Because
In view of the fact	Since, because
For the purpose of	For
At this point in time	Now
Due to the fact that	Because
In spite of the fact that	Although

ORGANIZATION AND LOGICAL DEVELOPMENT

Logical and Organized Presentation
Logical and organized presentation is systematic and orderly.

A report organized so that the development of ideas and arguments is clear and logical is easier for the reader to follow than a report that jumps from one idea to another. A **logical and organized presentation** can help to make even difficult material seem easier. On the other hand, fairly simple material can become confusing if points are not presented in logical progression. Let us compare the following two examples:

Organized Presentation
The good report writer plans his report before he begins writing. He asks a number of questions to bring the report into focus.

1. What is the purpose of the report?
2. What is the problem to be solved?
3. Who is the reader?
4. How much does the reader know?
5. How much does the reader *need* to know?
6. How will the reader use the report?

The answer to these questions will help the writer to choose the format, tone, level of formality, and depth of background information. The extent of planning will depend on the length of the report and the complexity of the problem. For long reports the writer will probably make a written plan; for reports of medium length he may simply jot down a few ideas; and for a short memo he may plan in his head. In any case, he will plan.

Unorganized Presentation

The extent of planning depends on the length of the report and the complexity of the problem, but the good report writer plans before he writes. For short reports less planning is necessary. He has to ask who the reader is and what the reader knows already about the problem. The answer to the question will help the writer to determine format, formality, tone, and depth of background information necessary. Medium-long reports and long reports require more detailed planning. Other questions the writer has to ask before he can start writing are: Who is the reader? How will the report be used? What is the problem to be solved? and What is the purpose of the report?

In the first example the arrangement of ideas makes sense, and the presentation flows naturally. The format also aids in making this sequence of ideas clear.

- Importance of Planning
- Elements of Planning—A Set of Questions
- Results of the Questioning Process—Determination of Type of Report to be Written
- Types of Planning—Types of Reports

In the second example the logical progression is interrupted as the writer jumps from one idea to another. An outline of the paragraph illustrates the lack of unity:

- Types of Planning—Types of Report
- Importance of Planning
- Short Reports
- Elements of Planning—A Set of Questions
- Results of the Questioning
- Medium Reports
- Long Reports
- More Questions for Planning

Even short reports benefit from a plan for presenting the information logically. Chapter 7 discusses planning in detail.

SUMMARY OF LEARNING OBJECTIVES

To write with clarity and precision.

Good writing is precise. The writer adapts his language to the level of the reader and chooses words that the reader understands. To ensure that the text is clear, the writer checks to see that words are used correctly.

To understand the use of business jargon.

The overuse of jargon distracts from the content of the message. The business writer should avoid jargon and buzzwords.

To use action verbs to make writing interesting and lively.

Action verbs make reports more interesting and concise. The report writer puts action into the verb and does not camouflage it in a noun. Although the passive voice is preferable in some cases, active voice is generally better writing.

To master correct sentence structure.

Shorter sentences are generally easier to read than longer sentences, but the level of difficulty is influenced by the complexity of the sentence and the relationship of ideas. A longer sentence that coordinates or subordinates ideas may be easier to read than a series of unrelated short sentences. Items in a series must be grammatically and logically parallel.

To review the rules of punctuation.

The effective writer knows the rules for punctuation and correct grammatical usage and takes care to follow them.

To write concisely.

Good writing is concise. The concise writer does not waste the reader's time.

To organize material logically.

To organization and the logical development of the material are major determinants in the level of difficulty.

KEY TERMS

Clear Writing	Active Voice
Difficult Words	Passive Voice
Jargon	Camouflaged Verbs
Communication Conventions	Logical and Organized Presentation

QUESTIONS AND DISCUSSION POINTS

1. What are elements of effective writing?
2. Discuss the importance of clarity and preciseness.
3. Discuss the use of simple and difficult words.
4. What makes a sentence simple or difficult?

5. Why should you use active rather than passive voice?
6. What is a camouflaged verb?
7. Discuss the rules for parallel structure in writing.
8. How do organization, page layout, and typeface help in making a text more readable?
9. How do you present numbers in reports?

EXERCISES

1. Correct the following sentences:

   The economy effects the performance of the firm.

   Like he said, the meeting did not last very long.

   The building cite was easily accessible.

   He decided to call the manager rather than writing to him.

   The company looked for someone who was experienced, had knowledge of computers, and an MBA.

   He passed the managers office.

   The instructor evaluated the students report.

   He rewarded his employee's very well.

   The job was difficult but he did complete it on time.

   Mrs. Semar the companys training director carefully read the participants evaluations.

   If he can get the job he will move to New York.

   To get the test results he went to the lab manager.

   He had told the manager "that he wanted to go to school."

   The supervisor said, I have very good workers in my group.

   The company celebrates their 25th anniversary this month.

   A series of problems are contributing to the loss of sales.

   Everyone knows their duty.

   Reading the report, the fire alarm went off.

   He should evaluate one's report carefully.

2. Identify whether the following sentences use active or passive voice. Change the passive voice to active voice.

   The decision was made by a special committee.

   The assembly line was slowed down by the supervisor for adjustment to the new product line.

   The office manager ordered new office equipment to accommodate the growing needs of the company.

   After much discussion it was decided that the training program should be adopted by the company.

3. Change the camouflaged verbs to action verbs.

The boss made the suggestion that the employees get back to work.

The department's recommendation is to buy three microcomputers with the necessary software packages.

The supervisor gave her permission for the line to be shut down.

4

THE WRITING PROCESS

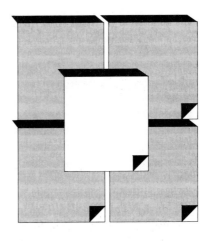

Learning Objectives

- To become familiar with the three stages of the writing process:

  Planning
  Writing
  Editing and revising

- To understand the impact of the computer on the writing process.
- To be able to apply readability measures in the writing process.
- To understand the process for collaborative writing.

The writing process can be divided into three parts: planning, writing, and editing and revising. The writer must understand that these stages overlap and are recursive. For example, in the writing and editing stages he must evaluate whether he addresses the problem identified in the planning stage. At the same time, he must recognize that the original plan may need revision in view of information collected after the initial planning.

PLANNING

Planning
Effective writing requires planning.

Some people write with a minimum of **planning;** others plan in great detail and prepare complex outlines. Some writers try to perfect the style and the tone of the message at the same time that they formulate their ideas; others initially concentrate on content and write fast.

Planning is a very individual task and you must find out what works best for you, but you must also be aware of some basic facts about the planning stage. Overplanning can be stifling to the writer who feels she must stick to the outline once it is finished. Lack of planning, however, also poses problems. The writer who does not plan at all may waste hours reorganizing a first draft or adapting it to a specific reader.

In the planning stage you should determine answers to the following questions:

1. What does the reader already know? You will not need to cover material that the reader is familiar with.
2. What does the reader need to know? You must include all necessary information.
3. How does the reader feel about the topic? This information will help you in adapting the message to the particular reader.
4. What is the purpose and the use of the report?

Computer Programs
They can facilitate the planning process.

You may find the computer helpful in the planning stage. **Computer programs** such as *ThinkTank®, MaxThink®,* and *Framework®* are especially designed for the planning task. Sometimes such programs are called idea processors. Of course, programs cannot process ideas; people do. However, the programs can help in organizing ideas. You can use these programs to make lists of concepts, ideas, facts, and tentative approaches to solving problems. You can organize, categorize, and establish hierarchical relationships between ideas.

Most planning programs allow you to view the entire outline, a single major heading with all its subheadings, or major headings only. For example, when you are working on a detailed outline of one section of a report, you can collapse the material so that you have only the major outline on the screen. If you are considering whether to rearrange material, you can examine the outline to see where a particular section might fit best. The planning programs encourage experimenting with the arrangement of material by examining the relationship between ideas. As a result, they help you to focus on the problem.

The planning process will be discussed in more detail in Chapter 7.

WRITING

Many writers suffer from writer's block—the inability to begin. They may worry that they do not have all the facts or that they are not up to the task. They may also be stalling while they look for a perfect beginning so they will not have to revise their writing later on.

Solid preparation in the planning stage and a good foundation in the writing principles discussed in Chapter 3 can help to overcome some of the fear that causes writer's block. A good report will go at least through one revision. Therefore, you should relax if your first draft is not perfect.

As you write, you may find that your outline needs changing. This is a natural process. As you become more familiar with the facts and as you examine the issues, the original approach and organization may no longer be appropriate. Writing is a creative process in which the final report evolves out of the original plan.

The Influence of the Computer on the Writing Stage

Microcomputers
They have influenced the writing process.

For centuries the writing process was essentially the same. People used pen and paper and more recently the typewriter to write a rough draft. Today more and more businesses place **microcomputers** on managers' desks in an effort to increase efficiency and productivity. The writing principles discussed in Chapter 3 apply whether you write a report with pen and paper or on the microcomputer, but the writing process itself may undergo some changes when you use a computer.

Writing with pen and paper is hampered by the impossibility of writing as fast as the ideas flow. Even a typewriter fails to keep up with the thought process for a number of reasons. For example, the time needed to return the carriage may appear insignificant, but it adds up. Each carriage return also tends to interrupt the flow of ideas. The awareness that typing errors mean retyping the page slows down the writing process even further.

Good keyboarding skills and a microcomputer help record ideas quickly. The speed also increases because you do not have to dread revisions. Errors can be easily corrected, and the automatic wraparound makes the carriage return superfluous. The only time the writer must push the return button is to start a new paragraph.

Many writing instructors in the past emphasized deliberate and careful writing. Consequently, revisions were often seen as punishment for not doing an acceptable job the first time. With the microcomputer, revision takes on a different dimension. The clear distinction between various drafts disappears unless you print out a hard copy after each revision. From planning to final copy, the drafts flow into one another.

When you first key your ideas into the computer, you should concentrate on the content and flow of ideas. You need not be particularly careful about spelling, grammar, or style because you can easily correct mistakes later. Editing is no longer seen as punishment for failing the first time but rather as an integrated part of the writing process.

It does not matter how you start the report. You do not have to wait for the perfect beginning. If you are not certain of a transition, you may simply type in the word *transition* to flag the spot so that you can work on it later. Because you can start at any point in the report, writing with a microcomputer may help you approach even long writing assignments with less apprehension.

Writing with a computer requires a different kind of memory and imagination from the traditional writing process. When composing on the screen, you never see an entire page. You cannot place three or four pages side by side. You must, therefore, visualize what you have written. Of course, you can reread a section, and a split screen will enable you to view two sections simultaneously. You can check for consistency of terminology and for contradictions. You can decide where a text segment fits best. Given the size of the screen, however, the sections you can view are fairly small. Looking at a split screen is not the same as looking simultaneously at different sections of a report on sheets of paper spread out in front of you. You must, therefore, keep in mind how the parts fit together and how a particular section fits into the whole.

Because you do not see an entire page and because the writing moves up as you enter material, you may forget when you started the current paragraph. When you edit your report later, you must, therefore, pay particular attention to paragraph length and paragraph unity.

Software for Writing

Many word processing packages are on the market to assist you in your writing tasks. Some of the most widely used word processing packages are

- *Ability*®
- *Edix/Wordix*®
- *MicroSoft Word*®
- *MultiMate*®
- *NewWord*®
- *PC-Write*®
- *Perfect Writer*®
- *Wordvision*®
- *PFS: Professional Write*®
- *Sidekick*®
- *VolksWriter*®
- *WordPerfect*®
- *WordStar*®
- *Writing Assistant*®
- *Super Writer*®

Although the specific features are different from package to package, most word processing programs perform the following functions:

- **Locate Any Point in the Text.** No matter how long your text is, you can easily move to the end or the beginning. You can either move the curser in increments of a specified number of lines or scroll the text up or down. Scrolling means to roll the text as if it were a scroll.
- **Delete and Add Letters, Words, and Paragraphs.** All word-processing packages allow you to delete and add text.
- **Find Words or Strings of Words and Replace Them.** Assume, for example, that you use the company name a number of times in a report about Wilson Sporting Goods. Rather than write it out each time, you

may write the letter *W* instead. After you finish the report, you can ask the computer to find each *W* and replace it automatically with the full company name.

- **Indent.** Whole sections are easy to indent and, unless you change the command, they remain indented.
- **Underline.** You can automatically underline words and sentences.
- **Highlight.** Most word-processing packages allow you to print material in boldface type for emphasis.
- **Center.** The computer will automatically center headings.
- **Insert Page Headings.** Most word processors will allow you to automatically insert special material such as the date, subject, and page number on the second and following pages of a letter or memo.
- **Reorganize Material.** You can change the sequence of paragraphs with a simple command. The specific commands vary, but all packages allow you to move blocks of material.
- **Vary the Print Type.** You may use italics, German script, or Gothic script. The special capabilities will depend on the compatibility of your computer, the software, and the printer. Special commands may be necessary to access particular capabilities.
- **Print Foreign Characters.** More and more packages allow you to use Greek letters, German umlauts, and French accents with ease. If you use foreign characters frequently, you may want to make the ease with which you can obtain them a major criterion for the software selection.

EDITING AND REVISION

Editing
The writer edits the report in sequential steps.

In the **editing** stage you will check your report for

- Completeness and accuracy of content
- Logical organization and appropriate format
- Appropriate style: tone, grammar, punctuation
- Correct spelling

Editing for content and organization should always precede editing for style and spelling.

Editing for Content

At this stage you check for completeness and correctness of the facts. You must ask yourself whether you have looked at the problem from all sides and whether you have included all the necessary detail. Your arguments may need strengthening. You may also find that some passages are too detailed and need tightening. Perhaps you have learned that the reader of your report knows more about the topic than you had originally assumed. In that case you may need to condense or even eliminate certain sections.

This is the time to check and double-check the accuracy of information. You should confirm numbers and validate your sources. If the company is going to invest thousands of dollars based on your calculations or your assessment of the competition, you must be sure of the facts and then copy them correctly from your notes or sources.

Editing for Organization and Format

After you have edited for completeness and accuracy, you can work on improving the logical flow of the presentation. Perhaps you reorganized some parts as you checked the content, but you still should carefully edit the organization of the report. A report organized so that the development of ideas and arguments is clear and logical is easier for the reader to follow than a report that jumps from one idea to another. A logical and organized presentation can help to make difficult material seem easier. Even fairly simple material can become confusing if points are not presented in logical progression.

The importance of organization, logical development, and format is illustrated in Exhibit 4.1, a memo written by an American manager to an employee at a foreign subsidiary. Clearly, the writer had not planned the organization and had not gone through any revisions before she faxed the report. The lack of organization and logical flow indicates that the writer changed her mind about the subject as she progressed. At the beginning she tells the reader that headquarters is definitely not interested in the proposed project. Yet at the end she seems to think that the project would be feasible and acceptable.

The lack of organization in the report is not the only problem. The lack of clear paragraphing and white space also hinders comprehension and readability. In addition, the format does not indicate any logical grouping of material. The style and presentation of the material need improvement also. The writer could have communicated much more effectively by making some changes as illustrated in Exhibit 4.2.

Editing for Style

Style
The style must be adapted to the reader and the situation.

Although **style** is an extension of a person's character and, therefore, highly individualistic, you should make certain that the style does not violate language conventions and that it fits the purpose of the report. You must check whether you applied the principles of good writing discussed in Chapter 3. In addition, you must decide whether the level of formality and the tone are appropriate. If the original reader will pass the report on to upper management, you may want to use a more formal style and format. For example, if only your immediate superior will read the report, you may refer to that person by name or as "you" and refer to yourself as "I." If the report will be sent to others as an official document, personal pronouns would not be appropriate.

As you edit for style, you will also check grammar and punctuation.

Style Checkers

Many people resent the time it takes to edit and proofread a report. Today numerous style checkers and spell checkers are on the market to take the drudgery out of editing and proofreading.

Exhibit 4.1　　　　　Confusing Organization and Weak Format

```
TO:            Noriko Kodate

FROM:          Stephanie Hollar

SUBJECT:       Development of Korean Vendors, Answer to Memo from
               May 10, 19xx

DATE:          May 12, 19xx

Regarding your memo on the possibility of Korean manufacturing,
here is the situation.
The U.S. is not currently interested in developing a Korean
vendor. However, as the Taiwanese dollar fluctuates, other
countries become more attractive for manufacturing. The
licensing agreement for manufacturing in Korea (considering the
problem we have getting into the market place) might be the
logical solution.
The product must meet Korean specifications for domestic sale.
At this point I am concerned about counterfeit products getting
into the Japanese market.
I will talk to John about the product. I am confident we can
count on support from the people in charge of technology. They
are pretty busy right now, but we can start talking to them. But
keep in mind that I cannot promise support.
The distribution of the product would have to be watched
closely. You should check the Korean regulations on what
percentage of production must be exported.
I will let you know what others think at headquarters.
```

Style evaluators, such as *Grammatik®* and *Rightwriter®*, examine writing style, consistency of terminology, and punctuation. They tend to check for problems in the following categories:

- Informal usage of a word
- Archaic usage
- Capitalization errors
- Gender-specific terms
- Jargon
- Awkward usage
- Overworked phrases
- Punctuation errors
- Vague adverbs
- Wordy phrases

Style evaluators do not uncover all stylistic problems, and they may flag phrases that are correct. When a writer uses the word *affect* correctly, the computer may still ask the writer whether she meant to use the word *affect* or *effect*. The writer must decide whether to make changes. The computer simply flags and makes suggestions; the ultimate decision always rests with the writer.

Exhibit 4.2   **Improved Organization and Format**

TO: Noriko Kodate

FROM: Stephanie Hollar

SUBJECT: Development of Korean Vendors, Answer to Memo from
                May 10, 19xx

DATE: May 12, 19xx

Thanks for your ideas about exploring Korean vendors.

Currently, the company does not have a great interest in
developing Korean vendors, but I like your ideas. Headquarters
might be willing to listen to convincing arguments; therefore, I
would suggest you prepare a more in-depth report and explore the
following points.

1. As the Taiwanese dollar fluctuates, a more stable currency
    would become more attractive. In that case a licensing
    agreement with a Korean company might be the logical way to
    go.

2. As you know, we have had problems with counterfeit products
    from Korea. You should address that problem carefully.

3. You should examine the time frame for product development.
    Even though the people in Technology are very cooperative,
    they are very busy right now. What timeframe did you have in
    mind?

4. The Korean government may have regulations saying that a
    certain percentage of goods manufactured in Korea must be
    exported. You should carefully examine the government
    regulations concerning this matter.

These are my thoughts right now. I will explore the "climate" for
your ideas at headquarters and will let you know what the feeling
is here. In the meantime, I suggest you address some of the
points and potential problems I have raised. Please keep me
informed.

Most style checkers provide a summary of the style analysis. *Rightwriter,* for example, provides the following information:

- **Readability Index.** Readability is measured in grade-level equivalent.
- **Strength Index.** A value of 1.0 indicates strong writing; a value of 0.0 indicates weak writing. Strong writing is clear, concise, and to the point.
- **Descriptive Index.** The use of adjectives and adverbs is measured.
- **Jargon Index.** A jargon index of 0.0 means that the writing has an acceptable level of jargon. If the jargon index is above 0.5, the writer should examine the use of jargon carefully.
- **Sentence Structure Analysis.** *Rightwriter* looks for repeated patterns in writing.
- **Words to Review List.** All uncommon, negative, slang, and misspelled words are listed.
- **Word Frequency List.** This category lists all the words used in the report. It also tells the writer how often each word has been used. This list could flag potential overuse of certain words.

In addition to providing the summary, *Rightwriter* also inserts comments into the text. George Napier, a tax accountant, has prepared the letter in Exhibit 4.3 for one of his clients. Before he sends the letter, he runs it through *Rightwriter* and receives the analysis illustrated in Exhibit 4.4.

George, after examining the comments, makes the changes illustrated in Exhibit 4.5. When he runs the revised version through *Rightwriter,* Exhibit 4.6 shows the analysis of the revised letter. Based on this analysis, George decides to send the revised letter to his client.

The exercise shows that there is no absolute right or wrong decision. You must evaluate the comments of the style checker and then decide which will improve your report the most.

Editing for Spelling

Spelling Errors
The checking for spelling errors is the last stage in the editing process.

In the last step, you look for **spelling errors.** Some people are very good at this, but others seem to miss even the most glaring errors. You should know that you can train yourself to become good at editing for spelling. To be proficient requires two major characteristics: good spelling and concentration. If your spelling is weak, you will have trouble finding errors. If you do not concentrate during the final stage of editing, you may find yourself reading for content rather than for spelling. In order to concentrate on spelling, you might try reading a text backward word for word. Because the text will be meaningless, you will be able concentrate on the individual words rather than on the flow of ideas. However, that approach will not eliminate the need to read in sequence. When you read backward, you will not catch typos such as *a* instead of *an* or *from* instead of *form.*

Spell Checkers

A number of software packages on the market will check spelling. Some spell checkers work in conjunction with word processing packages; others are integrated into style checkers. As with the style checkers, the spell checkers do

Exhibit 4.3   **Original Letter**

NAPIER AND WILLARD ACCOUNTING FIRM

707 East River Street
River Grove, IL 60171
(312) 555-5716

May 21, 19xx

Mr. William Hayes
303 Birch Lane
Winnetka, IL 60093

Dear Mr. Hayes:

Pursuant to our telephone conversation dated June 1, 19xx, I
attempted to determine if you were eligible for certain tax
deductions you want to claim on your federal and state returns
this fiscal year.

I examined the pertinent sections of the Code and even consulted
with our senior tax partner, who was of great help. He pointed
out several ideas for deductions I never would have thought of.

As you know, the rules and regulations of the Internal Revenue
Code are difficult and hard to interpret in many instances,
especially concerning travel expense deductions.

Your expenses to the convention are deductible if you spent at
least 50 percent of your time at business. Your wife's expenses
are not deductible. You should study Section XXX of the Code to
see why the deductions are not correct.

It is difficult to make a decision on the other area of deduction
you would like to claim. I will have to wait until Haggerty is
settled in the Federal District Court of the area.

If you have any questions regarding this or any other pertinent
matter, please do not hesitate to call us at the office.

Sincerely,

George Napier

George Napier

Exhibit 4.4   **Analysis of Original Letter**

Pursuant to our telephone conversation dated June 1, 19XX, I
attempted to determine if you were eligible for certain tax
deductions you want to claim on your federal and state returns
this fiscal year.
     ∧ < <* 17. LONG SENTENCE: 34 WORDS *> >
     ∧ < <* 31. COMPLEX SENTENCE *> >
I examined the pertinent sections of the Code and even
consulted with our senior tax partner, who was of great help. He
pointed
     ∧ < <* 8. CONSIDER OMITTING who was *> >
out several ideas for deductions I never would have thought of.

As you know, the rules and regulations of the Internal Revenue
     ∧ < <* 3. WEAK. CONSIDER REPHRASING As you know, *> >
Code are difficult and hard to interpret in many instances,
especially concerning travel expense deductions.
     < <* 17. LONG SENTENCE: 26 WORDS *> > ∧
     ∧ < <* 31. COMPLEX SENTENCE *> >
Your expenses to the convention are deductible if you spent at
least 50 percent of your time at business. Your wife's expenses
are not deductible. You should study Section XXX of the Code to
see why the deductions are not correct.

It is difficult to make a decision on the other area of
deduction you would like to claim. I will have to wait until
Haggerty is settled in the Federal District Court of the area.
     ∧ < <* 21. PASSIVE VOICE: is settled *> >
If you have any questions regarding this or any other pertinent
matter, please do not hesitate to call us at the office.
     < <** SUMMARY ** > >
     READABILITY INDEX: 10.64
*R1. Readers need an 11th grade level of education to
     understand the writing.
     STRENGTH INDEX: 0.34
*S2. The writing style is weak.
*S4. Passive voice is being used.
     DESCRIPTIVE INDEX: 0.55
*D2. The use of adjectives and adverbs is within the normal range.
     JARGON INDEX: 0.00
Most sentences begin with pronouns. Try using other sentence
start conditions.
     < < UNCOMMON WORD LIST > >
The following list contains uncommon words found in the
document. Will any of these words confuse the intended audience?

19XX	1	CONSULTED	1	CONVERSATION	1
DEDUCTIBLE	2	EXPENSE	1	EXPENSES	2
HAGGERTY	1	HESITATE	1	PERTINENT	2
PURSUANT	1	REGARD	1	REVENUE	1
WIFE'S	1	XXX	1		

     < < END OF UNCOMMON WORD LIST > >
     < <WORD FREQUENCY LIST > >

19XX	1	A	1	AND	4
ANY	2	ARE	4	AREA	3
AS	1	AT	3	ATTEMPTED	1
BUSINESS	1	CALL	1	CERTAIN	1
CLAIM	3	CODE	3	CONCERNING	1
CONSULTED	1	CONVENTION	1	CONVERSATION	1
CORRECT	1	COURT	1	DATED	1
DECISION	1	DEDUCTIBLE	2	DEDUCTION	1
DEDUCTIONS	5	DETERMINE	1	DIFFICULT	3
DISTRICT	1	DO	1	ELIGIBLE	1

continued

Exhibit 4.4

Analysis of Original Letter *continued*

ESPECIALLY	1	EVEN	1	EXAMINED	1
EXPENSE	1	EXPENSES	2	FEDERAL	3
FISCAL	1	FOR	2	GREAT	1
HAGGERTY	1	HARD	1	HAVE	3
HE	1	HELP	1	HESITATE	1
I	4	IDEAS	1	IF	3
IN	2	INSTANCES	1	INTERNAL	1
INTERPRET	1	IS	2	IT	1
JUNE	1	KNOW	1	LEAST	1
LIKE	1	MAKE	1	MANY	1
MATTER	1	NEVER	1	NOT	3
OF	8	OFFICE	1	ON	2
OR	1	OTHER	2	OUR	2
OUT	1	PARTNER	1	PERCENT	1
PERTINENT	2	PLEASE	1	POINT	1
PURSUANT	1	QUESTION	1	REGARD	1
REGULATIONS	1	RETURNS	1	REVENUE	1
RULES	1	SECTION	1	SECTIONS	1
SEE	1	SENIOR	1	SETTLED	1
SEVERAL	1	SHOULD	1	SPENT	1
STATE	1	STUDY	1	TAX	3
TELEPHONE	1	THE	11	THIS	2
THOUGHT	1	TIME	1	TO	10
TRAVEL	1	UNTIL	1	US	1
WAIT	1	WANT	1	WAS	1
WERE	1	WHO	1	WHY	1
WIFE'S	1	WILL	1	WITH	1
WOULD	2	XXX	1	YEAR	1
YOU	7	YOUR	4		

<<END OF WORD FREQUENCY LIST>>

not make the decisions for you. They flag words, but you must make the final decision on the spelling of the word. The checker matches the words you have used against its built-in dictionary. If the dictionary is not very large, you may receive the message that the computer cannot find any suggested corrections for a word that it flags. As a business writer you need a checker with a large business vocabulary. Most spell checkers can be expanded to meet your particular needs. For example, *Word Plus*® and *Random House Proofreader*® contain dictionaries ranging from 20,000 to 83,000 words. The larger the dictionary, the longer time the computer takes to check for errors. For most purposes a dictionary of 50,000 words should be sufficient.

Spell checkers also have difficulties with proper names, abbreviations, prefixes, and combination words. In addition, spell checkers will not flag the word *from* even if you meant to use the word *form*. Both are legitimate words, and the computer cannot decide which one you want. You must proofread your report even after you have run it through a spell checker.

Considerations for Editing

Revision cannot be an endless process. Businesses rarely ever permit the writer enough time to reach absolute perfection in a report. Business writers must meet deadlines. A report needed for determining a new advertising

Exhibit 4.5   **Revision of Original Letter**

NAPIER AND WILLARD ACCOUNTING FIRM

707 East River Street
River Grove, IL 60171
(312) 555-5716

May 21, 19xx

Mr. William Hayes
303 Birch Lane
Winnetka, IL 60093

Dear Mr. Hayes:

The following information will answer the questions you had about
tax deductions for this year's federal and state returns.

1. Your convention expenses are deductible if you spent at
    least 50 percent of your time at the convention.

2. Your wife's expenses are not deductible because she had
    no business reason to attend the convention.

3. Haggerty, the new Judge of the Federal District Court,
    should issue a ruling on your third area of concern
    within the next week. I will send you the information as
    soon as I receive it.

Let me know if you have any other questions.

Sincerely,

George Napier

George Napier

Exhibit 4.6

Analysis of Revised Letter

```
The following information will answer the questions you had
about tax deductions for this year's federal and state returns.
1. Your convention expenses are deductible if you spent at
   least 50 percent of your time at the convention.
2. Your wife's expenses are not deductible because she had no
   business reason to attend the convention.
3. Haggerty, the new Judge of the Federal District Court,
   should issue a ruling on your third area of concern within
   the next week. I will send you the information as
              ∧ < <* 17. LONG SENTENCE: 23 WORDS *> >
   soon as I receive it.
Let me know if you have any other questions.
                  < <** SUMMARY **> >
     READABILITY INDEX: 6.80
*R1. Readers need a 7th grade level of education to understand
     the writing.
     STRENGTH INDEX: 0.95
*S1. The writing has a strong style.
     DESCRIPTIVE INDEX: 0.50
*D2. The use of adjectives and adverbs is within the normal range.
     JARGON INDEX: 0.00
                 < < UNCOMMON WORD LIST  > >
The following list contains uncommon words found in the
document. Will any of these words confuse the intended audience?
     DEDUCTIBLE   2            EXPENSES   2          HAGGERTY   1
        WIFE'S   1
                 < < END OF UNCOMMON WORD LIST  > >
                 < <WORD FREQUENCY LIST> >
```

WORD			WORD			WORD	
A	1		ABOUT	1		AND	1
ANSWER	1		ANY	1		ARE	2
AREA	1		AS	2		AT	2
ATTEND	1		BECAUSE	1		BUSINESS	1
CONCERN	1		CONVENTION	3		COURT	1
DEDUCTIBLE	2		DEDUCTIONS	1		DISTRICT	1
EXPENSES	2		FEDERAL	3		FOLLOWING	1
FOR	1		HAD	2		HAGGERTY	1
HAVE	1		I	2		IF	2
INFORMATION	3		ISSUE	1		IT	1
JUDGE	1		KNOW	1		LEAST	1
LET	1		ME	1		NEW	1
NEXT	1		NO	1		NOT	1
OF	3		ON	1		OTHER	1
PERCENT	1		QUESTION	2		REASON	1
RECEIVE	1		RETURNS	1		RULING	1
SEND	1		SHE	1		SHOULD	1
SOON	1		SPENT	1		STATE	1
TAX	1		THE	8		THIRD	1
THIS	1		TIME	1		TO	1
WEEK	1		WIFE'S	1		WILL	2
WITHIN	1		YEAR'S	1		YOU	4
YOUR	4						

```
                 < <END OF WORD FREQUENCY LIST> >
```

campaign, for example, must be ready for the advertising managers' meeting. A perfect report that is not ready in time is useless.

The computer can help in reducing the time necessary for editing. As a result, writers may more readily give and accept criticism and suggestions for change. Let us assume that a manager looking over the third draft of a long typewritten report would like to add a few words on the second page and omit a sentence on page four. These minor changes would enhance clarity but would require the secretary to retype several pages, if not the entire report. The manager decides against the change, rationalizing that the report is good enough and that the additional time required for retyping could be better used. If the same report were on a word processor, the last-minute revisions would be so easy to make that the manager would likely go ahead with them and thus improve the report.

Writing with the microcomputer has many advantages, but it also creates some problems. Computers make the report look so perfect that problems in content and meaning may be overlooked. Visually, a computer-produced report is appealing. The centered headings, bold-faced captions, and justified margins add to the visual perception of readability, but they also can lull the writer into a false sense of security. A good-looking report is not necessarily a good report.

The writing process when using a computer is summarized in Exhibit 4.7. After keying in the report, the writer edits it on the screen and makes necessary

Exhibit 4.7

Summary of the Writing and Editing Process Using a PC

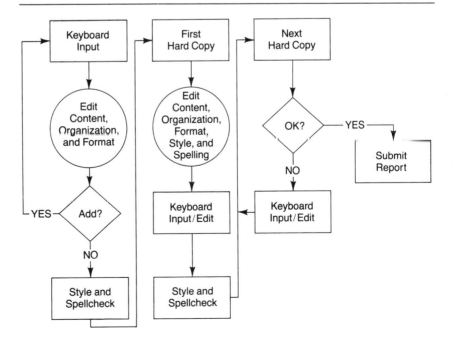

corrections. Next she checks the report for grammar and spelling. Then she prints the report and edits the hard copy. She keys in the changes and again edits and checks spelling. Then she prints a second hard copy and again edits and proofs the copy. If there are no errors, she can submit it; otherwise, she must key additional corrections into the computer. All reports should go through at least one hard copy for editing before the final copy is printed.

READABILITY MEASURES

The writer must adapt a report to the intended reader, as discussed in Chapter 2, but how does the writer know whether the level of writing is appropriate? Many factors determine the level of difficulty of a text. Among them are word choice, sentence length, sentence structure, paragraph length, paragraph structure, organization of material, logical development of material, difficulty of material, use of headings, page layout, typeface, and the number of illustrations. Most of these criteria are impossible to measure. We may agree that the organization of a report is good or weak, but we will probably never agree on a certain grade or numerical value for organization. The same is true for measuring the difficulty of material, the complexity of sentence structure, the organization of paragraphs, page layout, illustrations, difficulty of words, use of headings, and print.

Readability Formulas
Readability formulas measure the level of difficulty of a text.

Despite these problems, researchers have developed **readability formulas** for measuring difficulty. In the effort to quantify the level of difficulty, many of the criteria mentioned in the previous paragraph had to be discarded. All formulas that measure readability concentrate on word length and sentence length because they produce clear and undebatable numbers.

To get an acceptable measure of the readability of a text, the text sample must include at least 100 words and run to the end of a sentence. Let us examine three readability measures: the Gunning Fog Index, the Flesch Index, and the *Rightwriter* Index.

The Gunning Fog Index

The Gunning Fog Index measures the grade equivalent of a text. For example, if the readability measure is 10, the text is appropriate reading for someone in tenth grade. Examination of the following passage from an annual report will demonstrate how the index works.

> What does "maximizing shareholder value" really mean? Essentially it means giving shareholders more cash over time—in the form of dividends and capital appreciation —than they invested in our stock when they bought it. Our goal is to deliver this "value" at a level that meets or even goes beyond the initial expectation of the people who invest in Quaker. Cash flow is crucial to reaching this goal because the more cash we can generate today and in the future, the more cash our owners will get on a current basis and over the longer term—through dividend payout and the increase in our stock price.

The first step is to count words, number of sentences, and difficult words.

Number of Words	106
Number of Sentences	4
Number of Difficult Words	11

These figures are then used in two equations:

$$\text{Average Sentence Length} = \frac{\text{Number of Words}}{\text{Number of Sentences}} = \frac{106}{4} = 26.5$$

$$\text{Percentage of Difficult Words} = \frac{\text{Number of Difficult Words}}{\text{Number of Words in Sample}}$$

$$= \frac{11}{162} = .10377 \text{ or } 10.377\%$$

The final calculations are as follows:

Average Sentence Length	26.5
+ Percentage of Difficult Words	10.377
	36.877
× Multiplier of .4	.40
Readability Level	14.751

The text has a readability level of 14.751. It should be appropriate reading for students at the end of their sophomore year in college. When determining the percentage of difficult words, these rules must be followed precisely:

1. Words with three or more syllables are considered difficult words.
2. A word that appears twice is counted twice.
3. Exceptions:
   a. Words of three syllables that are compounds of two simple words are not considered difficult. Examples: *typewriter, lawnmower*.
   b. Simple verbs that become difficult by adding *-es, -ed,* or *-ing* are not counted. Examples: *repeated, conducted.*
   c. Proper names are never counted as difficult words.

The difficult words are *maximizing, really, essentially, dividends, capital, appreciation, deliver, initial, expectation, generate,* and *dividend*.

The Flesch Index

The Flesch Index is based on average sentence length and number of syllables per sample. It measures readability in a range from zero to 100, where zero is very difficult and 100 is very easy reading. The scale is as follows:

0– 30	Very Difficult
31– 50	Difficult
51– 60	Fairly Difficult
61– 70	Standard
71– 80	Easy
81–100	Very Easy

For the calculation of the Flesch Index you need the average sentence length and the number of syllables in the sample. You already have the sentence length, 26.5. The number of syllables in the sample is 162. The Flesch Index is calculated as follows:

Average Sentence Length × 1.015 = 26.5 × 1.015 =	26.898
+ Number of syllables × .846 = 162 × .846 =	137.052
	163.950
Subtract this sum from 206.835 (determined by Robert Flesch) =	206.835
	−163.950
Readability Level	43.139

Based on the ranges presented, this text is considered difficult.

The calculations for both the Gunning Fog Index and the Flesch Index are very tedious and time consuming, and in longer documents several samples would have to be analyzed. In addition, the chance of error is very high in manual calculations. Today the readability level can be calculated much faster with the help of a computer.

Computer-Generated Readability Checks

Many software packages on the market can calculate the readability of a text. Most of them are based on the Gunning Fog Index, the Flesch Index, or a combination or variation of these two. For example, the software package *Rightwriter* uses the Flesch-Kincaid formula, a combination of Gunning Fog and Flesch. It is based on the average sentence length and the average number of syllables per word. The result is given in grade-level equivalent. For the passage from the annual report in the above example, *Rightwriter* calculates a readability level of 12.89.

A comparison of the readability measures shows some differences:

Gunning Fog Index	14.751 or 15
Flesch-Kincaid used by Rightwriter	12.89 or 13
Flesch Index	43.139 or Difficult

The illustration shows that a writer must use readability formulas with caution. The formulas give a general idea of the level of the writing; they are not absolute.

Use of Readability Measures

Readability measures are used by a variety of businesses. Insurance companies use readability measures to comply with government requirements for readable and understandable policies. Financial institutions may use them to explain financial information more clearly to customers. Newspapers and magazines use them to see whether the readability level of their publications is appropriate for the target market. The military requires that contractors producing users' manuals for the armed forces meet definite readability specifications.

The readability level you choose depends on the purpose of the text. Many business people read newspapers on the way to and from work and understandably do not want to have to use a dictionary. They read quickly for information; therefore, newspapers are usually written below the readability level of their readers. Because *The Wall Street Journal* is read mostly by college graduates, the majority of its readers should be able to read at a level of 16, yet it has an average readability level of about 12. *Time* and *Newsweek* have levels of 8 and 10. Magazines such as *Sports Illustrated* and *Better Homes and Gardens* tend to have levels of about 6 to 8.

Considerations in Using Readability Formulas

As already discussed, readability formulas are only one aspect of measuring the difficulty of a text. Merely following readability formulas will not guarantee that a text is readable. They must be used with caution. Furthermore, readability formulas are language specific.

The Gunning Fog Index, for example, cannot be used in languages other than English. Difficult words are culture specific. German words, for example, tend to have more syllables than English words. As a result, even an easy text will have a higher percentage of long words than an English text. The following example illustrates the point.

	German	**English**	
	Textverarbeitung	Word processing	
Number of Syllables	5	1	3
	Autoreparaturwerkstatt	Garage	
	8	2	
	Gabelstaplerfahrer	Forklift driver	
	6	2	2

Based on the Gunning definitions of difficult words, all of these German words are difficult; in English none is difficult. (Processing falls under exception 3b.) Japanese and Chinese words are not written as letters grouped into syllables, and so the measure of difficulty would have to be based on completely different criteria.

The calculation of the readability level of your reports may help you adapt your reports to your readers. If a report intended for assembly-line supervisors is written at level 16, you may want to reexamine your writing. Although level 16 does not necessarily mean that the supervisors will have a hard time reading the report, the calculation certainly flags a potential problem. On closer examination you may find that you overused a few difficult words and that your sentences were strung together. That type of problem would be fairly easy to solve. You may also find, however, that the entire message is not geared to the level of the supervisors. In that case you might best put your report aside and start over.

COLLABORATIVE WRITING

You are used to your own approach to writing, and up to this point most of your writing has been an individual effort. You receive an assignment, and you sit down and do it: you plan, write, edit, revise. You are responsible for the content, the facts, the style, and the appearance.

Collaborative Writing
Collaborative writing affects the writing process.

[handwritten margin notes: Group structure, status (position each member holds), group norms of leadership, define leadership (who's leader)]

In business, however, much writing is done on a **collaborative** basis. The writing principles do not change, but the process itself may change. When you are involved in a group effort, you have to adjust schedules and take style preferences, backgrounds, and different abilities into consideration. Although the group report may be much better than a report you could have done on your own, its quality depends on the cooperation of several people. The following discussion details some aspects you must be aware of if the group effort is to be successful.

Group Dynamics

To write a good group report, the group members must understand the principles of group dynamics. Before people can work together, they must understand one another. The team members must be aware that there are two major aspects to group work: (1) the building of the group and (2) the performance of the group task. A group must invest in its own development before it can concentrate on completing a task.

For example, Laboratories United has just established a task force to examine quality control in the firm. In phase one of the project the task force is expected to prepare a status report. In phase two the group is expected to recommend improvements.

The team has four members from different departments and with different interests. Each member comes with a specific background and personal preferences. John, the member from production, is on the defensive. He thinks that his department will be blamed for all problems that may surface. Joanne, the marketing person, is poised and outgoing. She has many good ideas, but she can be rather domineering at times. Bob, the representative from planning, blames everyone for not following the original designs. His attitude is, "I told you so." Paul, the personnel representative, thinks it is all a waste of time. Why bother? Why look for problems unless they are glaringly apparent?

This group will have a hard time working on a report unless the members understand one another's attitudes and feelings. Groups have to work on the following aspects to function well: group structure, status and hierarchy of members, group norms, and leadership in the group. Only after the group has established some agreement on these aspects can it begin with the writing task.

Approaches to Group Planning

In the planning stage the group must discuss the problem, and all members must give their input. In addition, the group must discuss approaches to the report. What format is the report to take? What will be an effective outline?

Group writing
3 problems
- each member writes
an report.
- One member writes
report.
- everyone has to
write something from
one person's idea.

What information will go into the various sections? In fact, the group as a whole must discuss the entire process and the organization. At the end of the planning stage the group must have a clear understanding of the task, be aware of the strengths and weaknesses of the members, have an outline for the report, and assign specific tasks to each member. Planning is the foundation of successful group writing projects. Only after the group has discussed the issues and the writing plan should the writing stage begin.

In the planning stage the group must also set goals regarding the formality of the writing, the level of difficulty, the level of abstraction, and the use of active and passive voice.

Approaches to Group Writing

The group can take three approaches to writing: (1) one member writes the entire report, (2) each group member writes the complete report, (3) each group member writes one part of the report.

The first approach is most likely to produce a report with stylistic unity and effective transitions. Many groups use this approach. In reality, however, the project often becomes the project of one individual. The rest of the group easily loses interest, especially when members are not interested to begin with. In the team at Laboratories United, Paul does not care much. Joanne, who can be domineering, may simply take over. In turn, John may feel that he is pushed to the side. He believed that nobody was going to listen anyway. As a result, he may give up totally.

The advantage of the second approach is that every group member will be familiar with all aspects of the report. On the other hand, this approach wastes a lot of time. Furthermore, it complicates the reconciling and combining of various drafts from individual members. If group members are very sensitive about their writing, a discussion of the drafts, which will lead to a comparison of group members' writing, can cause fruitless arguments. This approach is the least functional of the three.

The advantage of the third approach is that each group member can work on a specific segment. They may be able to contribute their special skills. The member who is good at analysis may write that section. The one who is good at making recommendations may write that section.

For the third approach to be effective, the group must discuss the goals of each section and how the parts will fit together. A detailed outline must be available to all writers so that group members do not write in a vacuum.

Each group must decide which approach will be best for it and which will help to reach the goal most efficiently. The choice will be influenced by the dynamics of the group, the problem at hand, and the time available.

Approaches to Group Editing

During the editing stage, group members integrate the various sections. In preparation for successful group editing, members must understand that criticism must be factual, constructive, and goal oriented. Comments, such as "simplistic approach," "naive approach," or "ridiculous options" can put a severe strain on the group.

Groups must also realize when to stop editing. Some team members may try to vote on every sentence and change every phrase, and others may argue over editorial control and make it an ownership issue. The group must keep the goal clearly in mind at this stage: to create a single voice out of many different parts.

One group member should prepare the final draft after the group editing session. All group members will read the final report before it is submitted. The responsibility for final drafts can be rotated if the group must prepare several reports. The group must decide how much rewriting for the final draft the editor is to do. Should he merely work on transitions, or does he have authority to rewrite whole sections? To achieve stylistic unity, the editor may use a style checker.

Successful business people write as groups by approaching problems in a constructive and task-oriented manner.

SUMMARY OF LEARNING OBJECTIVES

To become familiar with the three stages of the writing process and to understand the impact of the computer on the writing process.

Planning. In the planning stage, the writer plans the message. She determines answers to questions such as who the writer is and what the purpose of the message is. Computer software can help in the planning stage.

Writing. Different writers use different strategies. Some are eager to get ideas on paper while others are concerned about style and careful organization from the very beginning. The computer has a marked influence on the writing process. Word processing software can help to reduce writer's block because the software makes it easy to reorganize, to add, and to delete text.

Editing and revising. Every writing project should be edited at least once. The writer should always edit for content and accuracy first. Editing for organization, style, and spelling follow. Many style and spell checkers can assist the writer during this stage; however, the writer must be aware that the computer can only make suggestions. The ultimate responsibility rests with the writer.

To be able to apply readability measures in the writing process.

Readability measures are an attempt to determine how well a text is adapted to the level of a particular reader or group of readers. Readability measures should be used with caution because they are culture specific and represent only one aspect of readability.

To understand the process for collaborative writing.

Business people frequently work in teams and have to prepare group reports. While the sequence of the process is basically the same for groups and individuals, the specific strategy is often different. For example, groups must reconcile style differences of various writers. They must reach a consensus as to the content, format, and use of the report. Most groups discuss the content and then have one member write the report. The entire group then works on editing and revising. In another approach every group member writes one segment of a report after the group has discussed the project. One person then reconciles style differences and edits the report. The entire group edits the final draft.

KEY TERMS

Planning	Style
Computer Programs	Spelling Errors
Microcomputers	Readability Formulas
Editing	Collaborative Writing

QUESTIONS AND DISCUSSION POINTS

1. What elements of a text determine whether it is easy or difficult to read?
2. Discuss the use of readability formulas.
3. Why are most readability formulas based on word length and sentence length?
4. Calculate the readability level of several business letters and reports. Based on the information you have about the reader, discuss how well the report is adapted to the level of the reader.
5. Why should you edit for content and accuracy of facts before you edit for style and spelling?

EXERCISES

1. Rewrite at least one sample for which you calculated the readability level. First raise and then lower the readability level. The revised passages should be at least two levels above and two levels below the original. Discuss the results. What did you do to achieve the change?

2. Revise the following report:

   Please review any project you are currently working on or that is in development and determine whether copies have been sent to headquarters. We need the information urgently. If your respective market centers submit materials that are utilized in your areas to headquarters, we can, when trademark infringement matters surface, readily submit the necessary proof of use to the trademark attorneys. Also, what you have developed in your center may be of use or generate ideas for other international markets—particularly for the Far East market that does not have its own marketing/advertising department. Reviewing what is done in the other markets is most helpful. To you that have been submitting items, keep up the good work.

3. Next month representatives will come from headquarters in Japan to visit your subsidiary. Your boss has formed a small committee of three people to arrange the first day. The executives will arrive at the airport at 9:00 a.m. The drive from the airport to the office will take about 45 minutes.

   You know that the Japanese executives have never before been to your subsidiary, and you are aware that in Japan the personal relationship is important in business.

   Your boss is rather nervous; he wants everything to go well. He has asked your group to work out an itinerary and to give him an overview of business etiquette in Japan. He does not intend to do everything the Japanese way, but he feels that it will help him if he knows something about Japanese ways.

   He has heard that the Japanese exchange a lot of gifts, and he wonders whether he should have official gifts ready. He wants the committee to prepare an itinerary and some background information on Japanese business customs.

   Address the committee report to your boss, Mark Theobald.

   On a separate sheet discuss the group process. What went well? What did not go so well? How would you approach the task next time?

4. Your department is going to buy new office furniture. You have $10,000 available for 12 people. You will need desks, chairs, lamps, file cabinets, and waste baskets.

   Your boss wants attractive furniture, but it must also be comfortable and functional. He has appointed a group of three people to prepare a report discussing the options.

   Address your group report to Mark Stroot, department manager.

   On a separate sheet provide a summary of how you worked as a group. What went well? What did not go so well? How would you approach the task next time?

ETHICAL ASPECTS
OF WRITING

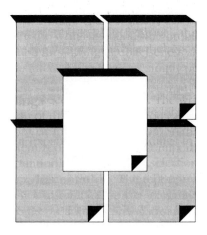

Learning Objectives

- To acquire a framework for ethics.
- To become aware of the ethical dimensions of organizations.
- To understand the ethical implications of word choice.
- To distinguish between factual and ethical data presentation.
- To examine questions of confidentiality and the law in report writing.

In order to discuss the ethical aspects of writing, we must first examine ethics. Ethics is one of the concepts we all think we know a great deal about, but when put to the test of defining the term precisely, we may not know where to begin.

To act ethically means to do the right thing. An ethical person's behavior could be written about in the newspaper for neighbors and friends to read, and the person would have nothing to be ashamed of. Ethical behavior is characterized by honesty, fairness, and good judgment. Some people argue that ethics are universal. What is ethical in Des Moines, Iowa, is ethical in Cairo and Singapore as well. What is not ethical here is not ethical anywhere else either. Others believe that ethical behavior depends on place and circumstance. According to this viewpoint, what is ethical in New York may be unethical in Berlin or Hong Kong.

In a way both groups are right. Most cultures agree to certain underlying principles of human behavior. For example, murder is considered unethical behavior in almost all cultures. On the other hand, ethical norms also change from culture to culture. Religion, history, and cultural values influence the definition of ethical behavior. Norms for ethical behavior in America, based on Christianity, Western philosophy, and Western values, have also been shaped by the environment of a new continent and life on the frontier. Moslems and Buddhists, who have different traditions, do not share all of our views on ethics.

For example, the United States government has declared that bribes are unethical, illegal, and punishable under the Foreign Corrupt Practices Act. In the Middle East and Latin America, on the other hand, bribes are an accepted cultural practice. People in those cultures have a feeling for the right time, place, and appropriate amount for a bribe. Outsiders, on the other hand, usually do not have that feeling because they did not grow up with the practice. They may go through the motions without really understanding the cultural underpinnings of bribes.

Most of us understand that people in business must make many decisions that involve ethics. We associate ethics with problems of bribery, shady deals, poor quality of products, lies about product performance, and false advertisements. However, we usually do not think of ethics in connection with writing.

Although we often think of writers as simply presenting facts objectively, writers cannot escape political pressures and realities. How should they handle the demand to "fix" data so that the details of questionable expenses do not show up? How should they phrase recommendations for employees who are lazy or unreliable? Is a good recommendation for a mediocre employee ethical?

Ethical behavior is a part of writing. Writing does not take place in a vacuum. A company does not hire some people as managers and others as writers. Writing is directly tied to actions. The personnel manager writes a performance appraisal; the production manager writes the production report; the advertising manager writes or evaluates the advertising copy. In a management course students concentrate on how to make decisions. The focus of this chapter is on how to communicate those decisions in writing.

A FRAMEWORK FOR ETHICS

Ethical decisions always involve judgment. A model or guide is needed to help people avoid the problem of circumstantial ethics. However, the several theories that scholars have developed are not prescriptions for ethical behavior; they are merely different ways of looking at a complicated concept. What may be ethical under one may not be ethical under another. The three most important are the utilitarian, the rights, and the justice theories. They help to determine answers in three areas of ethics: Is the action or decision good for the community (company)? Does the decision protect basic rights of all affected parties? Is the decision just?

Utilitarian Theory

Utilitarian Theory
Utilitarian theory considers as just that which serves the greatest good for the greatest number.

The **utilitarian theory** maintains that actions should be judged by their consequences; that means, if the outcome is good, the action is good. The utilitarian theory is also reflected in the statement that "the end justifies the means" and the concept of "the greatest good to the most people." If more people benefit from a questionable action than suffer from an ethical decision, the action is just. For example, if not promoting George means that harmony and, therefore, productivity in the department will be maintained, George should not be promoted.

As the example indicates, the utilitarian theory does not necessarily take individual justice into account. If George has worked much harder than anyone else and if he has the necessary qualifications for the position, one could argue that he should be promoted. The utilitarian theory does not necessarily concern itself with George's promotion; it concentrates on whether George's promotion is best for the welfare of the whole.

The Theory of Rights

Theory of Rights
Theory of rights emphasizes rights rather than obligations.

Due Process
Due process requires fair procedures and fair laws.

The **theory of rights** puts the issues of privacy, freedom of conscience, free speech, and **due process** at the center of ethical behavior. For example, free speech is a basic right, and, therefore, the exercise of free speech does not violate ethical principles. The right to due process is also a basic right and therefore, some argue, never violates ethical principles. As an example, assume that Pam Black finds out that Margery Rodway, who is a pillar in the community, was convicted of petty theft 20 years ago. She begins to spread the news to discredit Margery. Pam, under the theory of rights, could argue that she is simply exercising her right to free speech.

The difficulty with the theory of rights is that the emphasis on rights neglects to consider duties and obligations. The theory of rights does not pay enough attention to issues of social welfare and the benefit to others. It may result in an egotistic and selfish interpretation of ethical norms.

The Theory of Justice

Theory of Justice
Theory of justice concerns itself with fairness and justice rather than profitability.

The **theory of justice** emphasizes equity, objectivity, fairness, and impartiality. Concern for the well being of the other person enters the picture. The question is not so much whether an action is profitable but whether it is fair.

For example, special training programs for minorities may not be profitable in the short run, but they may be fair because they provide opportunities for employees who have been discriminated against in the past.

Stressing the principles of fairness, equity, and impartiality too much may lessen the incentive to produce and to do well. The theory of justice raises the question of whether equity and fairness require equity of opportunities or equity of results. For example, in addition to providing the opportunity for all students to attend high school, does the obligation exist to graduate all those who have attended regardless of level of achievement and credits earned?

Exhibit 5.1   **Model for Making Ethical Decisions**

Is the decision good for the company or community?

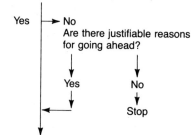

Does the decision protect the rights of all affected parties?

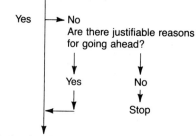

Is the decision just?

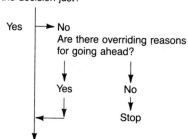

Implement the decision

Source: Adapted from Cavanaugh, G. F., Moberg, D. J., and Velasquez, M. (1980, August). *The ethics of organizational politics.* Paper presented at the 40th annual meeting of the Academy of Management, Detroit, MI.

The Integration of the Theories

Ideally an ethical decision would be in agreement with all three theories. However, this is rarely the case. A decision may be just, for example, but may violate the utilitarian theory or the rights theory. A business person must test each possible decision against all three theories, one by one. If it violates the principles under one theory, the question becomes whether justifiable reasons exist for still going ahead with the decision.

For example, management by asking to keep confidential a discussion on new-product development may violate the right of free speech (rights theory). Management might argue that the exercise of free speech would hurt the company in the competitive environment. Another argument might be that keeping the discussion confidential will benefit the employees (utilitarian theory) and therefore the request to curtail free speech is ethical.

In negotiations between countries secrecy is often necessary to achieve results. If the details of negotiations between two countries are published in newspapers, the parties may be reluctant to engage in any meaningful discussions.

The model in Exhibit 5.1 may help you in making ethical decisions and in communicating those decisions. Ethical decisions are, of course, more complex than the model indicates. In making ethical decisions, you must examine yourself and your motives to root out rationalizations and false justifications. Related to motives are values, judgments, behaviors, and attitudes.

The model implies that people will always think in terms of the well-being of others; however, what people invariably do is first decide what is good for themselves. The reality of self-interest is usually at the center and, therefore, a prime determinant in moral and ethical decisions. Self-interest does not necessarily mean selfishness; it also means the natural inclination toward self-preservation. Few people will sacrifice themselves for the betterment of a company or community—and, after all, only rarely will an act that benefits an individual clearly harm the company (except in cases of theft or embezzlement).

ETHICAL DIMENSIONS OF ORGANIZATION

After spending many weeks on a report, you want the reader to agree with your conclusions and recommendations. If you doubt this will happen, but you are convinced that your recommendations will ultimately benefit the company, the solution may lie in the organization of the material. Taking the reader through the inductive process—presentation of facts, analysis of facts, conclusions, recommendations—may result in acceptance of the recommendation. On the other hand, presenting the recommendation first might cause the reader to reject the report before even reading the analysis.

In this case you would be wise to choose the inductive arrangement. Is this ethical? Yes, if you believe in the soundness and truth of your conclusions and recommendations. You are in compliance with all three theories. The arrangement may benefit the future of the company. The presentation is fair. You have not changed anything; all you have done is rearrange the information. The reader is still free to agree or disagree with you. You are not trying to influence the reader by manipulation of the data itself.

When you organize material in a particular way, you must ask yourself why you are doing so. Do you choose an arrangement in order to further understanding or to manipulate? A fine line divides persuasion from manipulation. Persuasion presents the data in an arrangement that will help the reader see the facts in a certain order. Manipulation tries to influence the reader through a particular interpretation of the data, through editing and word choice, and even manipulation of the data itself.

As a report writer, you must realize that data is nothing per se. Most people do not know what to do with it. Businesses need people who place data in context, who signify its possible meanings, who hypothesize and project. Data only gains meaning when its patterns are perceived and interpreted. These two steps present a great challenge to the report writer.

Organization and presentation of information are closely related. For example, a company that is losing money still wants to present itself in a positive light to stockholders. The letter to stockholders in the annual report may begin with a positive element, such as reorganization of the firm for future growth. Based on the first sentence the reader might get the impression that the past year was actually good. Not until later in the letter may the stockholder realize that the company lost money or experienced a sharp decline in earnings. The following example illustrates the point:

> This is the year we celebrate the completion of the . . . mine. . . . It was completed on time, close to budget, and in a manner consistent with current environmental perceptions. It will be a profitable operation. Our stockholders will be the richer for it.

Several paragraphs later the letter continues:

> Net earnings for 1981 were $50,038,000, or $1.54 per common share, compared with $237,388,000, or $8.02 per share, in 1980. The reduction in earnings reflects the sharp deterioration in prices for . . . principal products.

Is this approach ethical? Some people argue that the facts are all somewhere in the report and that the figures must be correct to meet legal requirements. That may be true but, by starting as it does with very positive information, the report may also be misleading. Many stockholders may not look at the figures. They may simply glance at the opening of the letter and some of the graphs in the annual report. If the letter is positive, and if the lines in the graph go up, many will consider the performance satisfactory, if not excellent.

The presentation covered up negative news. The company wanted to present a positive image in order to attract and keep investors. The company acted out of narrow self-interest rather than in the interest of the stockholders and investors. Some will argue that the company manipulated the arrangement of data to present an image that did not reflect the whole truth, and that therefore the company acted unethically.

ETHICAL DIMENSIONS OF WORD CHOICE

The organization of material cannot be completely separated from the presentation and wording of the material. Word choice can influence the meaning of a message. Words like *outstanding, major, large majority, by a wide margin, enthusiastic, best, inferior, bargain,* and *special offer* are used to create a special impression. Although these words can describe a product or a person correctly, they may also be misleading.

Let us take the example of *special offer.* Intuitively you interpret the term to mean a large price cut, a substantial cut. Your supplier has lowered the price of an item from $100 to $99 for one month. In an advertisement the supplier refers to substantial savings to be gained by taking advantage of the special offer. You will indeed save money, but the question is whether the one-dollar reduction truly is a special offer.

If you read in a union report that the new union representatives were elected by a large majority, you have to ask what constitutes a large majority? To most people it is over 60 percent. Yet, in some elections, the terms *large majority* and *wide margin* are used when the candidate won by 52 percent. Fifty-one percent is a majority but does not constitute a win by a wide margin. Actually, the margin is very small.

Some words have more positive connotations than others with similar meanings. A research study showed that even a small change in the tone of a written communication directly affects a reader's perceptions of the material presented. To illustrate, an announcement of a company policy relating to social welfare, labor relations, and employment climate was written in two versions varying only in tone. One was intended to give the impression of a flexible company, the other of a strict company. Seven sentences distributed evenly throughout the material were selected for modification. In each of the seven sentences a nonsubstantive word was chosen for modification. Nonsubstantive words change only the climate of the text and not the factual content.

The seven word pairs used to present the strict–flexible image were:

- Asked—required
- Trying—driving
- Hesitant—willing
- Should—must
- Agreeable—forceful
- Offering—pushing
- Insightful—shrewd

The words on the left were considered more positive. The readers felt that the company described by using the words on the left was more flexible and responsive to people. The company described by the words on the right was seen as more authoritarian and strict (Kulhavy & Schwartz, 1981). The important point is that the facts were the same in both versions.

The example shows how much influence word choice can have on perceptions of the reader. This knowledge can be used positively to help present a positive image. It can also be used to manipulate perception. Management can use words to present a company as it is, as they perceive it, or as they want others to see it. The difficulty is that the three overlap and cannot always be separated.

A strict company can be presented as flexible, and a flexible company can be presented as strict, by changing some key words in the description. The writer must be aware of the impact of certain words and also the overall climate of the text, as the following example illustrates.

A university student who will graduate in May has applied for a job in your department. You look over the application and decide the student's credentials are impressive, but you have no openings. Remembering your difficulty in finding a job when you graduated, you do not want to discourage the student. After the interview you write a letter praising the resumé, adding that you do not have an opening now but will keep the application on file. You are absolutely certain that nothing will open up in the next few months, but you do not have the heart to say no.

Is your action ethical? Not completely. Someone who is familiar with the hiring process and with the style of rejection letters may recognize "keeping the application on file" as meaningless. Most readers understand the true meaning. Someone who is new to the job market may not, although no student is likely to expect to hear from you.

Now assume a different set of facts. You receive in the mail an application from a student who will graduate in May. You look at the resumé and the cover letter. The letter has numerous spelling and grammar errors, and the student is below average in academic performance. You would not hire that student under any circumstances. Your reply is the same letter that you wrote to the first student.

Is the behavior ethical? No. In this case you are lying. You may argue that the student can more easily take a polite and positive *maybe* than a definite *no,* but you are taking the easy way out. You may argue that it is not your responsibility to let that student know that his achievements are simply not sufficient to find a job with your company, but the point is that your message is deliberately wrong and untruthful. Your message violates the utilitarian and justice theories. Your message is not in the interest of your company or the student, and by being dishonest it also is unfair.

Ethical behavior takes courage. Writing a positive message is much more fun than writing a negative message; saying *yes* is much more fun than saying *no*. The conscientious report writer must strive for ethically acceptable reports.

ETHICAL DIMENSIONS OF FACTUAL PRESENTATION

Many people believe that a report meets ethical standards if the facts are correct. Some even say, "Let the facts speak for themselves." They believe that facts by themselves will present a true picture. Of course, the facts should be correct. However, situations are not usually that simplistic.

In a report on the financial performance of your company you cannot present every piece of financial information. You must summarize and concentrate on the major figures, which means you must select data for presentation. Everyone may agree that cost of raw materials, sales price, sales volume, and wages should be identified. However, you may feel pressure not to identify other costs. Do you identify what it costs the company to have a rejection rate of two percent? Do you include the cost of cars provided for executives? Do you itemize fringe benefits for executives, or do you lump them under "cost of doing business"? These costs may not look good to stockholders, investors, or employees. You must decide whether failing to identify them is ethical.

Deciding what to do is only part of the problem. Central to the decision is the consequence of the action, and again self-interest is involved. In deciding, you take into account the personal, social, and corporate effects of your actions. Once the decision has been made, you must act on it. Otherwise, you have not behaved ethically at all. Ethical behavior takes courage.

As you collect information for your report, you must be careful not to concentrate on facts that present a particular viewpoint. Reading only material that supports your views is tempting. Chapter 14 will discuss the problem of objective and unbiased analysis. Obviously the analysis can be unbiased only if your facts are correct and unbiased and complete.

Even if the facts are correct and all the important ones are included, the presentation still may not meet all ethical requirements. For example, a few years ago a national magazine carried the following article:

> The juvenile reading habits of American GIs stationed in West Germany have local authorities worried. It seems, according to the magazine *Der Spiegel,* that our soldiers have gone ape over World War II comic books that are published in New York and sold through army outlets abroad. The Germans depicted in these lurid publications are bestial and anti-American, and authorities fear that too many GIs are confusing these fictional characters with the present-day German public.

> The deplorable impression such war comics are making on lonely young GIs is evident even to casual observers. The youngsters are especially attracted to simplistic cartoon books because, *Der Spiegel* says, reading comprehension levels among post-Vietnam American recruits are so low: of 200,000 volunteers who signed up with the army, just 78,000 had a high school education.

> But whatever the reasons for the craze, war comics are a big business. *Der Spiegel* claims that 500,000 war-oriented comic books are sold yearly to American soldiers in European army installations. By contrast, *Playboy* sells 28,500 copies a month, and *Time* and *Newsweek* between them account for only 8,500 sales a week.

The two messages *Der Spiegel* wanted to convey were that GIs are poorly educated and have an incorrect picture of Germany and the Germans.

How did *Der Spiegel* get this message across?

The article depicts the GIs as poorly educated in that few have a high-school diploma. As a result, they can read and comprehend little above the level of a comic book. The issue of comic books also brings out a cultural prejudice. Germans are convinced that comic books foster illiteracy. Comic books are read only by people who cannot read well. In Germany educators are opposed to their sale.

As the magazine presents the story, the material that GIs read reinforces stereotypes of soldiers: (1) they are not very bright; (2) they are interested in sex—they read *Playboy;* and (3) few are interested in politics or anything else worth knowing.

The comparative popularity of the reading material supports the stereotype of the uneducated soldier. However, closer examination (Exhibit 5.2) shows that the sales figures are not presented objectively. They are in three different units: per year, per month, and per week. Are the figures correct? We have no reason to doubt the numbers. In that sense the facts are correct. However, they are neither unbiased nor presented fairly. They are presented to support a particular viewpoint. The impact of the numbers changes when they are converted to comparable units, that is, sales per year.

People reading a paper do not study every word. They assume that the bases of comparison are the same. After reading that GIs are buying 500,000 comic books per year, they skip to the next figure. Because the figures coincide with the perception of the reader, the reader sees no need to check more carefully.

The facts may be correct, but the presentation is unethical. The writer manipulated the information to support a particular viewpoint. The presentation violates the utilitarian and the justice theories, and possibly the rights theory. The article does not foster the common good, the cooperation between the two countries. It violates the rights of GIs to fairness. The misrepresentation also violates the principle of due process.

A United Press International news column on unemployment provides another example of unethical presentation of data:

JOBLESS RATE UP IN 42 STATES

Washington (UPI)—Unemployment increased in 42 states during January, according to raw data released Tuesday by the Labor Department, with 17 states suffering double-digit unemployment.

The largest over-the-month jump was in Indiana, where unemployment went from December's 8.9-percent level to 12 percent in January, a rise of 3.1 percentage points.

West Virginia, which leads the nation in unemployment, increased to 17 percent from December's 15.1-percent level but was below the 20.8 percent rate of a year ago.

Besides West Virginia, states with double-digit unemployment in January were: Alabama, 13.5 percent; Alaska, 13.3 percent; Michigan, 12.8 percent; Washington, 12.3 percent; Indiana, 12 percent; Kentucky, 11.7 percent; Oregon, 11.6 percent; Tennessee, 11.1 percent; Mississippi, 11 percent; Arkansas and Illinois, both 10.7 percent; Louisiana and Montana, both 10.4 percent; Ohio, 10.3 percent; Missouri, 10.2 percent; and Pennsylvania, 10.1 percent.

Exhibit 5.2	**Unethical Presentation of Facts**	
	As Presented	**Revised**
Comic Books	500,000 annually	500,000 annually
Playboy	28,500 monthly	342,000 annually
Time and *Newsweek*	8,500 weekly	442,000 annually

In addition, Puerto Rico had a 23-percent rate, and the District of Columbia, 12.2 percent.

The data was not adjusted for seasonal factors and compares to an unadjusted national rate dropped to 8.4 percent in February.

The seasonally adjusted national rate was 8 percent in January and dropped to 7.8 percent in February.

In addition to Indiana and West Virginia, six other jurisdictions had increases of 2 percentage points or more—Kentucky, Puerto Rico, Alaska, North Dakota, Alabama, and Arkansas (Jobless Rate, 1984).

What does the article really report? A careful reading reveals that the national unemployment rate dropped from 8 percent to 7.8 percent—a substantial drop for one month. This information is hidden, and the headline gives a different impression—unemployment has increased dramatically.

Again, no cause exists to doubt the basic accuracy of the data, but the reporting is selective and confusing. For example, the article does not give the adjusted and unadjusted national rate for December. In order to put the figures for January and February in perspective, those figures would be helpful. Most of the article concentrates on the 17 states worst hit, and only at the end is the reader told that all the figures are seasonally unadjusted. The article was published in March. The headline implies that the latest figures show a tremendous increase in unemployment, yet the article reports toward the end that the adjusted rate for February dropped from the January rate. The first four paragraphs discuss the increase, the final paragraph discusses increases in unemployment, and the information on the drop in February is buried in the middle.

The article does not present the information in perspective. The reason could be either incompetent reporting or willful confusion of information. In any case, the reader will have the impression that unemployment took a turn for the worse. The presentation is not fair and does not serve the common good; therefore, it violates utilitarian and justice theories.

As a final example, supermarkets in many states are required by law to provide **unit pricing** of items. The reason is to make comparison shopping easier for the consumer. Comparing prices is very difficult if one tall, thin bottle costs 65 cents; a short, stubby bottle costs 55 cents; and a cylinder-shaped bottle costs 57 cents. One approach is to consider the volume, but the first bottle might contain 12 ounces, the second 10 ounces, and the third 15 ounces. Most consumers would have difficulty calculating the cost per ounce for each bottle while shopping.

In the supermarkets that are required to provide unit price, the units of comparison are often different. The unit price is not helpful under those circumstances. For example, if one unit is 5 cents per ounce, another is 10 cents per pint, and a third is 3 cents per quart, the consumer cannot easily determine the least expensive one. The supermarket has complied with the law but has willfully twisted the intent of the law. The unjust practice does not help the consumer.

Unit Pricing

Unit pricing breaks down the price of an item to show the amount per unit, such as an ounce or a quart.

ETHICAL DIMENSIONS OF WRITING IN DECISION MAKING

You will always need to evaluate the political climate in an organization when you make decisions. You should examine how much the political pressures can, will, and should influence both the decisions you make and how you communicate them. If you think you are by nature totally objective, accept that all people at times have hidden agendas. They are after power, control, protectionism, or favoritism, and this influences their decisions and actions. As a first step in dealing with your own preferences and fears, you must recognize them. If you admit that you want a promotion and are afraid that you will put it

Exhibit 5.3

Ethics and Employee Evaluation

You are a first-line supervisor in a department in a large corporation. You and Lee each supervise ten clerks. One of the men you supervise is Jack.

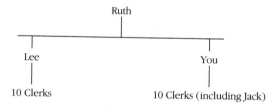

Job Performance:

Jack is, in your opinion, ready for promotion to Clerk II. He does the same amount of work as the other clerks in your unit. He is an efficient employee producing high-quality work. Because he has been with the company two years, he is eligible for 20 days of paid and 20 days of unpaid sick leave per year.

Problem:

You recommend Jack for promotion. Ruth reviews your request and informs you that his absentee rate exceeds the informal standard for the department of ten days per year. Jack has been absent 15 days—one and two days at a time. In addition Jack has been given time off for doctor's appointments. You do not feel Jack's absences are excessive, but Ruth will not okay the promotion.

Situation:

It is time for Jack's performance review, and you know the absences must be brought up.

1. How would you fill out the appraisal form?

2. Do you document Jack's absentee record?

3. What are the ramifications of documenting the file?

4. What are the ramifications of not documenting the file?

Appraisal Form:

1. List several strengths displayed on the job.

2. List several limitations to advancement.

3. Employee

_____ At present is ready for advancement
_____ Has potential for advancement
_____ Needs further development

4. Additional Comments

Source: This case was developed by Patricia Marcum Grogg, Professor of Business Communication, Illinois State University, and Beth Kranz, Personnel Communications.

in jeopardy by taking a stand against your supervisor, you at least know the factors that will influence your decisions. Once you have recognized them, you can deal with them.

The case study in Exhibit 5.3 involves an employee evaluation in which you are a supervisor. The evaluation process will require two stages: you must evaluate the employee and then communicate your conclusion. Although the communication takes place after reaching the conclusion, you may begin considering how you want to communicate some aspects of the evaluation as you evaluate.

At first glance you may not recognize the ethical ramifications of the process, but they are clearly present. In fact, all three theories of ethics are involved. The ethical questions relate to the good of the company, Jack's rights, and the issue of fairness and due process. Some of the factors you must weigh in making your decision are the following:

1. Formal versus informal absentee standards. According to written guidelines, Jack is ready for advancement. The question is whether an informal standard, which is tougher than the formal standard, can be applied. A complicating factor is that Jack may not even know about the informal standard. You might therefore conclude that Ruth is acting unethically in applying the informal standard.

   At the same time, you may want to find out why Jack was absent. Was he usually absent either on Monday or Friday? Was there any other pattern? You would also need to compare his record with that of other employees. In order to use the information against Jack, you need proof that he abused the sick-day policy. If he did, you might argue that his behavior is not in the best interest of the company and the other employees. In that case Jack acted unethically.

2. Quality of Jack's work. Based on the criterion of work quality, the promotion is in order.

3. Quantity of Jack's work. He produces the same quantity as others. On the other hand, if he were not absent so much, he might produce more.

4. Opinion of your supervisor. Ruth is against the promotion. Officially she bases her decision on the informal standard, but she may simply be using it to hide her real motives. She may realize that her insistence on standards will be perceived as laudable whereas the real motives might not. Ruth may have a hidden agenda, and so may you. Neither of you may be fully aware of the real motives of your actions; nevertheless, you must make a decision. Are you going to take a stand against Ruth on this issue? This question is related to the next factor.

5. Your own advancement in the company. What will happen to your own promotion if you defy Ruth? Does that concern enter into your decision? Should it? You must recognize and deal with the fact that it will be part of your decision process. Will you accept Ruth's decision? At first, making the decent decision appears to mean support of Jack's promotion. Suppose you find out that Jack was not sick at all but simply took the days off. Although he did not violate the allowable limit of absences, will the fact change your decision?

As a further complication, two people in your area may be considered for promotion at the same time. You must do some persuading in both cases. Knowing Ruth's feeling about Jack, should you concentrate on John's promotion? Ruth does not seem to be as concerned about it. If you support Jack, Ruth may block both promotions. Would it be better to settle for one than to risk both?

You may be tempted to dismiss this case study as capricious and unrealistic, believing that situations within companies are not that unfair. Actually, such situations do occur, and usually employees have a difficult time deciding what to do. Political power plays are a reality. The fact exists that you cannot divorce your own job completely from the situation. You have your career goals and wishes, and they will enter into the decision-making process.

You must weigh the alternatives and the implications of each. You must be honest with yourself about your reasons for choosing a certain alternative and then willing to accept the consequences of your actions. After you have evaluated the situation and filled out the appraisal form, you must still decide whether to document Jack's absences even though they did not exceed the allowed limit. If any reason exists to believe that Jack abused the sick-day privilege, his absences should be documented and he should be informed of the documentation. This case study points out the importance of keeping records of the absences of all employees so that no one will appear singled out. Fairness, honesty, and tact are the most important elements in evaluating employees. Standards must be uniform, and they must be enforced.

WRITING AND CONFIDENTIALITY

When you write reports, your research will often involve confidential information. It might relate to personnel, marketing, competitors, production runs, or product research. Secretaries, supervisors, and managers are all at one time or another entrusted with confidential information that somehow becomes generally known. Even the White House has problems with leaks of confidential material to unauthorized people, such as the press. Indeed, the people who give out the information know that they are not authorized to talk about it to outsiders.

Confidentiality is basically ethical. It protects the right to privacy and can be fair and just. Secrecy and confidentiality that are used to mislead and to harm require careful examination. On the other hand, confidentiality and secrecy are often important to the future of a company. A classic example is the company that has just developed a new product. A competitor that learns about it could copy and sell it without spending money on research and development. Keeping new-product information confidential will encourage more research and will reward the company that develops new products.

Some companies encourage employees to report the wrongdoings of other employees. Is whistle-blowing ethical? Do you do it in writing? Do you do it anonymously or do you give your name? Reporting the actions of another employee would seem to violate that person's right to privacy, but other issues are also at stake. If a crime is involved, the answer is easier because an employee who steals money from the company hurts the company and, therefore, other employees. The employee has clearly violated ethical and legal norms and should be held responsible.

Some decisions are obvious. An employee who sees safety violations in an atomic-energy plant has an obligation to the public to report them. The lives of many people may be at stake. In your everyday business the results of your decisions probably will be much less dramatic. The ethical issues may seem to be negligible in many cases, but they exist. Your duty as a writer is to present reports that can meet ethical standards. You will always need to weigh the issues of rights, public welfare, and justice.

LEGAL ISSUES IN WRITING

Many companies have codes for ethical conduct. If you examine these codes, you will find that most codes actually concentrate on legal rather than ethical issues, but the law and ethics are not the same. The law represents a base for acceptable behavior. An action that does not break the law is not necessarily ethical.

In report writing the legal issues will become important when you write proposals, contracts, employee evaluations, and job descriptions. The law gives you clear guidelines on what is permissible and what is not.

For example, the law addresses the following questions: What questions can an employer legally ask in a job interview? Is it legal to provide unsolicited information in a personnel report? Although you may want to leave the final decisions to company lawyers, you, as report writer, must be aware of the basics. You must be knowledgeable enough about the legal issues in report writing and business communication to know when to ask for expert legal advice. When preparing job descriptions or interview questions, you should check the law.

An important question the law addresses is, *What can an employer legally ask in a job interview?* The civil rights law prohibits discrimination in hiring on the basis of race, color, religion, sex, or national origin. Based on the law, questions per se are not illegal; discrimination is illegal. Because the information gained from certain questions can be used to discriminate, the interviewer must be careful about the questions asked.

An interviewer who asks about marital status and children might use the information to discriminate against women with small children, but discrimination must be proved. Courts will take all facts and circumstances into consideration in a case. Let us assume that a company has a job opening for a traveling salesperson. The job requires the employee to be on the road thirty-five weeks a year, three to four weeks at a time. Under these circumstances, a company could refuse to hire persons with small children or single parents with children at home. The interviewer asking applicants about children must ask all applicants. To ask women about their marital status and small children and not to ask men the same questions would be illegal discrimination. To give the job to a man with small children and refuse even to consider a woman with small children would also be illegal. Questions asked in a job interview must relate to the job and not expose the company to a charge of discrimination.

A second question of importance is, *Can report writers legally provide unsolicited information in personnel reports?* In writing a letter of recommendation or a personnel report, your moral duty is to state honestly what you know about an employee. If you provide unsolicited information, you should be sure that you speak the truth; otherwise you may be sued for libel. Even the truth does not necessarily protect you from a lawsuit if you acted maliciously in speaking the truth.

In one case, for example, a person was held liable for speaking the truth. The facts of the case show that the person had sent a letter to a supplier warning him not to sell goods to a competitor because the competitor was a bad credit risk. The court ruled that the writer had acted maliciously and for personal gain.

If you are asked for information about employees, you should basically have no fear of saying what you know and adding unsolicited information as long as you act in good faith. Good faith is the standard normally applied. When you are seeking information about an employee or potential employee, you, of course, want to know everything important and necessary. At the end of your inquiry you should ask whether the person would like to add anything else that you should be aware of.

If you understand some basic legal principles, you can avoid legal problems in report writing and business communication. For special cases you should, of course, consult a lawyer; however, an awareness of the law will help you understand when you need a lawyer and when you can solve the problem yourself.

SUMMARY OF LEARNING OBJECTIVES

To acquire a framework for ethics.

In order to write reports that are ethical, a report writer must understand the principles of ethics and the framework of ethical theory. The writer must answer three questions before making and communicating a decision:

1. Does the report protect the interest of the parties involved?
2. Does the report protect the rights of people?
3. Is the report fair and just?

The writer must weigh the answers and decide whether any special circumstances would allow a violation of any one of the three. After answering the basic questions, the writer can concentrate on the particulars of the presentation, which will require an examination of the organization, the word choice, and the facts.

To become aware of the ethical dimensions of organizations.

The report writer must be aware that decisions and implementations of decisions take place in complex reality. People have hidden agendas, are after power, and act out of self-interest. Although many people are capable of recognizing the ethical decision in a case, many are not willing or capable of following through with action. Ethical conduct takes courage.

To understand the ethical implications of word choice.

The writer must be aware that word pairs such as *asked–required, trying–driving,* and *should–must* create a climate in the presentation even though they do not change the factual presentation of the material.

To distinguish between factual and ethical data presentation.

Facts must be not only correct but also presented objectively and fairly. Both the decision-making process and the presentation of the decision are influenced by the political pressures and realities of an organization. The report writer must be aware of and must understand those pressures.

To examine questions of confidentiality and the law in report writing.

A report writer should know the legal ramifications of reporting. The law and ethics are not the same, but the law does provide a basis for acceptable behavior.

KEY TERMS

Utilitarian Theory
Theory of Rights
Due Process

Theory of Justice
Unit Pricing

QUESTIONS AND DISCUSSION POINTS

1. Discuss the utilitarian theory, the rights theory, and the justice theory in terms of ethics.
2. When are inductive and deductive orders of presentation not ethical?
3. Discuss the statement, "The facts speak for themselves."
4. Discuss some of the legal issues in report writing.
5. How does word choice influence the presentation in a report?
6. Discuss how a nonsubstantive word can influence the perception of the reader.

EXERCISES

1. Examine letters to stockholders in several annual reports and discuss the presentation and organization of the letters in terms of ethics.
2. Examine the codes of conduct of several companies. What are the major concerns of the companies? How do the companies try to solve ethical problems? To whom are the codes addressed? How do the codes define ethical behavior?
3. Select a newspaper or magazine article that violates the ethical norms of presentation of information. Write a brief discussion of the article.
4. Discuss the following:
   a. Is it ethical to have someone proofread a report for you that you must turn in for a grade?
   b. Mary is presenting a report on which she has worked a long time. The report is good, but you notice some minor mistakes. Should you speak up in the meeting and interrupt her presentation or wait until after the meeting?
   c. You are asked to write a recommendation for Ivan, who is an average employee at best. You do not think he will be able to do a good job in the position he has applied for, but you would like to get rid of him. You know that a good recommendation may get him the job. What do you do?
   d. You are interviewing Florence Chaplais for the position of district sales representative for your company, a major pharmaceutical firm. The job will involve substantial travel. Florence Chaplais has excellent credentials and references, but you would like to know more about her. Does she have small children? Is she married? What does her husband do? Although you know that you cannot discriminate against applicants based on family situation, you believe that Florence's personal situation may have a major impact on her job performance. The last woman you hired for the position missed work whenever her children were sick.

      In order to get the personal information you consider important, you plan the following strategy. You will ask your assistant, without explaining the details, to check with Florence about the type of insurance she would like: single or family. Florence's answer will tell at least something about her family status. During lunch with Florence, you and a coworker will talk about your carpool problems during the past week. You then will ask Florence whether she has had similar problems, adding that you yourself seem to constantly run into difficulties. You know from experience that Florence will relax and provide the personal information you want from her.

      Discuss the ethical implications of your strategy.

References

Jobless rate up in 43 states. (1984, March 21). *Vidette,* p. 2.

Kulhavy, R., & Schwartz, N. (1981). Tone of communication and climate perceptions. *Journal of Business Communication, 18*(1), 25–34.

THE PREPARATION OF BUSINESS REPORTS

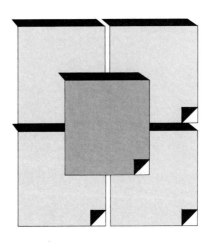

THE CLASSIFICATION OF BUSINESS REPORTS

6

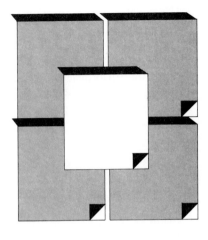

Learning Objectives

- To understand the role of report classification systems.
- To use the classification systems as a tool in report writing.
- To examine the most commonly used formats for short reports.

THE PURPOSE OF CLASSIFICATION

A business person preparing a report must determine whether it should be informational or analytical, long or short, formal or informal. The writer has to decide whether the report is a special or a periodic report and whether the report is best transmitted in a memo or a letter. In deciding what kind of report to write, the writer classifies it but keeps in mind that any classification system is a tool and not an end in itself.

Classification
In classifying, the writer describes the characteristics of the report.

Even though specific report classifications may vary from company to company, the basic **classification** systems are the same. For example, a manager who wants information on sales for the past month may simply ask for an informational report on sales. The writer who understands classification systems will know what an informational report is. A logical classification system saves time and improves communication. Classification systems also aid in filing and, therefore, in retrieving reports.

CLASSIFICATION BY FUNCTION

Based on function, we can distinguish two major types of reports—informational reports and analytical reports. The classification by function is illustrated in Exhibit 6.1.

Informational Reports

Informational Reports
Informational reports present facts.

At the beginning of your career you may write many **informational reports,** which present facts without interpretation. You will research the facts, organize them, and present them as shown in Exhibit 6.2. If the report is detailed, you should include a summary.

Exhibit 6.1   **Classification by Function**

Informational Report	Analytical Report		
Introduction	*Examination Report*		
Presentation of Facts	Introduction		
Summary	Presentation of Facts		
	Examination of Facts		
	Summary		
	Recommendation Report		
	Introduction		Introduction
	Presentation of Facts		Conclusions
	Examination of Facts		Recommendations
	Summary*	or	Presentation of Facts
	Conclusions		Examination of Facts
	Recommendations		

---

* Some report writers omit the summary in the recommendation report. They believe the summary material is included in the conclusions and recommendations.

Exhibit 6.2

Informational Report

TO: Cheryl Black

FROM: Todd Lozano ꞬL

SUBJECT: Use of Computer Lab

DATE: October 15, 19XX

The computer lab has been open for two months. Here is a summary of observations concerning the use of the lab during the second month. The first month is not included because all of the equipment had not arrived.

Equipment

The lab has 24 IBM Personal Computers and 6 printers. Software available at this point includes word processing, spreadsheets, and data-base management. Manuals on how to use the software are available.

Policy for Using the Lab

Students who are enrolled in a class that uses microcomputers have priority in using the lab. Instructors and graduate assistants may work in the lab if computers are available.

Seven classes with an enrollment of 30 students each have incorporated the microcomputer into the curriculum; therefore, the lab must serve 210 students.

During lab hours, students may work in the lab as long as they wish. Some students stay for four or five hours.

Lab Supervision

Shelly White organized the lab and set the schedules. She trained the ten students who are employed in the lab, and she coordinates their work schedules. She meets with the students once a week to discuss problems in procedure and policy.

Procedure

Students submit their IDs when they check out equipment. They are assigned a computer by the student worker. IDs are returned when students turn in the software.

A number of students ask the student worker for help, but in many cases the student worker does not have an answer. The student then often asks other students in the lab for help. This raises the noise level and interrupts the work of the other students.

Patterns for Lab Use

The lab is open from 8:00 a.m. until 9:00 p.m. Based on observations during the last month, the following pattern for use of the lab emerged.

Time	Number of Students
8- 9 a.m.	3
9-10	15
10-11	18
11-12	5
12- 1 p.m.	15

Exhibit 6.2   Informational Report (continued)

```
Use of Computer Lab                    p. 2                    October 15, 19XX


                                              Number
                               Time        of Students

                           1- 2 p.m.           20
                           2- 3                 30
                           3- 4                 35
                           4- 5                 25
                           5- 6                 20
                           6- 7                 37
                           7- 8                 48
                           8- 9                 45

        The number of students includes those in the lab and those trying to use it.  Some
        students wait almost an hour before they can get in.  Some come back several times
        before they find a place.
```

Analytical Reports

Analytical Reports
Analytical reports analyze facts.

The **analytical report** may be either an examination report or a recommendation report. The examination report examines or analyzes the data presented. Exhibit 6.3 is an examination report that analyzes the data on the use of the microcomputer lab.

The recommendation report is the most complete report. As illustrated in Exhibits 6.4 and 6.5, it expands on the informational and examination reports. It presents the data, examines it, draws conclusions, and makes recommendations. The information presented in Exhibits 6.4 and 6.5 is the same; the difference lies in the arrangement of the material. Many managers prefer to have the conclusions and recommendations early in the report, as is illustrated in Exhibit 6.5. Exhibit 6.4 uses an inductive order of presentation, whereas Exhibit 6.5 uses a deductive order.

Inductive
Inductive reports present conclusions and recommendations after the analysis of facts.

Inductive Presentation.   The **inductive** presentation closely matches the sequence in which you do your work. You lead the reader through the same steps in the same sequence in which you went through them. You present the facts, analyze the facts, draw conclusions, and make recommendations.

Let us assume you are the supervisor of an assembly line. The workers in your department assemble hand brakes for cars. For the brakes to function

Exhibit 6.3   **Examination Report**

TO: Cheryl Black

FROM: Todd Lozano JL

SUBJECT: Use of Computer Lab

DATE: October 15, 19XX

The computer lab has been open for two months. Here is a summary of observations concerning the use of the lab during the second month. The first month is not included because all of the equipment had not arrived.

Equipment

Policy for Using the Lab

Lab Supervision

Procedure

Patterns for Lab Use

Discussion

The use during morning hours is very light. In contrast, use after 2:00 p.m. is above capacity of the lab, with the exception of the dinner hour in the dorms. Many students have classes in the morning and in the early afternoon. This could account for the low user level during those times. One has to ask whether it makes sense to close the lab at 9:00 p.m. That is the time when many undergraduates begin to study.

Students are concerned about the policy for lab usage. It is difficult to justify the policy that a student may stay in the lab for as long as he wishes while others wait for hours to get in.

Students are frustrated about the level of computer knowledge of the student workers. They complain that it is difficult to get help and that there is general confusion in the lab.

Exhibit 6.4   Recommendation Report (Inductive)

TO: Cheryl Black

FROM: Todd Lozano

SUBJECT: Use of Computer Lab

DATE: October 15, 19XX

The computer lab has been open for two months. Here is a summary of observations concerning the use of the lab during the second month. The first month is not included because all of the equipment had not arrived.

Equipment

Policy for Using the Lab

Lab Supervision

Procedure

Patterns for Lab Use

Discussion

Conclusions

Based on the observations, one can draw the following conclusions:

Current lab hours are not efficiently used by students.
Current lab hours are not well coordinated with students' study habits.
The policy concerning length of usage causes problems.
The computer background of the student workers needs to be expanded.

Recommendations

The implementation of the following recommendations should help to solve some of the problems:

1. Sign-up sheets should be prepared for lab use. The maximum time for anybody using the lab should be two hours unless there are empty computers.

2. Lab hours should be publicized and students should be encouraged to use the lab in the morning.

3. The lab should be kept open until 10:00 p.m. on a trial basis.

4. The weekly meetings between supervisor and student workers should include additional training of the students on the equipment so they will be able to answer more questions.

Exhibit 6.5

Recommendation Report (Deductive)

TO: Cheryl Black

FROM: Todd Lozano *JL*

SUBJECT: Use of Computer Lab

DATE: October 15, 19XX

The computer lab has been open for two months. Here is a summary of observations concerning the use of the lab during the second month. The first month is not included because all of the equipment had not arrived.

Conclusions

Recommendations

Equipment

Policy for Using the Lab

Lab Supervision

Procedure

Patterns for Lab Use

Discussion

properly, all the steps in the assembly must be done correctly. Lately an increasing number of brakes have not met the standards. The brakes must be taken apart and reassembled, a time-consuming and costly procedure. Your boss wants a report on how to solve the problem. You investigate and present your findings in an inductive report. The elements of your report might include the following:

Problem: *An increasing number of brakes fail to meet production standards.*

Facts: *Carl Retton is absent very often. John Crotts, who is taking over for him, is not familiar with the process. In addition, several workers do not get along. They argue and disrupt the workflow.*

Conclusion: *The problem is caused by personnel difficulties and violations of company policies.*

Recommendation: *The workers should be reprimanded. If there is no improvement, they should be fired.*

The advantage of the inductive approach is that the reader becomes familiar with all the facts before being confronted with the conclusions and recommendations. The inductive approach is persuasive and guides the reader. On the other hand, it is time consuming for the readers who may be interested only or mostly in the conclusions but are forced to read all of the details.

If the writer knows that the reader is likely to agree with the facts, the inductive presentation may not be effective. Such a reader may become impatient and not finish the report. If the reader has to be persuaded, then the inductive approach can help in accomplishing the task.

Deductive

Deductive reports present conclusions and recommendations before the analysis of facts.

Deductive Presentation. The **deductive** report presents the problem, the conclusions, and recommendations, and finally the supporting facts and analysis. A deductive report on the assembly-line problem would be organized as follows:

Problem: *An increasing number of brakes fail to meet production standards.*

Conclusion: *The problem is caused by personnel difficulties and violations of company policies.*

Recommendation: *The workers should be reprimanded. If there is no improvement, they should be fired.*

Facts: *Carl Retton is absent very often. John Crotts, who is taking his place, is not familiar with the process. A number of workers do not get along. They argue and disrupt the workflow.*

Many businesses like this approach because of its directness. Its disadvantage is that readers who do not like the recommendations may simply quit reading the report before they reach the supporting data.

The following points should help you in choosing between the deductive and inductive presentations:

1. The deductive presentation saves time because it gives the important information first.

2. For a report intended to persuade the reader to a certain viewpoint, the inductive approach is advantageous because it presents all of the information before drawing any conclusions and making any recommendations. The presentation of the findings and the analysis of the data should lead the reader to the same conclusions as the ones presented by the writer.

3. If the writer knows that the reader will react negatively toward the conclusions and recommendations, they are best presented at the end. This order allows time to build arguments to convince the reader. Ideally, the reader will then accept conclusions he would not have accepted before the presentation of the data.

Determination of the Report Function

The writer must determine the kind of report the reader wants. The decision is not up to the writer. Sometimes the reader will specify whether she wants only information or also examination and recommendations. Sometimes the writer may have to ask the requester what she wants. In some cases the writer may know the potential reader well enough to know what the reader prefers.

Some managers prefer to get just the information; they do not want others to influence their decision. They prefer to analyze the information themselves, draw their own conclusions, and make their own recommendations. Some managers want the analysis input from others because they want to know how others interpret the data. Some managers may want to know the writer well before requesting a complete analytical report, which requires insight and analytical ability.

CLASSIFICATION BY TIME

 ## Periodic Reports

Some reports are written at regular intervals. For example, a sales representative may have to write weekly sales reports. An accountant may have to write monthly statements for clients. An affirmative-action officer may have to send reports to the government on a regular basis. Because these reports are written at regular intervals, they are also called **periodic reports.** In many cases they are part of the standard assignment of a particular job and included in the job description. For example, no one sends a request each Friday for a sales report on Monday. The sales representative is expected to have the report ready without any special request.

Periodic Reports
Periodic reports are written at regular intervals.

Progress Reports

To ensure that management knows whether long-term projects are on schedule, **progress reports** are written. They are usually written in connection with special projects; functions generating periodic reports rarely require progress reports. You will find more information on progress reports in Chapter 8.

Progress Reports
Progress reports provide an update on a project.

Special Reports

Special Reports
Special reports help in
solving special problems.

In contrast to periodic reports, **special reports** are written only on special request. For example, upper management may want a study of the feasibility of a new layout of the production line. Clearly, such a report would not be written on a regular basis but only when a particular problem exists. The solution may involve a team approach. For example, the manager of the production division may appoint a team to study the feasibility of a change in assembly-line layout. The team may include people from production, personnel, finance, and engineering. After the report is finished, the team will be dissolved.

CLASSIFICATION BY FORMALITY

Level of Formality
A formal report is less
personal than an informal
report.

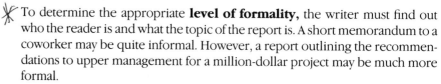 To determine the appropriate **level of formality,** the writer must find out who the reader is and what the topic of the report is. A short memorandum to a coworker may be quite informal. However, a report outlining the recommendations to upper management for a million-dollar project may be much more formal.

In an informal report, the writer may say: "These are my recommendations. What do you think, Tony? I would like to discuss the results with you during the coming week." In a formal report the writer uses a less personal style. The writer does not use the name of the recipient.

Personalization would be restricted to the cover letter that transmits the report. The letter might read: "I suggest a meeting to discuss the recommendations." In the report itself the writer might say: "Management should examine the results carefully before implementing any changes."

Some people insist that a formal business report should never use the personal pronouns *I, we,* and *you.* Although this may still be true for very formal reports, the avoidance of personal pronouns easily leads to an overuse of the passive voice. A report that uses personal pronouns is not necessarily less objective than a report that omits them. In most business reports the use of personal pronouns is acceptable and even preferable.

No absolute guidelines exist for determining when a report must be formal and when it can be less formal, but some general rules will help you in deciding on the level of formality:

1. Longer reports are more formal than shorter ones.

2. Special reports are more formal than periodic ones. The corporate annual report is an exception to this rule. The corporate annual report is very formal even though it is a periodic report.
3. Reports sent to a group of people rather than to only one person are more formal.
4. Reports that go up in the organization are usually more formal than reports to people at the same level in the organization.
5. Reports that go outside the work area or department are more formal than reports that stay inside the work area.

CLASSIFICATION BY FORMAT

Format
The format of the report
depends on its intended
use.

Standard Paper Sizes
The size of paper used in
business varies from
country to country.

The writer must know the kind of report that is wanted, the type of report is to address, and whether the report is periodic or special be she can determine the **format.** The format of the report is a function of the other classification areas. For example, a formal, in-depth examination of production costs will not be presented in a memo but on quality paper with a special cover and a title page. It may have a cover letter, a bibliography, a table of contents, and an executive summary. The periodic sales report, on the other hand, may be presented on a preprinted form or in a memo report.

The report forms illustrated in this chapter are representative of the ones used in many businesses. In some cases you may be allowed to develop your own format, but some companies insist on uniform formats. Your company may insist on a special size, color, and weight of paper for internal reports and a different paper and format for external reports. You will have to check to determine what your company expects you to do.

Paper size is of particular interest. Americans use an 8 1/2-inch by 11-inch sheet for most purposes, particularly for material that will be filed for future record. However, **standard paper sizes** vary from country to country. Germans use as standard size, DIN A4, that is about a quarter of an inch narrower and half an inch longer than American paper. This means envelopes do not fit, copy machines may need adjustment, and standard American filing cabinets are not usable for international correspondence. The problem can be particularly frustrating for multinational firms.

This chapter concentrates on the format of the memorandum, letter, bulletin, and form reports. The format of a long formal business report will be presented in Chapter 16.

Memorandum Reports

Memorandum Reports
Memorandum reports are
used internally.

The report writing principles of **memorandum reports** and letter reports are the same. The difference lies in the format of the presentation. Most companies have preprinted memorandum forms because memos are the most frequently written business reports. It would be a waste of time if the memo headings had to be typed each time. Preprinted memos are either full sheets or half sheets.

The length of memorandum reports ranges from one or two handwritten sentences to several typed pages. They can be quite personal or rather formal. The report on the Fall Kickoff Day in Exhibit 6.6 illustrates a typical memo format.

Format of Memo Heading. The memo heading identifies the sender, the receiver, the subject matter, and the date of writing. Three typical setups for this information are

TO:	Virginia Morris
FROM:	William Eick
SUBJECT:	Workflow in Word Processing Department
DATE:	December 15, 19XX

Exhibit 6.6   **Memo Report**

TO: Sharon Malone

FROM: Sandra Reese SR

SUBJECT: Chamber of Commerce Women's Division 19XX Kickoff Day

DATE: June 23, 19XX

Here is a status report on the preparation for 19XX Kickoff Day.

Place and Time

Kickoff Day is scheduled for September 20, 19XX. The Rolling Meadows Country Club will again be the site. The schedule for the day is as follows:

                    12 noon   - 4:00 p.m. Sports Activities
                    4:00 p.m. - 5:00 p.m. Relaxing Time
                    5:00 p.m. - 6:00 p.m. Cocktail Hour
                    6:00 p.m. - 7:30 p.m. Dinner
                    7:30 p.m. - 8:30 p.m. Dinner Speaker
                    8:30 p.m. - 8:45 p.m. Business Meeting

Sports Activities

I have tentatively arranged for golf, tennis, and badminton. Participants will have to provide their own equipment, but they may use the club facilities free of charge. In case of rain, outdoor activities will have to be cancelled.

Members may play bridge and other games in the clubhouse.

Cocktail Hour

Members and their guests can meet during the cocktail hour. Participants will pay for their own drinks. The cocktail hour has been a huge success in the past, and I expect many people to attend this year.

Dinner

The club has three choices for dinner:

    $9.00: Tossed salad, pork steak, french fries, mixed vegetables, vanilla
    pudding

    $10.00: Tossed salad, stuffed chicken breast on rice, mixed vegetables,
    chocolate cake

    $12.00: Jello salad, roast beef, potatoes, peas, ice cream

The menu decision has to be submitted by September 15.

After-Dinner Speaker

Because the theme for the coming year is professional self-development, I recommend we tie the after-dinner speech to the theme. Two possible speakers are:

    Susan Levine, Professor of Psychology at Midwest University
    Topic: How to Deal with Stress

Exhibit 6.6

Memo Report (continued)

Malone   p. 2   June 23, 19XX

Catherine Sullivan, President of Blooming Grove National Bank
Topic: Women and Financial Investments

Both women are well-known speakers.

<u>Publicity and Registration</u>

Information should be sent out around September 1. Reservations for dinner and activities must be made by September 15, either by mail or phone.

---

or

TO:	Virginia Morris	FROM:	William Eick
SUBJECT:	Workflow in Word Processing Department	DATE:	December 15, 19XX

or

December 15, 19XX
TO: Virginia Morris
FROM: William Eick
SUBJECT: Workflow in Word Processing Department

All three formats are acceptable and widely used.

Use of Titles in Memo Heading. In the memo heading, a complimentary title such as Mrs., Miss, Mr., or Ms. is not used with the writer's name. A complimentary title may precede the name of the receiver, but in most cases complimentary titles are omitted altogether. The receiver may be a group of people and might be identified as "all employees" or "sales managers."

If the writer does not know the name of the individual, she can use the position title of the receiver instead.

TO: Sales Agent

or

> TO: Affirmative Action Officer

In more formal memos the writer may add position titles following the names of the sender and the receiver.

> TO: Vivian Fernandez, Vice President Finance
> FROM: Mine Veral, Special Project Manager

Information in Subject Line.   The information in the subject line must be descriptive. Its purpose is to tell the reader what the memo is about.
A vague subject line such as this

> SUBJECT: Sales

can be improved by adding specific information:

> SUBJECT: Sales Data of District 5 for June 19XX

Subject lines should be constructed with care. They should answer when, where, why, what, and how whenever appropriate. The improved subject line in the example provides information on what (sales data), where (district 5), and when (June 19XX). The reader knows what the memo will be about.

Spacing and Paragraphing.   Memos are usually single-spaced with double spacing between paragraphs. Paragraphs are blocked rather than indented because the blocked style looks more modern, is easier to use, and saves time.

Headings within the Memo.   Headings help the reader to locate the main points of the memo report. Headings may be either centered or positioned at the left margin. In long memos, in which both headings and subheadings are appropriate, the major heading may be centered and the subheading placed on the left margin. Alternatively, both headings may be placed on the left margin. The major heading is often typed in all capital letters.

FISHER-PRICE TOYS

U.S. Division

or

FISHER-PRICE TOYS

U.S. Division

or

FISHER-PRICE TOYS

U.S. Division

Page Identification.   Memos longer than one page require page numbers. Headings for second pages always give the page number and the date; some also provide the subject or the name of the receiver. The following examples illustrate acceptable second-page headings:

Workflow in Word Processing Department	2	December 15, 19XX

or

Virginia Morris	2	December 15, 19XX

or

Virginia Morris
Page 2
December 15, 19XX

Signature of Sender.   Memos are not signed at the end. Writers should initial them after their typed names in the memo heading.

Letter Reports

Letter Reports

Letter reports are external reports in letter format.

Letter reports are used for external communication. They follow the same format as normal business letters, but they tend to be less personal and are usually longer. *(1-4 pages)*

The letter report has the following parts: letterhead, date line, inside address, salutation, body, complimentary close, signature block, information on attachments, carbon copies, and initials of the typist.

The letter report can be typed in blocked form or in modified blocked style. In blocked form all major parts of the letter begin on the left margin. In the modified blocked style the date, complimentary close, and signature block begin at the center of the page; paragraphs may be blocked or indented.

Letterhead.   The company letterhead is professionally designed. Traditionally it is centered at the top of the page although the letterhead of some companies is on the left margin. The letterhead includes the company name, mailing address, telephone number, and frequently the telex number and fax number.

Individuals writing business letters, such as job application letters, typically do not use stationery with a letterhead. Instead, they provide an address and telephone number in the return address. This is single-spaced and blocked on the left margin, just above the date line.

Date Line.   In the blocked style the date appears on the left margin. The name of the month should be spelled out to avoid misunderstanding, particularly in reports going to foreign branches or businesses.

Inside Address.   The inside address, also called the letter or envelope address, includes the name and title of the recipient, the name of the recipient's company, and the mailing address. A complimentary title should always precede the recipient's name (*Mr., Mrs., Miss,* or *Ms.*). As in the memorandum, a position title may follow the name.

As on the envelope, the name of the state is abbreviated using the two-letter form specified by the U.S. government for zip-code addresses:

Alabama	AL	Missouri	MO
Alaska	AK	Montana	MT
American Samoa	AS	Nebraska	NE
Arizona	AZ	Nevada	NV
Arkansas	AR	New Hampshire	NH
California	CA	New Jersey	NJ
Canal Zone	CZ	New Mexico	NM
Colorado	CO	New York	NY
Connecticut	CT	North Carolina	NC
Delaware	DE	North Dakota	ND
District of Columbia	DC	Ohio	OH
Florida	FL	Oklahoma	OK
Georgia	GA	Oregon	OR
Guam	GU	Pennsylvania	PA
Hawaii	HI	Puerto Rico	PR
Idaho	ID	Rhode Island	RI
Illinois	IL	South Carolina	SC
Indiana	IN	South Dakota	SD
Iowa	IA	Tennessee	TN
Kansas	KS	Texas	TX
Kentucky	KY	Utah	UT
Louisiana	LA	Vermont	VT
Maine	ME	Virginia	VA
Maryland	MD	Virgin Islands	VI
Massachusetts	MA	Washington	WA
Michigan	MI	West Virginia	WV
Minnesota	MN	Wisconsin	WI
Mississippi	MS	Wyoming	WY

Salutation. In most letter reports you will use the traditional salutation *Dear Mr., Dear Mrs., Dear Miss,* or *Dear Ms.* If you do not have the name of the recipient, you have several options, but none of them is completely satisfying.

1. Use of job title

   Dear Sales Agent:

   This salutation sounds impersonal and would not be appropriate for a warm and personal style.

2. Dear Sir:

   This salutation is not only old-fashioned but also objectionable because the receiver may be a woman. Unless you are certain that the receiver is a man, you should avoid this salutation.

   The salutation for men, regardless of age or marital status, is *Dear Mr.* When the recipient is a woman, you must choose from among *Mrs., Miss,* and *Ms.,* no easy task. Women who prefer a particular form of address should let people know. They can identify their preference in the signature block. In Europe, professional women are always addressed with the complimentary title *Mrs.,* regardless of whether they are married.

3. Subject line

   Some businesses are beginning to use a subject line when the name of the receiver is unknown. The subject line makes the letter report less personal, but it does identify the topic of the letter very clearly.

Body of the Letter Report.   The body of the letter report is single-spaced with double spacing between paragraphs. A letter report can employ headings to identify the material more effectively for the reader. For example, the headings in the letter report in Exhibit 6.7 clearly identify the problems, the possible solutions, and the costs. The rules for headings in letter reports are the same as in memo reports. As in the memo report, the writer may also use illustrations and itemization.

Complimentary Close and Signature Block.   The complimentary close, followed by a comma, is normally used at the end of the letter report. The typed name of the writer appears four lines below. Professional titles are added either after the name or underneath it. Some common complimentary closings in business correspondence are

> Sincerely,
>
> Sincerely yours,
>
> Yours sincerely,
>
> Respectfully,
>
> Respectfully yours,
>
> Cordially yours.

Secretary's Initials and Copies.   The secretary normally types her initials at the left margin. If the writer's initials appear also, they precede the secretary's initials.

To send copies of a letter to additional people, place their names below the secretary's initials, preceded by the notation *cc* for carbon copy, *xc* for Xerox copy, or "copy to." If you do not want the recipient to know that you are sending copies to other people, you may send blind copies. Use the notation *bcc* for blind carbon copy and the names of the additional recipients on the carbon copy only.

> Sincerely yours,
>
>
>
>
> William Shevrin
>
> WS/jp
>
> copy to: Fred Brown
>   Rose Bittner

Form Reports

Form Reports

The information on form reports is recorded on a preprinted form.

Form reports are used more and more frequently. The report writer fills in blanks on a preprinted form. Accident reports, sales reports, and sometimes job applications are examples of form reports. The lawn service company

Exhibit 6.7   Letter Report

SCHOLZ HOME IMPROVEMENT CO.
Hoopsten, WI 31761
312 Main Street
(315) 555-7681

September 20, 19XX

Mr. Chris Brons
541 Porter Avenue
Hoopsten, WI 31761

Dear Mr. Brons:

After inspection of your basement, I have decided that water-proofing is possible.

Problem

The water problem in your basement seems to result from several factors:

1. Rainwater on the paved driveway next to the house runs off against the foundation. Before the driveway was paved, the water could seep into the gravel.

2. Tests next to the foundation walls indicate that the tiling is either broken or was incorrectly laid. In any case, the tiling does not do its job. The problem is compounded by the paved driveway.

3. As you know, the sewers in many houses in your area back up after heavy rains. During the last 20 years we have averaged about two heavy storms every season. The storm sewers are inadequate for the size of the housing development.

Suggestions

My firm has been able to solve water problems similar to yours for many home owners. I recommend the following:

1. Create space between the house and the driveway. Because the rainwater runs directly from the driveway to the foundation, it is important that the driveway not touch the walls. I recommend taking out a two-foot-wide section of the driveway along the house. The area should be filled in with gravel. In addition, the outside of the foundation has to be waterproofed.

2. Replace the tiling. The changes in the driveway and the replacement of the tiling should be done at the same time. At this point the entire outside of the foundation can be waterproofed.

3. Install a valve in the drain in the basement. To solve the sewer problem, I can install a valve in your basement, so that the water cannot back up. I have installed several valves of this type, and they are working extremely well.

Exhibit 6.7   Letter Report (continued)

Brons   p. 2   September 20, 19XX

Cost and Time Frame

I could start with the work any time this month. It will take about one week from
start to finish.

The entire job--digging out around the foundation, replacing the old tile, and
installing the valve for the sewer--will cost $3,400.

Guarantee

The tiling work is guaranteed for ten years. After the job has been done, your
basement will be dry, and you can finish the area without having to worry about
water.

Sincerely,

Robert Scholz

Robert Scholz

RS/em

Exhibit 6.8

Form Reports

PERFECT LAWN
212 Garden Road
Deercreek, IL 61531
(309) 438-5796

Lawn Analysis

Customer:
Address:
Date:

Name of Inspector:

Cost per Treatment:

Number of Applications per Season:

	No Problem	Slight Problem	Severe Problem
Watering			
Mowing			
Thatching			
Density			
Crabgrass			
Dandelions			
Weeds			
Grubs			
Other Insects			

We will call you during the next few days to answer any questions you may have about our services.

Exhibit 6.9   **Bulletin Report**

October 26, 19XX

TAX BREAK SOON AVAILABLE TO ALL EMPLOYEES AT APPLIANCE INC.

If you have always wanted a legal way to reduce the bite of federal taxes, you can soon have it.

Starting in January, every employee at Appliance Inc. can sign up for the **DEFERRED PAY ACCOUNT.**

Here is how it will work:

1. You tell the company how much money you want placed in a new savings account in your name. The initial limit is 7 percent of your salary or wages.

2. The company deposits the amount you have specified into your account.

3. The company gives you a matching 50 percent contribution.

4. The company does not withhold any federal income tax on the earnings that go into the Deferred Pay Account.

5. Your deferred pay accumulates and grows over the years in your account.

6. You receive all your deferred pay plus its earnings when you retire or leave the company.

7. When you receive the payout, you will be eligible for special tax advantages.

You will be hearing more about this plan in the weeks ahead.

---

whose report is presented in Exhibit 6.8 chose a form report for communicating with customers. The form report is easily filled out by the employee inspecting the lawn. It is easily read by the customer, who immediately knows the condition of his lawn.

Form reports are useful when companies receive many reports on similar topics. For example, an insurance company uses forms for the reporting of accidents. When all accident reports are organized the same way, insurance clerks spend less time looking for location, time, and other details of the accident. The form also ensures that all important information is provided.

Bulletins

Bulletins are announcements. Because they go to a large audience, a memorandum report or letter report would not be as appropriate. The bulletin report tends to be about a page long. It has a title to identify the subject of the report. The date is also given, but neither writer nor receiver is identified. The announcement in Exhibit 6.9 was placed on bulletin boards in all departments of the company.

Bulletins
Bulletins are announcements to large audiences.

SUMMARY OF LEARNING OBJECTIVES

To understand the role of report classification systems.

With the help of the classification system, the writer determines whether the report is informational or analytical, formal or informal, internal or external, in memo or letter format. The classification system provides direction for the writer.

To use the classification systems as a tool in report writing.

Classification by Function. Reports can be divided into two major groups, informational and analytical. The analytical report can be further subdivided into examination and recommendation reports. The writer must consider the request for the report, the preference of the reader, and the topic to determine the report function.

Information can be presented either inductively or deductively. In inductive reports the conclusions and recommendations follow the analysis of data; in deductive reports the conclusions and recommendations precede the analysis of facts.

Classification by Time. Reports that are written at regular intervals are periodic reports. Reports that are written to help solve special problems are special reports.

Classification by Formality. Short reports tend to be less formal than long reports.

To examine the most commonly used formats for short reports.

Memorandum Report. Memorandum reports are the most frequently written reports in business. They are mostly used for communication within companies. Memo headings identify the receiver, sender, subject, and date. Memos are single-spaced and blocked.

Letter Reports. Letter reports are mostly used for communication outside the company. The letter report has the same parts as the regular business letter. It differs from the typical letter in that it uses headings and illustrations. It also tends to be longer and more formal.

Form Reports. Companies that process quantities of similar information often use form reports. Form reports guarantee uniformity of arrangement. They help the reader find and evaluate information.

Bulletins. Bulletins address a large audience. They are less personal than letter and memorandum reports. Company announcements are typically presented in bulletin format.

KEY TERMS

Classification   Level of Formality
Informational Reports   Format
Analytical Reports   Standard Paper Sizes
Inductive   Memorandum Reports
Deductive   Letter Reports
Periodic Reports   Form Reports
Progress Reports   Bulletins
Special Reports

QUESTIONS AND DISCUSSION POINTS

1. What is the purpose of classification systems in report writing?
2. Discuss the classification by function.
3. Discuss inductive and deductive arrangements of data.
4. What is the difference between periodic and special reports?
5. Discuss the difference between examination and recommendation reports.
6. When do you use a memorandum and when a letter report?
7. What is the purpose of form reports?
8. What is the purpose of bulletins?
9. Why do more and more businesses use blocked form for letters and memos?
10. What are the parts of the memorandum heading?

EXERCISES

1. Obtain a report from a local business and classify it according to the classification systems discussed in this chapter.
2. A majority of the employees in your department play on the department baseball team each summer. The ones who do not play generally help out in other ways. Practice will begin in three weeks, and players must sign up a week in advance. As usual, the company pays for uniforms and equipment. The location for practice has changed from Central High School to Sugar Creek Park. The department team will practice twice a week, Mondays and Wednesdays, from 5:00 to 7:00 p.m. Games will be either Friday at 5:00 p.m. or Saturday at 9:00 a.m. The final schedule will be posted as soon as all company teams have registered. Meanwhile, you would like to hold a meeting of all department members who want to play. The agenda will include the election of a new captain. As last year's captain you are in charge of the initial organization, and you have been talking to people individually. You also decide to post a bulletin on the board.

   Write a bulletin concerning this year's department team.

- a new practice location
- May 3 start date
- April 28 - a week in advance.

3. You are a college recruiter for a major firm. At the end of each interview you write a brief report. Later, as you evaluate and compare the candidates, you find that your reporting is inconsistent. You may comment on certain characteristics for one candidate but not for others, and your reports are organized differently. You want to be fair and as unbiased as possible in your evaluation.

   Design a form report that will enable you to be more consistent and objective.

4. Change the format of the following German business letter to a standard American format with blocked style.

Prof. Dr. Kathy Nink   Telephone: (05251) 601
College of Business   Extension 60 25 35
Department of Finance and Law

Central University
Normal, Illinois 61761
U S A

from the Dean of the College of Business
of the
Universitaet Paderborn   Paderborn, 14. 02. 1989
                                                        Kai/Ki

RE: Teaching Contract for the College of Business
Dear Professor Dr. Nink:
I am happy to inform you that the University has approved your teaching assignment for the summer semester. You will be teaching a seminar on the "American Market." Please sign the enclosed contract and send it back to us as soon as possible so that we can process the paperwork.
If you have any questions, please do not hesitate to call me.

Best wishes

Encl.

7

REPORT PLANNING

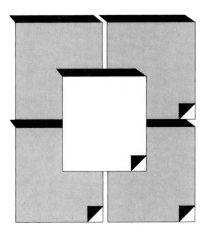

Learning Objectives

- To study the planning process for reports.
- To examine the parts of a report plan.
- To understand various organizational patterns.
- To become familiar with basic outlining systems.
- To construct effective headings.
- To examine three types of report plans.

In order to communicate successfully, the report writer must carefully study the biases, the needs, and the background of the reader. The writer furthermore must look at the report's intended use. In short, the writer must plan before beginning to write.

Planning is essential to successful communication, but a plan is exactly that, a plan. It provides a working basis, but it can never anticipate all eventualities. The plan, therefore, should be as complete as possible but also flexible. It is a tool, not an end in itself. It will always need revision and improvement before it is implemented. If the writer clings to the first draft because she has decided it is THE PLAN, the problem may remain unsolved. An architect makes many preliminary drawings before the final blueprints. Similarly, a report writer usually revises a plan several times before it is workable.

Planning is an essential element in good report writing, but the extent of planning in any given situation will depend on the complexity of the problem. In this chapter we will discuss three types of plans:

1. Informal plan—a simple outline, usually just a few notes for the writer's own use
2. Intermediate plan—usually no longer than one page
3. Formal proposal—a statement of several pages that becomes the organizational plan for a large project

Intermediate Plan
The intermediate plan is usually written in memo form.

Formal Proposal
The formal proposal is a written and formal report plan.

The writer can send an **intermediate plan** as a memo or a **formal proposal** as a formal planning document to the person who requested the report and ask for verification of the plan.

THE PLANNING PROCESS

If you have ever conducted an experiment in biology, planned a research report for marketing, or outlined a term paper for an English class, you have already used many of the tools necessary for successful planning.

You may ask yourself why a plan is necessary. You may argue that you are familiar with the problems you face on the job and are reluctant to waste time on planning when you could already work at solving the problem and write the report.

An article in *The Wall Street Journal* (Stengrevics, 1983, p. 28) reported the following about planning:

> In a work environment, where day-to-day pressures are extremely demanding, formal planning systems *require* managers to devote time to thinking about the future of their businesses. As a supplement to "gut feel," formal systems constitute an analytical, rigorous, and methodical approach to organization.

Planning helps to approach a problem rationally rather than emotionally. Planning helps to organize an approach to collecting the data, organizing the facts, analyzing alternatives, and communicating findings in a written report. Planning helps to arrive at conclusions that are based on facts rather than on feelings. Planning helps to arrive at a good decision based on a logical examination of all the facts. A plan provides guidance.

Assume, for example, that your company has decided to take advantage of new technology and automate the office. You are asked to evaluate word processing systems and present your findings and recommendations in a formal report to upper management. From the beginning of the investigation, you are excited about the available equipment, which you think can boost productivity and save money. After looking at all the cost factors, you recommend a centralized word processing system because it is most cost effective.

The system is installed, but the predicted boost in productivity and savings just does not materialize. You are asked to determine where the problem lies. When you talk to people and observe how they work, you find that most of them are used to working independently. The new system does not take this work style into consideration. Workers feel threatened and uncomfortable with the new arrangement. You come to the conclusion that a decentralized system would have been much better for your company.

This problem could have been avoided if you had talked to people at the beginning, observed their work styles, and made a recommendation that took those factors into consideration. You should have planned your investigation better.

The Scientific Method

Scientific Approach to Problem Solving
The scientific approach is an orderly and organized process for solving problems.

When you write a business report or when you carry out a business project, you apply the **scientific approach to problem solving.** In order to plan the report or the project well, you must be familiar with the steps of the scientific process as outlined below:

1. Identify the problem—To identify the problem correctly, you must distinguish between problem and symptom. Assume, for example, your business is losing money. At first thought you may say that the loss of money is the problem. It is more likely, however, that the loss of money is a symptom of other problems. Perhaps the declining profits are caused by poor marketing, lack of quality control, poor training of employees, or a combination of some or all of these factors.

2. Determine the methodology—How are you going to collect the necessary information? Will you talk to department supervisors? Will you call them? Will you look at past records? Will you send questionnaires to departments? Are you going to contact all departments, or will you select just a few?

3. Collect information and identify possible sources of the problem— Which departments lose money? How long has this been going on? What are possible reasons? What are possible solutions? What do the experts suggest?

4. Organize the information and the approach to solving the problem— What is the best or most appropriate order of investigation?

5. Evaluate the information—What do the facts mean? How are the facts related?
6. Draw conclusions and make recommendations—Based on the findings and the analysis, what is the best course of action to solve the problem?
7. Write the report and distribute it to the people who need the information.

These steps do not necessarily occur sequentially. You will more likely evaluate the information at every step and then redefine the previous steps based on the new information. The process is similar to a continuous loop, as presented in Exhibit 7.1, rather than one circle.

The actual plan will depend on the type of report you are writing. To aid you in writing a report that will meet the needs of the reader and will be ready on the requested date, a detailed report plan should include the following:

- Orientation to the Problem
- Definition of the Problem
- Problem Statement
- Purpose Statement

Exhibit 7.1   **The Problem-Solving Process as Applied to Report Writing**

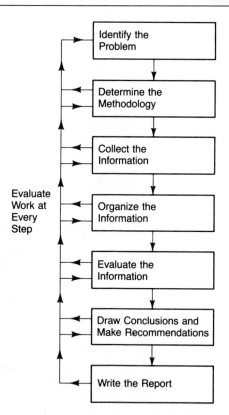

- Scope Statement
- Limitations
- Resources Required
- Time Schedule
- Method of Collecting Data
- Tentative Outline

The terminology may vary from organization to organization, but the content of the plan will be the same.

Orientation to the Problem

The orientation may give the history or chronology of earlier attempts to deal with the problem. This background information may be included to save time when considering options that were discussed at earlier times. The writer may help the organization avoid repeating mistakes by pointing out what has and what has not worked or why the company is looking at alternatives to present systems and practices.

For example, management may consider introducing word processing because of changes in the workflow, changes in space requirements and space availability, and cost and quality of clerical help. You may think this information is superfluous because everyone in the company knows about the problems. That is not necessarily true. Management may not be familiar with all the changes. Also, the readers of the report may need to be *reminded* of the reasons for the investigation. The orientation to the problem saves readers' time, because they will not need to find background information themselves.

Definition of the Problem

The clear identification of the problem is possibly the most difficult task. Yet, it is the most important step in the planning process. A problem that is not clearly understood cannot be solved. Defining the problem can mean a search through a labyrinth of parts and processes, departments, rules, organizational setups, and personalities.

You may know that your company's sales are down, but nobody will explain why. The cause could be in many areas. Should you examine advertising, personnel, marketing budget, product quality, production schedules, or customer relations? Should you look at the whole or at a combination of several factors, or is the problem in only one of the areas? If you concentrate on the marketing department and write a report on how to improve advertising, when in reality the problem is caused by a decline in product quality, you have written the wrong report.

Some preliminary research may help you put the problem into focus. Many business people say that at this point they physically tour the company, talk to many people, observe, ask questions, compare notes, and listen. No one way works best. Experience helps, but it alone is not enough.

Throughout this stage you must distinguish between symptoms, problems, and problem statement. A symptom is a sign of a deeper problem. For example, Susan Orrison is the marketing manager at a company where sales are down significantly. Everyone is pointing fingers, and nobody wants to take responsibility for the drop. After hours of discussions with department chairs and supervisors, observations, and examinations of records, Susan is convinced that a lack of quality control is at the root of the problem. As Susan sees it, quality must improve before sales will improve. Susan outlines the situation as follows:

Symptom: Sales are down by 30 percent.

Problem: Quality control is decreasing. The rate of rejects has increased by 40 percent. Turnover in the sales department has contributed to the difficulties, but a thorough investigation indicates that quality control is by far the overriding cause.

Therefore, the report Susan prepares for top management must answer the question of how to improve quality control. She formulates the problem statement in question form.

Problem Statement: How can the company improve quality control to increase sales?

Problem definition is time consuming and requires reflection. When you believe you have the problem clearly in mind, write it down, think about it further, and discuss it with others. But keep in mind that a committee agreement on what the problem is provides no guarantee that it has been correctly identified. Adjustments and changes may still be necessary as you collect more data.

When you are planning a report to solve complex problems, group discussions can help define the problem. Because major problems are seldom caused by one factor, the experience of people with different backgrounds may be needed for the task. Some companies form special committees or task forces to pinpoint problems.

If people from several departments are involved in planning, the departments will be more likely to accept the recommendations in the final report. If, for example, the marketing manager after much research defines the problem of declining sales as a production problem, production will be hesitant to accept the problem definition. If both the marketing and the production departments define the problem as a production problem, the report on how to solve the problem will be more readily accepted.

Brainstorming
In brainstorming either a group or an individual collects and organizes ideas to define the problem.

When group members first try to focus on the problem, they may engage in **brainstorming.** Usually brainstorming is thought of as a group effort, but the process also applies if you are working alone. In brainstorming the following guidelines are useful:

1. Write down whatever comes to mind as quickly as possible without stopping to analyze the ideas.
2. Continue brainstorming until you have exhausted all possible answers to the basic questions: what, where, when, how, why.

3. Examine basic assumptions, especially those you intend to use for value judgments.
4. Consider as many alternative solutions as possible.
5. Consider the implications to your organization of the problem and its potential solutions. What are the implications for cost, profit, procedures, people, materials, equipment, and legalities?

Problem Statement

When you believe that you have the problem clearly in mind, write it down again. You can use one of three formats: a question, a declarative sentence, or a fragment. If your assignment is to analyze a new training program, for example, you might state the problem in one of these ways:

Question form:　　　*How does the new program affect the departments in the company?*
　　　　　　　　　　or
　　　　　　　　　　What are the results of the new training program?

Declarative sentence:　　*This report examines the results of the new training program.*
　　　　　　　　　　or
　　　　　　　　　　This report analyzes the effect of the new training program on the departments in the company.

Infinitive phrase:　　*To examine the results of the new training program.*

All three types of problem statements are acceptable. If the writer asks a question such as "How can we measure the success of the new training program?" or "What elements have contributed to the success of the new training program?" then this question must be answered in the report. The writer can check the progress against the question and easily determine whether the focus is still on the problem. The question form tends to be more lively and interesting than the other two; it is concise and provides focus.

Questions that call for a *yes* or *no* answer do not get to the bottom of the problem, and they usually do not give much guidance in organizing and planning the report. For example, a better question than "Is the new training program successful?" would be "How successful is the new training program?" This problem statement forces the writer to examine the reasons for success or failure of the new training program and then conclude whether it is actually working or not. Ultimately, the reader wants to know not only *yes* or *no* but also *how, why, when,* and *where.*

The declarative form is best when the problem is stated as a hypothesis, as in the following examples:

The new advertising campaign has resulted in a 20 percent increase in sales.

No relationship exists between training and job satisfaction.

The first hypothesis is a positive hypothesis—there is a relationship. The second hypothesis is a null hypothesis—there is no relationship. (Chapter 11 will discuss hypothesis formation in detail.)

The fragment form, "to examine the results of the new training program," is a combination of purpose and problem statement. It works well for shorter and less complex reports. For difficult problems, which require more detailed planning, the writer may want to keep purpose and problem separate.

To continue the example, assume that you have decided the problem statement is "How does the new training program affect the departments in the company?" In the report you must examine the impact of training on each of the company's departments. In a list of all possible areas of impact, you might include the following:

- Salaries
- Mobility
- Job satisfaction
- Quality
- Cost
- Selection for programs
- Time spent in training
- Productivity
- Trends

When brainstorming to produce a tentative list, you should not be concerned about repetition and overlap. You can organize and refine the list later. The final list might look something like this:

Aspects of Inquiry	Possible Impact	Departments
Cost	Direct cost of training	Marketing Personnel Production Finance
	Indirect costs, time spent in training	Marketing Personnel Production Finance
Productivity	Impact on quality	Marketing Personnel Production Finance
	Impact on quantity	Marketing Personnel Production Finance
Selection process	Employees select	Marketing Personnel Production Finance
	Management selects	Marketing Personnel Production Finance
Mobility	Upward mobility	Marketing Personnel Production Finance
	Outward mobility	Marketing Personnel Production Finance

Salaries	People with training	Marketing Personnel Production Finance
	People without training	Marketing Personnel Production Finance
Satisfaction	Absenteeism	Marketing Personnel Production Finance
	Accidents	Marketing Personnel Production Finance
	Attitudes	Marketing Personnel Production Finance
Trends	National economy Competition Product line	

The breakdown of the problem statement into key components provides a tentative list for the investigation and report organization. A careful review of the list can show crucial omissions and signal the need for reorganization and grouping of aspects.

Purpose Statement

In a good request for a report, the purpose for the report will be clear. Often, however, the person requesting information may not know exactly how it will be used. The information requested may seem necessary, but the ultimate use may still be unclear. In this case it is the writer's task to formulate the purpose and show the purpose statement to the requester for verification. Without a clear purpose statement the writer may easily write the wrong report for the situation. Questions that may help in formulating the purpose are the following:

1. What is the purpose of this report? Is the report to inform, persuade, analyze data, compare options?
2. What is the problem?
3. Who will read the report?

Although the purpose statement needs to answer only the first question directly, the writer must know the answers to the other two. An example of a purpose statement would be "The purpose of this report is to examine available word processing systems and to recommend the system most appropriate for Grawe and Fine, Inc."

Some researchers use the words *problem* and *purpose* interchangeably. If the terms are used precisely, however, the purpose of the report is to do something: to solve the problem, to provide information, to evaluate data. The problem, on the other hand, is something that requires investigation. It may be a question that requires an answer. It may be a situation that as yet lacks focus but that clearly needs looking into. Conceptually, the problem and the purpose statements have different functions. The following examples may help to distinguish between the two:

Problem: *What is the best word processing system for the corporation?*

Purpose: *To recommend a system to upper management for implementation.*

Problem: *What are the major activities of the sales representatives in any given week?*

Purpose: *To summarize the major activities and present the report to the sales manager for training new sales representatives.*
or
To summarize the activities and present the report to upper management to show that the activities warrant a higher salary.

Scope Statement

Scope
Scope focuses on selected aspects of a problem.

Narrowing the problem to only those elements necessary to reach the stated purpose establishes the **scope** of the report. For example, there may not be a need to examine the impact of a proposed solution on all departments. The recipient of the report may need to know the impact on only the production and the advertising departments. Or headquarters may want a study of the impact of a training program in the eastern division only. Or the personnel manager may want to know the impact on job satisfaction and attitudes. In the scope statement the writer clearly states the aspects of the problem to be examined in detail. The scope statement can be part of the problem statement, or it can be a separate statement. The choice will depend on the amount of detail requested and considered necessary.

Limitations

Limitations
Limitations have a negative influence on the writing and planning process.

In the scope statement the writer consciously sets the boundaries for the report. **Limitations,** on the other hand, are beyond the control of the writer. Limitations affect the applicability and usefulness of the report. For example, the inability to collect information on the advertising budget of Company X is a limitation if the purpose of the report is to compare advertising of Company Y and Company X. An important aspect of the investigation is missing. The data on Company X may be based on press reports and hearsay, but the writer cannot verify the data by looking at the records of Company X. Conclusions concerning advertising expenditures by the two companies must therefore be considered with caution.

As another example, assume you are working under extreme time pressure. If you had three weeks, you could prepare an in-depth report. Because the report must be ready in three days, you can at best provide an overview and give an analysis of selected aspects of the problem. Still another type of limitation involves conflicting and inaccurate information. You might, for example, have to examine the possibility of establishing a subsi[diary in a] developing country where population and income statistics are oft[en un]available or are conflicting and inaccurate.

Because limitations affect the reliability of a report, they should be clearly stated. The writer must be aware of them in the planning process. Some projects may have to be terminated until major limitations can be overcome.

A statement of limitations might read: "Because of production deadlines this report has to be prepared in three weeks. For the investigation a budget of $XX is available."

Resources Required

A report must include information about the need for any special equipment, staff, time, or money. If a project will need two additional people for two months and you do not mention this fact, someone reviewing the proposal surely will ask, "How will the research be done and by whom?" If collecting your data on site selection for a new plant requires travel and on-site inspection, you must state the cost that will be involved in collecting the information. Management may want to postpone a project if the cost exceeds a certain limit. Therefore, you must determine the resources that are available, the resources you would need to do an exceptional job, and the minimum to do an acceptable job. You have to set priorities, rank the options available to solve the problem, and decide which aspects are most important. The budget should reflect the priorities established.

Time Schedule

In the time schedule, you spell out steps in the project along with corresponding dates. Be realistic and allow for a few more days than the minimum. The schedule will become a working schedule for the project and will also help your management to measure your progress. A typical timetable for a survey might be:

September 1	Finalize questionnaire
September 6	Mail questionnaire
September 30	Key responses into computer
October 1	Perform computer analysis
October 2–6	Analyze computer output
October 8–10	Write report
October 15	Complete report

Method of Collecting Data

Your written plan must describe how you will collect the information for the report. This description will usually be more detailed if you plan to use primary research or a combination of primary and secondary research than if you will rely on secondary research alone. For primary research you may need

a detailed description of sample size, sample selection, and type of investigation (that is, telephone, mail questionnaire, personal interview, type of statistical analysis). This information will help the reader decide if the methods you plan to use are valid and appropriate for the stated problem. For a detailed discussion of samples and data collection see Chapter 12.

Tentative Outline

The tentative outline will provide guidance in the research process and help with organizing the final report. It is a working outline; it will probably change as you progress. A knowledge of various organizational patterns will help you to develop an outline that fits the problem at hand.

ORGANIZATION PATTERNS

An effective organization of material will help the reader to understand it. The writer must shape the organization so that it will fit the problem and the needs and preferences of the reader.

The writer must also be aware that different cultures approach report organization differently. The Japanese tend to organize all reports in chronological order. They do not agree with the rearranging of the sequence of events. Germans tend to provide detailed discussions of background material regardless of the reader's needs or knowledge. A report without a detailed introductory section would be considered incomplete. An American who knows that the reader is familiar with the problem, on the other hand, will give little background information. The French begin with a presentation of the theory underlying the problem and then proceed to a background discussion. They tend to go from the abstract to the concrete. The American manager might be impatient with the slow start of such a report and the seemingly irrelevant information at the beginning.

This section is concerned with the order of presentation in the report, which is not necessarily the order in which the writer does the work. The writer summarizes the material only *after* all the research has been done and draws conclusions and makes recommendations only *after* a thorough examination of all the facts. In the actual report, however, the writer may want to use a different sequence. For example, he may begin with the conclusions and recommendations.

Inductive Presentation

The inductive report presents information in the sequence in which you did the work. The report leads the reader from the introduction to the presentation of facts, to the discussion of facts, and finally to conclusions and recommendations. You show the reader how you arrived at your conclusions and hope that the reader will agree with you.

As discussed in Chapter 6, the inductive approach is the best choice if you believe that the reader may resent the conclusions and recommendations. If you believe that the reader will accept the conclusions and recommendations, however, the inductive presentation may be too slow and time consuming.

Deductive Presentation

In the deductive presentation, you introduce the problem and then move directly to conclusions and recommendations. The facts and the analysis follow. The deductive arrangement is faster and more direct. Many business people prefer the deductive organization of reports because it immediately gives the crucial parts of the report. Chapter 6 provided a more detailed discussion of the deductive presentation.

Chronological Presentation

The chronological presentation is used when the sequence of occurrences and the historical development of the problem are important. Minutes of meetings are usually arranged chronologically.

> The meeting was called to order at 10:15 a.m. First item of business was. . . . The meeting was adjourned at 10:45 a.m.

Closely related to the chronological presentation is the step-by-step presentation. Instructions fall into this category. Strictly speaking, the sequence of a process rather than time is important in the step-by-step approach. Steps have to be done in a certain order to achieve the desired outcome.

For example, imagine that your parents have purchased a computer. They know nothing about computers. The instructions are written for technicians, and they ask you for help because you have worked with computers. You write out step-by-step instructions on how to get the computer, an IBM PC, ready for using the program *WordStar*. Your instructions might read:

1. Insert the *WordStar* disk into the left drive, usually called drive *a*.
2. Insert the work disk into the right drive, usually called drive *b*.
3. Turn on the computer.
4. When you see A>, type "ws" for *WordStar* and press RETURN.
5. You will then see a list (called a *menu*) of commands with the heading EDITING NO FILE.
6. Type "L" to change the disk drive to *b*.
7. When the prompt NEW LOGGED DISK DRIVE? appears, type "b:" and press RETURN.
8. When the EDITING NO FILE MENU appears on the screen, press d to create a file.
9. Type the name of your file (the title you want to give your document) when the prompt NAME OF FILE TO EDIT? appears and press RETURN.
10. You are ready to type your message.

A business that wants to examine its collection procedures for overdue accounts could also use the chronological organization to present the steps in the collection process:

1. The customer receives a friendly reminder as soon as the deadline has passed. Emphasis is on the positive. The assumption is that the customer will pay.
2. The customer receives a request to pay the bill promptly. This note follows two weeks after the first one. The emphasis is on payment of the bill and the benefits of a good credit rating.
3. The customer is informed that, unless the money is paid within one week, the account will be turned over to a collection agency. This letter follows two weeks after the second note.

The chronological presentation facilitates a comparison with collection efforts of other companies. The writer can research how many notes similar businesses send out. The timing of notes can also be compared. Chronological presentation lends itself to flowcharting. A diagram of the steps in the process can help in identifying strong and weak points in the process, as in the following step-by-step presentation:

Due Date
↓ 4 weeks
Reminder 1
↓ 4 to 6 weeks
Reminder 2
↓ 3 weeks
Reminder 3
↓ 6 to 7 weeks
Turn Over to Collection Agency

Presentation by Order of Importance

You can present your data either by starting with the least important and building up to the most important point or by starting with the most important and ending with the least important point. Much depends on your analysis of the reader. If the reader is impatient, you may want to begin with the most important point. Chances are the reader will not read the entire report if you build up slowly. On the other hand, some readers may want to know all the details. In that case, presenting the strongest point at the end may make more sense because readers will remember best the point that is made last.

Organization from least important to most important is illustrated in this example:

Advantages of proposed machine over present machine:
Less noise
10 percent lower electricity use
15 percent lower maintenance cost
30 percent higher productivity
Fewer workers (one rather than three operators)

A reversal of the order of the five advantages illustrates organization from the most important to least important.

Organization Based on Comparison

Your company may want to introduce computers into the office. After examining and analyzing three different computers, you will recommend one for adoption. In order to compare the computers, you have determined that the factors most important to your company are price, speed, complexity, and capacity.

In your report you could discuss each criterion for Computer A, then each for Computer B, and finally each for Computer C, but this would not facilitate comparisons. In your research you may have started that way, but in your analysis and in the presentation you may want to choose a different organization. The reader is more interested in finding out how the three computers rank under each criterion than in a detailed description of each computer. Your outline for the report would probably resemble the one at the left:

Outline 1	**Outline 2**
Cost	Computer 1
Computer 1	Cost
Computer 2	Speed
Computer 3	Capacity
	Complexity
Speed	
Computer 1	Computer 2
Computer 2	Cost
Computer 3	Speed
	Capacity
Capacity	Complexity
Computer 1	
Computer 2	Computer 3
Computer 3	Cost
	Speed
Complexity	Capacity
Computer 1	Complexity
Computer 2	
Computer 3	

Organization Based on Cause–Effect Relationship

If the major concern is, "What happens if . . .?" then you are dealing with cause–effect organization patterns. Managers ask this type of question frequently because they must make decisions under uncertainty. They hope that an examination of cause–effect relationships will help in answering such questions as how the new training program will affect motivation, what the result or the effect of the new training program will be, and what effect the reorganization of the assembly line will have on productivity.

The cause–effect organization moves from a known factor to the unknown. The process is linked to the chronological and step-by-step organization.

When you employ the cause–effect organization, you present the facts or options and then the possible outcomes. You want to show what might happen under certain circumstances. The cause–effect organization emphasizes future orientation and is useful in forecasting.

Organization Based on Effect–Cause Relationship

The effect–cause presentation is the exact opposite of the cause–effect presentation. Here you know the results. For example, productivity is low; sales are up; profits are down; absenteeism is down. You want to know the reasons or the cause behind certain phenomena that you have observed and examined. The organization pattern moves from the present to the past.

The relationship between cause–effect and effect–cause is shown in this diagram:

Past	**Present**	**Future**
Cause ←———	Effect	
	Cause ————→	Effect

As the diagram illustrates, you must look into the future if you know the cause and want to examine possible effects. On the other hand, if you search for possible causes, you must look at the past. In both the cause–effect and effect–cause orders, a clear problem statement is important. Otherwise, the investigation cannot be directed well.

Organization by Geographic Area

A sales manager may want to organize sales reports by districts. This order facilitates the comparison of sales performances in various territories. Multinational companies report their profits and losses by location of subsidiaries in other countries. Management can then see immediately whether investments in Southeast Asia have been profitable and how they compare to investments in Latin America or Europe.

Geographic organization can be combined with a number of other organizational patterns. The writer might present the historical development of the problem in each region and division. The writer might also arrange each region according to cause–effect relationships. The presentation within regions will depend on the nature of the problem and the needs of the reader.

OUTLINING SYSTEMS

If you choose a deductive order, it will be reflected in the outline of your report. The outline and the order of the presentation cannot be separated. The tentative outline that you put together in the proposal for the report may have undergone a number of changes as you progressed. It was a working outline. Now that you have completed the research, you are ready to complete the final outline. How detailed it will be depends on the complexity of the problem. A report of a few pages needs a less detailed outline than does a 30-page report. The two basic outline systems are (1) a combination of Roman numerals, Arabic numbers, and letters and (2) the decimal system.

The Combination System

Combination System
The combination system of outlining uses both numbers and letters.

The **combination system** is the traditional system, and it is probably used most frequently even today. Traditionally, the system uses indentations; however, it can also use the blocked form, with all headings and paragraphs on the left margin. The basic pattern for the combination system is as follows:

```
First-degree heading (usually the title)
  I. Second-degree heading
     A. Third-degree heading
        1. Fourth-degree heading
           a. Fifth-degree heading
              (1) Sixth-degree heading
                  (a) Seventh-degree heading
                  (b) Seventh-degree heading
              (2) Sixth-degree heading
           b. Fifth-degree heading
        2. Fourth-degree heading
     B. Third-degree heading
  II. Second-degree heading
     etc. . . .
```

The word *degree* refers to the level of importance of a heading.

The Decimal System

Decimal System
The decimal system of outlining uses only numbers. Decimal points identify the level of heading

The **decimal system** uses either indented or blocked format. The basic pattern is as follows:

```
First-degree heading (usually the title)
  1. Second-degree heading
     1.1 Third-degree heading
        1.1.1 Fourth-degree heading
        1.1.2 Fourth-degree heading
           1.1.2.1 Fifth-degree heading
              1.1.2.1.1 Sixth-degree heading
              1.1.2.1.2 Sixth-degree heading
```

The system you choose will depend, to some extent at least, on company practice. If everyone in your company uses the combination system, you should use it too. The sciences tend to use the decimal system. If you work with scientists or in a chemical firm, you may want to use the decimal system.

Some writers argue that the decimal system is better because it allows an infinite division into subtopics. Although that is true, an infinite number of subdivisions is not necessary. In most cases four parts (I.A.1.a or 1.1.1.1) are sufficient. The purpose of the divisions is to help the reader understand the problem and the report. The divisions are not meant to draw attention to themselves. Too many headings can confuse and break the continuity of the report.

Guidelines for Outlines

To effectively outline your report, you should observe these three guidelines:

Balanced Outline
A balanced outline subdivides report parts into approximately the same number of subparts.

The Outline Must Be Balanced.   In a **balanced outline,** divisions are fairly equal in length and all major parts have approximately the same number of subparts. Of course, you must use good judgment when applying this guideline, as these three outlines will illustrate:

```
Outline 1                  Outline 2                Outline 3

I. xxxxxxxxxx              I. xxxxxxxxxx            I. xxxxxxxxxx
  A. xxxxxxx                A. xxxxxxx               A. xxxxxxx
    1. xxxx                   1. xxxx                  1. xxxx
      a. x                    2. xxxx                    a. xxxxx
      b. x                      a. x                     b. xxxxx
    2. xxxx                     b. x                     c. xxxxx
      a. x                    3. xxxx                    d. xxxxx
      b. x                  B. xxxxxxx                   e. xxxxx
  B. xxxxxxx                  1. xxxx                  2. xxxx
    1. xxxx                   2. xxxx                 B. xxxxxxx
      a. x               II. xxxxxxxxxx           II. xxxxxxx
      b. x                 A. xxxxxxx            III. xxxxxxx
    2. xxxx                   1. xxxx                 A. xxxxxxx
      a. x                    2. xxxx                 B. xxxxxxx
      b. x                    3. xxxx                 C. xxxxxxx
II. xxxxxxxxxx             B. xxxxxxx               D. xxxxxxx
  A. xxxxxxx                  1. xxxx                 E. xxxxxxx
    1. xxxx                   2. xxxx                 F. xxxxxxx
      a. x                 C. xxxxxxx
      b. x                    1. xxxx
    2. xxxx                   2. xxxx
      a. x             III. xxxxxxxxxx
      b. x                 A. xxxxxxx
  B. 1. xxxx               B. xxxxxxx
      a. x                   1. xxxx
                            2. xxxx
The same
pattern
continues for
Chapter III.
```

Outline 1 is perfectly balanced. Every chapter has two divisions, and these, in turn, have two subdivisions each. It looks beautiful, but it is artificial, because few problems lend themselves to a perfect outline. The writer has probably forced the topic into this pattern. Outline 2 is more typical of a balanced outline that grows out of the material gathered for the report. The divisions are not even, but they are close. One chapter has two subdivisions, another has three. Differences exist, but they are not overwhelming.

Outline 3 has no balance at all. Point I.A.1 has been subdivided into five parts; I.A.2 has not been divided at all. Chapter II has no subdivisions, whereas Chapter III has six. A number of reasons may account for the imbalance. The writer may not have researched the material for Chapter II sufficiently. Perhaps Chapter II is not actually a separate chapter but a subdivision of Chapter I or Chapter III. Perhaps the writer had enough material for Chapter II but simply failed to show it in the outline. In any case, Outline 3 needs a lot of work. The entire approach to the problem might need to be rethought.

A Section, If Divided, Must Have at least Two Subdivisions.   If you have an *A,* you need a *B.* You cannot divide Chapter I into *A* only because subdivisions divide a whole into parts. One part or one subdivision can never present the whole. If you discuss the workforce in your company, for example, you can use as a heading the word *workforce,* which you then can divide into *management* and *labor.* The subheading *management* alone would not present the entire workforce. A single subdivision suggests carelessness on the part of the writer; it can also suggest that the writer has not thought the problem through properly.

Titles and Headings Must Be Parallel in Grammar and Thought.   All chapter titles must be parallel in structure. If you use a sentence for one chapter title, you need sentences for all chapter titles. This rule applies to all levels in the outline; therefore, headings within each subdivision under Chapter I must be parallel. This means that I.A must be parallel with I.B. On the other hand, II.A and II.B need not be parallel with I.A and I.B, nor must I.A and I.B be parallel with I and II. The diagram below illustrates an acceptable outline:

```
    I. Sentence
        A. Decapitated Sentence
        B. Decapitated Sentence
            1. Noun
            2. Noun
   II. Sentence
        A. Noun Phrase
        B. Noun Phrase
```

The following section of an outline illustrates violations of the principle of parallel structure:

1. Productivity is decreasing (sentence).
2. Delivery of raw material becoming unreliable (decapitated sentence).
3. Increase in cost of raw materials (noun phrase).

The writer could change all headings to sentences, all to noun phrases, all to decapitated sentences, or all to another consistent grammatical form. The point is that all three headings must be grammatically parallel. Improved wordings for the example are illustrated by the following:

All noun phrases:

1. Decrease in productivity
2. Unreliability of delivery of raw materials
3. Increase in cost of raw materials

All sentences:

1. Productivity is decreasing.
2. The delivery of raw materials is unreliable.
3. The cost of raw materials is increasing.

All decapitated sentences:

1. Productivity decreasing
2. Delivery of raw materials becoming unreliable
3. Cost of raw materials increasing

All participial phrases:

1. Decreasing productivity
2. Growing unreliability of delivery of raw materials
3. Increasing cost of raw materials

THE WORDING OF HEADINGS

All headings appear both in the table of contents and in the body of the report. They provide guidelines for the reader and should therefore be informative and precise. Because the reader may decide after looking at the headings whether to read a particular section, the wording of headings is extremely important.

The two main types are topic headings and talking headings. Which one you use will depend on the nature of your report, on the reader, and on the format your company uses for reports.

Topic Headings

Topic Headings
Topic headings tend to identify the function of the report parts.

In their most basic form, **topic headings** do not provide much information. The basic topic outline is abstract, as the following example illustrates:

Introduction
Presentation of Facts
Analysis of Facts
Conclusion
Recommendations

This outline does not tell the reader anything about the content of any of the parts. At best it would serve as a working outline for the writer. Some topic outlines are less abstract; for example, a writer examining difficulties in production might use headings such as:

> Motivation
> Workflow
> Absenteeism
> Training
> Quality of Raw Materials
> Working Conditions

This outline provides the reader at least with the major areas for discussion although it does not give any idea what the report will say about them.

Talking Headings

Talking Headings
Talking headings tend to emphasize the content of the report parts.

On the other hand, **talking headings** provide information about the content. The writer might expand the topic headings in the example to form these talking headings:

> Problem of poor motivation
> Inefficient workflow
> Frequent absences of employees
> Low level of training standards
> Poor quality of raw materials
> Outdated working conditions

The same headings could also be presented in sentence form:

> Employees lack motivation.
> The workflow is inefficient.
> Employees are absent too often.
> Training standards need improvement.
> The quality of raw materials is poor.
> Working conditions need improvement.

Talking headings help both the writer and the reader. After the writer has prepared a topic outline and completed the research, writing a talking outline might be a useful next step. The talking outline summarizes the major points of the discussion and may enable the writer to organize the report more effectively.

On the other hand, the writer must be careful not to provide the reader with too much information. Headings should be short and efficient. Too much information, as in the following example, may confuse the reader.

> Evaluation of motivational problems in Department Three of Subsidiary Midwest based on an examination of production records and interviews with employees and supervisors of the department.

The reader must read this heading several times in order to comprehend the content. Perhaps the writer should rearrange the entire section, as follows:

> Evaluation of motivational problems of Department Three in Subsidiary Midwest
> A. Interviews with employees and supervisors
> B. Examination of production records

If the department and the subsidiary have already been identified, perhaps even in the title of the report, the information does not need to be repeated in the subheadings. The heading could therefore be shortened to:

Evaluation of motivational problems
A. Interviews with employees and supervisors
B. Examination of production records

The development of talking headings can help some writers to overcome writer's block. Talking headings give the writer an opportunity to develop paragraphs and whole sections from the outline. The writer who chooses this approach, however, must be careful to reduce the final outline to an effective length for presentation in the table of contents.

THREE TYPES OF PLANS

The Informal Plan

To plan a one-page memo you may simply want to make a few notes for yourself. No official plan is necessary. In organizing your thoughts you should answer three questions:

What is the problem to be solved?
Who is going to read the report?
What use will the reader make of the information provided?

For short and simple reports you may plan in your head, but you do have to organize your thoughts.

The Intermediate Plan

An intermediate plan consisting of a statement of purpose, problem, and method may be all that is necessary for reports between two and eight pages long. This intermediate planning approach is illustrated in the following example.

Tim Richards, the new personnel vice president, wants a report on how the Women in Management program is doing. Terry Morris, his assistant, has two weeks to write a report. In view of the time frame and the wording of the request, Terry decides that she must write a short plan in order to clarify the purpose, state the problem, and outline her approach (method). She does not need special resources, there are no limitations, and the report is not so complex that she has to make a detailed time schedule.

The plan could look like this:

Purpose: *To inform management of the current status of the project*

Problem: *What is the status of the Equal Employment Opportunity (EEO) policy in the company.*
  1. To describe the EEO policy of the company
  2. To compare current figures concerning women in management with those of the past three years

3. To describe the current program
    a. Selection of participants
    b. Level of commitment
    c. Curriculum
4. To discuss appropriate methods for improving the effectiveness of the Women in Management program

Method: *Base the report on the company's current EEO report and on a report of the materials covered in the Women in Management program.*

The plan tells Tim Richards what Terry intends to do, and it has enough detail to help her collect the information and organize the report.

The Formal Proposal

Formal proposals are written when major projects are involved. They can serve several functions: they can become a guide for writing a report, they can be used to inform management or other interested persons of an intended project, or they may serve as a request to start a project. A formal proposal may include the following sections:

    Title Page
    Purpose or Objective
    Description of the Problem
    Orientation to the Problem
    Scope Statement
    Limitations
    Budget
    Timetable
    Methods
    Significance or Impact of the Study

Not all proposals have identical formats. Format, organization, and headings depend on the nature of the study and the guidelines established by those requesting a proposal or research plan. Most of the information provided in the proposal becomes part of the final report. Because the proposal is a plan for action, it is written in future tense; that is, "This report will examine. . . ." In the final report, after the research has been completed, this statement is changed to "The report examines the effects. . . ."

The formal proposal in Exhibit 7.2 is a report plan for examining the affirmative action plan at an insurance company.

SUMMARY OF LEARNING OBJECTIVES

To study the planning process for reports.

The planning process follows the scientific approach to problem solving. Planning helps the writer understand the problem and organize the material. As a memo to management, the plan helps the requester decide if the report will provide the necessary information.

Exhibit 7.2

Formal Proposal

UPDATING THE AFFIRMATIVE ACTION PLAN AT

AMERICAN INSURANCE COMPANY

A Proposal

Prepared for

Patricia Marcum

Personnel Manager

American Insurance Company

Prepared by

Melanie Woerly

Legal Staff Assistant

American Insurance Company

February 12, 19xx

Exhibit 7.2   Formal Proposal (continued)

UPDATING THE AFFIRMATIVE ACTION PLAN AT

AMERICAN INSURANCE COMPANY

<u>Purpose of the Study</u>

The purpose of this study is to analyze the current legal
rulings concerning affirmative action programs and to formulate
recommendations for updating the affirmative action program at
American Insurance Company.

<u>Background Information</u>

Affirmative action is in a state of change. The Reagan
Administration pushed strongly for a policy that would apply
affirmative action only to individuals who had been direct
victims of discrimination. The Supreme Court rejected this view
in two cases. In <u>Local Number 93, International Association of
Firefighters, AFL-CIO, C.L.C.</u> v. <u>City of Cleveland</u> and in <u>Local
28 of the Sheet Metal Worker's International Association</u> v. <u>Equal
Employment Opportunity Commission</u>, the Supreme Court ruled that
"numeric goals," also known as quotas, can be used in hiring
blacks and other minorities. In <u>Johnson</u> v. <u>Santa Clara County,
California,</u> the Supreme Court ruled that public and private
employers can voluntarily adopt hiring and promotion goals to
benefit minorities and women, even at the expense of more
qualified white men.

At the end of the Reagan Administration the Supreme Court
narrowly ruled in <u>City of Richmond</u> v. <u>J.A. Croson Company</u> that
affirmative action programs have to correct discrimination
problems that were encountered by specific individuals. The

1

Exhibit 7.2

Formal Proposal (continued)

Court ruled that affirmative action programs aimed at eliminating discrimination in general were not permissible. While experts insist that the ruling applies to a specific case only, there is concern about the direction of the Supreme Court.

Most of the Supreme Court cases on affirmative action programs deal with public, rather than private, employers. However, the decisions are important to private employers because the same laws apply to both groups, and cases against private employers may reach the Supreme Court in the future.

American Insurance Company has had an affirmative action program for the last ten years. In view of the Supreme Court rulings, the program needs to be reevaluated to ensure that it still complies with the law.

Problem Statement

What changes are necessary to bring American Insurance Company's affirmative action program up to date?

Scope Statement

The report will focus on a review of the literature and an examination of Supreme Court cases relating to affirmative action programs. The study will especially evaluate the implications for American Insurance Company.

A historical overview of the past Supreme Court decisions and the changing legal requirements will provide an understanding of the current legal environment that American Insurance Company must take into consideration in any changes in its program.

2

Exhibit 7.2   Formal Proposal (continued)

<u>Limitations</u>

The major limitation is that private affirmative action plans have not been brought to the Supreme Court. As a result, no precedents exist in the case literature. Furthermore, it is difficult to get information from other companies about their affirmative action programs because most companies consider details about their programs to be confidential information.

<u>Methodology</u>

The study will rely on thorough secondary research. Information about specific company programs will come from journals such as <u>Management World</u>, <u>Employment Relations Today</u>, and <u>Industry Week</u>. The <u>Corpus Juris Secundum</u> will be used to study recent Supreme Court cases in the area.

<u>Timetable and Budget</u>

American Insurance Company has the legal sources and the pertinent business publications in the company library. Therefore, no special financial resources are necessary to conduct the study.

In view of the changing environment of affirmative action programs, the company has put a high priority on this study. The following timetable provides a tentative schedule.

Research	2 weeks
First Draft	1 week
Revisions	3 days
Final Copy	2 days
Total Time	4 weeks

3

Exhibit 7.2   **Formal Proposal (continued)**

<u>Tentative</u> <u>Outline</u>

I. INTRODUCTION

    A. Background Information
    B. Problem Statement
    C. Scope Statement
    D. Limitations
    E. Methodology

II. HISTORY OF AFFIRMATIVE ACTION

    A. Title VII of the Civil Rights Act
    B. Equal Employment Opportunity Commission

III. ANALYSIS OF SUPREME COURT CASES

    A. Background of Supreme Court Decisions
    B. Recent Supreme Court Decisions
    C. Trend of Supreme Court Decisions

IV. ANALYSIS OF AFFIRMATIVE ACTION PROGRAMS

    A. Characteristics of Affirmative Action Plans
    B. Affirmative Action at American Insurance
    C. The Future of Affirmative Action at American Insurance

V. CONCLUSIONS AND RECOMMENDATIONS

    A. Necessary Changes at American Insurance Company
    B. Implementation Strategies

4

Exhibit 7.2   Formal Proposal (continued)

<u>Tentative Bibliography</u>

Bennett-Alexander, D. (1988). Can sex be considered in promotion determinations? <u>Labor Law Journal</u>, <u>39</u>, 99-123.

Civil Rights Act. Title 42. 1971 (1964). Amendments: Age Discrimination in Employment Act. (1973). Rehabilitation Act. (1973). Pregnancy Act. (1978).

Constitutional law: racial promotion quotas. (1987). <u>Harvard Journal of Law and Public Policy</u>, <u>10</u>, 746-752.

Cottam, K. (1987). Affirmative action: attitude makes a difference. <u>Library Journal</u>, <u>112</u>, 47-50.

Edwards, H. (1987). The future of affirmative action in employment. <u>Washington and Lee Law Review</u>, <u>44</u>, 763-787.

Friedman, J. (1987). <u>Employment discrimination</u>. New York: Foundation Press.

Furnco Construction v. Waters, 438 U.S. 567 (1978).

Griggs v. Duke Power Co., 401 U.S. 424 (1971).

Heart of Atlanta Motel v. U.S., 379 U.S. 241 (1964).

Is preferential treatment justified in voluntary affirmative action programs? (1988). <u>American Journal of Trial Advocates</u>, <u>12</u>, 232-241.

Local Number 93, International Association of Firefighters, AFL-CIO, C.L.C. v. City of Cleveland, 106 S.Ct. 3063 (1979).

Local 28 of the Sheet Metal Workers' International Association v. Equal Employment Opportunity Commission, 478 U.S. 421 (1986).

Meritor Savings Bank v. Vinson, 477 U.S. 52 (1986).

McGuire, C. (1989). <u>The Legal Environment of Business</u> (3rd ed.). Columbus: Merrill Publishing Co.

Price Waterhouse v. Hopkins, 109 S.Ct. 1775 (1989).

Smith, L., Roberson, G., Mann, R., & Roberts, B. (1988). <u>Business Law</u> (7th ed.). St. Paul: West Publishing Co.

5

To examine the parts of a report plan.

In the report plan the writer defines the problem and the scope of the report. He clearly states any limitations, required resources, time schedules, and the method for collecting data.

To understand various organizational patterns.

The final organization of the report is based on a reevaluation of the reader and the problem at hand. The choice of presentation will depend on company practice, reader bias, and preference. In inductive order the report progresses from problem presentation to presentation of data, analysis of data, conclusions, and recommendations. In the deductive report the writer presents the problem, conclusions, and recommendations first. The presentation and analysis come last.

Other organizational patterns are chronological presentation, presentation by order of importance, organization based on comparisons, organization based on cause–effect relationships, organization based on effect–cause relationships, and organization based on geographic area. For each report the writer must determine which organization presents the material most effectively.

To become familiar with basic outlining systems.

The writer must complete the outline of the report based on the organizational pattern chosen, using a combination system or the decimal system. Headings must be consistent and grammatically parallel. Although headings are necessary to guide the reader through the report, the writer must take care not to use too many. Too many headings make the report choppy and destroy the flow of ideas.

To construct effective headings.

Good headings are informative. The writer can use either topic or talking headings. Topic headings are shorter, but they do not provide much information about the material under the heading. When using talking headings, the writer should concentrate on the most important information. Headings must be concise and informative.

To examine three types of report plans.

The complexity of the plan depends on the complexity of the problem. Three types of plans are the formal proposal, the intermediate plan, and the informal plan. Planning is a tool, not an end in itself.

KEY TERMS

Intermediate Plan	Scientific Approach to
Formal Proposal	Problem Solving

Brainstorming   Decimal System
Scope   Balanced Outline
Limitations   Topic Headings
Combination System   Talking Headings

QUESTIONS AND DISCUSSION POINTS

1. Why is planning for report writing important?
2. Discuss the steps in the planning process. What are the functions of each step?
3. Discuss the difference between scope and limitations.
4. What is the purpose of stating the methodology in the report plan?
5. What is the difference between the report problem and the report purpose?
6. Contrast the planning process for short, medium-length, and long reports.
7. Discuss the inductive and deductive organization patterns. What are advantages and disadvantages of each?
8. What are the characteristics of organization based on comparison, cause–effect relationships, effect–cause relationships, geographic area, chronological sequence, order of importance?
9. Describe the characteristics of a balanced outline.
10. Discuss the advantages and disadvantages of using the combination or the decimal system for outlining a report.
11. Discuss the necessity for parallel headings.
12. Discuss the difference between talking and topic headings.

EXERCISES

1. Describe three situations that would require a business report and determine whether each situation demands an informal, intermediate, or formal plan.
2. Identify a problem of an organization to which you belong. Write a problem statement and scope statement to help you solve the problem.
3. Which one of the following headings does not fit?
   a. Growing sales
   b. Decreasing labor cost
   c. Materials unfinished
   d. Declining absenteeism
4. Which of the following does not fit?
   a. Production is holding steady.
   b. Negotiations progress smoothly.
   c. Competition making inroads.
   d. Advertising has to be improved.

5. Evaluate the following outlines. Are they logical and proportional? What improvements would you make in them?

   I. The Ranch-Style House
      A. Advantages
         1. No stairs to climb
         2. Modern in design
         3. Large roof area adds to construction cost.
      B. The Cape Cod-Style House
         1. Utilized to a large extent in New England
         2. Utilizes space to excellent advantage
  II. The Colonial-Style House
      A. Advantages
         1. Two floors make for low construction cost.
         2. Limited lot-size needed
      B. Disadvantages

   I. Directions of Communication in Industry
      A. Upward
         1. Purposes
            a. To inform
            b. To suggest action
      B. Downward
         1. Purposes
            a. To direct
            b. To inform
            c. To issue orders
      C. Laterally
         1. Purposes
            a. To inform
            b. To suggest

---

  1. The engineer's liberal education
    1.1 Necessary courses in the humanities
    1.2 Courses in the social sciences
    1.3 Physical-science courses
    1.4 Social-science courses
       1.4.1 History
       1.4.2 Economics
       1.4.3 Geography
  2. The engineer's professional education
    2.1 Courses in general engineering
       2.1.1 Mathematics
       2.1.2 Physics
       2.1.3 Mechanical engineering
    2.2 Courses in concentration area
       2.2.1 Electrical engineering
       2.2.2 Ceramic engineering
       2.2.3 Structural engineering
       2.2.4 Civil engineering

6. You have interviewed with a major marketing company for a position after graduation. The interview went well, and you think you have a

good chance of being hired. At the end of the interview the recruiter emphasized the importance of good communication skills and asked to see a sample of your writing. She suggested that you prepare a report identifying and describing a problem at an organization with which you are familiar. She would also like to see a tentative plan of possible solutions of the problem.

You decide to write about a problem you faced at a summer job. Your tentative outline is as follows:

Background of the Organization
My Position in the Organization
Description of the Problem
Possible Causes of the Problem
Tentative Outline for Solutions

You need to provide some detail because the recruiter is not familiar with the organization or the problem. When you are satisfied that you have done your best, use the outline to write a letter report. Address it to

Ms. Brigitte Martin
American Marketing, Inc.
350 Columbus Boulevard
Hinsdale, IL 60521

References

Stengrevics, J. M. (1983, September 26). Corporate planning needn't be an executive straitjacket. *The Wall Street Journal,* p. 28.

SHORT AND
SPECIAL REPORTS

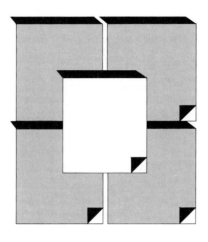

Learning Objectives

- To study the content and organization of the most frequently written business reports:

Minutes	Staff Reports
News Releases	Job Descriptions
Progress Reports	Policies and Procedures
Proposals	Instructions
Feasibility Studies	Annual and Quarterly Reports
Justification Reports	

Everyday business affairs require many more short reports than long reports. This chapter discusses the short reports most frequently written.

MINUTES

Minutes
Minutes are a record of a meeting.

Purpose of Minutes

The **minutes** of a meeting serve as a summary and a reminder for those who attended it. For those who were unable to attend, the minutes provide information about what went on. With the information from the minutes even people who did not attend the meeting can go into the next meeting well informed. Minutes are often distributed outside the group that was asked to attend the meeting because they contain information needed to coordinate efforts. They may also be sent to upper management.

Minutes are customarily approved at the following meeting after any necessary changes have been made.

Sometime during your career you will have to write minutes. A secretary is not always available to do the job. You may also be elected secretary for professional and civic organizations and be expected to take minutes in that position. Regardless of whether you write the minutes or simply approve them, you must know the elements of effective minutes.

One of the most important skills necessary for writing minutes is the ability to listen carefully. Although you might think that shorthand would help, shorthand alone does not guarantee the correctness or the accuracy of the minutes. In writing minutes you will need to summarize and selectively present information. Grasping key ideas and arguments is therefore much more important than the ability to record proceedings verbatim.

To record meetings on tape and write the minutes afterward is a waste of time. No company will want to pay you to listen to the same meeting twice. A recording can occasionally be helpful if you want to check or keep a complete record of some controversial points. In that case you must consider the legal ramifications of taping meetings. Unless you have permission to tape, you may be violating the law.

Ideally, the notes you take at a meeting will serve as a rough draft. To expedite the writing, minutes are normally written in chronological order. You may give the rough draft to the secretary or dictate the minutes so the secretary can type them. Minutes should be distributed as soon as possible after a meeting.

Format of Minutes

The two basic formats for minutes are the memo and the titled report. In either format the heading must give the subject, date, and place of the meeting. The following is an example of the heading for minutes in memo form:

TO: Patti Gahr
           Doris Gonzales
           Vivian Fernandes
           Bruce Milliard
           Frank Westphal
FROM: Cathy Bourke
RE: Minutes of Meeting of Training Supervisors, March 15, 19XX
DATE: March 16, 19XX

Present: Bourke, Gahr, Gonzales, Fernandes, Milliard
Absent: Westphal

Minutes for the same meeting, if written as a titled report, would be headed as follows:

Minutes of Meeting of Training Supervisors
March 15, 19XX

Present: Bourke, Gahr, Gonzales, Fernandes, Milliard
Absent: Westphal

The minutes must indicate who was present and who was absent. If the group is small, a list of people absent and present is usually included in the heading. If the list is long, it can be presented on a separate sheet at the end of the minutes.

People who make important contributions or who bring up an important argument should be identified by name. The writer can exercise some discretion in deciding whether to name and quote an individual. If there are any votes, the writer must identify the person who made the motion and the person who seconded it, the precise wording of the motion, and the precise outcome of the vote. A typical motion and vote might be reported in the minutes as follows:

Tanton moved to study the possible effects on workflow and turnaround time from centralizing word processing before any decision be made. (Chang seconded.) The motion passed: 5 yes, 1 no, 1 abstention.

Minutes are kept on file. Management may want to refer to them later to see, for example, who was present when a new policy was established. Members of the committee that established the policy may want to review the major arguments for or against it.

Minutes may have the following parts:

1. **Heading.** The writer can identify the subject of the report either with a title or as the subject line of a memo heading. The name of the group that met and the date of the meeting must be given.
2. **Attendance.** In the minutes, usually at the beginning, the writer lists the names of people present and absent. The names of guests, people who normally do not attend the meeting but who for a particular reason were present, are given too.
3. **Opening and Closing.** Minutes may start out by stating the beginning time of the meeting and close by providing the exact ending time. It is customary to approve the minutes of the last meeting at the beginning of the new session. The approval of the minutes guarantees that committee members agree to the content of the minutes.
4. **Record of the Meeting.** Minutes are arranged in chronological order. Topics discussed can be presented in itemized or paragraph form. Minutes must provide enough detail so that people who did not attend the meeting will know what took place.

5. **Votes.** If any voting takes place, the minutes have to state who made a motion, who seconded the motion. The minutes also have to provide the precise outcome of any vote.

The precise content of minutes depends on the nature of the meeting, the task of the group, and the formality of the meeting. Exhibit 8.1 illustrates one possible pattern for minutes.

NEWS RELEASES

News Release
A news release announces corporate news to the public. It may also be called a *press release*.

The **news release** is public-relations material. News releases often announce performance records, management decisions, awards to individual employees, the reasons for layoffs, or other information of interest to the public. They must be objective. Management, of course, wants to represent its actions in as positive a light as possible, but accuracy and ethical conduct are required when reporting information.

If you write a news release, you will usually write as a spokesperson for the company. Therefore, you refer to the writer as Company X rather than as *I*. You may say: "The company has decided" or "Management has determined."

To increase the probability that the release will be used, the message should be newsworthy, timely, and in proper form. The most important facts should be stated first. Because many people will read only the headline and the first paragraph, additional information should follow in descending order of importance.

If at all possible, you should limit the news release to one page. Longer releases are stapled so that the pages do not become separated. All news releases should be double-spaced and typed on company letterhead or on plain paper with the company name and address typed near the top. The end of the release should be marked clearly.

The name and telephone number of a person who can be contacted for more information should be included. Users occasionally want more detailed information than is given in the release.

Sometimes press releases are presented orally to the public or to employees before they are submitted to the media. You will need to check with particular newspapers for submission policies and deadlines. Large companies sometimes also send copies of news releases to stockholders.

News releases should have the following information:

1. **Identification.** You must identify the report as a news release, and write the words FOR RELEASE or FOR IMMEDIATE RELEASE at the top. You also must list the name of the company, the company address, and a contact person.
2. **Message.** The message has to be timely and newsworthy and answer *who, what, why, where, when,* and *how.* You should present the most important facts first. Additional facts should be given in descending order of importance.

Exhibit 8.1   **Minutes**

SPECIAL MEETING OF JOINT-APPRENTICESHIP COMMITTEE

January 16, 19XX, 2:00 p.m.

Members Present: Remmers, Ranney, Gonzales, DuBois, Gahr, Fox

This meeting was called for the purpose of evaluating David Swain, Maintenance Apprentice, because he is approaching the 6,999-hour mark.

The committee members were given Mr. Swain's evaluation sheets, which had been filled out by Selecting Shift Supervisors John Remmers, Mark Utendorf, and Vivian Grever. The Selecting Shift Supervisors evaluated Mr. Swain because they supervise him when he is working on shift rather than during the day. Miss Gahr informed the committee about the amount of time supervisors have spent with Mr. Swain for training on certain projects.

The evaluations were discussed. All of them showed a lack of improvement. The committee discussed the fact that at the previous meeting Mr. Swain was given up to 6,999 hours to show improvement. It had also been decided that the advancement to the 7,000-hour level would be withheld if Mr. Swain did not improve.

Mr. Swain was informed of the decision after the previous meeting. At that time he was offered the opportunity to move to the day shift in order to improve his performance. During the day he would be able to work with Journeymen Maintenance Mechanics. Mr. Swain turned the opportunity down.

Because of the most recent evaluations, the committee decided that Mr. Swain would be held at 6,999 hours and would not be allowed to advance to the 7,000-hour level. At the end of 1,000 hours (approximately six months) he will be evaluated again. If at this time he still does not show sufficient improvement, the Joint-Apprenticeship Committee will decide whether to keep Mr. Swain or remove him from the apprenticeship program.

The committee will once more offer Mr. Swain the opportunity to move to the day shift. Mr. Swain will have two weeks to consider this move.

The committee decision and recommendation will be discussed with Mr. Swain on January 17.

The meeting was adjourned at 3:00 p.m.

3. **Ending.** You should mark the end of the release clearly, so that the newspaper editor or the radio or television announcer knows that the release is complete.

An example of a news release is presented in Exhibit 8.2.

PROGRESS REPORTS

Progress Report
A progress report is an update on a project.

If you are working on a long project, you may be asked to write **progress reports.** Progress reports usually summarize what has been accomplished to date. The emphasis is on the interval between the last and the current progress report. The writer has to provide information on the tasks completed on time, tasks that are behind schedule, and tasks that are ahead of schedule. In addition, the writer must address any budget overruns. If there are discrepancies between the schedule and actual accomplishments, the reasons for the differences must be explained.

The writer of a progress report should identify what remains to be done, describe any foreseeable problems in detail, and analyze their impact on the schedule. If the project is off schedule, the report must include suggestions for making up time. Severe financial penalties are often incurred if a project is not completed as scheduled. For example, a construction firm may have to pay thousands of dollars in damages for every day a job goes beyond the scheduled completion date.

The progress report allows the reader to relate the progress of the project to overall company plans. Suppose, for example, that construction for K-Supermarket is not on schedule, as reported in Exhibit 8.3. Instead, the report indicates that work is three weeks behind schedule, and chances for making up the time are very slim. In that case the manager reading the report may need to reschedule the delivery date for merchandise to stock the store. Without a progress report, the manager would not have known to hold up delivery, and merchandise might have arrived long before the store was ready to open. The progress report also will help the manager to determine when to interview and hire employees for the new store.

PROPOSALS

Proposal
In a proposal the writer proposes to do a project.

In both business and government, **proposals** play an increasingly important part. For example, both provide money for research projects to universities and individual professors. In most cases the money is not simply handed out; universities and individuals must submit competitive proposals detailing their projects. Government and private businesses want to be certain that the money is spent for worthy projects. They also must account for spending tax or stockholders' money wisely.

Proposals also play a major role in everyday business practices. For example, suppose a company is expanding and needs more space. After evaluating

Exhibit 8.2   ## News Release

Further Information

Ronald G. Bottrell
Senior Manager
Corporate Communications
(312) 222-7388

**QUAKER ANNOUNCES EUROPEAN
PET FOODS CONSOLIDATION**

For Immediate Release

Chicago, Illinois, February 15, 1989 -- The Quaker Oats Company announced today that it plans to consolidate its European pet foods manufacturing through the closing of two older plants, and to centralize dry pet foods manufacturing at a new advanced technology plant to be built at Moerdijk in the Netherlands.

Philip A. Marineau, Executive Vice President -- International Grocery Products, said, "The consolidation of European pet food manufacturing will provide production efficiencies which will provide investment funds to strengthen Quaker's position in the highly competitive European market." Quaker is the number-two pet foods manufacturer in Europe where pet foods account for about 60 percent of the Company's European sales volume.

The phaseout of the two older plants, located at Etten-Leur in the Netherlands and Euskirchen, West Germany, will begin in October 1989 and is scheduled for completion by December 1990.

The consolidation will result in a one-time charge of $21 million, or 19 cents per share, which will be taken in the third quarter of fiscal 1989 which ends March 31, 1989.

Quaker is an international marketer of foods, pet foods, and toys.

# # #

Exhibit 8.3   **Progress Report**

```
TO:       John Lorenzen

FROM:     Joe Barrett

RE:       Progress on K-Supermarket Construction

DATE:     September 30, 19XX

The construction of K-Supermarket is on schedule.

By the beginning of September the construction of the building had been completed.
During September the following jobs were finished:

1.  Construction of interior walls.
2.  Installation of electricity, gas, and water.
3.  Application of insulation to outside walls.

The jobs left for October are:

1.  Painting.  The paint has not arrived yet; however, I called the dealer today
    and was promised it would be delivered within the next 3 days.  No schedule
    problems are anticipated as a result of the delay.
2.  Installation of light fixtures.
3.  Installation of counters, shelves, and freezers.

At this point I see no difficulty in completing the project by October 31, as
scheduled.
```

several options, management decides in favor of a new building. Rather than simply select a builder for the project, the company announces open bidding in an effort to assure that the building is constructed well and realistically priced. The company must observe legal requirements for soliciting bids. Bidding must be open to qualified companies, and affirmative action regulations may further influence the process. Exhibit 8.4 provides an example of a bid.

Most organizations that solicit proposals require a specific format that the bidder must follow exactly. Not following the format, not providing all background and supplementary information requested, or even double-spacing the proposal when single-spacing is requested may result in elimination of the proposal from consideration. The writer must follow all of the requirements for submitting a proposal even though they may seem unnecessarily rigid and arbitrary.

Sometimes a manager may ask for a proposal to solve a specific problem. Exhibit 8.5 is a proposal in response to a request by Florence Mazet, President, Student Affairs, at Prairie University. She wants to know why student participation in residency hall government and residency hall sponsored events is declining. Deepak Gupta submits a proposal on how to collect and analyze the data. Once the reasons are clear, solutions to the problem can be established.

Exhibit 8.4   **Proposal—Bid**

HERRMANN FIRE EQUIPMENT CO.
1615 S.W. Adams Street Scottsdale, CA 90123

January 7, 19XX

Mr. David Woodbury
Senior Programmer, Analyst
American Appliance Co.
1201 E. Bell Street
Oceanside, CA 93786

Dear Mr. Woodbury:

Here is our proposal for installing a fire-suppression system for your computer room. The proposal covers a Fenwal Total Flooding Suppression System designed for 5 percent concentration at 74°F and a fire detection system designed for early warning fire protection.

Scope of Work

The fire-suppression system will be provided in accordance with NFPA Pamphlet 12-a, "Halogenated Extinguishing Agent Systems, Halon 1301," and NFPA 72-E, "Standard on Automatic Fire Detectors."

All Fenwal equipment is designed to meet applicable requirements of Underwriters Laboratory Inc., and all items will bear the UL markings.

Equipment for this system will be supplied by Herrmann Fire Equipment Company. The system will be specifically designed to suppress fires in your computer room.

Automatic Operation

The system is designed to provide automatic protection. Any fire will be detected by cross-zoned ionization detectors in fire-suppression areas. These detectors will be located to conform to a standard spacing recommended by Underwriters Laboratory, Fenwal Inc., and all applicable codes and standards.

Manual Operation

The system can also be operated manually.

Services

Herrmann Fire Equipment Company will provide schematic drawings and calculations for the system and check the system after installation.

Price

The Fenwal Fire Suppression System will be supplied and installed for $15,806.00.

This price is based on a shipping date on or before March 1. The order must be received at least 30 days prior to the shipping date. The price does include freight charges.

Exhibit 8.4

Proposal—Bid (continued)

Woodbury   p. 2   January 7, 19XX

The price does not include:

1. Mechanical or electric fire dampers.
2. AC connection to the fire control panel.
3. Sealing of the rooms to be covered by the fire-suppression system.

<u>Terms</u>

One-third of the price has to be paid with the placement of the order. The remainder is due upon completion of the work.

This proposal shall become a contract agreement only when accepted by American Appliance Co. and approved in writing by an executive officer of Herrmann Fire Equipment Company.

Sincerely,

Robert Kuller

Robert Kuller
Herrmann Fire Equipment Company
Sales Engineer

P.S. Also see the attached "General Section," which is part of this proposal.

Exhibit 8.5 Proposal for Solving a Special Problem

IMPROVING STUDENT PARTICIPATION IN TTSA

A Proposal

Prepared for

Florence Mazet
President, Student Affairs

Prepared by

Deepak Gupta
Board Member, Tri-Towers Student Association

March 21, 19xx

Exhibit 8.5   Proposal for Solving a Special Problem (continued)

Problem

What are the reasons for the declining student participation in the activities of Tri-Towers Student Organization at Prairie University? How can the participation rate be improved?

Use of Results

Based on the analysis of the data, the Executive Board can examine the reasons for the decline in participation. They can look for possible solutions. The questionnaires, particularly the comments by the students, may hold some good suggestions for improvements.

Description of the Organization

Tri-Towers Student Association (TTSA) is the student government of West Campus at Prairie University. West Campus consists of three residence halls of ten floors each. Most of the 1,000 students living on West campus are freshmen and sophomores.

TTSA receives funds from the Office of Residential Life (ORL), the housing office at Prairie University. The purpose of TTSA and ORL is to provide housing and create an environment for individual growth and development. Student participation is essential in reaching that goal.

The representatives from each floor of Tri-Towers communicate the concerns of their floors to TTSA's General Assembly. The TTSA General Assembly consists of the floor representatives, members of the Executive Board, representatives from the Association of Residence Halls (ARH), and the chairpersons of three standing committees. The three committees are the

Service Committee:	responsible for providing students with services such as check cashing and educational materials.
Social Committee:	responsible for organizing social and cultural programs.
Finance Committee:	responsible for financial matters of the organization. This group allocates funds to the other two committees.

Description of the Problem

To justify receiving funds from ORL, TTSA must demonstrate a need for the funds. The criteria for allocation are the quality and quantity of student participation. ORL annually assesses the participation through a survey and bases the allocation on the survey results. If TTSA wants to keep the current level of funds or increase the funds, it must improve student participation.

For the past two semesters participation has declined by over 19

1

Exhibit 8.5   Proposal for Solving a Special Problem (continued)

percent. The percentage was determined by recording the number of
students who attended the TTSA General Assembly meetings, the
number of unexcused absences, and participation in programs and
services offered by the social and service committees.

In the past, committee members made program decisions with limited
or no input from residents. TTSA must determine to what extent
past programming has reflected the interests of the residents.
Based on the findings, TTSA can look at options to improve
participation.

Methodology

Data Collection
TTSA will use a questionnaire to collect data about student
interest and reasons or lack of reasons for participation. The
questionnaire will be distributed to a random sample of 500
students (50 percent of the total population) during the dinner
hour. The dinner hours are the best time to distribute the
questionnaires because most students go to the dining hall for
dinner.

The questionnaires will be handed out at the exit of the
cafeteria. The student volunteers will briefly explain the
purpose of the survey.

Data Analysis
Based on the results from question one, the percentage of
active students can be calculated. TTSA considers a participation
of 35 percent as ideal; therefore, all data will be evaluated
against this benchmark.

The answers to questions two and three will show whether students
who are involved in committees and residence hall government show
a higher participation rate than students who are not involved.

The answers to each Likert scale question will be tabulated
separately, and the average for each question will be calculated.
ORL and TTSA consider an average score of 3.75 acceptable on a 5-
point scale. The mean, median, and mode, and standard deviation
will provide information about the dispersion of the responses.

Visual aids such as pie graphs and bar charts will help the Board
members to visualize the results. The remarks made by the
students will be typed up and distributed to the board members
for discussion.

Resources Required

Time
The data collection and data analysis will require 12 hours. The
breakdown is as follows:

2

Exhibit 8.5   Proposal for Solving a Special Problem (continued)

Task	Hours
A. Typing, photocopying the surveys	2
B. Conducting the Survey	2
C. Compiling Data	4
D. Analyzing Data	2
E. Typing Comments and Preparing Graphs	2

Personnel
Four student volunteers will be needed for the project. One of the volunteers should be familiar with statistical concepts and be able to use Lotus for preparing the graphs. One volunteer should have good typing skills.

Money
The total cost of conducting the survey is $25.

Photocopying	$5.00
A gift certificate for each student	
$5.00 for each student	20.00

3

Exhibit 8.5   Proposal for Solving a Special Problem (continued)

TRI-TOWERS STUDENT ASSOCIATION

The Tri-Towers Student Association would like to collect
information about your interests in and opinions about the
services provided by TTSA. Please fill in the following
questionnaire and drop it in the box at the reception desk.

Please respond to questions 1 to 3 by circling the appropriate
choice.

1. How many programs organized by TTSA did you attend this year?

    0-2   2-4   4-6   6-8

2. Are you a floor representative?   YES   NO

3. Do you serve on any committee?   YES   NO

4. Rank the reasons for not attending more programs. (1 - most
    important reason)
    ___ Schedule Conflict   ___ Too Much Homework
    ___ No Interest in TTSA   ___ Program Choices
    ___ Atmosphere at Meetings___ Other, Please specify

5. Rank the types of programs you would like to see. (1 - highest
    choice)
    ___Political events   ___Study skills
    ___Foreign cultures   ___Social gatherings
    ___Guest speakers   ___Other

6. Tri-Towers Student Association represents the interests of
    the residents in Tri-Towers.

        Strongly Disagree   Strongly Agree
                  1   2   3   4   5

7. The programs are of high quality.

                  1   2   3   4   5

8. I feel welcome at TTSA functions.

                  1   2   3   4   5

9. I find it easy to get involved in TTSA.

                  1   2   3   4   5

10. I would attend more events if I had input in the selection
    and planning.
                  1   2   3   4   5

Please put any comments about TTSA on the back of the
questionnaire.

4

Deepak describes the method for collecting data, analyzing data, and drawing conclusions. He does not actually do the research; he presents a detailed description of his plan.

This proposal differs from the proposal in Exhibit 7.2 in Chapter 7, which is a plan and outline for an in-depth written report. The proposal in Exhibit 8.5 is a plan for conducting primary research. The results will be presented orally; Deepak Gupta will not necessarily prepare a written report.

The proposals discussed so far are examples of solicited proposals. Some proposals are unsolicited. The College of Business at Pacific University, for example, may submit a proposal to a multinational corporation for funding research in international business communication. In this case the proposal must show both that the research will be beneficial to the company and that the writer is capable of doing it. The writer must be convincing and persuasive.

Items that must be addressed in both solicited and unsolicited proposals are the following:

1. **Qualifications of People Doing the Project.** Proposals ask for money or other support and must show that the people who will be involved have the necessary experience.
2. **Purpose of the Proposal.** The reader must understand the objectives of the project. A clear and precise purpose statement is required.
3. **Significance.** The writer must show that the project is both viable and worthwhile by demonstrating that it will have a positive impact and will solve a problem.
4. **A Detailed Plan of Execution.** The proposal must provide a detailed methodology. If the proposal is for a survey, for example, it must be specific about plans to use a questionnaire, interview people, or observe people, and it must show plans for data analysis.
5. **A Detailed Time Schedule.** The reader must know how long it will take to complete the project. If the writer's company faces a crisis in production quality, for example, and the proposal suggests ways to solve the problem within the next two months, management must be able to judge whether the proposal is realistic. It may be too optimistic. With a few changes, however, it might be implemented in the proposed two-month period.
6. **An Itemized Budget.** The writer must show in detail how much the project will cost. The solution proposed may be more expensive but offer a higher quality result than other proposals. It is also possible that the problem could be solved with less money. In the proposal stage the budget is obviously based on estimates; therefore, in times of high inflation, the writer may want to include a clause that the budget will be increased if costs rise beyond a certain level. Budgets should be realistic. Construction bids have to include information on quality and cost of material to be used.

Proposals must be geared to the specific reader and to specific situations. The format and content of a proposal depend on the nature of the problem and the proposal guidelines. In Exhibit 8.4 the company wants to protect its computer room against fire; the proposal addresses the method and the cost of accomplishing that goal.

FEASIBILITY STUDIES

Feasibility Report
A feasibility report examines whether a project can be done.

A **feasibility report** investigates the chances of success of a project. For example, your boss might ask you to do a feasibility study of whether production schedules in the plant could be tightened. In this case you would concentrate on the possibilities of tightening the schedules. You would also examine ramifications of any changes in the schedules. While the feasibility study might outline the method for tightening the schedules, the method would not be the focus of the report.

Feasibility reports concentrate on this question: Is the undertaking possible and, if so, under what circumstances? Once the basic feasibility has been determined, the details of implementation must be examined. These include how long it would take and perhaps how it would affect the morale of employees. In many ways the feasibility report is a preliminary report on basic possibilities. The object is to find out the chances of success before making a more detailed investigation of solutions to a problem.

Assume your business has been expanding, and you need more space. Rather than move to another location or build an addition onto the present building, you may want to make increased use of the basement. Parts of it are already being used for storage. Before you plan the reorganization necessary to move offices into the basement, however, you need to know the feasibility of installing restrooms there. The building is 20 years old, you are the fifth owner, and you are not familiar with the construction and the plumbing layout. You contact a contractor and present your plan. After an examination of the basement, the contractor sends you the feasibility report presented in Exhibit 8.6.

Feasibility reports must give information on the following points:

1. **Feasibility.** The report must clearly indicate whether or not the project can be accomplished. This information is usually presented at the beginning of the report because it is the most important point.
2. **Problems.** The reader wants to know how easy or complicated the project will be. If the problems are staggering, the reader may determine that the project is not feasible financially even though it may be feasible technically.
3. **Time Frame.** The complexity of the problem will largely determine the amount of time required to complete a project. The reader must know how long it will take from beginning to end. A project requiring only a day might be done any time; one that will take two weeks requires careful planning so that ongoing business activities will not be unduly interrupted. The feasibility study gives an estimate of the time necessary to solve the problem or complete the task. It usually does not provide a detailed time study.

Exhibit 8.6

Feasibility Report

HOLLAND PLUMBING SERVICES

Pine Grove, WI 53705

August 20, 19XX

Mr. Robert Reiner
20 Main Street
Pine Grove, WI 53705

Dear Mr. Reiner:

It is possible to install restrooms in the southeast corner of the basement of your business, but the installation would be complicated and rather costly.

Water supply is no problem because there are water pipes within ten feet of the area of the planned restroom. The sewer lines are more complicated. The waste-water stack that is close to the planned restroom has a 2" pipe that is sufficient for sinks and water fountains, but not for toilets. Toilets have to drain into a 4" pipe. Unfortunately, the closest 4" pipe is at the other end of the building, roughly 50' away.

The pipe is deep enough so that the slope of the new pipe would not be a problem. The installation would, however, involve considerable work. The concrete floor would have to be cut open. The pipes could then be laid, and new concrete would have to be poured. The entire sub-floor work would take about a week.

You may want to reconsider the planned layout of the office area in the basement and consider putting the restrooms closer to the existing 4" sewer pipe.

I will be glad to give you estimates on both options.

Sincerely,

John Holland

John Holland

JUSTIFICATION REPORTS

Justification Report
The justification report is a
suggestion report.

A **justification report** is an unsolicited recommendation report. A manager, supervisor, or employee has observed a problem and writes a report to suggest ways of solving it. The reader, who did not ask for the report, may not be very interested in reading it. A justification report must, therefore, clearly and quickly identify the problem and offer a solution.

The typical justification report has the following parts:

1. **Purpose.** Here the writer identifies the problem and outlines the recommendation for solving it. Conciseness and clarity are necessary. Otherwise, the intended reader may simply put the report in the wastebasket.
2. **Benefits of the Recommendation.** The writer shows how implementation of the recommendation can save time and money, improve quality, or increase motivation. So that the points will be clear, they may be itemized. Giving the most important benefit first will capture the attention of the reader.
3. **Method of Implementation.** The report must demonstrate the feasibility of the recommendations and outline methods of implementation. Cost and time estimates must be realistic and supportable.
4. **Conclusion.** This section sums up the main reasons why the writer believes that the recommendations will work.
5. **Discussion.** This section may be very short. If the problem is complex, however, the writer may analyze it in more detail.

A justification report that describes in detail the benefits of a recommended purchase is illustrated in Exhibit 8.7.

STAFF REPORTS

Staff Report
Staff reports are written by
a manager's staff.

A **staff report** is a managerial recommendation report. It is usually written in memo form, often following a standardized format used throughout a company. The staff report can be arranged inductively or deductively. The term was first used in the military. In many businesses it now refers to reports written by a manager's staff. Business people write many different kinds of reports, however, and to group all of them under the label staff reports does not provide any information on the content of a particular report. It merely indicates which person or persons in the organization prepared the report. A personnel report for improving the hiring process or a report analyzing equipment, as in Exhibit 8.8, could be labeled a staff report.

JOB DESCRIPTIONS

Job Description
Job descriptions detail the
requirements for a job.

If you are in a supervisory position, you may need to write **job descriptions** for the people you supervise. In case of vacancies you will have to evaluate existing job descriptions and update them. A job description lists the qualifications necessary for a job and the duties to be performed.

Exhibit 8.7

Justification Report

TO: Michelle Clyne

FROM: Kent Waltz KW

RE: MAPPER 1100 Report Processing System

DATE: June 30, 19XX

I recommend the installation of the MAPPER system to increase efficiency and accuracy of work in Department 61.

What Is MAPPER?

MAPPER 1100 is a real-time, display-oriented report-processing system utilizing a report structured database.

MAPPER provides a unique user-oriented reporting capability. Reporting applications can be quickly implemented. An extensive set of report-processing functions is provided for searching, sorting, computing, and printing. A run language is available that provides functional sequencing with logical, computational, and formatted report generation.

What Can MAPPER Do?

MAPPER can help the company to save time and money in the following areas:

1. Analysis of Expenses
    The Sales Department would be able to compare expenses of each branch, region, and area. The sales manager has indicated that he would like to have comparisons every month. With MAPPER this task would take about 6 hours, whereas manually it would take at least 60 hours and even then the calculations would be in rough form.

2. Budget Preparation
    MAPPER could save the company up to 40 hours a year by making budget preparation easier and more routine. In addition, MAPPER would allow the company to make changes easily.

3. Partial Entries for Large Journal Vouchers
    Up to 32 hours of accounting time could be saved monthly. The greatest savings might be in computing the commission voucher, which would take run capability.

4. Burden Distribution
    The job now takes 15 to 20 hours monthly. MAPPER could save up to 15 hours.

5. Material at Vendor Inventory
    A major part of the time of one cost accountant is spent keeping track of material at vendor. MAPPER would save between 15 and 20 hours a month by selecting information directly from Accounts Payable and posting automatically. Returns from vendors could also be handled automatically.

6. Inventory Transfer
    MAPPER would save about 5 hours monthly in the calculation of figures to be used for the transfer of monthly production from In Process to Finished Goods inventory.

7. Fringe-Benefit Accrual
    The automatic computation and recording of fringe-benefit accrual should save approximately 5 hours monthly.

Exhibit 8.7   **Justification Report (continued)**

```
        Michelle Clyne                  p. 2                    June 30, 19XX


        Conclusion
        MAPPER would save the company up to 180 hours every month.  Precise figures are
        difficult to calculate because they will depend on the complexity of the jobs to
        be performed.  The company would also benefit in the area of quality.  Reports
        would be more complete, timely, and accurate.
```

The job description is a very common American report; it is found less frequently in other countries. Americans describe the position and look for the best-qualified person to fill it. In the Middle East, on the other hand, management tends to think in terms of whether a person would fit into the company rather than what the specific qualifications are. A manager in the Middle East often determines how and where to use a new employee only after the person is hired.

Job descriptions in the United States provide the following information:

1. **Job Title.**
2. **Responsibilities.** This section may be divided into routine and special tasks or main and secondary tasks.
3. **Job Classification.** The job description has to identify the level of the job. For example, it is necessary to identify whether the job opening is for a class I or class II typist. Salary ranges may also be specified.
4. **Lines of Authority.** Employees have to know who reports to them and to whom they report.
5. **Education and Experience.** Is a university degree necessary? What licenses or certificates are required? The education and experience levels specified have to be necessary to perform the job. If they are not necessary, the company may be accused of discrimination.

Exhibit 8.8   **Staff Report**

TO: Bob Morris

FROM: Dictionary Software Evaluation Committee

RE: Results of Software Trial

DATE: October 16, 19XX

We have completed our evaluation of two software packages:

1. Development Documentation Tool (DDT), DATAMANAGER, and First Structured
   Graphics

2. Excelerator

Recommendations

Based on the experience and reactions of the analysts and support personnel who
tested these products, we make the following recommendations:

1. We should not buy Development Documentation Tool, DATAMANAGER, or First
   Structured Graphics. These products should be returned to the vendor.

2. We should continue to explore the dictionary and text-documentation support
   capabilities of Excelerator.

3. A standard workstation for support of structured analysis should be developed.

4. A fully integrated data dictionary with the processes it is intended to support should be a long-range goal.

Rationale

While DDT and DATAMANAGER together form a dictionary that is easy to use, the
data-flow diagrams produced by First Structured Graphics are unacceptable.
Excelerator, on the other hand, is an outstanding graphic tool that includes a
very limited dictionary. The committee decided that the need was greater for a
drawing tool. Although time did not permit an in-depth evaluation of the
dictionary and documentation features of the Excelerator, they appear to be
adequate in the short term.

The committee concluded that the Excelerator would save time over manual methods
of preparing data-flow diagrams.

The librarian identified an additional use of Excelerator that would justify a
workstation. The presentation graphics feature of Excelerator can be used to
produce detail system flows, module call maps, and user view charts. Other
departments that have a need to document flows and hierarchical relationships may
also benefit from this feature of Excelerator.

6. **Personal Information.** Age, height, weight, and vision should be specified only if they affect performance of the job. If this information is not essential, the company may be accused of discrimination for requesting it.

The job description illustrated in Exhibit 8.9 emphasizes experience, knowledge, and ability rather than formal education. One can assume, however, that any serious candidate in today's banking environment would need a college background to function in that job. The job description specifically mentions effective communication, including the ability to make presentations and write business reports.

POLICIES AND PROCEDURES

Policies and Procedures
Policies and procedures inform employees of company rules.

Most companies have manuals that inform employees of **policies and procedures.** Employees can refer to a manual when questions arise about vacations, sick leave, and health insurance. The supervisor does not have to explain every policy to every employee. Manuals therefore save time, but only if they are clear, precise, detailed, and complete.

Assume for example, a company has a new policy on absences. The new policy has to be stated clearly. It must describe, as in Exhibit 8.10, what will happen to people who violate the policy. It has to detail what will happen to one-time offenders and to repeat offenders. Terms must be defined so that no misunderstandings will occur. Employee policy manuals are often regarded by the courts as equivalent to employment contracts, making precise language critical. Courts tend to interpret ambiguities against the employer.

Procedures manuals give a step-by-step description of processes. For example, a supervisor must know what to do in case of an accident. He has to know whom to inform, and what forms to fill out. The correct sequence of steps is important so that the process runs smoothly. The supervisor must fill out an accident report before notifying the insurance company of a claim. Not following procedures wastes time. Exhibit 8.11 illustrates typical procedures for processing an accident claim.

Policies and procedures that are clearly spelled out improve consistency of operations and fairness in personnel matters. They provide information that many employees need and instances that occur with a certain regularity.

INSTRUCTIONS

Instructions
Instructions provide a step-by-step outline of how to do a task.

All business people give **instructions** on a regular basis. A manager, for example, cannot do everything himself; he must delegate tasks. As he delegates the task, he will provide instructions on what he expects. The instructions clarify the job for both sides. For example, Christy Bland started as your administrative assistant yesterday. You want her to schedule meetings for you, screen your calls, prepare monthly reports on the progress of special projects, and represent you on several departmental teams.

Exhibit 8.9

Job Description

<u>Position</u>

Vice President of Pacific National Bank, Retail Division

The Retail Division Vice President reports to the President.

<u>Functions of the Job</u>

1. The Retail Division Vice President assumes the responsibility for planning, organizing, directing, and monitoring all retail banking activities; administering the sales management function; directing the Electronic Funds Transfer activities; and developing marketing concepts for retail banking products.

2. As Division Head, the Vice President ensures that all activities of the Retail Banking Division support the bank's overall business goals and objectives.

<u>Major Duties and Responsibilities</u>

1. The Vice President is in charge of the Retail Division. In this position he or she:
   a. Is in charge of personnel decisions including employment decisions, salary reviews, performance reviews, disciplinary actions.
   b. Administers the sales function, which includes selling bank products, developing incentive programs, providing sales training.
   c. Plans and directs all retail product development.
   d. Develops and coordinates media plans and marketing concepts for retail products.
   e. Serves as President's Circle Officer for selected customers.
   f. Attends the following meetings:
      (1) President's Circle Officers Meeting.
      (2) Bank Retail Division Committee Meeting.
   g. Prepares and monitors the Retail Division budget.

2. The Retail Division Vice President has additional responsibilities in the bank. He or she:
   a. Participates in the bank-wide planning process.
   b. Participates in Bank Marketing Committee meetings.
   c. Assists in bank-wide training programs.

<u>Necessary Knowledge and Skills</u>

The Retail Division Vice President has to be able to:
1. Relate to people.
2. Make effective oral presentations to internal and external groups.
3. Define problems precisely and clearly.
4. Prioritize multiple job responsibilities.
5. Work under pressure.
6. Handle confidential information.
7. Manage employees.
8. Write effective business letters.
9. Research, summarize, and write effective business reports.

Exhibit 8.10   Policies

PERSONNEL POLICY
ATTENDANCE IMPROVEMENT PROGRAM

Purpose

The purpose of this policy is to ensure the satisfactory attendance of all employees.

Policy

Punctuality and regular attendance are expected of all employees. This is important not only in maintaining high productivity but also in promoting morale among all employees.

General Rules

1. All employees must be in their assigned places and ready for work at the designated starting time.

2. All employees shall remain in their respective places of work during working hours. Employees shall not visit other employees or other departments except in the line of duty.

Reporting of Absences

1. If an employee cannot report to work, the supervisor should be informed a day in advance if possible or, in the case of an emergency, as soon as possible.

2. Reasons for absences or tardiness must be stated in writing.

3. If an absence of more than one day is likely, the employee has to inform the supervisor how many days he or she expects to be absent.

4. Absences exceeding three days will require a physician's statement before the employee may return to work.

Definition of Absences

1. Excused Absence - Any absence that is excused in writing by management prior to the occurrence and all absences covered by the current contract (jury duty, funeral leave, work-related injuries, vacations).

2. Unexcused Absence - Any absence that is not excused unless the employee calls the plant and reports off prior to the scheduled work time.

3. Absence Due to Sickness - Any unexcused absence during which the employee is under care of a physician. To qualify for this classification, the employee must present a doctor's certificate stating that the employee was under the doctor's care during the absence.

4. Occasion - Each day of an unexcused absence will be counted as one (1) occasion. Each occurrence of an absence due to sickness will be counted as one (1) occasion. If a doctor's certificate is not presented, each day of an absence will be counted as an unexcused absence.

Exhibit 8.10   **Policies (continued)**

```
Personnel Policy                    p. 2


Timetable

Each employee's attendance record will be measured on the basis of 12 consecutive
months.  After the first 12 months have elapsed, the first month will be dropped
from the measurement period upon the completion of each consecutive month.  For
example, at the conclusion of month 13, month 1 will be dropped.

Enforcement

The following disciplinary actions will be taken:

3 occasions -- verbal warning
6 occasions -- written warning
9 occasions -- 3-day suspension
12 occasions -- suspension with intent to terminate
```

Christy is new in the organization. She is bright, and you think she can learn very fast. To help her adjust and do a good job from the very beginning, you will give her some instructions on how you want reports prepared, calls handled, and meetings arranged. Some of that you may put in writing, but some you will tell her orally. So that Christy can follow your instructions, they must be clear and easy to follow.

Two examples will illustrate the importance of clarity in instructions:

1. An out-of-town consultant is scheduled to visit your office next week for the first time. Your office building is difficult to find, and you will need to furnish directions. If the consultant does not follow your directions, or if they are confusing, she may be late for the meeting.
2. Your office recently purchased new text editing software. Everyone received some training in using the program, but you know that not everyone feels comfortable with it. You ask your assistant to prepare an instruction sheet and distribute it to all employees.

Success in both examples depends on clear instructions and step-by-step implementation of the instructions. Good instructions tend to have the following characteristics:

1. The task is divided into sequential steps.

Exhibit 8.11   Procedures

Procedures for Processing Workers' Compensation Claims

1. When an accident occurs, the supervisor is responsible for filing an accident report with the Personnel Office.

2. The Personnel Office files Form 45 (state form).
   a. If the accident is recordable, the form is sent to the State Industrial Commission and to the insurance company.

   b. If the accident is not recordable, the form is only sent to the insurance company.

3. Medical bills are sent to the Personnel Office by the employee, the hospital, or the doctor. The amounts are recorded and then sent to the insurance company.

4. The insurance company sends payment to the Personnel Office, the hospital, or the doctor.

5. If lost time is involved, the insurance company sends the compensation check to the Personnel Office, which forwards the amount to the employee.

6. The insurance company is informed by telephone when the employee returns to work.

7. If a claim is questionable, the insurance company will be notified by the Personnel Office via telephone or letter. If necessary, the insurance company will conduct further inquiries. The insurance company will determine whether the claim is justified. The insurance company will send a justification to the Personnel Office if the claim is denied.

8. If an employee seeks a settlement for an injury, the employee has two options.
   a. The employee can obtain a lawyer who will file an adjustment with the State Industrial Commission. The Personnel Office will be notified and will forward the information to the insurance company. The insurance company will turn the case over to its lawyers. The insurance company's lawyers and the employee's lawyer will meet to settle the case. If they cannot agree, then the case will go before the arbitrator of the State Industrial Commission. Present at the hearing will be the employee, his or her lawyer, the insurance company's lawyer, the Personnel Office manager, and any necessary witnesses.
   b. The employee may contact the Personnel Office directly about a settlement. The Personnel Office will then contact the insurance company. The insurance company will make an initial settlement offer by phone based on the facts and the information provided by the Personnel Office. If the employee is not satisfied with the settlement, the insurance company will discuss the matter with the employee directly. If they reach an agreement, the arbitrator of the State Industrial Commission has to approve it. If the employee and the insurance company do not reach an agreement, the employee may go to a lawyer.

9. Settlement checks are usually sent to the Personnel Office. They are then recorded and forwarded to the employee.

2. The steps are itemized so that the user can easily carry out each step and immediately check for correctness.
3. Each task is written in command form. The verb is at the beginning and immediately tells the reader what needs to be done. (Insert the disk in drive A, Turn right at the third traffic light.)
4. The writer should check the instructions for accuracy. Before giving instructions on how to drive to your office, for example, you might actually try using your instructions. You may have forgotten to include a crucial step.

Exhibit 8.12 illustrates instructions for driving to Illinois State University in Normal, Illinois, from Chicago.

ANNUAL AND QUARTERLY REPORTS

Most organizations prepare regular reports on business activities to inform stockholders, employees, the government, and possible investors. The systematic review and summary of events also help management in the decision-making process.

Annual Reports
Annual reports are accounts of organizations' activities and performance during the previous year.

Many organizations, government offices, and universities write **annual reports.** They provide an update on activities, accomplishments, use of resources, and future plans. Annual reports are group efforts, compiled from information in departmental reports.

Department reports contain more detail than composite annual reports. A production department report, for example, may include production quotas, level and quality of productivity, price and quality of resources used. It may comment on quality standards in the department. The report may list the names of the people in the department, recognize outstanding performances, and record turnover in personnel. It documents financial performance relating to cost of labor, cost of raw materials, overhead, and profit. Information from the departmental reports is then used for the company's annual report.

Corporate annual reports are required by law to contain comparative financial statements and an auditor's report. Almost all go beyond these legal requirements. Most companies use their annual reports to give a history of their performance through pictures, graphs, and stories about products, employees, and customers. Most annual reports begin with a letter to the stockholders. Typically written by the chairman of the board, it gives an overview of the company's performance.

Quarterly Reports
Quarterly reports summarize an organization's performance for three months.

Most organizations also prepare **quarterly reports,** which are less detailed than annual reports. Corporate quarterly reports, for example, present a summary of the financial performance and a brief letter written by the president. The quarterly report seldom includes pictures, graphs, or detailed descriptions and reviews of management, marketing, or production activities. Exhibit 8.13 illustrates a quarterly report.

Exhibit 8.12   **Instructions**

June 21, 19xx

Mr. John Cheng
Consultant
341 Wikert Drive
Chicago, IL

Dear Mr. Cheng:

Thank you for agreeing to speak on June 29, 19xx, to the Alumni
Council on fundraising at public institutions. I look forward to
meeting you next week.

The following instructions should help you find my office without
any difficulties.

    Take the second exit off I-55 in the Bloomington-Normal
    area. The exit is labeled Normal. It takes you to Route
    51, Main Street.

    Follow Main Street South until you reach College Avenue.
    (4th stop light)

    Turn left on College and go to School Street. (2nd stop
    light)

    Turn right on School Street.

    Follow School Street until you reach the Stevenson Hall
    Parking lot on the left (1 1/2 blocks). With the enclosed
    parking sticker, you can park anywhere in that lot.

    Enter Stevenson Hall from the South (parking lot side). My
    office, STV 206, is in the hallway to the left as you come
    up the steps.

The enclosed map of the campus should help you in locating
Stevenson Hall. Please attach the enclosed parking sticker to
your windshield when you park on campus.

If you have any questions, please call me at (309) 555-5885.

Sincerely,

Paula Pomerenke

Paula Pomerenke
Workshop Coordinator

Exhibit 8.13   **Quarterly Report**

FIRST BOSTON INCOME FUND, INC.

FELLOW SHAREHOLDER:

The past three months have been challenging months, but we are pleased to report that your management's disciplined approach to investing in the fixed income market has allowed your Fund to continue providing high current income consistent with preservation of capital.

As we enter the second quarter of 1989, our assets are allocated 33% to high yield corporate bonds, 61% to U.S. Government agencies and the remainder to cash and preferred stock. The net asset value as of March 31, 1989 is $8.43.

During 1988, the decline in bond prices, and the Fund's net asset value, was a direct result of rising U.S. interest rates. The Federal Reserve's monetary policy throughout most of the year focused on restraining excessive economic strength and combating inflationary pressures. In the quarter just ended, the U.S. economy showed signs of slower growth thus reducing the need by the Federal Reserve to raise interest rates further. Mortgage backed securities become more attractive in this environment because the higher short term interest rates discourage refinancing and reduce pre-payment risk. Corporate debt also benefits from slower, more sustainable growth in the economy.

Looking ahead to the next two quarters, we believe interest rates are at or near a peak. We don't think a recession is likely and, as always, we will continue to monitor fully both the economy and interest rate trends in order to anticipate their impact on our investments.

As the new Chairman of the Board and Chief Executive Officer of the Fund, I am pleased to report to you that Mr. Edward N. McMillan, Managing Director of The First Boston Corporation, has been elected President of the Fund, replacing Mr. Donald J. McDonough, Jr. The team of professionals responsible for your Fund's investment decisions remains the same and will now report to Mr. McMillan and myself. Thank you for your continued confidence.

Sincerely,

James C. Freeman   *Edward N. McMillan*

JAMES L. FREEMAN   EDWARD N. MCMILLAN
Chairman of the Board   *President*
May 16, 1989

	Face Amount (000)	Market Value (000)
REMIC		
10.0%, 4/15/18	$ 5,000	$ 4,785
Federal National Mortgage Association		
11.0%, 12/25/03	4,945	4,970
REMIC		
10.3%, 3/25/18	10,000	9,725
Government National Mortgage Association		
9.5%, 6/15/16-6/15/17	14,339	13,524
10.0%, 1/15/17-11/15/18	66,246	64,052
10.5%, 3/15/18-9/15/18	17,853	17,764
Graduated Payment Mortgages		
12.75%, 10/15/13-11/15/13	488	512
Group Total		124,387

	Shares	
WARRANTS (0.1%)		
Braniff Inc.	30,000	180

TOTAL INCOME SECURITIES
(Cost $205,232)   197,185

TEMPORARY CASH INVESTMENTS (3.7%)

	Face Amount (000)	
Repurchase Agreement		
Morgan Stanley & Co., Inc.		
9.3%, 4/3/89		
(Collateralized by U.S. Treasury		
Notes 8.625%, 10/15/95)		
(Cost $7,632)	$ 7,632	7,632

TOTAL INVESTMENTS (100.5%)
(Cost $212,864)   204,817

OTHER ASSETS AND LIABILITIES (-0.5%)

Other Assets		6,324
Liabilities		(7,411)
		(1,087)

NET ASSETS (100%)
    $203,730

NET ASSET VALUE PER SHARE
Applicable to 24,159,827 issued
and outstanding $.001 par value
shares (authorized 100,000,000
shares) $8.43

* Market Value Includes Accrued Interest.

SUMMARY OF LEARNING OBJECTIVES

To study the content and organization of the most frequently written business reports.

Minutes are summaries of meetings. They are arranged chronologically.

News releases inform the public of important company events and decisions. Accuracy is essential.

Progress reports inform the reader whether or not a project is on schedule. They are organized deductively.

Proposals may be solicited or unsolicited. They identify the qualifications of the person who will do the project. The reader needs a detailed plan for execution and a budget, particularly when comparing several proposals.

Feasibility studies examine whether or not a project can be done. The report should be arranged deductively.

Justification reports are unsolicited recommendation reports. They are presented in deductive order to hold the interest of the reader.

Staff reports are written for management by management staff.

Job Descriptions must clearly identify tasks to be performed and the qualifications considered necessary to perform them.

Policies and procedures inform employees of rights, obligations, and company rules. They must be clear and unambiguous.

Instructions explain step by step how to do a specific task.

Annual and quarterly reports are periodic and systematic summaries of an organization's activities and performance. They are used both internally and externally.

KEY TERMS

Minutes	Staff Report
News Release	Job Description
Progress Report	Policies and Procedures
Proposal	Instructions
Feasibility Report	Annual Reports
Justification Report	Quarterly Reports

QUESTIONS AND DISCUSSION POINTS

1. What is a staff report?
2. What are the major parts in a progress report and in a justification report?
3. Discuss the main parts of a job description.
4. Familiarize yourself with *The Wall Street Journal Index* or any other index. Write instructions (procedures) for its use.

EXERCISES

Select one of these & prepare a short report.

1. Locate and examine at least two short reports that are typical for your major field of study.

2. Write a progress report on a project you are doing for one of your classes.

3. Write a report on the feasibility of your going to Europe next summer.

4. Write a job description for the officers of a student organization of which you are a member.

5. Your university is in the process of establishing quiet dorm floors where students can study without the typical dorm noise. Write policies for those quiet floors.

6. Take minutes of the next club meeting you attend. Review your minutes several days after the meeting to check how much they help you in reconstructing what went on during the meeting.

7. As program chair for a student organization, you are confirming arrangements and directions to your campus (include parking, and do not forget the building and the room number) for a speaker who has already agreed to come. The speaker will be driving to your campus from the nearest major city. The speech is scheduled for 5:00 p.m. on a business day, and the speaker will arrive just a few minutes before the presentation. You will meet the speaker at the speech site. Following the presentation, you and other club officers will be taking the speaker to dinner. It is your understanding that the speaker has already made overnight reservations and will be spending the next day on campus for the purpose of recruiting June graduates.

    Using the letter format, write instructions for the speaker on how to best get to campus.

8. You have been asked by the dean of the college to write to a student who is transferring to your university from Alfalfa Community College. This student is the daughter of an alum who has been most generous to the college, and the dean wants to be certain the student feels welcome and understands the transfer process. The student will be coming by car from a small town 150 miles east of the campus. You will be meeting her for lunch, but she plans to arrive by 10:30 a.m.

    In a letter, give instructions for parking and for the overall transfer procedure. Include advice you believe will be helpful.

9. You are the host/hostess for a guest of the college. This "business person of the day" will be arriving on a 7:30 a.m. flight and prefers to pick up a rental car and meet you at the Student Union for an 8:30 breakfast with the dean of the college.

    Write giving directions from the airport; include parking and campus information.

Additional short report assignments are in the cases at the end of the book.

RESEARCH FOR
BUSINESS REPORTS

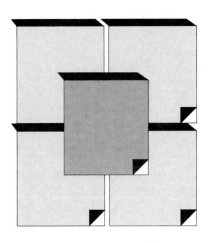

CHAPTER
9

SECONDARY RESEARCH

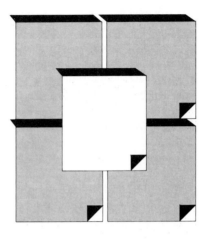

Learning Objectives

- To understand the role of secondary research in report writing.
- To recognize different types of libraries.
- To understand the organization of libraries.
- To become familiar with secondary sources useful to the business writer.
- To become familiar with computer searches.
- To be able to evaluate sources and compile bibliography and note cards.

THE ROLE OF SECONDARY RESEARCH IN REPORT WRITING

Secondary research is a study of printed sources. It involves going to the library to find out what may already have been written about solutions to problems similar to the one you are researching. There is no point in sending out questionnaires, going through interviews, and conducting surveys to find out what type of insurance new graduates need if the results of a similar study are available in the latest issue of *The Journal of Risk Management* or another insurance journal. You would be wasting time reinventing the wheel.

Studying the published results of the insurance investigation would provide you with basic information. After determining how the published study is similar to or different from your company's problem, you could concentrate your research on how your company could best attract recent graduates and what types of policies you would have to develop to fill their needs. The study of published materials allows you to spend most of your time on the aspects unique to your problem.

Secondary research sources are not limited to materials in libraries. Your company has numerous reports on operations, personnel matters, marketing strategies, and other topics. These reports have not been published in the sense that they have appeared in journals, but they are readily available to you. Government reports, tax reports, pamphlets, employee manuals, and customer-relation materials are all source materials for secondary research.

TYPES OF LIBRARIES

To the beginner a library may be a confusing place. To the regular user, it is a source of detailed information from around the world, available in minutes. The kind of information varies however, depending on the type of library.

GENERAL LIBRARIES

Only the Library of Congress carries all of the books, magazines, and journals published in the United States. Other libraries carry only the materials that best meet the needs and wants of their users. Public libraries, which have clients with many different interests, are rather diversified. They have materials on many topics, but most of the books and periodicals are geared to the general user rather than the expert in a particular area. Public libraries are *general libraries.*

RESEARCH LIBRARIES

Most universities have extensive libraries. The materials are selected to complement the work in the classroom and facilitate research by students and faculty. These libraries are more academically oriented than public libraries. They have collections of journals in such specialized areas as science, business, and history. They carry materials that serious scholars would need in their research; therefore, these libraries are sometimes referred to as *research libraries.* They have different clients than public libraries.

SPECIAL PURPOSE LIBRARIES

More and more companies are establishing their own libraries. This development shows that secondary research does play an important role in business. Managers have found that a library saves them time. During the past decade the number of company libraries has increased from 5,000 to 7,200. In addition, many companies are enlarging their libraries.

Of course, company libraries are specialized. They carry only those materials that are essential for the company's business. State Farm Insurance, for example, concentrates on materials that are related to insurance, such as insurance journals, government regulations relating to insurance, data processing materials, and legal documents. Most accounting firms and law firms have libraries for their special needs. Company librarians would not spend money on fiction, philosophy, or ancient history because they are building *special purpose libraries.* Whether a report writer concentrates on the company library or goes to other libraries will depend on the quality of the company library and the problem she is trying to solve.

LIBRARY SYSTEMS

Fortunately, most libraries belong to a library system. Libraries within the system have an agreement that they will share their materials. In central Illinois, for example, a resident of Peoria can visit the public library and request materials from Illinois State University. In addition to the regional systems there is the interlibrary loan system. Students at Illinois State University may request a book from any library in the country through interlibrary loan. The fast, reliable service increases the available sources tremendously.

THE ORGANIZATION OF LIBRARIES

A library is a superb example of excellent organization. To use the library efficiently, however, the user must understand how it works. Some things are organized similarly in all libraries, and some things are different.

Libraries use either the Dewey Decimal or the Library of Congress system for cataloging their holdings. Under the Dewey Decimal System, knowledge is divided into 10 categories using numbers 000 through 900.

In recent years many libraries have switched to the Library of Congress cataloging system because it provides a more detailed breakdown of the areas of knowledge. It uses letters of the alphabet and thus allows for the creation of more categories. Business is grouped with the social sciences under the subcategories *HD* and *HF* (see Exhibit 9.1).

Exhibit 9.1

Classification Systems

The classifications under the Dewey Decimal System:

000	General Works	500	Pure Science
100	Philosophy	600	Useful Arts
200	Religion	700	Fine Arts
300	Social Sciences	800	Literature
400	Philology	900	History

The classifications under the Library of Congress System:

A	General Works	O	not used yet
B	Philosophy and Religion	P	Language and Literature
C	History	Q	Science
D	Universal and Old World History	R	Medicine
E,F	America	S	Agriculture
G	Geography, Anthropology, Sports	T	Technology
H	Social Sciences	U	Military Science
I	not used yet	V	Naval Science
J	Political Science	W	not used yet
K	Law	X	not used yet
L	Education	Y	not used yet
M	Music	Z	Bibliography and Library Science
N	Fine Arts		

THE CARD CATALOG

The card catalog is most useful for finding books. The two types of card catalogs are the author–title catalog and the subject catalog. If you have either the title of the book you need or the author's name, you can locate the book by using the **author–title catalog**. Cards for authors and titles are in alphabetical order. If there is no card, the book is not available in the library, but the librarian may be able to obtain if for you through interlibrary loan.

Author–Title Catalog
The author–title catalog lists books by author or title.

In many cases you may know the topic you want to investigate but not the titles or authors of any books on the topic. In that case your options are to refer either to the two-volume *Library of Congress Subject Headings* or to the **subject catalog.** The *Library of Congress Subject Headings*, usually located near the reference desk, will provide you with a list of subject headings and subheadings that are used in cataloging books. Knowing the terms may save you time when you use the subject catalog.

Subject Catalog
Books are listed according to subject matter.

COMPUTER RETRIEVAL SYSTEM

Technology has changed the work of the researcher tremendously over the past decade as many libraries have switched to a computerized catalog system. Rather than physically thumb through the catalog, you may key the name of the author and sometimes the subject you are looking for into the computer in order to locate useful material.

One computer program widely used in libraries throughout the United States is Ohio College Library Center (OCLC). OCLC allows you to search for books by name of author, title, or a combination of author and title. With it you can also search for books in a series and for periodicals by title; however, the system does not have the capability to search for individual articles in periodicals or to do a subject search.

Database
A database is a collection of files integrated into a file system.

OCLC's **database** contains the titles of all holdings of OCLC libraries and is, therefore, very useful for interlibrary loans. If your library does not have a particular book, OCLC can locate it for you at another library.

Not all libraries can afford computer technology, which is expensive. To spend your library time efficiently, you should check with the librarian about the types of cataloging and retrieval system your library offers.

TYPES OF SECONDARY RESOURCES USEFUL IN REPORT WRITING

The goal of your secondary research is to find the most pertinent and current information available for solving your particular business problem. In many cases, a search through the library card catalog will give you the information you need; however, some books may be too outdated to be useful in business research. If you want the latest information on advertising, for example, you will not find it in books. Although the lag time between collecting the material for a book, the writing, and the printing has shortened, it can still be about two years. For up-to-date information you should look at the **periodical literature**.

Periodical Literature
Periodicals include professional journals, magazines, and newspapers.

Books do have their place in business research, of course. They provide background information and detailed discussions of timeless principles. They will be helpful if you are looking for the foundations of a theory in marketing, a discussion of the principles of advertising, for research on the similarities and differences between various management theories, or for information on standard accounting practices.

Much of the information you are looking for may not be in books. You must be familiar with the index system for articles, reference books, and government publications if you need to research such topics as government regulations, the latest Supreme Court decisions, economic statistics for the past year, trade figures on import and export for the past 12 months, or population statistics for a specific area. The librarian can help you find data you are looking for, but you should also be familiar with the types of resources available. Some of the most useful sources for business research are the following.

Almanacs

Almanacs are helpful in locating statistical information on a variety of topics such as income, population, and production. Two almanacs that business researchers often find useful are these:

Dow Jones–Irwin business and investment almanac. (Annual). Homewood, IL: Dow Jones–Irwin.

The world almanac and book of facts. (Annual). New York: Doubleday.

Directories

Business directories are especially helpful if you need information on a particular company. They typically provide the address of a company, the names of major officers, location of subsidiaries, lists of products manufactured, and figures on sales and profit. Some directories provide credit ratings of corporations. Most directories are published yearly and are updated regularly throughout the year. Exhibits 9.2 and 9.3 illustrate listings in *Standard & Poor's Register.*

If, for example, you want information on Penn Engineering & Manufacturing Corporation, you would look first in the index to find the page number, as shown in Exhibit 9.2. The detailed information to which the index refers is shown in Exhibit 9.3.

You may find the following list of directories useful.

Wood, D. (Ed.). (Annual). *Trade names dictionary.* Detroit, MI: Gale.

Directory of American savings and loan associations.(Annual). Baltimore, MD: T.K. Sanderson Organization.

Directory of corporate affiliations. (Annual). Skokie, IL: National Register Publishing.

Dun & Bradstreet reference book. (Annual). New York: Dun & Bradstreet.

Dun & Bradstreet reference book of corporate management. (Annual). New York: Dun & Bradstreet.

Towell, J.E. (Ed.). (1989). *Directories in print* (6th ed.). Detroit, MI: Gale.

Forbes annual directory issue. (Annual). New York: Forbes.

Fortune directory of the 500 largest U.S. industrial corporations. (Annual). New York: Fortune Magazine.

Kelly's business directory. (Annual). London: Kelly's Directories.

Million dollar directory. (Annual). New York: Dun & Bradstreet.

Moody's manuals. (Annual). New York: Moody's Investors Service.

National trade and professional associations of the United States. (Annual). Washington, DC: Columbia Books.

Standard & Poor's register of corporations, directors, and executives, United States and Canada. (Annual). New York: Standard & Poor's.

Stopford, J.M., & Dunning, J.H. (Eds.). (1983). *World directory of multinational enterprises.* (2nd ed.). New York: Facts on File.

Exhibit 9.2

Standard & Poor's Corporation Records: Index Section

PENN ENGINEERING & MFG. CORP	**4966**
Interim Consol. Earns.: Sept. '88	5677
Interim Consol. Earns.: June '88	6046
Interim Consol. Earns.: Mar. '88	6494

Source: Copyright ©1989 *Standard & Poor's Corporation Records.* Reprinted with permission.

Exhibit 9.3   *Standard & Poor's Corporation Records*: Index Section

Penn Engineering & Mfg. Corp.

CAPITALIZATION (Dec. 31 '88)

LONG TERM DEBT- None.

STOCK-	Auth. Shs.	Outstg. Shs.
Common $1 par	3,000,000	*1,732,097

*Excl. 39,928 in treas.

UNUSED LINES OF CREDIT (short-term) totalled $12,500,000 at Dec. 31, 1988.

CORPORATE BACKGROUND

Company makes self-clinching and broaching fasteners, and automatic insertion equipment for such fasteners sold under the names PEM and Pemserter, respectively. Self clinching fasteners, which become a permanent part of the material to which they are attached, provide strong threads in materials too thin or ductile to tap. Broaching type fasteners provide permanent threads in non-ductile materials such as plastics and printed circuit boards. Co. also makes and sells inserts for use in certain plastic products. In addition, Co. makes permanent magnet field, brush-commutated direct current motors sold under the Pittman and Pitmo names; and electronically commutated direct current servomotors and controls sold under the Elcom name. In 1988, fasteners provided 72.6% of net sales and 55.3% of operating profit (74.0% & 59.4% in 1987); and electric motors 27.4% and 44.7% (26.0% & 40.6%).

SUBSIDIARIES- wholly owned- PEM International, Ltd.; Standard Insert Co., Inc.

PROPERTY- Co. owns plants in Danboro and Harleysville, Pa., and Winston-Salem, N.C.; and a warehouse in Doncaster, England. A warehouse is leased in Horsham, Pa. Co. expected to complete construction of a plant in Suffolk, Va., in the summer of 1989.

BACKLOG, Dec. 31: Thou. $
1988 16,027   1987 11,390   1986 7,950

CAPITAL EXPENDITURES, Yrs. End. Dec. 31: Thou.$
1988 3,437   1987 1,440   1986 1,804

EMPLOYEES- Dec. 31, 1988, 784.

INCORPORATED in Del. Dec. 23, 1942.

CHAIRMAN & CHIEF EXEC OFFICER, K.A. Swanstrom; PRES & CHIEF OPER OFFICER, Kenneth A. Swanstrom; V-P, SECY & TREAS, M.W. Simon; V-Ps, R.B. Ernest, P.M. Hall, J.W. Segraves; CONTR & ASST SECY, W.E. Sarnese.

DIRECTORS- W.S. Boothby, Jr., L.W. Hull, T.M. Hyndman, Jr., G.H. McNeely III, M.W. Simon, K.A. Swanstrom, Kenneth A. Swanstrom, Daryl L. Swanstrom.

MAILING ADDRESS- Box 1000, Danboro, PA 18916 (Tel.: 215-766-8853). ANNUAL MEETING- In May.

STOCK DATA

STOCKHOLDERS- Dec. 1, 1988, 810 (of record). Mar. 15, 1989, K.A., Kenneth A. and Daryl L. Swanstrom, T.M. Hyndman, Jr. and related trusts owned or controlled 53.1% of the Com.

TRANSFER AGENT & REGISTRAR- Philadelphia Natl. Bank, Pa.

LISTED- American SE (Symbol PNN); also traded Midwest SE:

1988	36¼	21⅛	1987	34½	19¼
1986	34⅛	25	1985	45⅛	23
1984	42¼	32¼	1983	36½	21¼
1982	23	17	1981	31⅜	16¾
1980	38⅜	16¾	1979	21½	11

RECENT DIVIDENDS- Com. $1 par: $

1989 (to July 6)	*0.40	1988	1.50
1987 .... 0.75	1986 .... 0.60	1985-84 ...	1.45
1983 .... 1.10	1982 .... 1.00	1981	0.60
1980 .... 1.00	1979 .... 0.90		

*Incl. $0.20 pay. July 6 to record June 15.

EARNINGS AND FINANCES

AUDITORS- Deloitte Haskins & Sells, Philadelphia, Pa.

CONSOL. EARNS., Y-E Dec. 31: Thou. $

	Net Sales	Inc. Taxes	*Net Inc.	*Sh. Earns.
1988	66,130	3,065	5,842	3.37
1987	55,039	3,422	3,649	2.11
1986	44,702	2,456	2,570	1.48
1985	43,361	1,673	2,421	1.40
1984	52,086	6,371	7,217	4.17
1983	41,827	5,336	5,599	3.23
1982	28,511	2,847	3,134	1.81
1981	28,983	3,151	3,655	2.12
1980	29,461	4,051	4,328	2.50
1979	26,923	4,413	5,037	2.91

*Bef. extraord. items (Thou. $): 1979, cr55 or $0.03.

Sh. earns. are as reported by Co.

Annual Report- Consol. Inc. Acct., Yrs. End. Dec. 31: Thou. $

	1988	1987	1986
Net sales	66,130	55,039	44,702
Cost & exps	55,557	46,126	38,462
Oper. income ...	10,573	8,913	6,240
Other income...	482	166	510
Total income ...	11,055	9,079	6,750
Depreciation....	2,148	2,008	1,724
Income tax	3,065	3,422	2,456
Net income	5,842	3,649	2,570
Dividends.........	1,905	1,472	1,299
Bal. after divds	3,937	2,177	1,271
*Sh. earns.......	$3.37	$2.11	$1.48

*Avge. shs.: 1,732,000.

Consol. Bal. Sheet, Dec. 31: Thou. $

Assets—	1988	1987
Cash & short-term invests	6,420	5,947
Accts. rec	9,494	9,504
Inventories	14,188	11,676
Prepayments, etc	307	340
Tot. curr. assets.	30,409	27,467
Investments	500	...
*Net property	19,545	18,395
Total assets	50,454	45,862
Liabilities—		
Accts. pay	1,820	1,329
Accruals	4,761	3,412
Divds. pay	---	693
Tot. curr. liabs	6,581	5,434
Defr. inc. tax............	2,216	2,778
†Com. stk. p. $1.......	1,772	1,772
aTreas. stk.	dr352	dr351
Paid-in cap	932	932
Retain. earns	39,260	35,323
Fgn. currency transl. adjtmts	cr45	dr26
Total liabs	50,454	45,862
Net wkg. cap	23,828	22,033
Equity per sh	$24.05	$21.74
*Depr. res	15,180	13,168
†Shs.:	1,772,025	1,772,025
aShs.:	39,928	39,928

Thomas register of American manufacturers. (Annual). New York: Thomas Publishing.

World wide chamber of commerce directory. (Annual). Washington, DC: World Bank.

Encyclopedias

Both general and specialized encyclopedias are useful at the start of your research. They provide pertinent background information and often help in developing a clearer focus of the problem.

Bittel, L.R. (Ed.). (1979). *Encyclopedia of professional management.* New York: McGraw-Hill.

Childs, J.F. (1976). *Encyclopedia of long term financing and capital management.* Englewood Cliffs, NJ: Prentice-Hall.

Graham, I. (Ed.). (1969). *Encyclopedia of advertising* (2nd ed.). New York: Fairchild Publications.

Greenwald, D. (Ed.). (1982). *Encyclopedia of economics.* New York: McGraw-Hill.

Lucas, A. (Ed.). (1990). *Encyclopedia of information systems and services.* Detroit, MI: Gale.

Garcia, F.L., & Munn, C.G. (Eds.). (1983). *Encyclopedia of banking and finance* (8th ed.). Chicago: Bank Administration Institute.

Thorndike, D. (Ed.). (1987). *Thorndike encyclopedia of banking and financial tables* (rev. ed.). Boston: Warren Gorham & Lamont.

Woy, J. (Ed.). (1989). *Encyclopedia of business information sources* (7th ed.). Detroit, MI: Gale.

Guides to Books

If you want to know the titles of the latest publications in your area of research, you many find guides to books helpful.

Cumulative book index. (Annual). New York: H.W. Wilson.

Daniells, L.M. (Ed.). (1985). *Business information sources* (rev. ed.). Berkeley, CA: University of California Press.

Publishers' weekly. New York: Bowker.

Subject guide to books in print. (Annual). New York: Bowker.

Guides to Government Publications

The business researcher will find current information on trade figures, population statistics, business trends, import–export regulations, and trade legislation in government publications. The government also publishes committee reports and transcripts of congressional hearings.

American statistical index. Washington, DC: Congressional Information Service.

Guide to U.S. government publications. (Annual). McLean, VA: Documents Index.

Monthly catalog of United States government publications. Washington, DC: Government Printing Office.

Monthly checklist to state publications. Washington, DC: Government Printing Office.

Statistical abstract of the United States. Washington, DC: Government Printing Office.

U.S. Department of Commerce publications. Washington, DC: Department of Commerce.

Handbooks

Handbooks provide an overview on many topics. The researcher may use them as background information before starting an in-depth search.

Agent's and buyer's guide: the markets handbook. (Annual). Cincinnati, OH: National Underwriter.

Area handbook series. (Annual). Washington, DC: U.S. Department of the Army.

Farrell, P.V. (Ed.). (1982). *Aljian's purchasing handbook* (4th ed.). New York: McGraw-Hill.

Farrell, M. (Ed.). (Annual). *Dow Jones investors' handbook.* Princeton, NJ: Dow Jones.

Handbook of basic economic statistics. (Annual). Washington, DC: Bureau of Economic Statistics.

Hodgson, R.S. (1980). *Direct mail and mail order handbook* (3rd ed.). New York: Dartnell.

Heyel, C. (Ed.). (1980). *Handbook of modern office management and administrative services.* New York: Krieger.

Scheer, W. (1985). *Personnel administration handbook* (3rd ed.). Chicago: Dartnell.

U.S. Bureau of Domestic Commerce. (Annual). *Franchise opportunities handbook.* Washington, DC: Government Printing Office.

U.S. Bureau of Labor Statistics. (Annual). *Handbook of labor statistics.* Washington, DC: Government Printing Office.

International Business Sources

As business becomes more international, the business researcher must be familiar with international trade statistics and economic performances of major countries. The United States government regularly publishes international business information. In addition, foreign governments make available many reports on the business, economic, and political climate in their respective countries.

Canadian trade index. Toronto: Canadian Manufacturers' Association.

Dun & Bradstreet's principal international businesses. New York: Dun & Bradstreet.

Europa yearbook: a world survey. (Annual). Detroit, MI: Gale.

Foreign economic trends and their implications for the United States. Washington, DC: Government Printing Office.

Johannsen, H., & Page, T., eds. (1986). *International dictionary of management.* New York: Nichols.

Marconi's international register. (Annual). New York: Telegraphic Cable & Radio Registration.

Overseas business reports. Washington, DC: Government Printing Office.

Ulrich's international periodicals directory. (Annual). New York: Bowker.

United Nations. (Annual). *Yearbook of international trade statistics.* New York: International Publications Service.

Newspaper Indexes

Many newspapers carry extensive business information; however, because the number of newspapers is so great and because most newspapers are published daily, finding information in past issues can be tedious and time consuming. The business researcher, therefore, will find the indexes to major newspapers an invaluable research tool.

The Wall Street Journal Index is organized in two volumes, one by subject and one by corporations. If you want to read about automobile manufacturing at General Motors, for example, you can look under either "General Motors" or "auto" (Exhibits 9.4 and 9.5). The index provides a short abstract of every article so that you can determine at once whether it will be useful.

Bell and Howell newspaper indexes. Wooster, OH: Bell & Howell.

The New York Times index. New York: New York Times Co.

The Wall Street Journal index. Princeton, NJ: Dow Jones Books.

Periodical Indexes

For your search of the periodical literature, you must be familiar with the periodicals index system, which catalogs periodical articles by particular fields of interest. The index you will probably use most is the *Business Periodicals Index.*

Most periodicals indexes provide, in every volume, detailed instructions on their organization and use. For example, information on how to use the *Business Periodicals Index* is shown in Exhibit 9.6.

Exhibit 9.4	*The Wall Street Journal Index: Corporate News*

GENERAL MOTORS CORP.
(see also **Hughes Aircraft Co.**)

GM, with hoopla, seeks to trade in its current image: a big exhibit from Jan. 5 through Jan. 7 at the Waldorf-Astoria Hotel in New York will open costly effort; a skeptic: 'Basic Insanity.' 1/4-1;4

GM expects in 1988 to reverse its market-share declines of the past two years, company executives said; also Jan. 5. GM's Chevrolet division will cut base prices on its 1988-model pickup trucks an average of 0.4% from prices announced earlier in the model year. 1/6-7;1

GM produced 330,317 cars and truck-buses for December; produced 5,129,322 cars and truck-buses in 1987 to date. 1/6-7;1

GM named a vice president, finance, for the Motors Insurance Corp. subsidary of firm's General Motors Acceptance Corp. unit; he was also elected a Motors Insurance Corp. director and member of its executive and finance committees. 1/6-21;3

A GM unit, Saturn Corp., has narrowed to just a handful the list of ad agencies that will compete for the Saturn account, the largest up for grabs in the ad industry. 1/7-22;3

GM produced no cars in week ended Jan. 2; produced 53,282 cars in 1988 to date. 1/8-8;2

Sold 92,792 cars in Dec. 21-31 period; sold 263,997 cars in December; sold 3,555,538 cars in 1987 to date. 1/8-8;5

Firm will indefinitely halve production and staffing at its Van Nuys, Calif., assembly plant, a move that will affect 1,800 jobs beginning Feb. 1. 1/11-14;3

GM is planning further production cuts on certain slow-selling models to bring down high inventories. 1/12-12;2

GM's Chevrolet division will extend most of its sales incentives to Feb. 29, while GM's other divisions are considering continuing their plans, which were set to expire Jan. 11. 1/12-12;5

Sold 95,694 cars in Jan. 1-10 period; 1/26-4;2

GM agreed to recall 77,000 cars and pickup trucks in California that may have faulty anti-smog devices, according to California officials. 1/26-4;4

Fiat S.p.A. hopes to become Europe's No. 1 auto maker with its new mid-sized car, called the Tipo, meant to compete with Volkswagen's leading Golf model and cars by Ford and a GM unit. 1/26-31;4

GM's new compensation plan reflects general trend tying pay to performance; firm hopes new program, which will affect 112,000 employees, will get people to try harder. 1/26-39;4

Units were given Navy contracts totaling $10.3 million for aircraft-engine parts and missile equipment. 1/26-59;3

The Electronic Data Systems Corp. unit of General Motors Corp. signed a 12-year extension of its contract to manage the information processing operations of Security Mutual Life Insurance Co. 1/27-8;2

GM narrowly averted a strike at its truck and bus complex in Pontiac, Mich., reaching a tentative settlement with UAW local 594 just five minutes before the scheduled walkout at 10 a.m. EST Jan. 26. 1/27-28;6

Profits for the Big Three auto makers, GM, Ford and Chrysler, have jumped as much as 68% in the fourth quarter compared with a year earlier, though auto sales fell significantly. 1/28-4;2

GM's General Motors Acceptance Corp. unit announced several executive appointments, effective Feb. 1. 1/29-26;1

GM produced 54,217 cars in week ended Jan. 23; produced 200,389 cars in 1988 to date. 1/29-33;2

GM's Chevrolet division would give a $1,200 cash rebate to owners of foreign cars and trucks who buy a Chevrolet Nova by Feb. 29. 1/29-33;3

Responding to strong earnings at its nonautomotive units, boosted the dividends for its Class H and Class E common stocks and declared a 2-for-1 stock split of the

---

Source: The Wall Street Journal Index: Corporate News, 1988. Reprinted by permission of *The Wall Street Journal,* © Dow Jones & Company, Inc., 1988. All Rights Reserved Worldwide.

Exhibit 9.5   *The Wall Street Journal Index: General News*

AUTOS
(*see also* **Buses, Emergency Vehicles, Recreational Vehicles, Trucks & Vans**)

GM, with hoopla, seeks to trade in its current image; a big exhibit called 'GM Teamwork & Technology--for Today & Tomorrow' at Waldorf-Astoria Hotel will open estimated $20 million effort; a skeptic: 'basic insanity.' 1/4-1;4

General Motors Corp. expects in 1988 to reverse its market-share declines of the past two years, firm's executives said; also, GM's Chevrolet division will cut base prices on its 1988-model pickup trucks an average of 0.4% from prices announced earlier in model year. 1/6-7;1

Car stereo systems get harder for thieves to find as installers are finding big business in learning to hide them; for example, Beverly Hills Motoring Accessories sells a $200 device that makes a stereo recede into the dash behind a plain locking flap. (Business Bulletin) 1/7-1;5

Slower growth in credit-card debt and auto loans held the November increase in consumer credit outstanding to $2.22 billion, or a 4.4% annual rate, Federal Reserve Board said. 1/8-7;5

A longstanding feud between car audio industry and auto makers reopened Jan. 7 with an antitrust lawsuit by four audio firms alleging Chrysler Corp. is making it difficult for consumers to buy cars without factory-installed sound systems. 1/8-8;5

After the Spree: Consumers' spending shows signs of stalling in first quarter of '88; auto, airline and retail firms act to counter problems; 'promote a little harder'; failing engine for economy; includes charts. 1/13-1;6

William Popejoy, chairman of Financial Corp. of America, went out of his home in Newport Beach, Calif. and found a new Lincoln Continental Mark VII with ribbon on it in driveway; Popejoy was stunned and dismayed; Ford Motor Co. had been trying to acquire Financial's main unit, American S&L Association, so he thought deal had gone through and Lincoln was his new company car; to Popejoy's relief, car was a surprise gift being hidden from woman next door. (Shop Talk) 1/13-23;2

Source: The Wall Street Journal Index: General News, 1988. Reprinted by permission of *The Wall Street Journal,* © Dow Jones & Company, Inc., 1988. All Rights Reserved Worldwide.

Some indexes, such as the *Accountant's Index,* are organized by both subject and author, whereas the *Business Periodicals Index* and others are organized by subject, as illustrated in Exhibit 9.7. To use the *Business Periodicals Index* effectively, you should follow these steps:

1. Starting with the most recent volume, look up your subject in the index. You may have to try several subject headings and cross-references.

2. Pick out all promising articles under your subject and copy all the information listed. If the title of the periodical is abbreviated, check the abbreviations in the front of the index for the complete title.

3. Repeat the process using the most recent volumes, and work your way back through as many volumes as necessary. This system will assure you of finding the most up-to-date material.

4. Use the *Periodical Directory* at the library to find the location of the periodicals you need. Copy the location for each. Some libraries assign **call numbers** to periodicals. If your library does, you need to check the call number only once. The *Harvard Business Review,* for example,

Call Number
The call number is the identification number for each book in the library.

Exhibit 9.6   *Business Periodicals Index* Instructions

Explanatory Notes

ARRANGEMENT. *Business Periodicals Index* is a subject index and all entries are arranged in one alphabet. Subject headings beginning with numerals appear before those beginning with the letter A.

SUBJECT HEADINGS. This Index uses specific headings and subheadings. Biographical articles are indexed under biographees. An article describing a company is indexed under the name of the company.

REFERENCES. *See* references guide the user from a term not used as a heading to a term that is used. *See also* references guide the user from a term used as a heading to related headings under which additional material may be found. *See also* references have been made for most companies from their primary industry.

Sample entries:

Money management firms *See* Investment management firms
Investment management firms
    See also
        Capital Guardian Trust Company
    Spotlight put on fiduciaries [pension fiduciary voting of
        fund shares] B. L. Krikorian. *Pensions Investm Age* 16:61+
        Ja 25 '88   **Advertising**
    Campaign draws heavily on trust [Lincoln National] D. C.
        Jones. *Natl Underwrit* (*Life Health Financ Serv Ed*) 92:13
        Mr 14 '88   **Investments**
    Market beat. See issues of Pensions & Investment Age

EXPLANATION. The first line in the sample entry directs the user from a term not used as a heading to the established heading Investment management firms. On the second line is the subject heading **Investment management firms.** Under this heading the user is referred by a *see also* reference to an article which is about a particular company in the industry, Capital Guardian Trust Company. After the *see also* is an article about investment management firms entitled "Spotlight put on fiduciaries," by Betty L. Krikorian. This article will be found in the periodical *Pensions & Investment Age,* volume 16, page 61 and continuing on later pages of the January 25, 1988 issue. A title enhancement, "pension fiduciary voting of fund shares," has been added by the indexer to clarify the meaning of the title. Square brackets are used to indicate these editorial interpolations. On the next line the user will find the subheading **Advertising.** This is a subdivision of the heading **Investment management firms.** Under this subheading appears an entry about the advertising aspects of the industry. The last entry—**Investments**—is another subheading for this industry and the reader will find the entry entitled "Market beat" which is a regular feature in *Pensions & Investment Age.*

Exhibit 9.7   **Arrangement of** *Business Periodicals Index*

---

746   **BUSINESS PERIODICALS INDEX**

Technical education—*cont.*
Technical training in America: how much and who gets it? A. P. Carnevale and E. R. Schulz. il tabs *Train Dev J* 42:18-28+ N '88
Technical information
  See also
  Product manuals
Change the way you think about using information. M. Maccoby. *Res Technol Manage* 31:56-7 Jl-Ag '88
Technical information, Communication of *See* Technical communication
Technical innovations *See* Technological innovations
Technical literature
The international professional marketplace. G. Feldman. il *Publ Wkly* 234:55-6 O 28 '88
The technology booklet: a new form of product literature. L. C. Hawes and H. B. Michaelson. tabs *Tech Commun* 35:108-11 My '88
When Johnny won't read [dealing with engineering staff that doesn't use literature effectively] W. G. Cutler. *Res Technol Manage* 31:53 S-O '88
             Editing
  See Technical editing
Technical managers
Evaluating the technical operation. L. W. Steele. *Res Technol Manage* 31:11-18 S-O '88
Technical reports
             Editing
  See Technical editing
Technical schools *See* Technical education
Technical societies
  See also
  American Vacuum Society
Technical workers
  See also
  Technical managers
What we've learned: managing human resources. M. K. Badawy. *Res Technol Manage* 31:19-35 S-O '88
When Johnny won't read [dealing with engineering staff that doesn't use literature effectively] W. G. Cutler. *Res Technol Manage* 31:53 S-O '88
             Training
Performance testing for technical trainers. R. L. Sullivan and M. J. Elenburg. il *Train Dev J* 42:38-40 N '88
Technical training in America: how much and who gets it? A. P. Carnevale and E. R. Schulz. il tabs *Train Dev J* 42:18-28+ N '88
Technical writers
The business of technical pubs. P. Caernarven-Smith. *Tech Commun* 35:228-30 Ag '88
The challenges we face [editorial] F. R. Smith. *Tech Commun* 35:84-8 My '88
The freelance writer and marketing. E. Slatkin. tabs *Tech Commun* 35:112-17 My '88
Marketing your services [freelance technical writers] D. R. Young. tab *Tech Commun* 35:123-4 My '88
Professionalism [editorial] E. W. Smith. *Tech Commun* 35:164-6 Ag '88
Technical writing
Technical editors deserve respect, too. R. Reinhart. *Tech Commun* 35:126+ My '88
Usable instructions based on research and theory [special section] *Tech Commun* 35:89-107 My '88; 35:167-93 Ag '88
             Bibliography
Bibliography on the writing of instructions, excluding sources on computer documentation. S. Southard. bibl *Tech Commun* 35:101-4 My '88
Recent and relevant. J. S. Patterson. bibl *Tech Commun* 35:132-5 My '88; 35:218-21 Ag '88
Writing instructions for computer documentation: an annotated bibliography. C. H. Sides. bibl *Tech Commun* 35:105-7 My '88
             Study and teaching
Rewiring the English teacher. D. F. Beer. *Tech Commun* 35:152-4 My '88
Technocracy
Education for modernization: meritocratic myths in China, Mexico, the United States, and Japan. B. Ranson. bibl *J Econ Issues* 22:747-62 S '88
Technological change *See* Technological innovations
Technological change in agriculture *See* Agricultural innovations
Technological forecasting
  See also
  New products
  Technology assessment
  Technology transfer
Technological innovations
  See also
  Agricultural innovations

  Automation
  Diffusion of innovations
  Industrial research
  Innovation centers
  New products
  Technology assessment
  Technology transfer
Awards: ten innovators are honored for being industry builders [National Medals of Technology] *Res Dev* 30:25 S '88
The capital-investment appraisal of new technology: problems, misconceptions and research directions. R. W. Ashford and others. *J Oper Res Soc* 39:637-42 Jl '88
Capturing value from technological innovation: integration, strategic partnering, and licensing decisions. D. J. Teece. bibl flowchart graphs *Interfaces* 18:46-61 My-Je '88
Charting a course to superior technology evaluation. B. Gold. graph *Sloan Manage Rev* 30:19-27 Fall '88
Choice of technology and long-run technical change in energy-intensive industries. F. R. Forsund and L. Hjalmarsson. bibl graphs tabs *Energy J* 9:79-97 Jl '88
The financial linkages between the development and acquisition of technology. S. C. Justice. bibl *J Econ Issues* 22:355-62 Je '88
Fostering creativity and innovation in an industrial R&D laboratory. A. R. C. Westwood and Y. Sekine. *Res Technol Manage* 31:16-20 Jl-Ag '88
How can I use cost accounting in the new high-tech environment? J. F. Towey. *Manage Account* 70:61 Ag '88
Innovate! Quick! J. Case. *Inc* 10:19-20 Ag '88
Innovation in large and small firms: an empirical analysis. Z. J. Acs and D. B. Audretsch. bibl tabs *Am Econ Rev* 78:678-90 S '88
Innovation—a state of mind. I. M. Wood. diags tabs *Manage Decis* 26 no4:17-24 '88 Entrepreneurs: a Blueprint for Action issue
Limitation is the mother of innovation. G. L. Shostack. *J Bus Strategy* 9:51-2 N-D '88
Look beyond the lab for sources of innovation [views of E. Von Hippol] R. Cassidy. graph *Res Dev* 30:13-14 Ag '88
The new globalization [increased competition, capital mobility, technological sophistication] M. A. Cohen. *Can Bus Rev* 15:37-8 Aut '88
R&D marketing linkage and innovation strategy: some West German experience. K. Brockhoff and A. K. Chakrabarti. bibl tabs *IEEE Trans Eng Manage* 35:167-75 Ag '88
The role of politics in technological innovation [presidential candidates G. Bush and M. Dukakis] A. Furst. *Electron Bus* 14:162 S 15 '88
Scientific innovations [best of 1988] il *Bus Week* p116-17 Ja 9 '89
Significant technology: 100 new products from the past year [1988 award winners] il tab *Res Dev* 30:60-104 O '88
Technological change: disaggregation and overseas production. J. R. Munkirs. tabs *J Econ Issues* 22:469-75 Je '88
Technological innovation and development: prospects for China. X.-Y. Jin and A. L. Porter. bibl tabs *IEEE Trans Eng Manage* 35:258-64 N '88
Technological unemployment *See* Technology and labor
Technology
  See also
  Engineering
  Information technology
  Inventions
  Medical technology
  Membranes (Technology)
  Separation (Technology)
  Technocracy
  Technological innovations
  Technology and labor
Technology, regulation and the financial services industry in the year 2000. B. Ely. graphs *Issues Bank Regul* 12:13-19 Fall '88
             International aspects
  See also
  Foreign licensing agreements
  High technology industries—International aspects
  Technology transfer
Keeping in touch with technology. T. M. Rohan. *Ind Week* 237:39-42 O 3 '88
OECD report raises science policy issues [Science and technology policy—1988] D. A. O'Sullivan. *Chem Eng News* 66:7-8 S 26 '88

Source: Business Periodicals Index, Vol. 31, April 1989. Copyright © 1989 by The H. W. Wilson Company. Material reproduced with permission of the publisher.

has the same call number regardless of whether you are looking for an article published in June 1967 or July 1991.

Accountants' index. New York: American Institute of Certified Public Accountants.

American statistics index. Washington: Congressional Information Service.

Applied science and technology index. New York: Wilson.

Business periodicals index. New York: Wilson. Prior to 1958 the index was part of the Industrial Arts Index.

Education index. New York: Wilson.

Engineering index. New York: Engineering Index.

Index to legal periodicals. New York: Wilson.

Index to supermarket articles. Chicago: Supermarket Institute.

Index to labor union periodicals. Ann Arbor: University of Michigan, School of Business Administration.

Personnel management abstracts. Ann Arbor: University of Michigan.

Readers' guide to periodical literature. New York: Wilson.

Small business index. Metuchen, NJ: Scarecrow.

Social science index. New York: Wilson.

COMPUTER SEARCHES

Computerized search systems allow for a fast, comprehensive, and up-to-date search through all kinds of information. An online search of numerous databases can provide you with titles of periodical articles, listings of government publications, trade directories, and news services within minutes. Because it may take you some time to become efficient in online searches, you should in the beginning seek the help of librarians who have had training in computer searches.

Systems Available

Most databases are prepared by private companies that sell or lease them to vendors. BRS, DATA-STAR, ORBIT, DIALOG, SCD, ITT Dialsom, ESA, and IRS Information Service are examples of the computer services available. Some companies sell the access to their database to several vendors. The *Harvard Business Review,* for example, can be accessed through BRS and DIALOG.

The development in the field is dynamic and, in order to conduct searches efficiently, the user must be aware of frequent changes. For example, in January 1989, ORBIT and BRS merged into Pergamon ORBIT InfoLine. The two services had some of the same databases, but sometimes they were in different form. The two systems are being integrated.

To facilitate the use of computer search systems, many vendors publish guides to their databases. For example, DIALOG publishes guides, database chapters, Bluesheet listings of databases, software packages, and the monthly *Chronolog.* These and other publications can be ordered online or by mail.

The fee users pay for an online search is usually based on the length of the search and/or the time of day when the search is conducted. The cost is easily offset by the time the researcher saves in finding necessary information.

Some databases, such as the *Accountants' Index,* will provide you with only the title, author, and publication data. Others, such as *Management Contents,* also provide an abstract of the information. In all cases you can request a complete printout of an article for an additional fee.

Use of the Systems

Descriptor
A descriptor is a phrase or word you enter to find information.

If you want to find information through a computer search, you must use valid **descriptors**. Assume, for example, that you are researching the reasons for declining sales. You suspect that the decline is caused by problems in quality control and ineffective advertising. To find information in these two areas, you can use several descriptors.

Quality or advertising: This descriptor will provide a listing of articles that mention either quality or advertising but not both.

Quality and advertising: This descriptor will produce a listing of articles that mention both areas.

Quality not advertising: This descriptor will give a listing of articles that mention quality; it will not list articles that mention advertising.

You must decide which descriptor will be most helpful. You might want to use the descriptors "quality and advertising" and "quality or advertising," for example.

Databases cover legal, governmental, technical, educational, and business information. Exhibit 9.8 illustrates the variety of databases you can access through DIALOG. The business researcher must determine which specific databases will be most appropriate for solving the problem at hand.

EVALUATION OF SOURCES

Once you have identified potentially useful sources, you must decide which ones to read. The answers to these three questions will help you to decide:

1. How old is the source? Was it published several months ago, one year ago, five years ago?
2. Who is the author? Is the author a recognized expert in the field? Is the author a member of, or prominent spokesperson for, a special-interest group?
3. Is the article published in a scholarly journal, a popular magazine, or a special-interest group publication?

Finding the answer to the first question is easy, because the periodical or book carries the date of publication. That will not tell when the material was actually researched and written, but you can assume that at the time of publication the material was not outdated.

Exhibit 9.8 | Dialog Databases

BANKNEWS	BANKNEWS (AMERICAN BANKER NEWS)	3/87
390	BEILSTEIN	10/89
297	BIBLE (KING JAMES VERSION)	12/86
285	BIOBUSINESS™	10/88
286	BIOCOMMERCE ABSTRACTS AND DIRECTORY	2/89
287, 288	BIOGRAPHY MASTER INDEX	10/84
5, 55, 205	BIOSIS PREVIEWS*	9/88
357	BIOTECHNOLOGY ABSTRACTS	8/88
626	BOND BUYER FULL TEXT	3/88
470	BOOKS IN PRINT	10/89
137	BOOK REVIEW INDEX	5/82
430	BRITISH BOOKS IN PRINT	1/87
121	BRITISH EDUCATION INDEX	8/88
227	BRITISH OFFICIAL PUBLICATIONS (HMSO)	2/90
228	BRITISH OFFICIAL PUBLICATIONS (NONHMSO)	5/87
635	BUSINESS DATELINE*	11/86
256	BUSINESS SOFTWARE DATABASE™	6/89
610	BUSINESSWIRE	6/86
308-312, 399*	CA SEARCH	3/88
50, 53	CAB ABSTRACTS	4/86
262	CANADIAN BUSINESS AND CURRENT AFFAIRS	8/88
159	CANCERLIT*	4/88
491	CANCORP CANADIAN CORPORATIONS	3/89
162	CAREER PLACEMENT REGISTRY	12/85
580	CENDATA™	5/88
CENDATA	CENDATA™	5/86
335	CERAMIC ABSTRACTS	7/88
318	CHEM-INTELL	12/87
319	CHEMICAL BUSINESS NEWSBASE	7/88
315	CHEMICAL ENGINEERING ABSTRACTS	5/88
138	CHEMICAL EXPOSURE	5/83
19*	CHEMICAL INDUSTRY NOTES	6/85
174	CHEMICAL REGULATIONS & GUIDELINES	11/81
317	CHEMICAL SAFETY NEWSBASE	5/89
301, 398, 231*	CHEMNAME™ CHEMSEARCH™ ONTAP™ CHEMNAME™	8/89
632	CHICAGO TRIBUNE	12/88
64	CHILD ABUSE & NEGLECT	8/80
344*	CHINESE PATENT ABSTRACTS IN ENGLISH	6/87
410	CHRONOLOG* NEWSLETTER–INTERNATIONAL ED	5/81
101	CIS	8/80
220-222*	CLAIMS™/CITATION	12/85
242*	CLAIMS™ COMPOUND REGISTRY	11/82
123*	CLAIMS™/REASSIGNMENT & REEXAMINATION	1/90
124*	CLAIMS™/REFERENCE	10/86
23-25, 125, 340*	CLAIMS™/U.S. PATENTS	10/87
223-225, 341*		
219	CLINICAL ABSTRACTS	9/85
164	COFFEELINE*	7/82
194, 195*	COMMERCE BUSINESS DAILY	8/88
479	COMPANY INTELLIGENCE™	10/89
8	COMPENDEX* PLUS	2/88
675	COMPUTER ASAP™	9/88
230	COMPUTER-READABLE DATABASES	9/89

QUOTES*	DIALOG* QUOTES AND TRADING	3/86
158	DIOGENES*	11/87
100	DISCLOSURE* DATABASE	9/89
540*	DISCLOSURE*/SPECTRUM OWNERSHIP	10/86
35	DISSERTATION ABSTRACTS ONLINE	7/89
588,289*	DMS CONTRACT AWARDS	12/88
984*	DMS CONTRACTORS	3/87
988*	DMS MARKET INTELLIGENCE REPORTS*	1/87
103,104,803*§	DOE ENERGY	3/89
229	DRUG INFORMATION FULLTEXT	11/87
22	EBIS™ – EMPLOYEE BENEFITS INFOSOURCE	5/89
565	ECONBASE: TIME SERIES AND FORECASTS	10/89
139	ECONOMIC LITERATURE INDEX	10/89
511	THE EDUCATIONAL DIRECTORY	6/89
241	ELECTRIC POWER DATABASE	7/86
72,172,173	EMBASE (Excerpta Medica)	7/88
114	ENCYCLOPEDIA OF ASSOCIATIONS	2/89
69	ENERGYLINE*	8/88
293	ENGINEERED MATERIALS ABSTRACTS™	8/87
40	ENVIROLINE*	8/88
68	ENVIRONMENTAL BIBLIOGRAPHY	7/80
1	ERIC	2/87
316	EUROPEAN DIRECTORY OF AGROCHEMICAL PRODS	10/88
182	EVERYMAN'S ENCYCLOPAEDIA	11/85
54	EXCEPTIONAL CHILD EDUCATION RESOURCES	10/89
183*	EXPERTNET*	10/88
264	FACTS ON FILE*	1/86
291	FAMILY RESOURCES	12/83
187	F-D-C REPORTS	10/89
20	FEDERAL INDEX	10/80
699	FEDERAL REGISTER	8/89
136	FEDERAL REGISTER ABSTRACTS	11/88
265,266	FEDERAL RESEARCH IN PROGRESS	7/88
560	FINANCIAL TIMES COMPANY ABSTRACTS	9/86
622*	FINANCIAL TIMES FULLTEXT	12/86
196	FINDEX	5/88
268	FINIS: FINANCIAL INDUSTRY INFORMATION SERVICE	2/90
96	FLUIDEX	12/80
51,251	FOOD SCIENCE & TECHNOLOGY ABSTRACTS	6/89
79	FOODS ADLIBRA™	5/84
90*	FOREIGN TRADE & ECON ABSTRACTS	9/88
26	FOUNDATION DIRECTORY	9/89
27	FOUNDATION GRANTS INDEX	5/82
58	GEOARCHIVE	6/80
292	GEOBASE™	4/87
89	GEOREF	2/81
66	GPO MONTHLY CATALOG	7/83
166	GPO PUBLICATIONS REFERENCE FILE	11/87
273*	GRADLINE	4/88
85	GRANTS	2/86
122	HARVARD BUSINESS REVIEW	7/83
198	HEALTH DEVICES ALERTS*	7/89

*Databases not available under the Classroom Instruction Program.
†Available to U.S. users only.

§Available in the U.S., Canada, Denmark, Finland, France, Italy, Japan, Netherlands, Norway, Spain, Sweden, Great Britain, and Northern Ireland only.

(February 1990)   B-1

Questions about the author may be more difficult to answer. Sometimes periodicals provide a profile of the writer, including company or university affiliation and research interests. You might also check various *Who's Who* directories to find more information.

The third question is the most difficult. Scholarly journals by their very nature should be unbiased. They tend to be published by or affiliated with universities. The editing board of a scholarly journal checks the quality of the articles submitted and tries to assure objectivity. With magazines you must be more careful. No strict rules exist for determining whether a periodical is classified as a journal or as a magazine, but the information in Exhibit 9.9 should help you to make a decision. You might query the editor of a magazine

Exhibit 9.9

Distinction between Journals and Magazines

	Journal	Magazine
Publisher	University Professional organization	Commercial enterprise
Editor	Professor	Full-time paid
Review	Peer review, review-panel names often listed	Different from magazine to magazine
Frequency	Usually quarterly	Often biweekly or monthly
Advertising	Few paid ads	Many paid ads
Authorship	Authors almost always listed	Many anonymous or staff written articles, some authors identified

from a commercial publisher about the selection process for articles. Some publications are produced by special-interest groups such as political parties, labor unions, and churches. The articles might be useful, but you must evaluate the materials and the source carefully for bias.

After deciding which sources will be useful and appropriate, the next step is to compile a preliminary **bibliography** on cards. For every source you should include the following information:

Bibliography
A bibliography is an alphabetized list of sources on a given topic.

Books	Articles
Names(s) of author(s)	Name(s) of author(s)
Title of book	Title of article
Name of publisher	Title of periodical
Place of publication	Volume number
Year of publication	Month and year of publication
Edition number	Page numbers
Call number	Call number of periodical

So that you can type your bibliography for the report directly from the bibliography cards, you should use the format of the stylebook that you intend to use for the completed report. Documentation will be discussed in detail in Chapter 10.

The two samples in Exhibit 9.10 show how to enter bibliography information on the card. You may put the call number in any corner as long as you are consistent. You may want to add a brief **annotation**. This will help you later in determining whether you have information on all areas of your topic. It can also serve as a starting point in future research projects. In the annotation you might identify the major topics, compare the positions taken with other sources, and list particularly helpful features.

Annotation
An annotation provides a very short summary or comment of a source.

A detailed discussion of how to analyze secondary research sources is presented in Chapter 13.

Exhibit 9.10   Sample Bibliography Cards

HF 5718.J6

Haworth, D., & Savage, G. (1989). A channel-ratio model of intercultural communication: the trains won't sell, fix them please. *The Journal of Business Communication, 26*(3), 231–254.

The model is based on concept of high context/low context cultures. It discusses use of the model and provides a useful framework for business people dealing with different cultures. Specific examples and applications of model to practical situations are particularly helpful.

HD 30.28 .42 1983

Amara, Roy, and Andrew J. Lipinski.
Business Planning for an Uncertain Future, Scenarios & Strategies.
New York: Pergamon Press, 1983.

Gives step-by-step strategies for planning in corporate settings; develops a model for planning and provides guidelines for using the model; gives case examples and political framework of planning. The political aspects of planning and communicating in the planning process are particularly helpful.

SUMMARY OF LEARNING OBJECTIVES

To understand the role of secondary research in report writing.

Secondary research tells the writer what research has been done to solve similar problems; therefore, secondary research saves time.

To recognize different types of libraries.

There are general purpose libraries, research libraries, and special-purpose libraries.

To understand the organization of libraries.

Libraries have author–title catalogs and subject catalogs that help in finding books. Index systems help in the search for periodical articles. For the business writer the *Business Periodicals Index* is probably the most useful. Many libraries also have an OCLC computer program.

To become familiar with secondary sources useful to the business writer.

The sources listed at the end of the text of this chapter will help the researcher find secondary information more efficiently.

To become familiar with computer searches.

Computer searches can save time and allow an in-depth search for information.

To be able to evaluate sources and compile bibliography and note cards.

The researcher must determine whether an article or a book is useful for the project at hand. The name of the author, name and reputation of the periodical, date of publication, and the reviewing system can help to evaluate the credibility of an article.

On the bibliography card are written the name of author, title of article, title of book or periodical, place of publication, name of publisher, date of publication, and page numbers. An annotation of the source may be added.

KEY TERMS

Author–Title Catalog   Call Number
Subject Catalog   Descriptor
Database   Bibliography
Periodical Literature   Annotation

QUESTIONS AND DISCUSSION POINTS

1. Prepare an annotated bibliography of at least ten sources for a topic in your area of study.
2. Why have many libraries switched to the Library of Congress cataloging system?
3. What is the organization of the *Business Periodicals Index*?
4. Discuss the use of computers in secondary research.

EXERCISES

1. Look at the research plan for a report you are preparing to determine subject headings under which you may find material for your report. Check those subjects in the library.
2. Compile a list of journals in your major. Give a brief description of the focus of each journal.
3. Examine several journals in your field for currently popular topics.
4. You have an employment interview with a corporation two weeks from now. Find out about the financial position of the company, major products, and location of subsidiaries. List the sources you consult and record the findings.
5. Compile an annotated bibliography of books and articles on business communication published during the past year.

10

DOCUMENTATION OF SOURCES

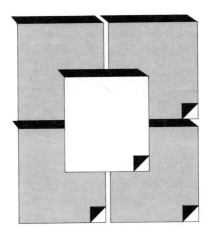

Learning Objectives

- To understand the reasons for documentation and the problem of plagiarism.
- To become familiar with the APA style for quotations and documentation of sources.
- To understand the principles for compiling bibliographies.

DOCUMENTATION

All secondary sources that you use in your report must be documented regardless of whether you quote or **paraphrase.** Documentation is important for these reasons:

..rase is a summary
ui—or comment on—a
source, in the writer's own
words.

1. Documentation allows the reader to check the sources you have used in your report. The reader may want to see the material in context or know who wrote the article or report. The reader may even want to read the entire article from which you quoted.
2. Documentation indicates that you researched what others have written about the same topic. It shows that you are up-to-date, and, therefore, documentation lends credibility to your work.
3. Documentation is necessary for legal reasons. Not giving credit where credit is due can cause legal problems. To use material without giving the source is unethical.

Plagiarism

Plagiarism
Plagiarism is the
unauthorized or
unacknowledged use of
secondary material.

Using material without documentation is called **plagiarism** and is punishable by law. If you refer in your report to interviews, lectures, unpublished papers, television or radio broadcasts, books, magazines, or journals, you must credit the source.

Information that is considered general knowledge, however, need not be documented. For example, you do not have to document the fact that the United States has 50 states. You would not need to document the statement that Saudi Arabia is a principal producer of crude oil, but you would have to document the source for specific production statistics. The reader must know whether the source is the Saudi government, the U.S. government, a private research firm, or the Soviet Union. Each of these entities would look at the statistics from its own frame of reference and have a different definition for production of crude oil. If you are not certain whether an item is general knowledge, you should document it.

Copyright Laws

Copyright Laws
Copyright laws are
intended to prevent the
illegal use of secondary
sources.

Copyright laws provide protection for published material. If you write a book, for example, you copyright the book. Anybody who wants to duplicate or photocopy material from your book must obtain your permission. You may legally charge the user of the material.

Under copyright laws material is protected for the author's life plus 50 years. After that time the material is in the public domain. Once the copyright has expired, you need not pay for material used, but you still must document the source.

Copyright laws allow for the educational use of material. For example, if you quote material from a copyrighted book in a term paper report, you do not have to ask for permission. If you photocopy an article for your own use, you do not have to ask permission or pay the author. If, however, you use the material in a book that will be published and sold, you must obtain permission. In most cases you will be allowed the use of a limited amount of material, usually a paragraph, free of charge, but you may have to pay for longer quotations.

STYLE MANUALS

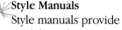
Style Manuals
Style manuals provide guidelines for writing and editing, including documentation.

If your company has specified a particular documentation format, you must follow it precisely. If you are allowed to make format decisions, you may choose one of a number of **style manuals** on the market. A style manual provides guidance in preparing manuscripts. Most style manuals discuss margins, indentations, headings, capitalization, and formats for footnotes and bibliographies. The style manuals most frequently used are

The Chicago manual of style (13th ed.). (1982). Chicago: University of Chicago Press.

Gibaldi, J., & Achtert, W. S. (1984). *MLA handbook for writers of research papers* (2nd ed.). New York: Modern Language Association of America.

Publication Manual of the American Psychological Association (3rd ed.). (1983). Washington: American Psychological Association.

Turabian, K. L. (1973). *A Manual for writers of term papers, theses, and dissertations* (4th ed.). Chicago: University of Chicago Press.

Documentation consists of two basic components: citations in the text and complete entries in the notes or bibliography. The precise format depends on the style manual you use.

Business journals tend to use the American Psychological Association (APA) style, whereas language journals tend to use the Modern Language Association (MLA) style. This chapter presents APA style. MLA style is illustrated in the appendix to the chapter.

FORMAT FOR QUOTATIONS

Short Quotations

The writer may integrate short quotations (up to 40 words) into the text. The name of the author may appear at the beginning or the end of the quoted material.

> March (1988) maintains that "the Japanese do not like negotiation. It has disagreeable connotations of confrontation, to be avoided whenever possible" (p. 15).

or

> It has been argued that "the Japanese do not like negotiation. It has disagreeable connotations of confrontation, to be avoided whenever possible" (March, 1988, p. 15).

Long Quotations

Long quotations (more than 40 words) are indented five spaces. The quoted material is not enclosed in quotation marks. The source, as for short quotations, may appear in the introductory text or at the end of the quote.

> March (1988) gives a detailed account of Japanese negotiation practices. In his opinion The Japanese do not like negotiation. It has disagreeable connotations of confrontation, to be avoided whenever possible. The Japanese instinct is for agreements worked out behind the scenes, on the basis of give and take, harmony and long-term interest. In fact, except for a handful with extensive international experience, very few Japanese even know how to negotiate in the Western sense (p. 15).

Using APA style, long quotations are normally double spaced. If the report is single spaced, however, you may single space the long quotation.

Ellipses

The ellipses—a series of three periods with spaces between them—indicate that something has been omitted from the original text. Because omissions from the original text can change the meaning, the writer must make it clear when material is omitted. An omission in the middle of a sentence is indicated by three periods with spaces between.

> Verbal contracts remain widespread because Japanese men continue to value their public reputations . . . as men of honor (March, 1988, p. 32).

An omission at the end of a sentence is indicated by the ellipses plus a fourth period to mark the end of the sentence.

> The older managers wished to follow conventional Japanese practice, with senior managers in charge . . . . Problems like this threatened the smooth operation of the new management team (March, 1988, p. 39).

Additions

Sometimes the writer may want to add a comment or clarify a term in the quotation. The writer's own comments or additions within a quotation are set off by brackets. If the typewriter does not have a key for brackets, they must be added by hand.

> In Germany you "need to be absolutely factual in any claims for your product. There are laws against exaggeration [no superlatives are allowed in ads]. You cannot claim to be the leader in the field" (Hall, 1983, p. 78).

Emphasis

Emphasized or italicized words in the original must be emphasized or italicized in the quotation. On the other hand, if the writer wants to *add* emphasis, he has to indicate that the emphasis was not present in the original.

> In Germany you "need to be *absolutely factual* [emphasis added] in any claims for your product" (Hall, 1983, p. 78).

PLACEMENT OF DOCUMENTATION

Reports using the APA style do not have endnotes or footnotes. The citations in the text include the name of the author, year of publication, and page reference. A bibliography at the end of the report identifies all sources, whether

Exhibit 10.1	**Sample Bibliography Based on APA Style**

References

Bennet, J. C., & Olney, R. (1986). Executive priorities for efficient communication in an information society. *The Journal of Business Communication, 23*(2), 13–22.

Computers: the new look. (1987, November 30). *Business Week,* p. 112.

Pomerenke, P. (1987). Process: More than a fad. *The Journal of Business Communication, 24*(1), 37–39.

Varner, I., & Grogg, P. M. (1987). Business writing with the microcomputer: what do the users report? *Journal of Education for Business, 61,* 259–263.

Zinsser, W. (1983). *Writing with a word processor.* New York: Harper & Row.

they specifically support the report or were used as background information. They are listed alphabetically by last names of authors. If all of the entries in the bibliography specifically support the report, the list is called "References."

Bibliographies use hanging indentations; that is, the first line of an entry is on the left margin and the remaining lines are indented. When the report is written in blocked style, the bibliography may be blocked also. The name of the author appears in reverse order: last name, first name. Only the initials of the first and middle name of the author are given. Exhibit 10.1 illustrates the APA format for the bibliography.

When bibliographies are annotated, the annotations start on a new line (see Exhibit 10.2).

FORMAT FOR DOCUMENTATION USING APA STYLE

Book with One Author

March, R. M. (1988). *The Japanese negotiator.* Tokyo: Kodansha International.

Exhibit 10.2	**Annotated Bibliography**

References

Bennet, J. C., & Olney, R. (1986). Executive priorities for efficient communication in an information society. *The Journal of Business Communication, 23*(2), 13–22.
An examination of the frequency and type of written communication in businesses.

Computers: the new look. (1987, November 30). *Business Week,* p. 112.
A look at the impact of the switch from the mainframe to the microcomputer.

Pomerenke, P. (1987). Process: More than a fad. *The Journal of Business Communication, 24*(1), 37–39.
An examination of the writing and editing process with emphasis on the sequence of steps.

Varner, I., & Grogg, P. M. (1987). Business writing with the microcomputer: what do the users report? *Journal of Education for Business, 61,* 259–263.
An empirical study of the impact of the microcomputer on writing attitudes and writing performance.

Zinsser, W. (1983). *Writing with a word processor.* New York: Harper & Row.
An examination of the role of talent and technology in writing.

Book with Two Authors

Smeltzer, L. R., & Waltman, J. L. (1984). *Managerial communication.* New York: Wiley.

Anonymous Book

The 1990 information please almanac. (1990). Boston: Houghton Mifflin.

An Edited Book

Luce, L. F., & Smith, E. C. (Eds.). (1987). *Toward internationalism* (2nd ed.). Cambridge, MA: Newbury House.

Journal Article with One Author

Hagge, J. (1989). The spurious paternity of business communication principles. *The Journal of Business Communication, 26*(4), 33–55.

Journal Article with More Than Two Authors

Gatewood, R., Lahiff, J., Deter, R., & Hargrove, L. (1989). Effects of training on behaviors of the selection interview. *Journal of Business Communication, 26*(1), 17–31.

Magazine Article

Carlson, M. (1989, February 9). Friendship has limits. *Time,* pp. 30–31.

Newspaper Article without Author

Status of the Senate. (1989, February 21). *The Wall Street Journal,* p. A18.

Computer Software

Rightwriter 2.1. (1987). [Computer program]. Sarasota, FL: RightSoft, Inc.

Unpublished Speeches and Lectures

Hoss, E. (1989, April). *An analysis of visual aids in annual reports.* Paper presented at the Midwest regional meeting of the Association for Business Communication, Cincinnati, OH.

Government Reports Available from the Government Printing Office (GPO)

United States Department of Commerce, National Technical Information Service. *Directory of federally supported information analysis centers* (3rd ed.). (1974). Washington: U.S. Government Printing Office.

Personal Interviews

(Format suggested by author; APA does not cover interviews.)

Pomerenke, P. (1989, March 15). Personal interview.

Radio and Television Programs

(Format suggested by author; APA does not cover radio and television programs.)

This Week With David Brinkley. (1989, March 12). New York: ABC.

SUMMARY OF LEARNING OBJECTIVES

To understand the reasons for documentation and the problem of plagiarism.

The report writer must document the sources she uses for both ethical and legal reasons. If the writer uses a large amount of copyrighted material, she may need permission from the author.

To become familiar with the APA style for quotations and documentation of sources.

Regardless of which style manual is used, quotations must be precise. The writer must indicate whether he has added to, deleted from, or changed emphasis of the material quoted. Short quotations can be incorporated in the text; long quotations, which are set off as indented blocks, are not enclosed in quotation marks.

Using APA style, sources are always listed alphabetically at the end of the report. The text citation includes the author's name, year of publication, and page number.

To understand the principles for compiling bibliographies.

All reports using material from secondary sources require documentation, whether the sources specifically support the report or were used as background information. Following APA style, both types are combined in the bibliography. Other style manuals specify the use of footnotes or endnotes; if footnotes, a bibliography may also be required.

KEY TERMS

Paraphrase
Plagiarism

Copyright Laws
Style Manuals

QUESTIONS AND DISCUSSION POINTS

1. Discuss the term **plagiarism.**
2. What are some of the reasons for documenting sources used in writing reports?
3. Discuss the use of style manuals.
4. How do you handle omissions, additions, and emphasis in quotations?
5. What is the format for long quotations?
6. Where in the report can you put reference listings?
7. What is a hanging indentation? When do you use it?

APPENDIX 10A

MLA STYLE

FORMAT FOR QUOTATIONS

The *MLA Handbook* format for quotations is the same as the *APA Manual* format discussed in the chapter text, except that MLA indents long quotations ten spaces. According to MLA, long quotations are double spaced. If the report is single spaced, the writer using MLA style may also single space the long quotation.

PLACEMENT OF DOCUMENTATION

Reference Notes

Reference notes are traditionally called footnotes because they were originally placed at the bottom, or foot, of the page. Today, they can be in the text, at the bottom of the page, or at the end of the report or chapter.

Complete Notes in the Text. If the report has only one or two reference notes, the writer may choose to place them within the text. The following example illustrates this option:

> The research found (Varner, Iris, and Patricia Marcum-Grogg, "Microcomputers and the Writing Process." *The Journal of the Association for Business Communication: 25.3 (1988): 70) that many writing instructors "have moved away from a prescriptive, grammatical approach to an emphasis on interactive methods which stress . . . planning, clarification of purpose, and development of concepts."*

The reader has complete source information, but the sentence flow is interrupted. This option should be used sparingly.

Footnotes. Placement of the footnote at the bottom of the page requires a note number in the text following the quoted or paraphrased material. This number is raised half a line above the typed text. It follows all punctuation except a dash. When all cited information in a paragraph is from a single source, a single footnote can be used. Its number follows the last sentence in the paragraph containing information from that source. In practice, this sentence is often the last one in the paragraph. Footnoted material is numbered sequentially throughout a report; in books the numbering is often by chapter.

The proper placement of footnotes and numbers is shown in Exhibit 10A.1. The footnote is separated from the last line of the text by a solid line usually about 1½ inches long. The line is a single space below the last line of text. The footnote entry is indented the same amount as paragraphs in the text. The

Exhibit 10A.1   **Footnotes Based on MLA Style**

German law prohibits any defaming reference to a competitor or his goods and services in ad campaigns. For example, it would be totally unacceptable to make remarks about a competitor's status in the market, history, or nationality. The competitor's name need not be included in the advertisement to cause such statements to be considered unfair. The mere mention of the competitor's business category is considered a violation of the law.[1]

American advertising law, on the other hand, does not forbid the use of a competitor's trademark or trade name in an ad.[2] It was because of this difference in advertising law that Burger King ran into legal problems when it promoted its international advertising campaign, the "Battle of the Burgers," in Germany. The ad's headline read: "Let the others stew in their own fat." Underneath were the captions: "Burger King grills" and "It tastes better from the fire." Burger King knew the ad campaign was illegal, but it was considered necessary to educate German customers who "don't yet know there's any difference between hamburgers."[3] This indirect reference to other hamburger restaurants that fry their hamburgers violated German law and had to be discontinued.

[1] Rudolf Mueller, _Doing Business in Germany: A Legal Manual_ (Frankfurt/Main: Fritz Knapp Verlag, 1971) 66.

[2] Louis W. Stern and Thomas L. Eovaldi, _Legal Aspects of Marketing Strategy_ (Englewood Cliffs: Prentice-Hall, 1984) 57.

[3] Wellington Long, "Burger Battle Goes Overseas," _Advertising Age_ 20 Aug. 1984: 44.

number of the footnote is typed half a line above the entry. Footnotes in double-spaced reports can be either single- or double-spaced. If the footnote entry is longer than one line, the following lines start on the left margin. Two footnotes on the same page are separated by a line of space.

A complete footnote entry is necessary only when a work is cited the first time. Later an abbreviated form, giving the name of the author and the page number, is sufficient. If the article does not list the name of the author, the second citation gives the title of the article and the page number. If the second immediately follows the first, the writer may use *Ibid.* for the second citation:

[1] Wilson T. Price, <u>Microcomputer Applications</u> (Hinsdale: Dryden, 1989) 27.

[2] William A. Simcox, "A Design Method for Graphic Communication," <u>ABCA Bulletin</u> 47.1 (1984): 5.

[3] <u>Ibid.</u> 3.

[4] Price 60.

When footnotes are used, a bibliography is required at the end of the report or book to list in one place all the sources cited.

Endnotes.   Endnote references are at the end of the report or chapter. Most journals use endnotes because they are easier to type and print. The disadvantage is that the reader must turn back and forth between the endnotes and the text. As a result, most readers do not check references.

The format for endnotes is the same as the format for footnotes. Published articles that use endnotes do not include a separate bibliography. The text citation for endnotes may give the name of the author or may be simply an assigned endnote number.

Endnotes Cited by Name of Author.   When endnotes are cited in the text by name of author, an example would read as follows:

> The research found that many writing instructors "have moved away from a prescriptive, grammatical approach to an emphasis on interactive methods which stress . . . planning, clarification of purpose, and development of concepts. (Varner and Marcum-Grogg 70).

The writer may also use the author's name in the text and place the page number in parentheses. Referring to the author by name in the text may give more credibility to the information. In this case the example would read as follows:

> Varner and Marcum-Grogg found that many writing instructors "have moved away from a prescriptive, grammatical approach to an emphasis on interactive methods which stress . . . planning, clarification of purpose, and development of concepts" (70).

Identification of the Reference by Number.   If the reference is cited in the text by number, the example would be written as follows:

> The research found that many writing instructors "have moved away from a prescriptive, grammatical approach to an emphasis on interactive methods which stress . . . planning, clarification of purpose, and development of concepts" (6:70).

Exhibit 10A.2   **Bibliography Based on MLA Style**

Bennet, James C., and Robert Olney. "Executive Priorities for Efficient Communication in an Information Society." *The Journal of Business Communication* 23.2 (1986): 13–22.

"Computers: the New Look." *Business Week* 30 Nov. 1987: 112.

Pomerenke, Paula. "Process: More than a Fad." *The Journal of Business Communication* 24.1 (1987): 37–39.

Varner, Iris, and Patricia Marcum-Grogg. "Business Writing with the Microcomputer: What Do the Users Report?" *Journal of Education for Business* 61 (1987): 259–63.

Zinsser, William. *Writing with a Word Processor.* New York: Harper & Row, 1983.

With this notation the reader has no idea that the quotation is from an article by Varner and Marcum-Grogg. The number 6 refers to the bibliography. The quoted material is taken from the sixth entry in the bibliography, page 70. Reference notes treated this way are easy to type, but the reader is given no useful reference information in the text.

Bibliography

Bibliographies list all of the works used in the report alphabetically by the last name of the author. Bibliography entries are numbered if the references in the text refer to works by number. Bibliographies use hanging indentation; that is, the first line of an entry is on the left margin and the remaining lines are indented. When the report is written in blocked style, the bibliography may be blocked also. The name of the author appears in reverse order: last name, first name. Although the second edition of the *MLA Handbook* says that bibliography entries are to be double-spaced, it may be more appropriate to single-space bibliography entries in a single-spaced business report. Bibliography entries in a double-spaced report can be either double- or single-spaced. Exhibit 10A.2 illustrates a bibliography using the MLA style.

FORMAT FOR DOCUMENTATION USING MLA STYLE

The MLA style uses different formats for footnotes/endnotes and bibliography entries. In the paired examples that follow, the first entry is the footnote or endnote; the second entry is the bibliography.

Book with One Author

[1] Robert M. March, *The Japanese Negotiator* (Tokyo: Kodansha International, 1988) 70.

March, Robert M. *The Japanese Negotiator.* Tokyo: Kodansha International, 1988.

Book with Two Authors

[2] Larry R. Smeltzer and John L. Waltman, *Managerial Communication* (New York: Wiley, 1984) 59.

Smeltzer, Larry R., and John L. Waltman. *Managerial Communication.* New York: Wiley, 1984.

Anonymous Book

[3] *The Information Please Almanac* (Boston: Houghton Mifflin, 1988) 36.

The Information Please Almanac. Boston: Houghton Mifflin, 1988.

An Edited Book

[4] Louise Fiber Luce and Elise C. Smith, eds., *Toward Internationalism,* 2nd ed. (Cambridge: Newbury House, 1987) 22.

Luce, Louise Fiber, and Elise C. Smith, eds. *Toward Internationalism.* Cambridge: Newbury House, 1987.

Journal Article with One Author

[5] John Hagge, "The Spurious Paternity of Business Communication Principles," *The Journal of Business Communication,* 26.1 (1989): 34.

Hagge, John. "The Spurious Paternity of Business Communication Principles." *The Journal of Business Communication* 26.1 (1989): 33–55.

Journal Article with Two or Three Authors

[6] John M. Penrose, Joel P. Bowman, and Marie E. Flatley, "The Impact of Microcomputers on ABC Recommendations for Teaching, Writing, and Research," *The Journal of Business Communication,* 24.4 (1987): 81.

Penrose, John M., Joel P. Bowman, and Marie E. Flatley. "The Impact of Microcomputers on ABC Recommendations for Teaching, Research, and Writing." *The Journal of Business Communication* 24.4 (1987): 79–91.

Journal Article with More Than Three Authors

[7] Robert Gatewood et al., "Effects of Training on Behaviors of the Selection Interview," *The Journal of Business Communication,* 26.1 (1989): 18.

Gatewood, Robert, et al. "The Effects of Training on Behaviors of the Selection Interview." *The Journal of Business Communication* 26.1 (1989): 17–31.

Magazine Article

[8] Margaret Carlson, "Friendship Has Limits," *Time* 20 Feb. 1989: 30.

Carlson, Margaret. "Friendship Has Limits." *Time* 20 Feb. 1989: 30–31.

Newspaper Article

[9] Karen Elliott House, "As Power Is Dispersed among Nations, Need for Leadership Grows," *The Wall Street Journal* 21 Feb. 1989: A1.

House, Karen Elliott. "As Power Is Dispersed among Nations, Need for Leadership Grows." *The Wall Street Journal* 21 Feb. 1989: A1.

Newspaper Article without Author

[10] "Status of the Senate," *The Wall Street Journal* 21 Feb. 1989: A18.

"Status of the Senate." *The Wall Street Journal* 21 Feb. 1989: A18.

Personal Interviews

[11] Paula Pomerenke, Professor of Business Communication, Personal interview, 14 Mar. 1989.

Pomerenke, Paula. Professor of Business Communication. Personal interview. 14 Mar. 1989.

Computer Software

[12] *Rightwriter 2.1,* computer software, Sarasota: Rightsoft, Inc., 1987.

Rightwriter 2.1. Computer software. Sarasota: RightSoft, Inc., 1987.

Radio and Television Programs

[13] *This Week with David Brinkley,* ABC Television, New York, 12 Mar. 1989.

This Week with David Brinkley. ABC Television, New York. 12 Mar. 1989.

Unpublished Speeches and Lectures

[14] Eric Hoss, "An Analysis of Visual Aids in Annual Reports," Midwest Regional Meeting of the Association for Business Communication, Cincinnati, 14 Apr. 1989.

Hoss, Eric. "An Analysis of Visual Aids in Annual Reports." Midwest Regional Meeting of the Association for Business Communication. Cincinnati, 14 Apr. 1989.

Government Reports Available from the Government Printing Office (GPO)

[15] United States Department of Commerce, National Technical Information Service, *Directory of Federally Supported Information Analysis Centers,* 3rd ed. (Washington: GPO, February 1984) 3.

United States Department of Commerce. National Technical Service. *Directory of Federally Supported Information Analysis Centers.* 3rd ed. Washington: GPO, 1984.

PRIMARY RESEARCH

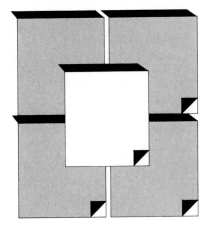

Learning Objectives

- To become familiar with the characteristics of and the research designs for primary research, such as search through company records, observation, surveys, and experiments.
- To understand the steps involved in conducting primary research.
- To understand the advantages and disadvantages of the different types of primary research.

In many cases the research studies you find through secondary research in the library are related to your problem, but they do not fit exactly. Your product may be different, and thus pricing strategies may be different. Your labor force may be larger, hold different values, and live in a different environment from that in the studies you have read; therefore, your labor force may react differently to training programs, job sharing, and job enrichment.

Secondary research is a starting point and will save you time, but it will seldom completely solve a problem. Primary research furnishes the rest of the information needed.

Descriptive or Ex Post Facto Research
The researcher describes the characteristics of a population.

Experimental Research
The researcher interferes to test a hypothesis.

This chapter will discuss the search through company records, observation research, survey research, and experimental research. The first three of these are also called **descriptive** or **ex post facto research** because they describe findings. The researcher, collecting material, does not interfere or change any conditions to influence the outcome. In **experimental research**, on the other hand, the researcher changes the environment and then tests the influence of the interference.

The role of primary research depends to some extent on the type and size of the company. For example, a small manufacturing firm usually does not have the expertise and financial resources to conduct in-depth research on the latest technological developments. Such a company will probably rely on readily available research. The management of a small department store, not feeling comfortable conducting detailed research, might want to hire a marketing research firm to conduct surveys and tests for merchandising strategies. Rather than compile a mailing list on its own, a local business may purchase a list to meet its needs. Large companies conduct more of their own research, but even they may hire experts at times. Even though a manager may not actually do the research and even though he is mostly interested in using the results in his decision making, he must be familiar with various research techniques so he can judge whether the research will actually meet his needs.

SEARCH THROUGH COMPANY RECORDS

The researcher checks through company records for the answers to many questions. What were hiring practices in the past? How does the company deal with late accounts? What were sales for each of the past five years, and how do they compare with the current year? When was the policy manual last revised? All of that information should be available in company records. Exhibit 11.1 details the steps involved in this type of research.

Planning

Before examining any company files, the researcher must define the problem and determine exactly what is needed. At each stage it may be helpful to talk to people who are knowledgeable about the history of the company. If Pat Long is examining the hiring and promotion practices at Illington Glass Company, for example, she should not only look at the personnel records but also talk to

Exhibit 11.1   **Steps in Conducting the Search through Company Records**

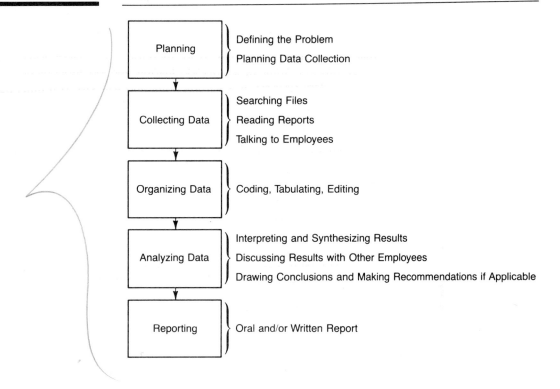

people in personnel. They can tell her where old personnel records are stored and how they were kept. If she is examining the reasons for declining sales, however, she will examine past sales records and talk to people in sales in order to be efficient in her search.

Collecting Data

Some pieces of information will be easy to find; others may take longer. For example, 25 years ago few companies kept records on the hiring and promoting of minorities and women. A search through the records for that type of information would be time consuming and not very productive. The search might have to be supplemented by personal interviews with people who were involved at that time. Filing systems, too, have changed. Different keywords may be used for the same subject, and older files may be stored in a warehouse. Even so, company records provide helpful information on past practices and can also serve as a guideline in determining what is acceptable and unacceptable in a company. By showing what has worked in the past and what has not, they help management to avoid repeating past mistakes.

Organizing and Analyzing Data

Based on past records, Pat Long can determine whether sales follow a cyclical pattern or whether there is a long-term or short-term pattern of decline. Once she has established a pattern, she can look for the reasons. At this point she may go through additional records. She might also decide to search the literature at the library for information on how to combat declining sales.

Reporting

Depending on the nature of the problem and the use of the material, the search through company records may result in a written report, an oral report, or both. The report could be informational or analytical.

Advantages of the Search through Company Records

- The search is conducted at the company; therefore, it is inexpensive.
- The search can be tailored to the specific problem. For example, the company's own past sales figures can be used in analyzing a decline in sales. If the researcher studies problems of declining sales through secondary research, on the other hand, the data and the conditions described may not be valid for the company.

Disadvantages of the Search through Company Records

- Company records, especially older ones, are often not well organized.
- Needed data may not have been kept.
- People who might help may not be with the company any longer.

Guidelines

The following guidelines will help you to make an efficient search through company records:

1. Define the problem clearly.
2. Plan the approach. Decide which records might be most helpful.
3. Identify people in the company who might know about similar problems and who might know where and how records have been kept in the past.
4. Concentrate on relevant information.
5. If necessary, discuss findings with knowledgeable employees.

OBSERVATION RESEARCH

Observation research is used frequently in business. You may have driven through an intersection and noticed a person recording on a pad of paper each time a car passed. Usually, traffic counts are now done automatically.

However, if it is important to know the traffic pattern in the intersection and not just the raw count, manual observation is still used in many cases. The data might be needed to decide whether the intersection should have a traffic light, a stop sign, or nothing. In a shopping mall you may see people observing shoppers and recording their observations. They may observe what fashions are popular in the area, how many men carry purses, or what shoes women wear.

At first glance, observation might appear to be casual and almost haphazard, but it is highly structured. Exhibit 11.2 presents an overview of the steps in observation research.

Planning

Research requires planning. The researcher must clearly understand the problem and purpose of the study. Assume, for example, that the problem is increasing traffic on the west side of town resulting from a new subdivision.

Exhibit 11.2   **Steps in Conducting Observation Research**

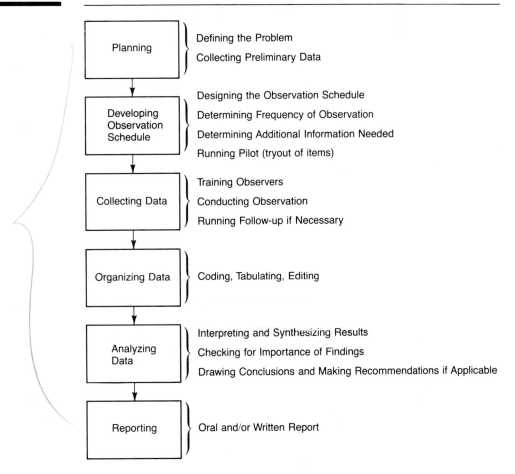

Planning	Defining the Problem Collecting Preliminary Data
Developing Observation Schedule	Designing the Observation Schedule Determining Frequency of Observation Determining Additional Information Needed Running Pilot (tryout of items)
Collecting Data	Training Observers Conducting Observation Running Follow-up if Necessary
Organizing Data	Coding, Tabulating, Editing
Analyzing Data	Interpreting and Synthesizing Results Checking for Importance of Findings Drawing Conclusions and Making Recommendations if Applicable
Reporting	Oral and/or Written Report

The purpose of the study is to determine whether a traffic light is needed between Center and Main streets to help improve traffic flow. To fulfill that purpose, someone must observe the traffic flow and record the findings.

Developing the Observation Schedule

Once you have decided an observation is the best way to collect the data, you must choose a **research design**, and you must design an observation instrument. The sample **observation instrument** presented in Exhibit 11.3 continues the example of the traffic study. The pattern of the intersection, as illustrated in Exhibit 11.4, might also be on the sheet together with a code for the various route possibilities. The instrument asks for information in addition to the actual count of cars. The time of observation is necessary because it obviously makes a difference whether the count is taken during rush hour or during midmorning. The date is also important. The traffic flow may vary during the week, and Saturdays and Sundays may have a different traffic pattern from weekdays.

The observation instrument must provide space for recording special occurrences during the observation. If a traffic accident blocked the intersection for half an hour, for example, the traffic count will be lower than under normal circumstances. The weather may have an influence on traffic flow. Rain, sunshine, heat, and cold may affect the number of people driving. The person who will evaluate the data must know about the special conditions.

Research Design
The design is the plan for collecting and analyzing data.

Observation Instrument
The observation instrument is the form on which the data is recorded.

Exhibit 11.3　　　Observation Instrument

Traffic Count

Observer _____ Date _____

Location _____ Time _____

Weather _____

Special Occurrences _____

NM SM	NM WC	NM EC	SM NM	SM WC	SM EC	EC WC	EC NM	EC SM	WC EC	WC NM	WC SM

Exhibit 11.4	**Key to Observation Schedule**

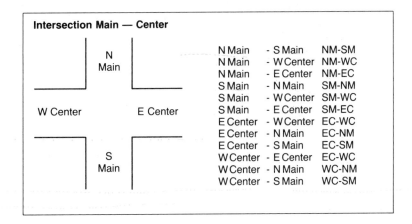

Intersection Main — Center

N Main	- S Main	NM-SM
N Main	- W Center	NM-WC
N Main	- E Center	NM-EC
S Main	- N Main	SM-NM
S Main	- W Center	SM-WC
S Main	- E Center	SM-EC
E Center	- W Center	EC-WC
E Center	- N Main	EC-NM
E Center	- S Main	EC-SM
W Center	- E Center	EC-WC
W Center	- N Main	WC-NM
W Center	- S Main	WC-SM

The name of the person who records the observation should be on the instrument so that the evaluator can ask questions, if necessary. The name is also useful in comparing instruments. Let us assume the city has three observers for the same intersection observing at different times and on different days. When reviewing the instruments, the evaluator may notice that the recordings of observers A and B show similar patterns, whereas the ones for observer C are different. It is possible that during C's time something special was going on, but it is also possible that C simply did not record accurately. The name of the observer on the instrument serves as a check for accuracy.

Collecting Data

Observation research is observing with a particular purpose. The observer records *exactly* what happens, leaving out nothing, adding nothing, and changing nothing.

If the phenomenon occurs too frequently to be recorded each time, the researcher can ask the observer either to record every *nth* item or to record in predetermined intervals. The fashion observer in a shopping mall, for example, may record the shoe fashions of every fifth woman passing by. The person observing consumer behavior at the checkout counter may observe for two minutes, record for one minute, observe for two minutes. That decision is *not* made by the observer but by the researcher in charge of the project. The observer must follow all procedural instructions carefully.

Organizing and Analyzing Data

The evaluator tabulates the data and determines any patterns in the observation. In the traffic count example, the evaluator would summarize the number of cars that went in each possible direction through the intersection and, based on the pattern for various times of the day, recommend whether to install a traffic light, a stop sign, or nothing.

Reporting

The results of observation research are reported in written or oral form or both.

Advantages of Observation Research

- Observations are comparatively inexpensive and fast.
- The data is well organized on the instrument and easy to tabulate in most cases.
- Observation of traffic or fashion patterns does not require extensive training.

Disadvantages of Observation Research

- The observation is limited in its use. To count the traffic is easy; however, to observe the reasons for certain behaviors is impossible. You can observe students going into a certain store, for example, but you cannot tell why they go there. Is it the atmosphere, the prices, the selection of goods, or the proximity to dorms? Other forms of primary research would have to be used to answer these questions.
- Physical phenomena such as fashions are easy to record. More difficult to observe and record are various types of behavior, such as the interaction between an instructor and students. You can record how many people participate and how many women versus men enter into discussions. If you want to observe how the instructor motivates students to participate, however, you must define what you mean by motivation and determine what constitutes motivating behavior on the part of the instructor. The observation of behavior, when not impossible, takes more preparation than a traffic count.
- In observing behavior, two observers may record the same situation differently. Observers of behavior must, therefore, be carefully trained.

Guidelines

These guidelines should help you in conducting observation research:

1. Define the problem clearly.
2. Plan the observation form carefully to make certain that all necessary information will be recorded.
3. Select reliable observers who will observe and record accurately. If you act as an observer yourself, be accurate.
4. Repeat observations to check reliability and accuracy.

✳ SURVEY RESEARCH

Like all research, survey research must be planned carefully. Exhibit 11.5 outlines the steps involved.

Planning

Many problems do not lend themselves to conducting an experiment or observation. For example, the best way to find out why people watch certain TV programs or buy certain products is to ask them. A candidate wanting to

Exhibit 11.5   **Steps in Conducting Survey Research**

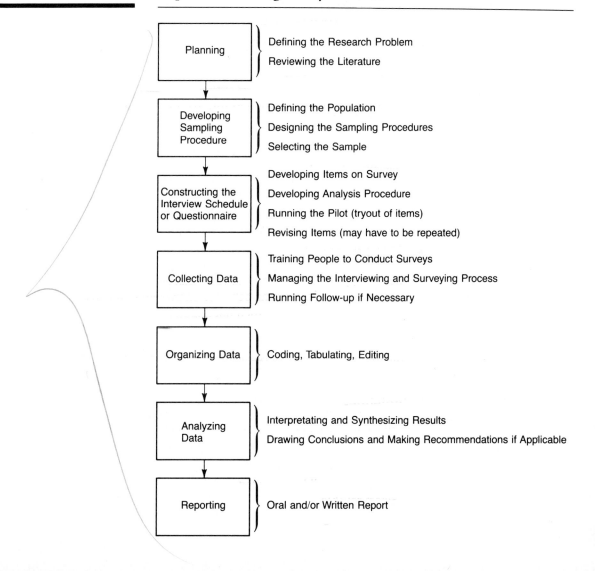

| Planning | Defining the Research Problem |
| | Reviewing the Literature |

Developing Sampling Procedure	Defining the Population
	Designing the Sampling Procedures
	Selecting the Sample

Constructing the Interview Schedule or Questionnaire	Developing Items on Survey
	Developing Analysis Procedure
	Running the Pilot (tryout of items)
	Revising Items (may have to be repeated)

Collecting Data	Training People to Conduct Surveys
	Managing the Interviewing and Surveying Process
	Running Follow-up if Necessary

| Organizing Data | Coding, Tabulating, Editing |

| Analyzing Data | Interpretating and Synthesizing Results |
| | Drawing Conclusions and Making Recommendations if Applicable |

| Reporting | Oral and/or Written Report |

know how people will vote in the next election must ask them how they would vote if the election were today. City officials must ask people how they would react to an increase in taxes or to a bond issue to build a new park or hospital.

In all of these situations the researcher would conduct a survey. Surveys focus on people. They concentrate on people's attitudes and opinions about their environment, their experiences, their communities. With the help of a survey, the researcher tries to assess the characteristics of large groups.

Sampling Procedures and Questionnaire Design

Sample
A sample is a subset of a larger population.

The researcher will seldom survey the entire population of a city, state, or country. Surveying a **sample** of the population is less costly and more efficient. Sampling procedures and the construction of questionnaires are discussed in detail in Chapter 12.

Organizing and Analyzing Data

The researcher, in interpreting the data, tries to generalize from the sample to the population as a whole. That is possible only if the sample is representative of the population from which it was drawn. A survey of workers about the relationship between the workers and management, for example, cannot be generalized to all companies. It can only be generalized to the one plant. If the survey is conducted in a random sample of auto manufacturing plants, then the results can be generalized to all auto manufacturing plants. Care still must be taken, however, because other variables such as geographic location could influence the results. In any case, the researcher could not generalize from auto plants to the steel industry or the computer industry.

Reporting

The researcher will report the results in an informational or analytical report to be used by management in the decision-making process.

Types of Surveys

The three ways to collect data with a survey are by telephone interview, mail survey, and personal interview.

Telephone Interviews.   Many researchers seem to think only of the advantages of the telephone interview, for it is used extensively. You and your friends have probably been interviewed by telephone at least once. The topics of telephone interviews range from consumer surveys to political opinion polls and sales pitches for new products.

The Advantages.   The advantages of the telephone interview are that

- The telephone interview is fast. The surveyor can reach many people in a short period of time and obtain immediate answers. No danger exists that information might not be returned, as is the case with the mail survey.

- The telephone interview is inexpensive.
- The telephone interview is convenient for the interviewer, who can simply call again later if people are not at home.

The Disadvantages.   The disadvantages of the telephone interview by far outweigh its advantages.

- The call may come at an inconvenient time, and the person may refuse to answer questions or, even worse, give careless answers. Obviously the results of such an interview are not very usable.
- Most people refuse to give personal information over the telephone. They may be reluctant to talk about their income, political or religious affliation, educational background, or products they buy.
- The telephone interview forces an immediate response, even though the interviewee might need to think about the answer for a while. Maybe the interviewee does not immediately remember data the interviewer asks for, but, feeling pressured, the interviewee gives an answer. Few people, for example, can give the exact number of dollars they spend on groceries or clothing every month.
- Telephone samples are not representative of the population because only people with telephones can be reached.
- People may be impatient because they are tired of being interviewed by telephone. They argue that they have the telephone for their private use and not for the convenience of researchers.
- Much nonverbal communication is lost over the telephone. The interviewer cannot observe facial expressions and hand movements, yet nonverbal signs can give distinct meanings to the verbal responses. Posture and body movements could indicate whether the person is telling the truth or simply wants to finish the interview.

Guidelines.   These guidelines will help you in conducting successful telephone interviews:

1. Plan the telephone interview carefully. Have the list of questions ready.
2. Time how long the telephone interview will take and then adjust the timeframe. The interview should not be longer than five to ten minutes.
3. Call at a time that might be convenient for the person you want to interview. Dinnertime and lunchtime are not convenient.
4. Avoid very personal questions. Ask only questions to which the respondent can be reasonably expected to know the answer.
5. Introduce yourself at the beginning of the survey and clearly state the purpose of your call. Name the organization you are working for.
6. Call a day before the interview to introduce yourself and the organization and to ask for an interview, if you think this might be helpful. At that point you can set a time when you will call. People may appreciate your thoughtfulness and be more willing to cooperate.

7. State your questions clearly and pleasantly. If your voice indicates that you are serious about the interview, the respondent may be more serious too.
8. At the end of the interview thank the person for the time and cooperation given to you.

Mail Surveys.   Many researchers send out questionnaires in order to collect data. Because bulk mailings are inexpensive, mail surveys are used extensively. A growing concern exists, however, about the effectiveness of mail surveys.

The Advantages.   The advantages of mail surveys are that

- Mail surveys are comparatively inexpensive. Many people can be reached with the same mailing.
- People can answer their own convenience. They are not pressured to answer immediately.
- People can think about the question and the answer. This can increase accuracy and objectivity.
- With a good sample the results can be generalized to large groups of the population.

The Disadvantages.   The disadvantages of mail surveys are that

- It may be difficult to reach the target group. People resent being inundated with junk mail, and the overuse of mailing lists has added to the problem. Many companies buy mailing lists from mailing-list companies, competitors, or banks. Often they are outdated or addressees do not have the characteristics that the researcher is seeking. Many people, like the college student who receives a questionnaire about retirement communities, are on mailing lists by mistake.
- Even people who are willing to answer a questionnaire often put it at the bottom of a pile of mail and forget it.
- The response rate to questionnaires can be as low as 10 percent and is seldom higher than 60 percent. Even if the researcher starts with a representative sample, the sample may not be representative after all the responses are in. Whole groups with certain characteristics might not answer and would not be represented in the final data. Furthermore, to determine which groups did not respond might be very difficult.
- People who answer may have characteristics that are not common in the population as a whole.
- People may exaggerate in their answers. For example, successful people tend to overstate their earnings. They may give answers that reflect their feelings and desire for prestige. They may say they go to the theater, donate money to charities, travel, and buy new cars every two years, simply because they think they should be doing these things. The results are therefore not reliable.

✳ *Guidelines.*   These guidelines will be helpful in working with mail surveys:

1. Plan the questionnaire very carefully. Organize the questions logically.
2. State the purpose of the questionnaire.
3. Select the sample carefully. The target group for a seminar to improve secretaries' business communication skills, for example, would be the secretaries themselves if the seminar is scheduled after work hours and the secretaries are to pay the fee. The target group might be office managers if the seminar is scheduled during work hours and the company is to pay.
4. Provide a stamped envelope for the return of the questionnaire.
5. Send the questionnaires via first class mail and make sure that they do not look like advertisements.
6. Consider giving a token of your appreciation; some companies enclose a quarter or a pencil.
7. Consider calling the people in the sample ahead of time, if the sample is not too large, and ask for their cooperation.

✳ **Personal Interviews.**   If conducted well, the personal interview is a powerful tool for collecting data. There are two types of personal interviews, the **structured interview** and the **unstructured interview.** In the structured interview, such as a census, the interviewer follows a set of questions written on an interview schedule. The interviewer does not rephrase questions or change the order of the questions because even the slightest change in wording can distort the meaning of the question and influence the results of the study. The interviewer must also be careful not to allow his intonation to suggest a certain answer or preference.

Structured and Unstructured Interviews
The structured interview asks questions in predetermined form and sequence. The unstructured interview resembles a conversation.

Sometimes the interviewee may fail to understand a term or even the entire question. When this happens, the interviewer should repeat the question. He should not, however, provide his own definition or clarification of the question.

In the unstructured interview the interviewer creates the atmosphere of a conversation. He is not bound to follow a certain pattern for the questions. The interviewer may repeat the question, repeat the answer, ask additional neutral questions, make comments to clarify answers, or get the interviewee to explain a response in more detail. A neutral question, for example, might be, "Anything else?"

The unstructured interview (the name is actually misleading) might seem to be much easier to conduct than the structured interview, but the opposite is true. The temptation in the unstructured interview is to have a friendly chat. Lacking a preset list of questions, the interviewer must remember what has been discussed in the interview and what is still to be covered. To conduct an unstructured interview properly requires training.

During a job interview you are in an unstructured interview situation. The interviewer asks personalized questions that relate to you and your background. A good job interview, however, has an invisible structure. The first few minutes are devoted to making you feel at ease. Next the interviewer may ask you questions, but they usually are worded to create the feeling of a relaxed conversation. Then you are given an opportunity to ask questions. The interviewer closes the interview and, after you have gone, writes down her observations, impressions, and perhaps a decision. The unstructured interview is really highly structured.

The interview is often used as a follow-up to other types of investigation, but it can also be used at the beginning of the research project. At the beginning, it serves the purpose of setting the scope of the study, clarifying the problem, and formulating the hypothesis. At the end, it helps interpret unusual findings, examine some aspects of the problem in more depth, and put into perspective some major groups in the sample. The interview can also be used as the major research plan, especially if the target group is small.

In many cases you will get information by talking to people without setting up a special interview. For example, you might discuss a new product with consumers or talk with the participants of a training program about their thoughts. Even though these conversations are not interviews, strictly speaking, they can provide much useful information.

The Advantages.   The advantages of the personal interview are that

- The interview is flexible and adaptable to individual situations.
- The interview permits probing into the reasons and the context for attitudes. The interviewer finds out not only the attitudes people have but why they have them.
- The interviewer can observe the nonverbal behavior of the respondent in addition to the verbal responses.
- Ambiguous words can be clarified.

The Disadvantages.   The disadvantages of the personal interview are that

- The personal interview is expensive and takes much time.
- Interviewer bias can creep into the questions and the answers. The intonation, dress, and nonverbal behavior of the interviewer may elicit a certain response.
- Clarifying statements may influence the respondent.
- Noise in the office or incoming telephone calls can interrupt the interview and interfere with the interview process.

Guidelines.   These guidelines will help in conducting successful personal interviews:

1. Prepare for the interview by going over the questions beforehand.
2. If the interview is lengthy—half an hour or more—always make an appointment. Unstructured interviews should always be scheduled.
3. When you make the appointment, say how long the interview will take.
4. Arrive on time.
5. If you have not done so before, ask at the beginning of the interview whether you may take notes or record the interview.

6. If you want to quote the person afterward, obtain permission.
7. Be courteous.
8. Stick to the topic of the interview, and do not waste the interviewee's time.
9. At the end thank the person for the time and cooperation given to you.

EXPERIMENTAL RESEARCH

The two basic types of experiments are the lab experiment and the field experiment. The research principles are the same for both, but in the lab environment the researcher has more control over the experiment than in the field environment, that is, the real world. The basic steps for conducting experimental research are illustrated in Exhibit 11.6.

Planning

At the beginning of every experiment is a problem. For example, Peggy Rehm may notice that the secretaries in her office who write on the new microcomputers seem to be more productive and have a more positive attitude toward their work than those who do not use a microcomputer. She may also notice an improvement in the quality of the work. Based on her observations, she believes a relationship between the microcomputers and the work performance may indeed exist. Of course, at this point she cannot be certain. Perhaps the secretaries writing on microcomputers received a pay raise or have a new supervisor. To determine the impact of the microcomputer, Peggy can formulate a **hypothesis.**

Hypothesis
A hypothesis is an unproven supposition that is testable.

Formulating the Hypothesis

Unlike the problem statement, which is usually stated as a question, the hypothesis is always stated in declarative form. These are examples of hypotheses:

> Secretaries who write on microcomputers are more productive than those who do not.
>
> Secretaries who write on microcomputers have a positive attitude toward their work.
>
> Secretaries who write on microcomputers produce higher quality work than those who use typewriters.
>
> Advertising has a positive impact on sales.
>
> Advertising increases sales.

A hypothesis is never based simply on guessing and is never randomly picked. The researcher formulates a hypothesis only when reasonably certain that the results of the experiment will support it. A hypothesis is based on theory, observation, past research, and practical problems. The researcher or other people may have observed, for example, that customers tend to select items on the shelf that are in front and at eye level. Of course, there may be

Exhibit 11.6   **Steps in Conducting Experimental Research**

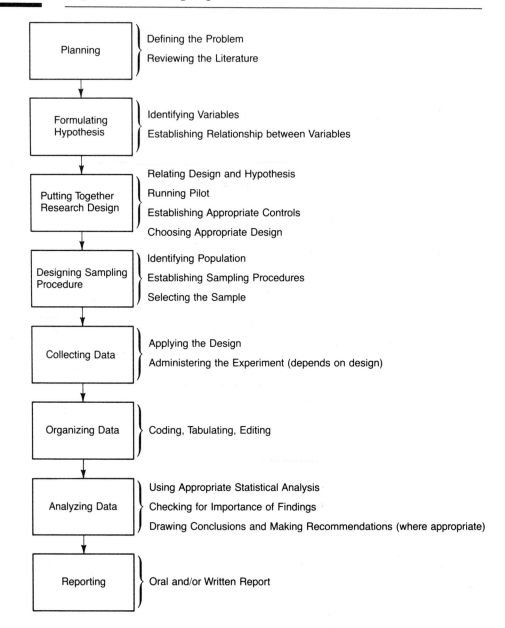

other reasons than location to explain why the products are selected. Perhaps the color is more attractive or perhaps the customer's preferred brand simply happens to be in that location. Because there may be a relationship that is worth testing, the researcher may formulate the hypothesis: shelf location influences sales. A good hypothesis gives guidance in the experiment by stating precisely what is to be tested.

The three hypotheses stating that a positive relationship exists between the use of microcomputers and work performance can be labeled hypothesis 1 (H_1), hypothesis 2 (H_2), hypothesis 3 (H_3) so that they are not confused. A hypothesis can also be formulated that no relationship exists between the use of microcomputers and work performance and attitude. This is called a **null hypothesis** (H_0). The positive hypotheses and the null hypotheses for the example would be:

Null Hypothesis
Any change in the relationship between variables in a null hypothesis is not due to the experiment.

H_1:   *Secretaries who write on microcomputers are more productive than those who do not.*

H_0:   *Microcomputers have no influence on productivity of secretaries.*

H_2:   *Secretaries who write on microcomputers have a positive attitude toward work.*

H_0:   *There is no relationship between the use of microcomputers and attitude toward work.*

H_3:   *Secretaries who write on the microcomputer produce higher quality work than those who use typewriters.*

H_0:   *There is no relationship between the use of microcomputers and the quality of work.*

The null hypothesis is the opposite of the positive hypothesis. It is not always explicitly stated, but it is always implied. The outcome of hypothesis testing confirms or disconfirms a hypothesis. A hypothesis must therefore be testable. If the problem statement does not lend itself to a hypothesis that can be tested, then the problem is not amenable to scientific investigation. The value statement that American companies should adopt the Japanese practice of making decisions by consensus, for example, cannot be tested scientifically. The statement does not establish a relationship between **variables** or point toward a way to test them. Value words such as *should, ought, better,* or *best* should not be used in a hypothesis because they cannot be measured.

Variables
A variable is a characteristic that can be measured.

Hypothesis testing involves the testing of the relationship between variables. In the example, the hypotheses clearly state the relationship between the use of a microcomputer (a variable), quantity (a variable), quality of work (a variable), and attitude toward work (a variable).

Identifying Variables.   Each hypothesis in the example establishes a specific relationship between two of the variables: *microcomputer, quantity of work, quality of work,* and *attitude toward work.* So that they can be measured and related to each other, variables must be specific. They must be *operationalized;* that is, they must be stated in quantifiable terms.

The researcher in the example must define *higher quality* exactly. It may be the number of errors in a business letter or report or the number of retypes required because of errors. *Quantity* is easier to measure because output can be counted in numbers of pages or letters. *Attitude toward work* is difficult to measure. It might be measured in the number of sick days that secretaries take, the length of coffee breaks, the number of arguments in the office, or the number of complaints to supervisors about coworkers or work environment. The researcher can list a number of attributes of attitude but will probably never be able to list them all. To resolve the problem, the researcher could use a validated attitude survey that has been tested for accurately measuring attitudes.

Dependent and Independent Variables
The dependent variable is expected to change as a result of change in the independent variable.

Establishing Relationships Between Variables.   The two types of variables in an experiment are: **dependent** and **independent variables.** In the example, the *use of the microcomputer* is the independent variable, whereas *quantity, quality,* and *attitude* are the dependent variables. The independent variable is presumed to be the cause of the dependent variable. The dependent variable is supposed to occur as a result of the independent variable; it is influenced by the independent variable.

In an experiment the independent variable is manipulated by the researcher, who might introduce microcomputers into one office but not in the other or increase or reduce advertising outlays. The dependent variable, on the other hand, is *not* manipulated. It is observed for changes. The researcher manipulates the use of microcomputers and then observes work performance and attitudes.

While the independent variable is manipulated, all other variables must be held constant. If the researcher introduces microcomputers and at the same time changes the furniture in the office and introduces flextime, he cannot test whether changes in work performance and attitude are the result of the use of the microcomputer, of flextime, or of the new furniture. If the researcher changes advertising outlay for a product and at the same time changes the packaging of the product, he will not know whether sales change as a result of advertising or changes in packaging.

One of the basic requirements is to manipulate only one variable and to keep all of the others constant. This is, of course, possible in a lab environment. There the researcher can change the light, for example, while keeping the temperature constant and the amount and quality of food the same. In the field, control is much more difficult. The researcher may not be able to keep everything constant. The supervisor may resign in the middle of the experiment and a new one may be hired. Furthermore, business activity does not stand still until an experiment is completed.

Putting Together the Research Design

In order to test the hypothesis, the researcher must have an experimental design. The design is the plan, the structure, or the strategy for testing the hypothesis and defines the method of collecting and analyzing the data. We will discuss two basic designs: the controlled before–after design and the time design. The design is dependent on the problem statement and the hypothesis. Once you understand the principles of research design, you can consult books on research to familiarize yourself with more details.

Control Group
No treatment is given to the control group in an experiment.

Experimental Group
The treatment is administered to the experimental group.

The Controlled Before–After Design.   In the controlled before–after design there are a **control group** and an **experimental group.** After both groups take a pretest, the independent variable is manipulated in the experimental group only. Then both groups take a posttest as illustrated in the following example:

Experimental Group	Control Group
Pretest	Pretest
Manipulation of Independent Variable	
Posttest	Posttest

As an example, assume that a report-writing instructor would like to test what impact the use of a microcomputer has on writing anxiety. The hypothesis is that the use of a microcomputer decreases writing anxiety. In this case both groups take the writing anxiety test as a pretest at the beginning of the semester. Then the experimental group writes all assignments for the semester on the microcomputer, whereas the control group writes all assignments as before—with paper and pencil and typewriter. At the end of the semester, both groups take another writing anxiety test. The scores for the tests are as follows:

	Experimental Group	Control Group
Pretest	90 average	95 average
Manipulation	yes	no
Posttest	45 average	65 average

The lowest possible score on the writing anxiety test is 26 points; the highest is 130. The higher score means higher writing anxiety.

There is a difference of 5 points in the pretest and a difference of 20 points in the posttest. The difference in the pretest is due to factors that are beyond the researcher's control. They may be due to natural differences between students. The difference in the posttest is due to differences beyond the control of the researcher *and* to the impact of the experiment, namely, the microcomputer used in writing. Both groups have less anxiety at the end of the semester than at the beginning.

The researcher must ask whether the decrease in writing anxiety resulting from the manipulation is significant. If the control group improves by 30 points, and the experimental group by 31 points, the one point is assumed to be due to the manipulation. The researcher could argue, however, that a one-point difference is not significant enough to count. That one point could be the result of error or it could be the result of the manipulation. However, one point may not be enough to justify the spending of thousands of dollars for microcomputers in order to decrease writing anxiety.

Researchers set guidelines for expected results, and the changes must be significant enough to ensure that the additional cost of equipment will be balanced by higher output. For example, cost factors will play a role in the acceptance criteria of a new package design. Even if a new design increases sales significantly, management still must determine whether the sales increases are high enough to pay for the new design and also increase profits.

The validity of the controlled before–after design depends on an important assumption: that the control group and the experimental group have the same characteristics. This is a big assumption indeed. The people must be randomly assigned to the groups to assure that they have the same characteristics, and even then the researcher cannot be absolutely certain. There is always a degree of error because people are always different.

The maturity factor also influences the results. The instructor would expect that during the semester both groups would change their attitude toward writing. The instructor is interested in whether the difference between the groups narrows or widens.

Another problem is that the pretest–posttest system may sensitize people to the experiment, both those in the control group and those in the experimental group. They become aware of what the researcher is looking for. At the very minimum they know that they are part of some project, and that in itself may change their behavior.

The design can be extended to a controlled before–after design with one experimental group and two control groups or even with one experimental and three control groups.

Time Design.   The time design has the same setup as the controlled before–after design, except that the dependent variable is again measured at a later date. Both groups in the example would take another writing anxiety test, perhaps two months after the posttest:

$$\text{Measure} \rightarrow \text{Manipulate} \rightarrow \text{Measure} \rightarrow \text{Measure}$$

In a variation of the time design, the dependent variable is measured twice before the manipulation of the independent variable and twice after the manipulation:

$$\text{Measure} \rightarrow \text{Measure} \rightarrow \text{Manipulate} \rightarrow \text{Measure} \rightarrow \text{Measure}$$

This design allows for a closer monitoring for changes over time. Between the first and the second measurements both groups should change at the same rate. The third measurement, after the manipulation, should show different results. The fourth measurement, then, will show whether the manipulation has long-lasting results. If the manipulation has a lasting influence, the two groups will change at different rates. If the manipulation produces short-term results, the two groups will change at approximately the same rate again.

The remaining steps in experimental research will be discussed in greater detail in the following chapters: sampling and data collection in Chapter 12 and the organization and analysis of data in Chapters 13 and 14.

Advantages of Experimental Research

Lab Experiment.   The advantages of the lab experiment are that

- There is a high level of control of variables.
- Subjects or items can be randomly chosen and assigned to control and experimental groups.

- The manipulation of the independent variable can be closely monitored.
- The lab experiment is precise and lends itself to duplication.

Field Experiment. The advantages of the field experiment are that

- There is the possibility of some random selection and assignment into groups.
- Strong manipulation of the independent variable is possible.
- The experimental situation reflects the complex situation of real life and business environment.
- Broad hypotheses can be tested.
- The field experiment is flexible and applicable to actual business situations.

Disadvantages of Experimental Research

Lab Experiment. The disadvantages of the lab experiment are that

- The lab situation is artificial.
- Because the lab situation is artificial, the results cannot easily be generalized. For example, do the results of tests of drugs with animals really apply to humans? Most business problems simply cannot be tested in a lab environment.

Field Experiment. The disadvantages of the field experiment are that

- There is a problem with random selection and assignment.
- Variables are difficult to isolate and manipulate.
- Any experiments with people raise ethical questions. Is it ethical to put people into a control group if the hypothesis states that the new training program accelerates the upward mobility of participants? Because a hypothesis is formulated only after some reason exists to believe that an experiment will support it, the people who are randomly assigned to the control group are automatically at a disadvantage.

Because the experiment is limited in its use, it is often replaced by or supplemented with field studies, which permit no randomization and very little control. The examination comes *ex post facto*. This means that the researcher not only has no influence on the variables but also cannot study how the relationship of dependent and independent variables has changed. Yet often a field study is all that is possible. After examining the possible advantages of a new training program, for example, hardly any company would continue the old program and at the same time start the new program in order to set up an experimental design. It is even less likely that people would be assigned randomly into the two programs. In most cases the company will adopt the new program. It is impossible to determine the effectiveness of the training program with an experiment.

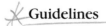
Guidelines

These guidelines will help in conducting experimental research:

1. Carefully define the problem.
2. Formulate the hypothesis you want to test. You may have one or several hypotheses.
3. Identify the independent and dependent variables clearly. Put the variables in testable form, and establish the relationship between the variables.
4. Formulate a testable hypothesis.
5. Choose an appropriate research design. The design will depend on the problem and the hypothesis.
6. Choose your sample according to the rules of sampling. Assign subjects to the control and experimental group to ensure reliability.
7. Be aware of the ethical implications of using people in experimental research.
8. Be aware of the problems of generalizing from a sample to the population in general.
9. Conduct your research with honesty and integrity.

SUMMARY OF LEARNING OBJECTIVES

To become familiar with the characteristics of and the research designs for primary research.

Search through Company Records. This often is the starting point of the data collection.

Observation Research. Data is recorded on an observation instrument. The observer records phenomena as he sees them. There is no manipulation of variables.

Survey Research. This can be done by telephone, mail, or interview. The interview is the most expensive of the three. For surveys to be valid, researchers need training in data gathering. The questionnaire is used extensively in survey research.

The Experiment. The researcher manipulates variables. The development of an appropriate research design is crucial. A widely used design is the controlled before–after design, in which a pretest is administered to a control and an experimental group. Then the variable is manipulated in the experimental group. A posttest is administered. The difference between the changes in the two groups is assumed to be caused by the experiment. A basic assumption in experimental research is that the experimental and control groups have the same characteristics.

To understand the steps involved in conducting primary research.

All primary research starts with planning and the definition of the problem. The research design and the method for data collection depend on the type of research to be conducted. The data must be organized and analyzed before it can be reported.

To understand the advantages and disadvantages of the different types of primary research.

The researcher must know the advantages and disadvantages of the research approach he selects so that he can choose the most appropriate method for solving the problem. The telephone survey, for example, is fast and inexpensive but not very accurate. The experiment is more accurate but raises ethical questions concerning the random selection and manipulation of people.

KEY TERMS

Descriptive or Ex Post Facto
   Research
Experimental Research
Research Design
Observation Instrument
Sample
Structured and Unstructured
   Interviews

Hypothesis
Null Hypothesis
Variables
Dependent and Independent
   Variables
Control Group
Experimental Group

QUESTIONS AND DISCUSSION POINTS

1. Discuss the major differences between primary and secondary research.
2. Define the terms *ex post facto* research and experimental research.
3. What are some of the shortcomings of experimental research in business?
4. What are some of the advantages and disadvantages of the telephone interview, the mail survey, and the personal interview?
5. When would you use a telephone interview, a mail questionnaire, or a personal interview?
6. What is the role of the research design?
7. What are major differences between the field and the lab experiments?
8. Discuss some of the ethical considerations in experimental research.

EXERCISES

How would you test the following hypotheses? Explain and justify your choice.

1. Pub II is a bar with patrons who are more working class than white collar.

2. Saturday is the biggest shopping day in Campus Town.
3. Of the students who spend an evening at the university library, fewer than 50 percent appear to be studying.
4. Food service in the cafeteria would be smoother with an additional food line.
5. The college male prefers to date women who are four inches shorter than he.
6. The average shopping time before making a purchase in the university book store is ten minutes.
7. Most shoppers go to the university book store because of its proximity to classrooms and dorms.
8. Men and women exhibit different classroom behaviors in accounting classes.
9. Fax machines have significantly reduced the volume of business correspondence.
10. Ninety percent of all consumers make purchasing decisions based on information in advertisements.
11. Graduates with good writing skills get better jobs than graduates with poor writing skills.

TOOLS FOR PRIMARY RESEARCH: SAMPLING AND QUESTIONNAIRE

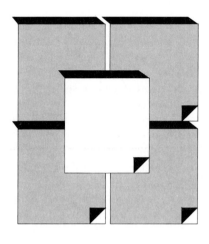

Learning Objectives

- To examine various types of samples and become familiar with the sampling procedure.
- To apply the principles of questionnaire design.
- To write effective questions for a questionnaire.
- To tabulate results.

This chapter and the previous one complement each other. Good primary research requires mastering the tools presented in this chapter: sampling techniques, questionnaire design, and editing and tabulating questionnaire results.

SAMPLING

Theoretically, a marketer could interview all customers or test his product in every city with every consumer group, but, of course, time and cost constraints make such a procedure undesirable and impossible. The researcher may therefore decide to select only a small group out of the population. This small group is the sample. Any research results apply to this sample only. If the researcher wants to draw conclusions and generalize the conclusions to the entire population, the sample must be comparable to the population or representative of it.

Representative Sample
The sample must have the characteristics of the population.

The larger the sample, the greater is the likelihood that it is a **representative sample** of the population. If a population of 100 people has a sample of 2 people, then it is unlikely that the sample is representative of the 100. A sample of 60, on the other hand, makes representativeness likely but is more expensive, of course. A researcher must weigh accuracy against cost and decide on the best balance, that is, how much accuracy to sacrifice to keep the cost down.

As an example, assume that a marketer has to draw a sample in a city with more than 500,000 people. In order to be 95 percent certain that the sample does not have an error larger than 3 percent, the researcher needs a sample of 544 people. This assumes that the population is rather homogeneous in the characteristics relevant to the research. In a town of 10,000 people, the researcher would need a sample of 516. Exhibit 12.1 illustrates the sample size

Exhibit 12.1

Sample Size for Various Population Sizes and Percentages of Error

Population Size	Error			
	±1%	±2%	±3%	±5%
1,000	a	a	353	235
2,000	a	760	428	266
3,000	a	890	461	278
4,000	a	938	479	284
5,000	a	984	491	289
10,000	3288	1091	516	297
20,000	3935	1154	530	302
50,000	4461	1195	538	304
100,000	4669	1210	541	305
500,000 to ∞	4850	1222	544	306

[a] In these cases more that 50 percent of the population is required in the sample. Since the normal approximation of the hypergeometric distribution is a poor approximation in such instances, no sample value is given.

Source: Adapted from Lin, N. (1976). *Foundations of social research,* p. 477. New York: McGraw-Hill, Inc. Reprinted with permission.

for various population sizes and percentages of error. The table applies to fairly homogeneous groups. If the populations are heterogeneous, the samples would need to be larger.

Random Sample

Random sampling gives every member of the population an equal chance of being selected for the sample.

For example, assume you work in quality control. At the end of the assembly line, a worker puts electric switches into boxes, 50 in each box. You examine five switches in every box; that is, you draw a sample of five switches out of each box. Each switch in the box has an equal chance of being selected. If your samples of five are truly random, you should have the same percentage of faulty switches from each box.

Random Sample
Each item in the population has an even chance to be selected.

The researcher, no matter how careful, can never be certain that the **random sample** is representative of the population. If the sample is random, however, the chances that the sample is representative are greater than if the sample is not randomly drawn.

Reliability
Successive tests will bring the same results.

The researcher wants the sample to be reliable as well as random. **Reliability** means that successive samples from the population will have the same characteristics. If the researcher draws several samples of ten screws out of a box of screws, the first few samples may be quite different. As more samples are drawn, this difference decreases. In the context of a questionnaire, reliability means that samples from the same population will answer the questionnaire with the same results.

Validity
The valid test measures what the researcher wants it to measure.

Validity, on the other hand, means that the test actually measures what the researcher wants to measure. For example, the assumption is that a test to measure writing anxiety actually measures writing anxiety and not writing ability or vocabulary level. On first thought, validity might not seem to be a problem because the researcher will design an experiment or a questionnaire that measures what he wants to measure. In reality this can be quite difficult. Think of the controversy surrounding intelligence tests.

Many people argue that intelligence tests do not actually test intelligence but rather measure adaptation to the particular culture of a person. If you decide to go to graduate school for an MBA, you must take the Graduate Management Aptitude Test. Presumably the GMAT measures how well you will do later in management, but critics argue the test measures how well you will do in graduate school. Although many highly educated people work on designing these costly tests, serious doubts exist about their validity.

Systematic Random Sample

On first thought, the term *systematic random sample* does not seem to make much sense. You may think that a sample is either random or systematic. Actually, the two can be combined.

Suppose, for example, that you want to draw a sample of the members of the Association of Business Communication (ABC). You want to study the educational background of business communication instructors and the courses they teach. You could cut up a printed list of the names, put them all in a bowl, and draw your sample. However, you can obtain a random sample with less work than that. You can randomly choose a starting point on the list of names and then select every nth name on the list after that. You can obtain a membership list from the ABC office at the University of Illinois. It contains 1,200 names in alphabetical order, and you want a sample of 250 names for your research.

The systematic random sample in this case is based on the assumption that people whose last names start with M do not have different characteristics from people whose last names start with R, E, or any other letter in the alphabet. Last names are assumed to have no bearing on the variables important to the study.

One important limitation has to do with the outcome of the study. You may generalize your findings only to members of ABC. You cannot generalize to all business communication instructors because the people who are members may have different characteristics from the instructors who are not members.

Stratified Random Sample

The population is divided into strata, or layers. Each stratum has its own characteristics: income, education, values, and lifestyles. The researcher determines which characteristics are important for the study and then draws a random sample from each stratum. In stratified random sampling the final sample should have the same proportion of men, women, college graduates, Hispanics—if those are the important characteristics in the study—as in the population.

Cluster Sample

Cluster sampling, used frequently in surveys, is a successive random sampling of groups in the population. For example, a researcher may draw a random sample of chambers of commerce in the country, then draw a sample of small businesses from the sample of chambers of commerce, and finally draw a sample of individual employees in those businesses.

Quota Sample

Quota sampling is nonrandom. It is based on knowledge of various strata or characteristics in the population that are suitable for the research. The purpose of quota sampling is to ensure that various subgroups in a population, such as young people, old people, or middle- aged people, are represented to the extent the researcher desires. The researcher will decide how to select the sample and how to meet the quota. Thus the process may introduce bias, as the following example shows.

A research firm hired students to conduct a quota sample based on age. When the researchers began to analyze the sample, they found that most of the people under 25 were students. The student workers had included other students in the sample to fill the quota. Quota samples tend to include people who are easy to find and willing to be interviewed.

Summary of Sampling Techniques

Random sampling is assumed to result in a sample that is representative of the population from which the sample is drawn. Once the sample has been selected, people or items should be randomly assigned to experimental or control groups if an experiment is conducted.

Research findings, based on samples, can be generalized only to the population from which the sample was drawn. A sample based on names in the telephone book, for example, is representative of the people listed in the book and *not* of all people living in the city, not even of all people owning telephones, because the book does not give the names of people with unlisted numbers.

THE QUESTIONNAIRE

The purpose of the questionnaire is to help answer the research question or solve the research problem. The questionnaire is the instrument used to collect the necessary data for testing a hypothesis through surveys. It is the tool to gather data on opinions, attitudes, and facts.

Questionnaire design takes time and care. Because good questionnaires are difficult to write for a number of reasons, many questionnaires are weak. The data they collect is biased and often unreliable. The questions may be ambiguous, may be leading, or may play on the emotions and prejudices of the respondent. An understanding of the steps in conducting survey research, discussed in Chapter 11, is important to good questionnaire design.

The Overall Planning of the Questionnaire

Before writing specific questions, the researcher must determine the precise goal of the questionnaire. Does the researcher, for example, need facts on which automobile-care products, over-the-counter drugs, cleaning products, or processed foods consumers use? Does she want to collect information about people's attitudes toward drugs, processed food, or pollution? Does she want both facts and attitudes? In any case, the purpose and the goal of the questionnaire, which are determined by the problem, must be clarified before the researcher writes any questions.

To save time and to help in writing the questions, the researcher must also determine the key areas to be investigated, a process similar to breaking a problem down into subfactors.

Many people think that questionnaires are mostly used in marketing and consumer research; however, questionnaires can be successfully used in a variety of situations. For example, a company may use a questionnaire to measure employee satisfaction and attitudes or to get input for developing training programs for new supervisors. By guaranteeing anonymity, the questionnaire may encourage open and honest comments.

A major insurance company, for example, wanted to determine what lower level managers think of their superiors and what upper middle management expects from subordinates. The executives were particularly interested in collecting information on perceptions about promotion guidelines, fairness, clarity of company policy, and continuing education opportunities. The results were to be used in improving employee morale.

The executives were particularly concerned about anonymity and honest responses. They knew that employees would be reluctant to answer the questions if they felt that the purpose of the questionnaire was to punish critical employees. To avoid any perception of manipulation, the company hired an outside consultant to talk to employees. Based on these initial interviews, the consultant then designed and administered a questionnaire. After he had analyzed and summarized the findings, he shared the results with both the employees and management. Throughout the process the company worked hard to present the study as an attempt to improve the environment rather than to punish and identify problem employees. The careful preparation paid off because the results of the questionnaire led to in-depth discussions and special seminars among managers from different levels.

Unfortunately, many companies attempting a similar survey do not take enough time to clarify the purpose of the questionnaire and to communicate the purpose to employees, even though research shows that a poorly constructed questionnaire can do much harm.

Questionnaires are most helpful in collecting data from many people. If only ten people work in your group, the number is too small to warrant a statistical survey. Establishing trends, correlations, and causal relations is difficult with a small sample.

Questionnaires must take into consideration the cultural background of the respondent. What is considered an appropriate question in the United States may be considered offensive in some other country. Americans are fairly willing to disclose information about their sex life, private feelings, and personal beliefs. However, a pharmaceutical company that wants to collect such information for marketing purposes will not be able to ask this type of question in the Middle East or India. On the other hand, in many countries people openly talk about their income; that information is considered more off-limits in the United States.

The questionnaire designer must also take into consideration the political climate of a country. A totalitarian country may not allow survey research. If it is allowed, people may not give honest answers. A business that relies on the results of questionnaires administered under such circumstances may easily make inappropriate decisions.

An added problem is the translation of questionnaires. A literal translation may not mean that questions are interpreted the same way in two different cultures. For example, the question "Do you drink?" is an acceptable question in the United States. Some people drink; some don't. It basically asks whether a person drinks at all. The same question in Germany or France would be considered insulting. Most people would interpret it to mean "Are you an alcoholic?" Even though this is not what the researcher wanted to ask, it is a very likely interpretation. The assumption is that everyone drinks unless overriding medical reasons exist.

The researcher conducting an international survey must test the validity and reliability of questions carefully. Most researchers hire an interpreter who is comfortable with both cultures and fluent in both languages. He will translate the original questionnaire and point out problem spots. Another person will then back-translate the questionnaire into the original language to see whether it conveys the same meaning as the original.

As you can see, questionnaires in an international setting pose many problems that are both time consuming and expensive to solve.

The Sequence of Questions

When collecting data, the researcher is usually interested not simply in what people think in general, but also whether patterns exist in the attitudes of people. For example, the researcher may want to distinguish between what young and old people think about ways to solve pollution problems. A problem may require finding out whether men and women have different attitudes toward advertising. A solution may depend on knowing whether political affiliation, religious affiliation, or educational level makes a difference in attitudes toward collective bargaining or affirmative action.

Profile of Respondent
The profile establishes the personal data of the respondent.

Where does the researcher put those questions? On many questionnaires the **profile of the respondent** is established at the beginning. Some people resent giving this kind of information, however, and may discard a questionnaire that begins with personal questions. If profile questions are put at the end of the questionnaire, the respondent may have become interested in the topic, and the profile questions may appear to be a natural extension of the other questions. The profile questions may also make more sense after the respondent has read the entire questionnaire. The researcher should include only those personal questions that relate directly to the hypothesis and problem.

The designer of the questionnaire also must consider the sequence of the main questions. Questions should follow each other in a logical order. If question 8 asks about the use of personal-hygiene products and question 9 asks about attitudes toward company profits, the respondent will have a difficult time seeing a logical connection between them and may become frustrated.

Finally, a questionnaire must concentrate on a central issue that relates to the problem. A title at the top of the questionnaire is helpful in identifying this central issue.

The Wording of Questions

The wording of questions is probably the most difficult aspect of designing a questionnaire. The overriding consideration is clarity. Questions must be absolutely clear and unambiguous. The question "How much did you make last year?" is so personal that many people might resent it. The question is also unclear. Most people would assume that they are supposed to give information on their income. They might wonder, however, whether the question asked for before-tax income or after-tax income and whether they were to include income from wages, from investments, or both.

The question "How much did you make last year?" creates another problem. How many people actually remember their exact income? They probably would need to refer to their tax-return records, and most will not go to that much trouble for a questionnaire. Therefore, they will either leave the question blank or give a *ballpark* figure that may be a poor guess. The researcher might increase the response rate by asking for income ranges, such as $10,000 to $14,999, $15,000 to $19,999, and higher.

The following example illustrates the difference between ambiguous and clear questions:

Poor: How do you bank?

Better: What banking conveniences do you use?
               Mark all that apply.
               _____ Drive-up window
               _____ Lobby
               _____ Automatic teller
               _____ Other, please specify ____

It is possible that the researcher actually wanted to find out what kinds of accounts people have. In that case the question might be:

Better: What types of bank accounts do you have?
               Mark all that apply.
               _____ Checking Account
               _____ Now Account
               _____ Savings Account
               _____ Other, please specify ____

The first question of the next pair is ambiguous:

Poor: Which organizations do you support?

Better: Which of the following organizations did you financially support last year?
               Mark all that apply.
               _____ Heart Fund
               _____ Easter Seal
               _____ March of Dimes
               _____ Other, please specify ____

The improved questions make it easier for the researcher to tabulate the answers.

The researcher must consider whether the respondent can be reasonably expected to have the necessary background information to be able to answer. If a question asks "Do you support the U.S. decision to leave UNESCO?" then the respondent must be familiar with UNESCO and the problems that led up to the decision to leave UNESCO in order to give an intelligent opinion. To ask people "How do LIFO and FIFO affect the income statement and balance sheet in inflationary times?" is pointless if they do not know what the terms LIFO and FIFO mean.

Leading Questions
Leading questions suggest
the desired answer.

A researcher must be alert for **leading questions** that suggest the answer. Leading questions come in many forms and disguises. Some researchers may not be aware that they are suggesting an answer, yet they may be so personally involved in the issue that their own beliefs influence the wording of the question. In other cases the answer may be suggested more openly. The question "You are concerned about inflation, aren't you?" has the answer built in.

"Do you watch educational TV?" will draw many "yes" answers. Even if people do not watch educational television, they may say "yes" because they think they should watch it. Moreover, this question is ambiguous. What is educational television? Is PBS educational television by definition? What types of programs are educational? Educational television would need to be defined or, even better, the term should not be used at all.

Poor: Do your children watch educational television?
        _____ Yes
        _____ No
        _____ Don't know

Better: Which of the following television programs do your children watch?
        _____ Sesame Street
        _____ 3-2-1 Contact
        _____ Bugs Bunny
        _____ The Cosby Show
        _____ Other, please specify ___

The question "Do you watch educational television?" also appeals to what is called social desirability. Many people will give the answer they think is socially acceptable rather than describe what they actually do or believe. A question that asks whether people support local charities will not receive many valid responses because most people, regardless of what they actually do, will say they support local charities. They feel they are expected to support them; admitting they did not would reflect poorly on them.

Poor: Do you support charities to help the poor?
        _____ Yes
        _____ No
        _____ Don't know

Better: Which of the following charities did you support last year, either with money or volunteer help? Mark all that apply.
        _____ United Way
        _____ Salvation Army
        _____ Goodwill Industries
        _____ Other, please specify ___

Each question should address only one topic. The question "What do you like best about herb tea?" assumes that you like herb tea. It also asks what you like best about it. This is two questions in one. The respondent does not know which of the two questions he is expected to answer.

Poor: What do you like about herb tea? ___

Better: Do you like herb tea?
         _____ Yes
         _____ No
         _____ Don't know
         If your answer was yes, then complete this question. Otherwise go to number *X*.
         What do you like about herb tea? Mark all responses that apply.
         _____ Flavor
         _____ Lack of caffeine
         _____ Price
         _____ Other, please specify ___

In summary, questions must be nonoffensive and unbiased.

The Form of Questions

The information sought will partially dictate the form of the question.

Fixed-Alternative Items.   The most popular forms of the fixed-alternative type are either–or and multiple-choice questions. The respondent is given a choice of several alternatives from which to choose one.

Either–Or Questions.   The either–or question is the simplest of the fixed-alternative types:

Does your city have a public transportation system?
_____ Yes
_____ No
_____Don't know

Do you support mandatory drug testing in the workplace?
_____ Yes
_____ No
_____ Don't know

This type of question polarizes the responses. The true–false, agree–disagree, and approve–disapprove questions also fall into this category.

The either–or question has two distinctive advantages. It helps in achieving uniformity and reliability; the respondent's answer is based on previously established response categories. Fixed-alternative questions are easy to code and tabulate.

The major disadvantage is that the questions tend to be superficial. Many problems are too complex to lend themselves to a yes–no type of question. The respondent may become discouraged by being forced to choose one of the options without being able to give an explanation.

Multiple-Choice Questions.   A respondent given multiple choices must choose one, as the following examples illustrate.

Which of the following best describes your occupation?

_____ Secretary	_____ Sales
_____ Professional/Technical	_____ Manager/Owner
_____ Farmer	_____ Retired/Unemployed
_____ Housewife	_____ Skilled/Unskilled Laborer
_____ Other, please specify ___	

Check the category that best approximates your *total* pretax household income.

_____ under $9,999   _____ $30,000 to $34,999
_____ $10,000 to $14,999   _____ $35,000 to $39,999
_____ $15,000 to $19,999   _____ $40,000 to $49,999
_____ $20,000 to $24,999   _____ $50,000 or over
_____ $25,000 to $29,999

Multiple-choice questions, like either–or questions, do not probe for reasons behind the responses. A respondent may simply check an alternative to conceal ignorance. None of the options may fit the attitudes or the facts relating to that particular respondent.

Open-Ended Questions.   Open-ended questions overcome some of the disadvantages of the first two question forms. Here the respondent can be asked for his reasons for certain attitudes, and he can also express his opinions. This advantage has a built-in disadvantage. Because open-ended questions take time and great care to answer, many people may simply skip them. If respondents answer them in great detail, on the other hand, the researcher is confronted with the time-consuming task of tabulating the responses. The following examples illustrate that open-ended questions are broad.

In your opinion, what can cultural organizations do to better serve *your* particular needs?

What types of activities do you enjoy most during your leisure time?

What techniques do you use in motivating your subordinates?

All of these questions might be easier to answer if they were asked in the form of a checklist.

Checklist.   In a checklist the respondent is given a number of alternatives. He marks as many as apply to him.

I use a terminal to keyboard (check all that apply)
_____ Business letters sent outside the company.
_____ Interoffice memos.
_____ In-house reports.
_____ Reports sent outside the company.
_____ Other, please explain _

During the last month, I went to
_____ the movies.
_____ a restaurant.
_____ a museum.
_____ a sports event.
_____ Other, please explain. ___

A checklist should include an *other* category because rarely will all possibilities be given. Many respondents like this form because they are not forced to decide what they like best or least. They simply check all responses that pertain. Checklists are easy to tabulate.

Fill-in Questions.   The fill-in question is a variation of the open-ended question; however, the respondent is not asked to write a lengthy comment.

Usually the fill-in question asks for specific numbers, as the examples illustrate.

> How many people live in your household? ___
>
> How many years of schooling have you completed? ___

The tabulation of this form takes longer than if the question provided categories from which to choose. Moreover, this form lends itself only to short and factual answers.

Scales.   Scales help in measuring the intensity of feelings, agreements, and disagreements. The goal of the scale is to put the answers of an individual on some continuum of the attitude in question. The scores of a respondent on a particular topic can be added and averaged. In this way the researcher can obtain a profile of the attitude toward a certain topic. A manager who wants to find out secretaries' attitudes toward word processors, for example, can use a scale-type question. The attitude for each individual is determined by adding up the scores for every individual and then averaging them. The manager can also average the scores of the group to get a feel for attitudes.

The use of a microcomputer in writing helps to overcome writer's block.

Strongly Agree	Agree	Don't Know	Disagree	Strongly Disagree
1	2	3	4	5

If the tabulation is

Respondent	**Response**
A	2
B	2
C	3
D	4
E	2

the average is 2.6. However, researchers must be careful with using averages. Perhaps 10 employees mark 2, and 10 employees mark 4. The average, 3, is misleading. The score is polarized, and the result would have to be reported as polarized rather than as an average.

Some researchers prefer a scale of seven items. They think that a more detailed scale, as in the example below, is more accurate and differentiates the answers better.

The instructions for the word-processing package are

Excellent	Very Good	Good	Average	Fair	Bad	Very Bad
1	2	3	4	5	6	7

Some researchers think that even a scale of seven items is not discriminating enough. They believe a scale should have ten items, but providing appropriate labels for ten options may be a problem. When a scale has more than seven categories, researchers usually do not label each one. They may simply write as follows:

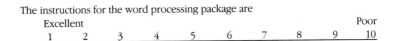

The instructions for the word processing package are

Excellent									Poor
1	2	3	4	5	6	7	8	9	10

An advantage of scales is that the response labels can be geared toward the question. Appropriate labels can help the respondent in answering the questions. Scales can emphasize level of interest, frequency, importance, quality, and satisfaction, as in these examples:

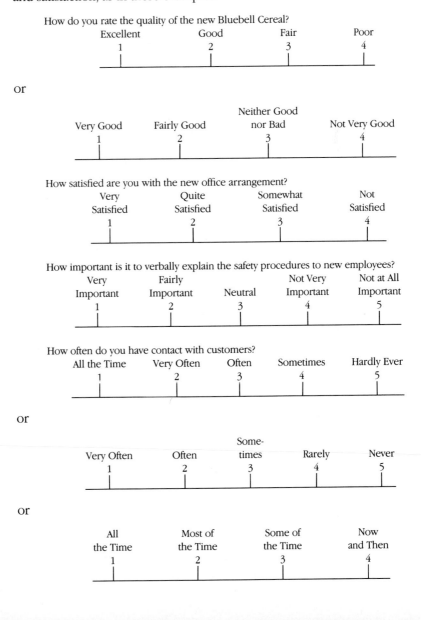

How do you rate the quality of the new Bluebell Cereal?

Excellent	Good	Fair	Poor
1	2	3	4

or

Very Good	Fairly Good	Neither Good nor Bad	Not Very Good
1	2	3	4

How satisfied are you with the new office arrangement?

Very Satisfied	Quite Satisfied	Somewhat Satisfied	Not Satisfied
1	2	3	4

How important is it to verbally explain the safety procedures to new employees?

Very Important	Fairly Important	Neutral	Not Very Important	Not at All Important
1	2	3	4	5

How often do you have contact with customers?

All the Time	Very Often	Often	Sometimes	Hardly Ever
1	2	3	4	5

or

Very Often	Often	Some-times	Rarely	Never
1	2	3	4	5

or

All the Time	Most of the Time	Some of the Time	Now and Then
1	2	3	4

Ranking.   In scaling, a respondent could give every item on the questionnaire the same number. In ranking, on the other hand, the respondent is forced to put items in a certain order. No ties are allowed.

Rank the following cities in order of preference (one is highest) for living:

_____ New York	_____ Chicago
_____ Atlanta	_____ Boston
_____ San Francisco	_____ Los Angeles
_____ Dallas	_____ Denver
_____ Houston	_____ Phoenix

Rank the universities according to your preference for obtaining an MBA.

_____ University of Illinois
_____ University of Michigan
_____ University of California/Berkeley
_____ University of Texas
_____ University of Colorado

To establish whether certain population groups share certain preferences is fairly easy. Women students and men students, for example, may have different preferences for a university.

Two assumptions concerning ranking can cause difficulty. First, the preference of a respondent is assumed to decrease or increase in equal intervals. Second, the preference is assumed to decline or increase in equal segments for all respondents. In reality, one respondent may possibly, and in fact may likely, rank the University of Illinois and the University of Michigan about the same. The same respondent may not have much of an opinion about the University of California, Berkeley, but may be totally uninterested in the University of Texas and the University of Colorado. The ranking does not indicate all the attitudes.

The Appearance of the Questionnaire

The questionnaire should have visual appeal to the person who is asked to answer it. If the questionnaire looks disorganized and confusing, the response rate will probably be affected negatively. A questionnaire should not be unnecessarily long, but at the same time the questions should not be crowded together. Enough white space is needed on the page and between the questions to distinguish various items.

The design should be consistent. If the answer boxes for one yes–no question are at the right of the question, they should be on that side for all other yes–no questions. If they are at the left, they should always be there. Consistency in the placing of response space is most important. It helps not only the person who answers the questions but also the person who will tabulate the answers.

The Cover Letter

The cover letter presents the questionnaire to the person who is asked to answer the questions. It should explain the purpose of the questionnaire and motivate the recipient to answer and return it. A cover letter that stresses the benefit of the research to the recipient may encourage a high response rate. A cover letter accompanying a service department survey might begin, "So that we can serve you better, we would like to ask you to take a few minutes to answer the attached questionnaire." The implication is that if customers give their opinions of the service, the service can be improved. The researcher should supply an addressed and stamped envelope for use in returning the questionnaire.

The cover letter in Exhibit 12.2 encourages the reader to respond in several ways:

1. It shows a reader benefit.
2. It gives the purpose of the study.
3. It tells the reader how the results will be used.
4. It identifies the groups being surveyed.
5. It promises confidentiality.
6. It encourages the reader to respond by a specific date.
7. It directs the reader to use the enclosed envelope.

The Pilot Questionnaire

Before the questionnaire is sent to the printer, it is a good idea to test the questions. You may first want to show it to some friends and colleagues to eliminate obvious ambiguities and awkward wordings. You should also try to tabulate a few questionnaires to see whether there are any difficulties with the questions. After you have made revisions based on the feedback from friends, you may want to run a full pilot study with a small sample to further revise and refine the questionnaire. Only after this process should you send the questionnaire to the complete sample.

Set a date when you will close the collection and begin the tabulation. Actually, you may find that most of the returned questionnaires come back fairly fast. You may receive more after a follow-up letter or a reminder, but usually the response rate to follow-ups is fairly low.

The Tabulation and Editing of Results

Tabulating the responses by computer is advantageous because computerized data can be easily reused. As you code the responses, or even before, check for obviously wrong or invalid answers. The answers of people who are careless in filling in the blanks, for example, may not reflect their true attitudes. You would like to eliminate those questionnaires or, at least, the carelessly answered questions. In some questionnaires the researchers include *test* questions to test the honesty of the respondent. They may include items that are wrong:

Which one of the following television shows do you watch at least once a month?
_____ Night Court
_____ Designing Women
_____ LA Law
_____ Cheers
_____ Family Connections

Exhibit 12.2   **Cover Letter for Questionnaire**

September 15, 19XX

Dear Educator:

Does your school have computers that are not used?

Many schools have started the school year with additional electronic equipment for their business classes. Yet, research indicates that many teachers will not use the available technology because they do not feel comfortable with it.

This survey attempts to do three things:

1. Determine the current status of the use of technology in business courses in secondary and post-secondary schools.

2. Determine the level of computer literacy and technological skills of teachers.

3. Identify what methods state departments of education, schools, and departments use to aid teachers in developing technological skills.

The following groups are being surveyed: state departments of education, National Association of Business Teacher Education schools, and secondary schools.

Please take a few moments to complete the enclosed questionnaire. This study will help in the development of training seminars and training packages for teachers who are interested in using the new technology effectively.

Your comments will be held in strictest confidence. Coding is used for group identification only.

You may make additional comments in the margins of the survey form. So that we can complete the study and use the results to effectively train teachers in the use of technology, please return the questionnaire by October 10 in the enclosed envelope.

Sincerely,

Marcy Hayes

Marcy Hayes, Ph.D.
Professor of Business Education

Because the program listed last does not exist, the questionnaires of those people who mark the last option should be checked carefully for inconsistencies. Editing is time consuming and yet is a necessary process.

A questionnaire response on attitudes toward the use of terminals in writing is illustrated in Exhibit 12.3. The exhibit is a copy from respondent 1. The tabulation for respondent 1 on the op-scan sheet is shown in Exhibit 12.4. Columns 1 to 23 are the recordings of the answers. Because this respondent has a terminal at her desk, she did not answer question 13, and so column 13 is blank. Columns 24 and 25 identify the respondent (01).

Exhibit 12.5 illustrates the frequency count of question 23. It shows that 37 people believe writing takes less time with the help of a terminal, 14 people believe it takes about the same amount of time, and 4 people think it takes more time. The statistical analysis of the data will be described in Chapter 13.

The questionnaire in Exhibit 12.6 was designed by a marketing research class. You may want to analyze the questions and see where some improvements could be made.

SUMMARY OF LEARNING OBJECTIVES

To examine types of samples and become familiar with the sampling procedure.

Reliable samples have the characteristics of the population from which they are drawn. The larger the sample, the greater is the likelihood that it is representative of the population. In determining sample size, the researcher has to balance accuracy and cost of sampling.

To achieve representativeness, the sample should be drawn randomly. The systematic random sample, the stratified sample, and the cluster sample are types of random samples. The quota sample is a nonrandom sample.

To apply the principles of questionnaire design.

The questionnaire should ask only questions that are related to the research problem. Personal questions must be handled tactfully. A cover letter must explain the purpose of the questionnaire and the benefit to the respondent. The instructions must be clear and unambiguous.

To write effective questions for a questionnaire.

Questions must be clear and easy to answer. The questionnaire form must provide space for the answers. The questions can take a variety of forms, such as yes–no questions, open-ended questions, fill-in questions, scales, and rankings.

To tabulate results.

Before tabulating, the researcher must edit the returned questionnaires. Results can be tabulated by computer or by hand.

Exhibit 12.3   Questionnaire Response

USE OF VIDEO DISPLAY TERMINAL FOR COMMUNICATING
IN BUSINESS

The results of this questionnaire will be used to study the use of terminals in communication. We would very much appreciate your help in providing information by answering the following questions. Please complete the questionnaire by using a check mark to indicate the most appropriate answer(s).

1. What is your sex?
      √ Male   ___ Female

2. What is your age?
      ___ under 21   ___ 36-40   ___ 51-55
      ___ 21-25   ___ 41-45   ___ 56-60
      ___ 26-30   √ 46-50   ___ 61 plus
      ___ 31-35

3. In what type of business firm do you work?
      ___ Food   ___ Paper, fiber, and wood products
      √ Publishing, printing   ___ Metal products
      ___ Petroleum refining   ___ Motor vehicles
      ___ Electronics, appliances   ___ Office equipment (includes computers)
      ___ Aerospace   ___ Soaps, cosmetics
      ___ Pharmaceuticals   ___ Other (Please identify)_____
      ___ Tobacco   _____

4. What is your job title? (Check the title which describes your job best.)
      ___ Supervisor   √ Manager   ___ Systems Analyst/Designer
      ___ President   ___ Programmer   ___ Instructor/Trainer
      ___ Admin. Ass't.   ___ Project Leader ___ Other_____

5. On the average, I use the terminal to type letters, reports, and/or other types of information approximately
            ___ 1-3 times daily.   ___ 7-9 times daily.
            √ 4-6 times daily.   ___ 10 or more times daily. (Give approximate number)_____

6. I have used a terminal for
      ___ 1-6 months.   ___ 25 months to 3 years.
      ___ 7-12 months.   ___ Over 3 years (Specify number of years.)____
      √ 13 months to 2 years.

7. My keyboarding (typing) skills are
            √ Excellent (know proper fingering for the keyboard, type rapidly, seldom make
              typing errors).
            ___ Good (know proper fingering, have fairly good speed, make minimal number of
              typing errors).
            ___ Fair (know proper fingering, type slowly, make more than average number of
              errors).
            ___ Poor (use "hunt and peck" system, type slowly, make too many errors).

8. Which of the following applies to you?
            √ I have a terminal at my desk to use whenever I need to use it.
            ___ I share the use of a terminal with 1-3 people.
            ___ I share the use of a terminal with more than 3 people.

Exhibit 12.3   **Questionnaire Response (*continued*)**

2

9. How is the information typed by you printed?
    ✓ I have a printer at the desk.
    ____ The unit shares three or four terminals.
    ____ The printer is in a central location shared by many.
    ____ Other (Please explain)

10. I prefer to
    ____ Work in longhand and have secretary type my work.
    ____ Dictate using a recorder/have typing done by word processing.
    ____ Dictate to a secretary.
    ✓ Keyboard myself.

11. I am more creative
    ____ Using paper and pencil.
    ✓ Using the terminal.
    ____ Dictating to a secretary.
    ____ Dictating to a recording device.

12. Which best expresses your feelings about the use of terminals? (Check all that apply.)
    ____ I am apprehensive about terminals.
    ____ Terminals are cold and impersonal.
    ____ Terminals help in personalizing my communications.
    ____ Terminals help me in communicating faster and more efficiently.
    ✓ I don't have any special opinion on the use of terminals.

13. (Answer this question only if you share a terminal.) How would your attitude towards the
    use of a terminal differ if you had one at your desk and did not share it?
    ____ I would feel more positive about using a terminal.
    ____ I don't mind sharing the use of a terminal with others.
    ____ It would not change my feeling; I dislike using terminals.

14. The use of a terminal
    ✓ Has increased the number of my written communications.
    ____ Has decreased the number of my written communications.
    ____ Has held constant the number of my written communications.

15. Use of the video display terminal to produce written communications has
    ✓ Increased the sharing of ideas with colleagues.
    ____ Discourages the sharing of ideas with colleagues.
    ____ Does not change the frequency of sharing ideas.

16. When using the terminal for communicating, I believe I am
    ✓ More concise
    ____ Less concise
    ____ No difference

17. When using the terminal for communicating, I believe I am
    ____ Inhibited in the flow of ideas
    ✓ Relaxed
    ____ Unaffected (unchanged)

Exhibit 12.3   Questionnaire Response (*continued*)

3

18. I use the terminal to keyboard (check all that apply)
    ✓ Business letters sent outside of the company.
    ____ Inter-office memos, letters, and reports.
    ____ Memos, letters, and reports sent outside of the company.
    ____ Other (Please explain)_____

19. Before I input information, I
    ✓ Put key points on a piece of paper.
    ____ Make a detailed outline.
    ____ Write key paragraphs out in longhand.
    ____ Write entire report out in longhand.
    ____ Compose directly on the keyboard and do not make any notes.

20. I find it easier to
    ✓ Plan with pencil and paper.
    ____ Put the plan on the video display terminal.

21. I find it easier to organize the flow of thought and presentation
    ____ On paper.
    ✓ On the terminal.

22. I revise material
    ✓ Always on a printout.
    ____ Always directly on the screen.
    ____ Sometimes on the printout.
    ____ Sometimes on the screen.

23. Using the terminal to prepare my communications
    ✓ Takes less time than the method I used previously.
    ____ Seems to take about the same time as I spent previously.
    ____ Takes more time than the method I used previously.

NOTE: Please attach or staple to this questionnaire a sample of a <u>recent</u> business letter or memo
      that was written by you. Please block out any confidential information. You may also
      block out your company name, if you desire.

RETURN THIS QUESTIONNAIRE AND THE ATTACHED SAMPLE OF YOUR COMMUNICATION TO:

Dr. Jean Grever & Dr. Iris Varner
Department of Business Education and
    Administrative Services
Illinois State University
Normal, IL 61761

Exhibit 12.4   **Op-Scan for Exhibit 12.3**

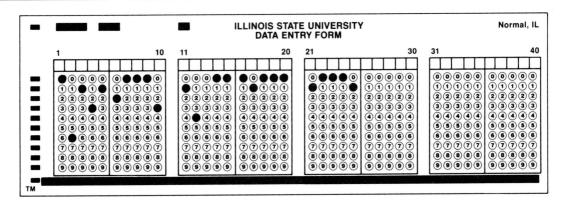

KEY TERMS

Representative Sample   Validity
Random Sample   Profile of Respondent
Reliability   Leading Questions

QUESTIONS AND DISCUSSION POINTS

1. Give at least ten guidelines for preparing a questionnaire.
2. Define the terms *randomness, validity,* and *reliability.*
3. Discuss some of the difficulties in ranking questions.
4. What are some of the shortcomings of either–or questions?

Exhibit 12.5   **Frequency Count for One Question**

SPSS BATCH SYSTEM

FILE   NONAME   (CREATION DATE = 01/31/XX)

Q23

CATEGORY LABEL	CCDE	ABSOLUTE FREQ	RELATIVE FREQ (PCT)	ADJUSTED FREQ (PCT)	CUM FREQ (PCT)
	0.	37	67.3	67.3	67.3
	1.	14	25.5	25.5	92.7
	2.	4	7.3	7.3	100.0
	TOTAL	55	100.0	100.0	

VALID CASES 55   MISSING CASES 0

Exhibit 12.6   Questionnaire

Dear Recipient:

This questionnaire is being conducted to obtain information that will be utilized by various non-profit McLean County cultural organizations to design programming which better reflects the needs of this community. Your full cooperation is needed if this project is to be successfully completed.

The questionnaire must be completed by the husband, wife, or head of the household. Upon completion, please fold and mail it in the postage-paid and pre-addressed envelope provided. It is very important to the success of the project that you return the completed questionnaire as promptly as possible. You were selected through a random process, and your responses are completely anonymous.

Along with the questionnaire you will find enclosed a pre-addressed postage-paid postcard. Upon completion of the survey, please fill out the card and drop it in the mail so that we might send you a package of premiums and discounts for various community events as a token of our appreciation for your participation.

This study, a learning exercise for a marketing research class, is being conducted by Illinois State University with the anticipation that the results will be of value to the McLean County organizations which sponsor cultural programs and activities for the community.

Thank you for your time and your cooperation.

Sincerely,

Jon F. Bibb, Professor of Marketing

Gary R. Sudano, Professor of Music

Source: Reprinted with permission of the College of Fine Arts, Illinois State University.

Exhibit 12.6   **Questionnaire (*continued*)**

Questionnaire   p. 2

ARTS COUNT: A McLEAN COUNTY SURVEY

INSTRUCTIONS: For this study, cultural activities and programs will include
Visual Arts (e.g. painting, sculpture, photo, crafts), Performing Arts (e.g.
dance, theater, music) and Museum and Gallery Exhibitions.

1. Within the past year, have you attended any cultural activity(s) (Visual Arts,
    Performing Arts, Museum and Gallery Exhibitions) in McLean County? (including
    those offered by high schools, colleges and local organizations)

                YES _____   NO _____   If NO, please proceed to question #4.

2. Please check which type(s) of cultural activities you have attended in McLean
    County:

    ____ Visual Art exhibits (e.g. painting, sculpture, photography, crafts)

    ____ Dance performances (e.g. folk, ballet, modern, jazz)

    ____ Theater productions (e.g. plays, musicals, poetry readings)

    ____ Musical performances (e.g. symphony, band, solo recitals, chamber music,
          chorus)

    ____ Museums (e.g. historical items, artifacts, exhibits)

    ____ Other (please specify) _____
          _____

3. Please indicate the number of times within the past year you have attended
    each of these activities in McLean County:

    Visual Arts exhibits   ____ times   Music performances   ____ times
    Dance performances   ____ times   Museums   ____ times
    Theater productions   ____ times   Others (please specify)   ____ times
                                          _____

4. Please rank the following categories within each cultural activity in the
    order which you are most likely to attend, ranging from 1, most likely to
    attend to 4, least likely to attend.

    Art Exhibits   Dance Performances:
    ____ Paintings   ____ Folk (ethnic)
    ____ Sculpture   ____ Ballet
    ____ Photography   ____ Modern
    ____ Crafts   ____ Jazz
    ____ Other (please specify)   ____ Other (please specify)

    ____ Would not attend art exhibits   ____ Would not attend dance performances

Exhibit 12.6   Questionnaire (*continued*)

Questionnaire   p. 3

Theater Productions: Musical Performances:
____ Dramas   ____ Symphonic Music
____ Comedies   ____ Opera
____ Musicals   ____ Solo Recitals and Chamber Music
____ Poetry Readings   ____ Choral Music
____ Other (please specify)   ____ Other (please specify)

____ Would not attend theater   ____ Would not attend musical
       productions   performances

9. Please check the cultural activity(s) in which you would like to see addi-
    tional programs. (Please check all that apply) (If additional programs are
    desired, please specify)

    ____ painting (specify) _____   ____ dance (specify) _____

    ____ sculpture (specify) _____   ____ theater (specify) _____

    ____ photography (specify) _____   ____ music (specify) _____

    ____ crafts (specify) _____   ____ other (please specify) _____

                                           _____

10. Are you interested in any additional classes in the arts areas?

            YES _____   NO _____

11. If YES, please elaborate. _____

    _____

5. How can you check whether respondents answer accurately?
6. Discuss the role of the cover letter when sending out questionnaires.
7. What are some advantages and some disadvantages of using questionnaires in research?

EXERCISES

1. Find a questionnaire in a magazine or newspaper and evaluate the design.
2. Design a questionnaire for solving a research problem you have defined. Try the questionnaire out on some friends. Tabulate the results.
3. Critique the following questions and try to reword them. They were used by an organization called ASH (Action on Smoking and Health).
   a. As research has proven, tobacco smoke can and does cause lung cancer in nonsmokers. Given this information, do you think
   _____ government should ban all smoking in most public places,
   _____ permit smoking only in separate sections,
   _____ only enforce decisions made by owners of buildings,
   _____ do nothing?
   b. Tobacco kills more people each year than alcohol, guns, AIDS, automobile and plane accidents combined. Yet as a society, we spend far more money educating the public about each of these other problems. Do you feel it is time the government should
   _____ spend more money on antismoking education,
   _____ spend comparable money on antismoking education,
   _____ continue the same level of spending,
   _____ reduce or eliminate spending on antismoking education?
4. A few years ago, a pro-gun organization conducted a survey which used the following question. Evaluate the question.
   Do you believe agents of the government should have the power to crash into your home, seize and confiscate your guns you keep for the protection of your wife and children, and thus leave them at the mercy of rapists and robbers?
   _____ Yes
   _____ No
5. A survey on salary increases for Congress asked the following question. Evaluate the question.
   Do you feel that members of Congress, who already receive expensive perquisites and a lush retirement, should vote themselves a 51 percent raise in pay?
   _____ Yes
   _____ No

6. Which responses would the next two questions most likely elicit?

   a. Do you feel the United States should have got involved in Vietnam in the first place?

      _____ Yes

      _____ No

   b. Do you feel the United States should have helped South Vietnam to defend itself?

      _____ Yes

      _____ No

PART

V

EVALUATION OF DATA

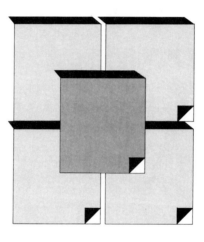

ANALYSIS WITH STATISTICS

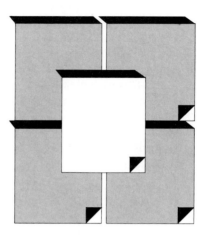

Learning Objectives

- To understand the purpose of statistics.
- To be able to differentiate between qualitative and quantitative data.
- To use measures of central tendency and measures of dispersion effectively.
- To use measures of correlation correctly.
- To understand the meaning and purpose of simple and multiple regression.

When the research has been completed, analysis of the data still remains to be done. This is a challenging and exciting part of the report-writing process.

Some people argue that a report writer has no need for statistical tools. A statistician, they believe, does the statistical work, and the report writer uses the results. Even if this were true, report writers must know enough about statistical techniques to understand when a simple correlation should be used, when a simple regression is appropriate, or when multiple regression analysis is needed—even though someone else does the actual work. To intelligently report statistical information obtained from secondary sources, report writers must understand what the statistics mean. They must also determine how to use the statistical results.

This chapter will present some of the most frequently used statistical tools. It will examine the use and meaning of measures of central tendency, measures of dispersion, correlation measures, and basic inferential statistics. The emphasis is on the meaning of statistical results rather than on actual computation. For a detailed treatment of statistics, you may consult one of the following books:

Bradley, Iver E., and J. B. South. (1981). *Introductory statistics for business and economics.* Hinsdale, IL: Dryden.

Huff, Darrell. (1954). *How to lie with statistics.* New York: Norton.

Zikmund, W. G. (1991). *Business research methods.* Hinsdale, IL: Dryden.

THE PURPOSE OF STATISTICS

Statistical analysis will help you in the interpretation of your research. The four major purposes of statistics are to help in:

1. Reducing large volumes of data to a manageable size.
2. Studying populations and samples.
3. Making decisions.
4. Making inferences.

With the help of statistics you can draw conclusions. Of course, the possibility of error always exists, but statistics help in determining the probability of error and the level of uncertainty in the results. You can determine that a certain inference is correct at a certain level of significance.

The two basic forms of research data are qualitative and quantitative data.

Qualitative Data

Qualitative Data
Qualitative data is nonnumeric data.

As the term indicates, **qualitative data** is related to the "quality," or the attributes, of data. Assume, for example, you are working on a report determining the new site for a subsidiary. You have collected data from the library and visited the sites under consideration. As the result of your work, you have information on cost of land, availability of workers, water supply, tax structure, transportation networks, cultural opportunities, schools, and recreational facilities. You can organize, present, and discuss your material according to those categories.

Some of the data you collected will be in the form of numbers, but some will not. For example, the caliber of the schools will be difficult to assess. You may look at graduation requirements, extracurricular activities, athletic programs, scores on national aptitude tests, and the percentage of students going on to college. Ultimately you will have to judge whether the schools are good, bad, or average on the basis of this qualitative information.

Many people argue that, in order to overcome pay discrimination between men and women, every job should be assigned a number of points. Jobs of equal value—that is, jobs with equal points—should pay the same salary. The difficulty lies in determining the points and agreeing on the criteria used to describe a job. Once there is agreement on those things, the rest is indeed easy. No matter how many criteria are used—education, social benefits, work hours, and work hazards, to name a few–the decision is ultimately a qualitative one. It is qualitative, even though a job is given a specified number of points for each criterion, because someone must decide how many points to assign.

Your search for a lucrative and rewarding job after graduation will be an attempt to quantify qualitative data. You may spend many hours researching the companies you are interested in. You may also read a number of books on how best to sell your skills and prepare your resumé. The authors of the job-hunting books you may consult often provide step-by-step procedures for choosing the right position. They may suggest drawing up a list of all the things to consider: pay, location, advancement possibilities, fringe benefits, and size of company.

Because these factors are not likely to be equally important to you, you will assign weights (a number) to each factor. All factors together represent the job characteristics you consider important. The factors, therefore, must add up to one, and their weights are always the same. Regardless of where the job is, for example, location carries the same weight each time you examine a job opportunity.

For each job you analyze, you evaluate the factors and assign points to each factor. You decide beforehand the highest number of points you want to give. In the example that follows, the highest number of points for the pay factor is 50. In comparing two jobs, one with high pay and one with lower pay, you may assign 50 points to one and only 30 points to the other. You then assign points to the other job factors for each job.

By multiplying the weights by the points, you get weighted values. When you add the weighted values, you will get weighted averages, which makes possible a clear ranking of the job offers. The weighted average is influenced by the two decisions you make: (1) the assigning of weights to the job factors and (2) the assigning of points to each job factor.

As an example, assume that you are evaluating two job offers, one in Chicago and one in Denver. The pay is about the same. You like to ski; in fact, that is your favorite winter pastime. Denver is the better location for skiing. Advancement within the Denver firm appears more promising, but the Chicago job offers much better fringe benefits. The company in Denver is fairly

Exhibit 13.1

Quantifying Qualitative Data: The Calculation of
Weighted Averages

	Weights	Denver		Chicago	
		Points	Average Value	Points	Average Value
Pay	.5	40	20	40	20
Location	.2	50	10	30	6
Advancement	.2	40	8	30	6
Fringe benefits	.05	30	1.5	50	2.5
Size	.05	30	1.5	50	2.5
			41		37

small, whereas the Chicago firm is large, and you have always wanted to work for a large corporation.

You have to rank your priorities and assign points. You then multiply and add the scores (Exhibit 13.1). Based on your analysis, you should take the job in Denver.

In this example you worked with qualitative data. Because you worked with numbers, you may think the data was quantitative. The fact is that you converted qualities to numbers. This process allows you to apply statistical analysis to qualitative data. You have "clean" data; the outcome looks clear and convincing and has the illusion of scientific certainty. The process can be very helpful as long as you are aware of its shortcomings.

Because qualitative data is connected to subjective judgment, you have to be careful in its use. If you are not certain exactly what you are looking for in a job, for example, you cannot assign weights and points intelligently. If you have had a bad day and want to get far away, Denver may seem to provide that distance. The results of your analysis may therefore show a clear preference for Denver, but intuitively you are not convinced.

In your career, you will write many reports weighing several alternatives. A clear understanding of weighted averages is, therefore, essential.

Quantitative Data

Quantitative Data
Quantitative data is numeric data.

In contrast to qualitative data, **quantitative data** is entirely objective. If you want to find the average height of the students in your class, you simply measure everyone and compute the average. Scores on an objective test in your report-writing class are quantitative data. You either marked the correct answer or you did not. You either understood the point or you did not. Based on the scores, the instructor can calculate the average for the class.

A score on a writing assignment may at first seem to be a quantitative measure as well, but that score is actually based on qualitative judgment. The instructor may have a scale for certain mistakes: spelling, 2 points off; grammar, 3 points off; punctuation, 1 point off; lack of reader adaptation, up to 20 points off. The instructor decides whether a report loses, for example, 15 or 20 points on reader adaptation. Two instructors may be very close in their scoring and evaluating of a report, yet their scores may also differ. To overcome these differences, instructors can grade papers together so that they will use the same standards and give identical or close to identical scores. This technique is called the establishing of interrater reliability.

In working with quantitative data you will have to examine carefully the sample and the variables you want to measure. You also must check the data for accuracy, reliability, and validity. Those terms were discussed, along with sampling, in Chapter 12. If the sample is not representative of the population, your findings cannot be generalized to the population. If you do not control the independent variables carefully, your results may be misleading.

DESCRIPTIVE STATISTICS

After you have collected and organized the data, you may have rows and columns of numbers. In this form the information is not particularly useful. To make it meaningful, you need a way to summarize the overall tendencies of particular sets of data and to establish relationships between sets.

Measures of Central Tendency

One way to summarize the general shape of raw data is to indicate where the midpoint occurs—the point statisticians call the *mean* or the *median*—or to indicate the most frequently occurring number, the *mode*. These devices are called **measures of central tendency.**

Measures of Central Tendency
Measures of central tendency examine the clustering of data.

Newspapers and news broadcasts often carry reports about average income, average cost of living, average cost of housing, and average medical costs. In our everyday language we use the term *average* rather loosely. Average can have three meanings: arithmetic mean, median, or mode.

Mean
The mean is the arithmetic average.

Arithmetic Mean.   The arithmetic **mean** is probably used most frequently and, of all the measures of central tendency, is probably the best understood. To determine the mean income of a sample, simply add all the income figures of the sample (X) and then divide the sum by the number of observations (N). The symbol used for the arithmetic mean is the lower case Greek letter *mu*, written as μ. The mean of a sample is expressed as $\overline{X}$.

As an example, assume that you have collected the following data on incomes:

$$
\begin{array}{rl}
X = & \$15,000 \\
X = & 17,000 \\
X = & 20,000 \\
X = & \underline{22,000} \\
\text{Sum} & \$74,000
\end{array}
$$

The mean income is:

$$\mu = \frac{\$74,000}{4} = \$18,500.$$

In this example the mean is a fair representation of the income of the surveyed group. The lowest and highest figures are not far apart, and the mean is the midpoint between the two middle figures.

In many cases, as in the following example, the mean by itself may be misleading and may not give a very realistic picture.

$$
\begin{aligned}
X &= \$\ 12,000 \\
X &= \quad 12,000 \\
X &= \quad 13,000 \\
X &= \quad 15,000 \\
X &= \quad 18,000 \\
X &= \quad 19,000 \\
X &= \quad 20,000 \\
X &= \quad 20,000 \\
X &= \quad 20,000 \\
X &= \quad 55,000 \\
X &= \quad \underline{60,000} \\
&\quad \$264,000
\end{aligned}
$$

The mean value is:

$$\mu = \frac{\$264,000}{11} = \$24,000.$$

This mean value is misleading. The two high-income figures cause the mean to fall between the nine lowest and the two highest figures. Because the mean gives no indication of this fact, the median might be a more accurate representation of the data.

Median

The median is the midpoint—half the data is above, half the data is below.

Median.   The **median,** which is depicted by the letter M, gives the central value when all values are arranged in increasing or decreasing sequence.

Of 11 income figures, the sixth one is the central value. In the example for calculating the mean, half of the sample was above $19,000 and half below. The median was therefore $19,000.

If you have an even number of observations in your sample, you average the two central values. For example, assume that you have two incomes of $60,000. This raises the number of observations from 11 to 12. You have two central income figures: $19,000 and $20,000. You calculate the median by averaging these two figures to arrive at a median of $19,500.

The formula for finding the median can be expressed as:

$$M = \frac{n+1}{2}$$

In the example the difference between the mean and the median is $5,000. The two high-income figures that raise the mean for the sample actually distort what the average person makes. In this case the report writer might provide both of the figures and thus show that the sample is half above and half below $19,000 and that the mean income is $24,000. The comparison puts both figures in perspective.

If income is important for marketing a particular product, management should know more than the mean income. For example, assume that the target market is an income range of $20,000 to $30,000. The mean falls within this range. Based on this information only, management should market the product to this group. The median, however, indicates that half the families are under the specified threshold. Before making a decision, management may want to study the situation in more detail.

Mode
The mode is the most frequently occurring value.

Mode. The **mode,** another measure of central tendency, tells which value occurs most frequently. In the example, three families make $20,000. No other income level applies to as many families; therefore, the mode is $20,000. The mode may be helpful but must be used carefully. A researcher who presents only the mode may misrepresent the data because the mode may, and often does, represent a minority of the total population. The following example illustrates the point:

$X = \$14,000$	$X = 30,000$
$X = \ 15,000$	$X = 33,000$
$X = \ 17,000$	$X = 45,000$
$X = \ 17,000$	$X = 50,000$
$X = \ 17,000$	$X = 50,000$
$X = \ 17,000$	$X = 60,000$
$X = \ 20,000$	$X = 70,000$
$X = \ 22,000$	$X = 72,000$
$X = \ 25,000$	

The mode in this case is $17,000. The median, which is the ninth value on the list, is $25,000, and the mean income is $33,764.70.

No relationship exists between those numbers. They can all be helpful, but the report writer must understand the meaning and know when and how to use each one. So that the reader of a report can put measures of central tendency in perspective and judge whether the mean, median, and mode fairly represent the facts, the report writer should include the actual figures in a report table or appendix.

Bimodal Distribution
The bimodal distribution has more than one cluster.

The Bimodal Distribution. In a **bimodal distribution,** which has two or more clusters, a calculation of the mean may be senseless. The following example of test results illustrates the point. As the results in the example show, the highest score of a 100-point test was 93, the lowest 75.

$$
\begin{array}{rrr}
2 & 75 = & 150 \\
4 & 77 = & 308 \\
5 & 79 = & 395 \\
3 & 81 = & 243 \\
1 & 83 = & 83 \\
4 & 88 = & 352 \\
5 & 90 = & 450 \\
5 & 91 = & 455 \\
2 & 93 = & \underline{186} \\
& & 2,622
\end{array}
$$

Based on these scores, the mean is 84.58, or 85 points. The median is 88 points. There is no mode.

The mean value in this case does not help the instructor in analyzing the results of the test. Based on the popular interpretation of the mean, the instructor might assume that the scores are clustered around that value and that many test scores would be at or around 85. The data shows that this is not the case at all. There are two distinct groups in the class. One group performed in the upper 70s and the other in the upper 80s and lower 90s. Almost half of the class did not do well.

The graphic distribution of the test scores in Exhibit 13.2 clearly shows the two clusters.

Skewed Distribution
The values are clustered at one extreme.

The Skewed Distribution.   The scores of a test may be **skewed** to a particular side. A test might result in the following scores:

$$
\begin{array}{rr}
1 \times 62 = & 62 \\
1 \times 67 = & 67 \\
1 \times 71 = & 71 \\
2 \times 75 = & 150 \\
2 \times 77 = & 154 \\
3 \times 83 = & 249 \\
3 \times 84 = & 252 \\
4 \times 87 = & 348 \\
5 \times 88 = & 440 \\
5 \times 90 = & 450 \\
4 \times 93 = & 372 \\
1 \times 94 = & 94 \\
1 \times 96 = & \underline{96} \\
& 2,805
\end{array}
$$

These test results are skewed toward the upper scores, as the results and also the graphic illustration in Exhibit 13.3 show. If the scores are skewed, measures of central tendency are not particularly helpful in understanding the results. The mean of 85 and the median of 87 (there is no mode) do not indicate that the distribution is skewed.

The instructor must look at the actual scores to determine whether to calculate a measure of central tendency. With a class of 30 this may be fairly easy to do. If the instructor has 200 scores, the trends may not be that clear. In that case, calculating both a measure of central tendency and a measure of dispersion might be best.

Exhibit 13.2   **Bimodal Distribution**

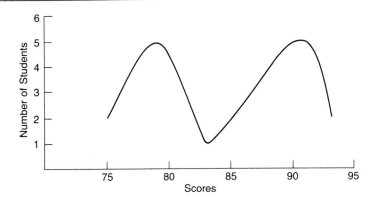

Exhibit 13.3   **Skewed Distribution**

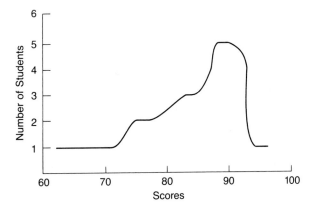

Measures of Dispersion

As indicated by the example of skewed data, measures of central tendency by themselves are usually not enough to describe the pattern of data. Management may want to know not only the average sales for the entire company and each district but also the differences between the various districts. An instruc-

Measures of Dispersion
Measures of dispersion examine the scattering of data.

tor may want to find out not only the average score but also the distance between the highest and the lowest scores. Measuring those differences can be as important as measuring the central points. To examine the differences, the researcher uses **measures of dispersion.**

Range

The range gives the extreme values.

Range.   The most frequently used measure of dispersion is the **range.** If the highest score on the test is 90 and the lowest is 75, then the range is:

$$90 - 75 = 15$$

The range provides a concise summary of the variation of the values. It tells how far the highest and lowest values are apart, but it neglects all the values in between. It does not tell anything about the pattern of the distribution. To overcome this shortcoming, a researcher might also need to calculate the mean and the median.

Most scores on a test might be fairly close together except for one very high and one very low score. Perhaps the lowest score is 50 and the highest is 100, but the majority of scores are around 85. In that case the range is somewhat misleading. It tells the extremes, but only two scores are at those points. No other score is even close. To avoid an emphasis on the extremes, which happens if the absolute range is stated, researchers will often give a range within which 80 percent or 90 percent of all scores fall. In this way the reader or user of the data has more accurate information on the distribution of the data.

Variance.   The variance is another measure of dispersion. The range shows the distance between highest and lowest scores, whereas the variance shows the average distance between the mean and the actual test scores. The variance is more useful because it tells more about the distribution of the data than does the range.

In calculating the variance, all the individual variances between observations and mean are squared. The squared variances are added and then divided by the number of observations. The formula for calculating the variance is as follows:

$$\text{Variance} = \frac{\Sigma \, (\text{Observation} - \text{Mean})^2}{N \text{ of Observations} - 1} = \frac{\Sigma \, (x - \bar{x})^2}{n - 1}.$$

Note: To use population rather than sample data, the denominator is n rather than $n - 1$.

The following is a calculation of the variance for the same test results used in the bimodal-distribution example:

$$
\begin{aligned}
(x - \bar{x})^2 \\
(75 - 83)^2 &= -8^2 = 64 \\
(75 - 83)^2 &= -8^2 = 64 \\
(76 - 83)^2 &= -7^2 = 49 \\
(77 - 83)^2 &= -6^2 = 36 \\
(78 - 83)^2 &= -5^2 = 25 \\
(78 - 83)^2 &= -5^2 = 25 \\
(79 - 83)^2 &= -4^2 = 16 \\
(81 - 83)^2 &= -2^2 = 4 \\
(88 - 83)^2 &= 5^2 = 25
\end{aligned}
$$

$$(88 - 83)^2 = 5^2 = 25$$
$$(89 - 83)^2 = 6^2 = 36$$
$$(89 - 83)^2 = 6^2 = 36$$
$$(90 - 83)^2 = 7^2 = \underline{49}$$
$$\Sigma(x - \bar{x})^2 = \quad 454 \text{ square points}$$

$$S^2 = \frac{454 \text{ Square Points}}{13 - 1} = 37.83 \text{ Square Points.}$$

You can see the numbers are getting high. Imagine the calculation of the variance if you deal with millions of dollars. Another difficulty is that the variance is not expressed in the same units as the observations. The observations, in this case the test results, are expressed in points. Because all deviations are squared when calculating the variance, the variance is expressed in square points, a rather meaningless designation.

To overcome the difficulty of high numbers and squared deviations, statisticians take the square root of the variance. The result is the standard deviation.

Standard Deviation
The standard deviation calculates the distance from the sample mean.

Standard Deviation.   The **standard deviation** is a practical and descriptive measure of dispersion. Its major advantage over the variance is that it is expressed in the same units as the data. The standard deviation is, therefore, easier to use and easier to understand. The standard deviation for the example is computed as follows:

$$\text{Standard Deviation} = S = \sqrt{\frac{\Sigma(x - \bar{x})^2}{n - 1}} = \sqrt{37.83} = 6.15.$$

Normal Curve
The normal curve is a theoretical probability distribution. It is bell-shaped.

The standard deviation is particularly helpful if the population has a special distribution called the **normal curve.** The normal curve is a theoretical distribution of sample means. It is bell-shaped. Under a normal curve, 99.7 percent of all observations fall within ±3 standard deviations of the mean, 95.5 percent fall within ±2 standard deviations of the mean, and 68 percent fall within ±1 standard deviation of the mean (Exhibit 13.4). For the business person, the standard deviation together with the normal curve can be an important statistical tool.

A manufacturer for men's clothing, for example, has to make sure that the clothes produced actually fit the men in the population. He might take a sample of men and measure their height. If the average height of the men in the sample is 5 feet 10 inches with a standard deviation of ±2 inches, under the normal curve the manufacturer would calculate the following results:

68 percent of the men are within one standard deviation of the mean. They are between 5 feet 8 inches and 6 feet tall.

95.5 percent are within two standard deviations of the mean. They are between 5 feet 6 inches and 6 feet 2 inches tall.

99.7 percent are within three standard deviations of the mean. They are between 5 feet 4 inches and 6 feet 4 inches tall.

Exhibit 13.4   **Normal Curve**

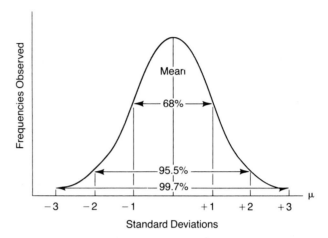

With this information the manufacturer can determine how much fabric he needs. He knows what percentage of slacks should have short or long legs. These calculations influence the manufacturing, budgeting, pricing, and marketing decisions.

Both the clustering and the variability of data are useful for the business person to know. A production manager who wants to improve quality control must know the numbers of acceptable and unacceptable products and by how many units of measurements the faulty products are outside the specified tolerance levels. If 95 percent of production is meeting the standard, the manager must determine by how much the 5 percent miss the standard. Based on the results of a measurement of dispersion, the production manager may learn how much improvement is needed. A low standard deviation indicates that the variability is fairly low. If the standard deviation in the quality check is high, production may need major attention and quality improvements.

When you collect data for business reports, you will find many references to standard deviation in connection with results of primary research. You must, therefore, understand the standard deviation so that you can communicate its meaning and implications ethically and effectively.

Measures of Correlation

Usually managers want to know not only sales or advertising costs but also the relationship between sales and advertising. They want to find the relationship between the successful completion of training courses and productivity or between bonuses and job satisfaction.

In many cases researchers may know intuitively that certain phenomena are related. For example, it makes sense that relationships exist between the

Correlation
Correlation measures examine the strength of the relationship between variables.

number of finished houses and the sale of appliances and carpeting, between the birth of new babies and the sale of baby food, and between hot weather and the consumption of soft drinks. They usually do not know, however, how strong or weak the relationships are. Most people do not care about the details of **correlation,** but in the business situation observation or intuition is not enough. Business people must know the nature and the strength of the relationship to gauge future product planning, marketing campaigns, expansion projects, and personnel forecasts.

A number of statistical techniques such as the simple correlation coefficient, the coefficient of determination, and the chi-square test can measure the relationship between variables. Because descriptions of all these measures exceed the scope of this chapter, the discussion will concentrate on the simple correlation coefficient and concentrate on its meaning.

The simple correlation coefficient measures the correlation between two variables. The value for the correlation can range from $+1$ to -1. A correlation of $+1$ indicates perfect correlation between two variables. If a company's sales go up along a straight line as advertising dollars go up, for example, the correlation is $+1$. A value of -1 indicates an inverse relationship. A company may find that sales go up as the price goes down. A value of zero means that no relationship exists between the variables.

Usually you hope for a high correlation between a new training program and job performance. If you find that the correlation coefficient between the training and job performance is very low or zero, your business would have to reevaluate the program. Perhaps the wrong people are participating in the program or it is not well designed. Perhaps the sessions are at the wrong time of the day.

Correlational research indicates only the strength and the direction of a relationship between two variables; it does *not* show whether there is a causal relationship, that is, whether one variable causes the other. A simple correlation may show a relationship between sales of soft drinks and hot weather, for example, but the report writer cannot say that hot weather causes the sales of soft drinks to go up. When looking at correlation research, the writer obviously has to keep the limitations of correlations in mind.

Correlations are nevertheless useful. They show the business writer which variables are related, and they help in exploring the nature of the relationship. If no relationship whatsoever exists, the writer may dismiss further investigation. If, based on common sense, a relationship could be expected, the writer should investigate why the statistical analysis does not show a correlation. If a relationship does exist, the writer may want to formulate a hypothesis and conduct experimental research to test whether the relationship is causal. Correlations can help to eliminate irrelevant variables and focus on the important ones.

Variables may appear to be statistically related even though no actual relationship exists. Some things happen coincidentally. A correlation of the length of skirts and the movement of the stock market, for example, would be a chance correlation.

The correlation may be caused by a third factor. A correlation study may show that the sale of soft drinks is related to vacations, but more likely the correlation is based on hot weather. Most people take vacations during the summer, and in hot weather people drink more soft drinks.

Users of correlational research in the decision-making process should be aware of the shortcomings of this statistical tool. It can be helpful, but by itself it may not be enough. A wrong interpretation of the results may lead to poor planning and poor decisions. In many cases the report writer has to use more powerful statistical tools.

Some questions the report writer should ask when examining correlation research are as follows:

1. Was there a reason to assume that the variables were indeed related, or does it appear that the researcher blindly investigated any two variables? Did the researcher use a shotgun approach?
2. Did the researcher in any way imply a causal relationship between the variables?
3. Did the researcher repeat the study?
4. What other means did the researcher use to validate the results?

INFERENTIAL STATISTICS

Inferential Statistics
Inferential statistics are used to make predictions about a population based on a sample.

As we have seen, descriptive statistics describe and summarize data. For decision making and forecasting, businesses use descriptive statistics together with **inferential statistics.** In inferential statistics, investigators make generalizations about the whole by examining a part. For example, the business person examines a sample and then projects the results to the entire population. Inferential statistics are subject to error, and the report writer must be aware of that possibility when reporting, analyzing, and presenting data. Because inferential statistics are based on probability, no certainty exists that the generalizations are true.

Level of Significance
The level of significance indicates the probability level that the results are due to chance.

With the help of inferential statistics the writer can say that a forecast is true at a certain **level of significance.** Although he may assume that a hypothesis he tests is correct, he must keep the possibility in mind that it may not be correct. For example, he might find that the statistical results of a study support the hypothesis that—at a .05 level of significance—the use of microcomputers reduces writing anxiety. This finding really means that, given the sample size and the data derived from the testing program, he has found support for his hypothesis with this qualification: A 5 percent possibility exists that the sample is not typical of the entire population about which he is generalizing. Thus, conclusions drawn by using inferential statistics are, to a certain degree, always tentative.

Simple Regression Analysis
Simple regression predicts the causal relationship between an independent and a dependent variable.

Simple Regression Analysis

With a correlation you can measure the strength of the relationship between variables. With a **simple regression** you can measure whether this relationship is causal, that is, whether changes in the independent variable produce

Exhibit 13.5   **Data on Sales and Building Permits**

Wholesaler	Number of Permits	Sales in $000
1	$x = 86$	$y = 77$
2	$x = 92$	$y = 79$
3	$x = 93$	$y = 81$
4	$x = 102$	$y = 82$
5	$x = 140$	$y = 105$
6	$x = 120$	$y = 130$
7	$x = 130$	$y = 120$
8	$x = 145$	$y = 115$
9	$x = 120$	$y = 100$
10	$x = 105$	$y = 100$
11	$x = 103$	$y = 94$
12	$x = 160$	$y = 150$
13	$x = 158$	$y = 130$

changes in the dependent variable. Regression, because it examines the causal relationship, is a more powerful tool than the correlation measures.

As an example, assume that a lumberyard wholesaler thinks a relationship exists between sales and the number of building permits issued. He does a simple correlation that shows a strong correlation between sales and building permits but does not establish a causal relationship. He may decide to perform a simple regression analysis. The number of permits issued is the independent variable; sales are the dependent variable. Looking at past data, the wholesaler hopes to make inferences about future sales. He hopes to determine how well sales can be predicted from the number of building permits issued. If he can calculate future sales, he can make better decisions about inventory, number of employees, and size of buildings needed.

The wholesaler decides to collect data on building permits and sales from 13 wholesalers in the area. His findings are presented in Exhibit 13.5.

The figures can be plotted in a diagram (Exhibit 13.6). The values are not on a straight line, but the linear regression is based on the concept that there is a straight line. As Exhibit 13.6 shows, it is possible to draw more than one straight line based on the data.

The problem is to determine which line is most accurate for forecasting sales. Line *a* suggests a higher increase of sales than does line *b*. Because the difference is rather great, the wholesaler would like to have a more accurate measure. He can use a simple regression analysis. The formula is as follows:

$$\hat{Y} = \hat{a} + \hat{\beta}X$$
$$\hat{a} = \hat{Y} - \hat{\beta}X$$
$$\hat{\beta} = \frac{n(\Sigma XY) - (\Sigma X)(\Sigma Y)}{n(\Sigma X^2) - (\Sigma X)^2}$$

where:

$\hat{\beta}$ = the estimated slope of the line,
$\hat{a}$ = estimated intercept of the y-axis,
Y = dependent variable (sales),
$\bar{Y}$ = mean of dependent variable,
X = independent variable (permits),
$\bar{X}$ = mean of independent variable, and
n = number of observations.

The calculations are shown in Exhibit 13.7.

$$\bar{Y} = 104.846$$
$$\bar{X} = 113.54$$

Calculate $\hat{a}$ and $\hat{\beta}$:

$$\hat{\beta} = \frac{13(169084) - 2118102}{13(193436) - 2414916} = \frac{7990}{99752} = .8$$

$$\hat{a} = 104.846 - 95.63 = 9.216$$

Exhibit 13.6   **Relation of Sales Outlook and Building Permits**

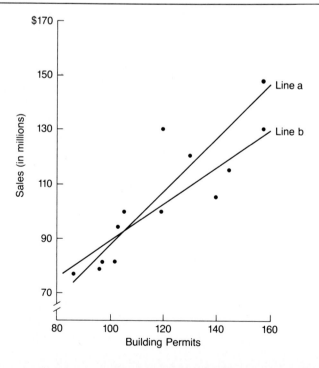

Exhibit 13.7

Calculation of Regression

Y	Y^2	X	X^2	XY
77	5929	86	7396	6622
79	6241	92	8464	7268
81	6561	93	8649	7533
82	6724	102	10404	8364
105	11025	140	19600	14700
130	16900	120	14400	15600
120	14400	130	16900	15600
115	13225	145	21025	16675
100	10000	129	14400	12000
100	10000	105	11025	10500
94	8836	103	10609	9682
150	22500	160	25600	24000
130	16900	158	24964	20540
ΣY	$\Sigma(Y^2)$	ΣX	$\Sigma(X^2)$	ΣXY
1363	149241	1554	193436	169084

Forecast sales with the regression formula:

$$\hat{Y} = \hat{a} + \hat{\beta}X = 9.216 + .8X$$

With the results shown in Exhibit 13.6, the wholesaler can forecast sales. If 80 permits are issued, he can expect sales of $73,216.

$$\hat{Y} = 9.216 + .8\,(80) = 73.216.$$

The report writer must be aware that linear regression or, for that matter, any statistical technique cannot promise that the forecast is correct in all details. Although no promise of certainty exists, statistical techniques do measure the likelihood of the relationship. Even with precise numbers, the business person has to make the final decision. The statistical techniques are merely an aid in the process.

The lumber wholesaler must examine more than the causal relationship between sales of building supplies and the issue of building permits. Before he begins to expand, he has to look at his current and long-range debts, examine space requirements, take into account the cost of a larger inventory, and determine whether the building boom in the area will last or will be short lived. The causal relationship between sales and building permits is only one factor in the decision-making process.

Multiple Regression Analysis

Few business problems are two dimensional, that is, have one dependent and one independent variable. Usually many variables influence sales; for example, a consumer deciding whether to buy a new car will consider not only price but also rate of interest, cost of keeping the old car, style, cost of maintaining the new car, and probably several other factors. With the help of multivariate analysis the consumer can examine all those variables at the same time. In contrast to the simple regression analysis that is two dimensional, the **multiple regression analysis** is multidimensional.

Multiple Regression Analysis
Multiple regression predicts the causal relationship between one dependent and two or more independent variables.

Before computers were in common use, an analysis of more than three variables was nearly impossible because the calculations became too complex. Computers, which have made multiple regression analysis possible, have given the business person a more accurate tool for forecasting.

A business person who tries to predict sales of cars solely on the basis of price leaves out important factors. With the help of multiple regression analysis the business person can determine how the various factors that make up the purchasing decision are related. The lumberyard wholesaler, for example, has to consider the income level in the area, prices, and general economic outlook in addition to the number of permits issued. Multiple regression analysis, because it takes more factors into account than the simple regression, is more realistic and has higher predictive powers.

The business person is guided not only by demands for accuracy but also by cost considerations. Both play an important role in collecting and analyzing data. The business person has to weigh the cost of additional accuracy. The sample may have to be larger; the study may have to be repeated for reliability and validity. Each attempt to raise accuracy also raises the cost. If an additional $10,000 is expected to increase revenue by $500,000, then the cost may be justified. If the $10,000 is expected to raise revenue by only $15,000, however, management may be hesitant to spend the additional money.

Time is a factor, too, particularly for a new product. More research and detailed analysis might add certainty but will also delay entering the market. Six months from now the competitive edge may have disappeared, and the added accuracy may have cost the company a share of the market. Statistics contribute to accuracy, but accuracy costs both time and money.

The report writer must be aware of the power and also of the limitations of regression analysis. She may, for example, discuss the cost and time factors of collecting and analyzing data and their influence on accuracy in the section on limitations (see Chapter 7).

SUMMARY OF LEARNING OBJECTIVES

To understand the purpose of statistics.

Statistics help in summarizing data, manipulating data, and making inferences from data.

To be able to differentiate between qualitative and quantitative data.

Quantitative data is numeric data. Qualitative data is nonnumeric data. Qualitative data can be converted into quantitative data, but an element of subjectivity is always involved.

To use measures of central tendency and measures of dispersion effectively.

The three measures of central tendency are the mean, the median, and the mode. The report writer may have to show all three to present data accurately. Measures of central tendency emphasize the clustering of data.

Measures of dispersion emphasize the distribution of data. The most important measure of dispersion is the standard deviation. The standard deviation is particularly useful in connection with the normal curve.

To use measures of correlation correctly.

Correlation studies measure the direction and the strength of the relationship between variables. They do not measure any causal links between variables.

To understand the meaning and purpose of simple and multiple regression.

Regression analysis establishes causal relationships between variables. It can be used in forecasting. The simple regression analysis makes predictions based on one independent variable; the multiple regression analysis makes predictions based on two or more independent variables. Multiple regression analysis is a more powerful forecasting tool.

KEY TERMS

Qualitative Data	Range
Quantitative Data	Standard Deviation
Measures of Central Tendency	Normal Curve
Mean	Correlation
Median	Inferential Statistics
Mode	Level of Significance
Bimodal Distribution	Simple Regression Analysis
Skewed Distribution	Multiple Regression Analysis
Measures of Dispersion	

QUESTIONS AND DISCUSSION POINTS

1. Define *mean, median,* and *mode.* What are disadvantages and advantages of each measure?
2. Name several measures of dispersion. Explain why the researcher may want to calculate measures of central tendency and measures of dispersion.

3. What are the characteristics of correlation research? What can correlation research do and not do?
4. When would you use a correlation and when a linear regression?
5. When would you use a multiple regression analysis?
6. What are the differences between quantitative and qualitative data?
7. Discuss the role of statistics in writing good reports.
8. What is the purpose of statistics?
9. A report writer argues that, based on his study, sales will go up by 30 percent next year if the company increases its advertising budget by $50,000. Discuss this statement.
10. Someone has found that a high correlation exists between teachers' salaries and the consumption of liquor over a number of years. Discuss this correlation.

EXERCISES

1. You received a score of 78 on your last report in business report writing, and you want to find out where you stand in relation to the class. The scores for the class were as follows: 75, 84, 90, 64, 82, 58, 76, 80, 73, 71, 74, 69, 61, and 93. Find out where you stand in relationship to the other students. Are you above or below the mean?
2. You are a newly-appointed manager in charge of a production line. Your goal is to achieve an average production rate of 60 units per hour. On your first day, the hourly production output (for eight hours) was 53, 55, 58, 61, 59, 63, 66, and 65. You will meet with your boss to discuss the results. Prepare for the meeting by determining whether you have achieved the goal.
3. The daily sales of the ABC Grocery Store for the first week of March were recorded as $5,200, $3,820, $4,140, $3,970, $4,210, $6,280, and $7,030. What was the daily average for the week? What was the standard deviation? How meaningful is the daily average?

14

REASONING WITH DATA: ANALYSIS, CONCLUSIONS, RECOMMENDATIONS

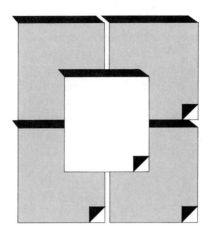

Learning Objectives

- To be familiar with analysis aids.
- To become aware of problems in analyzing data.
- To analyze data.
- To draw conclusions.
- To make logical recommendations.

At this point in your work you have collected and statistically analyzed the data, but a mere presentation of the statistical results is usually not enough. The statistics do not speak for themselves. They must be seen in the context of the overall problem.

Analysis
The analysis examines the data and establishes patterns.

Analysis is never a completely objective process; subjective elements always come into play. Two people looking at the same set of data may analyze the figures differently, as when economists disagree on the effect of tax cuts. Some argue that tax cuts favor the rich more than the poor and, in addition, lower the revenue of the government. Other economists argue that tax cuts will raise the revenues and do not unduly favor or benefit rich people. Both have the same set of data, but they look at the figures differently.

Even if two people with the same background and the same goals agree on the major points of an analysis, they will seldom agree on everything. So that the problems of analysis can be minimized, every researcher has to be aware of the most common problems in analysis. A knowledge of the difficulties is a step toward eliminating them.

AIDS IN ANALYSIS

To avoid the problems of faulty analysis, you can take a number of steps. Experience, an open mind, and talking with others will help, although none is a cure-all. The struggle starts anew with every report you write, with every research project you undertake.

Awareness of the History of the Problem. You may find it helpful to examine other research studies that explored similar problems. What have other companies done, for example, to improve inventory control? You might also look at the history of the problem in your company. How long has the company had the present system? How many people work in the area? What kind of training do they have? You asked similar questions when you first defined the problem for the report and made your research plan or proposal.

The report-writing process is not totally linear. You will do a number of the steps simultaneously, and you may repeat a number of them. Going back over your notes to refamiliarize yourself with the precise problem statement is particularly important at the beginning of the analysis.

Consultation with Others. Before you decide on a particular interpretation, you may want to find out how others interpret the findings. If you are good at interpreting, you are also aware of the difficulties and know that it is easy to overlook some aspects. Another person can also provide a fresh approach to the analysis. Perhaps in your analysis of a new training program you have overlooked the attitudes of the supervisors. Perhaps someone else can suggest how to make employees more open in their responses to questions about the program. Perhaps you should use a different statistical tool.

Understanding of Statistics.   Without a clear understanding of major statistical techniques discussed in Chapter 13, you will have difficulty understanding what the data means and putting the results in context.

Critical Viewpoint.   Applying a critical viewpoint involves reevaluating your findings, your research design, your grouping of data, and your results. You must then reevaluate your interpretation of the data and the conclusions. You should constantly ask yourself whether you can justify your analysis. Are there any items you have overlooked? If you have strong feelings on a particular point and your interpretation conforms to your viewpoint, reevaluation is imperative.

Assume for example, that you firmly believe training programs are a waste of money and do not benefit the company. Asked to research the effect of current training programs, you come to the conclusion that they are not worth the money the company spends on them. Upper management, however, believes they are an excellent tool for motivating and training employees, and several people have advanced successfully after undergoing special training. Given those circumstances, you should reexamine your results.

Knowledge of Logic.   The interpretation of data must be logical. Knowing the basic rules of logic will help you avoid some of the major flaws in interpreting data.

FLAWS IN INTERPRETING DATA

Some of the points in this discussion will overlap because one flaw in reasoning is often closely connected with another one. As in real life, it is difficult to separate all items neatly from one another.

Differing Views of Reality.   The problem of people's differing views of reality relates to the discussion of the communication process in Chapter 2. Two people never perceive a phenomenon identically. Both bring their own backgrounds, feelings, and values to the interpretation. Travel brochures from Iceland describe summer temperatures as mild or even warm, for example, but a person from Singapore would probably disagree with that description. To the Singaporean, Iceland's summers are rather cold.

If differing viewpoints are considered wrong or unimportant, they may be neglected in an analysis. This neglect may not be done consciously. If it is a subconscious process, the problem is unlikely to be corrected, because, in order to correct a problem, the researcher must know that it exists.

The data may also be interpreted on the basis of emotions and feelings rather than a rational examination. Someone violently opposed to smoking has a different perception of nonsmokers' rights than a smoker. If the researcher has a particular perception of a situation, finding data to support that viewpoint is not difficult.

A Craving for the Sensational.   Most people want to show that their work is important, and it is tempting to convey the message by implication. If a report sounds important, the writer may feel important.

As an example, assume that 53 percent of the sample studied in a market research project like a new product. In a spectacular interpretation the writer would not be satisfied with the presentation of the fact that a majority of the sample liked the product; he might report that an overwhelming majority liked it. The word *overwhelming* presents the problem, especially if the exact percentage is not given. Because most readers would not define 53 percent as an overwhelming majority, the writer longing for the spectacular might be tempted to omit the number. Similarly, in the late 1970s a number of people criticized business profits and labeled them *obscene*. The word certainly catches attention, but it conveys little meaning. It is emotional rather than factual. The report writer has to avoid language that overstates the situation and may influence management to make the *wrong* decision.

Preference for a Particular Viewpoint.   A writer with a strong personal opinion about a situation may look only at data that will support that viewpoint or may simply neglect "unfriendly" data.

To guard against this possibility, the writer should look at all points of view and weigh all evidence carefully. Making a list of all advantages and disadvantages of a particular decision would be helpful. If the list contains mostly advantages, and the writer at the same time emotionally favors the decision, the signal should be clear: reevaluate.

For example, in an employee-performance review the supervisor concludes that the employee should receive a rating of outstanding. Ready to go on to the next case, the supervisor remembers receiving a number of complaints about that particular employee. The supervisor and the employee are personal friends, see each other socially, and their children play together. Despite the pressure to give this employee an outstanding rating, the supervisor must consider the complaints and reevaluate the entire file.

Value Judgments.   Value judgments are usually based on emotions and insufficient data. The person making a value judgment is often unaware of making it.

Consider the following example. You are about to go to China on a business trip. To prepare for the trip, you read a number of books on cultural practices, including table manners and eating habits. You learn that in China people eat dogs. Thinking of your pet dog, you are absolutely horrified. You consider the eating of dogs to be outrageous and uncivilized. Obviously, the Chinese do not share your feelings.

In declaring the practice uncivilized and outrageous, you have made a value judgment based on your own cultural background and feeling of what is appropriate or acceptable. You may say that you would not want to eat this type of food. You might try it and decide you do not like it, but you may not condemn others for liking it. The Hindus are outraged that Americans eat beef. Try to explain that to a meat-loving American and the cattle industry.

Value judgments readily lead to generalizations. Basically there is nothing wrong with generalizations. In fact, unless you want to tailor every product to individual tastes, you have to generalize tastes. For example, you may find that college-educated single women in the 25 to 30 age group like a certain type of car. You will not please everyone in that group. If you have done your research well, however, enough women will like your company's car so that many will be sold.

When you make value judgments, be aware of what you are doing and learn to separate feelings from facts.

Inability to Distinguish the Important from the Unimportant.   Some writers are afraid of omitting any data from their reports; they want to include every finding. All, they may argue, are related to the problem. Unfortunately, the major points may get lost in the mass of minor details. The report may be useless because it is confused, disorganized, and difficult to read.

Insufficient Data.   Often the report writer must generalize on the basis of a limited sample. In the 1970s many academic journals examined Japanese management practices, for example, and usually concluded that Japan's success was attributable in part to the lifetime-employment system. Scholars and journalists argued that this provided stability to the corporations. Often the writers had not been to Japan at all or had only visited major corporations.

A more critical examination showed that the lifetime-employment system affects only employees at large corporations; small corporations do not have the system at all. In addition, lifetime employment usually stops at age 55, the traditional retirement age in Japan. Women are never part of the system because they are expected to leave the workforce when they marry. Clearly the interpretation of the lifetime-employment system was based on insufficient data.

Comparison of Noncomparable Data.   Numerous studies on both sides of the Atlantic show that, based on tests given to high-school or college students, German students are superior to American students. This data is taken as proof that American students and the American system are not as good as the German. The difficulty lies in the sample selection for the tests. Although the sample may have been selected randomly and the research design may be good, the results are still misleading because the groups cannot be compared.

In the United States, the young people who enroll in high school include students who will go to college, will have technical jobs, or will become unskilled workers. A number of students will drop out along the way. All attend the same school and are usually together in the same classrooms for many subjects.

In Germany, it is still common practice that after fourth grade students have to decide whether they will later attend a university, have a technical job, or become unskilled workers. Obviously one cannot compare test results of German university-bound high school students with American high school students. Those types of inaccurate studies continue to appear at regular intervals.

Statistical competency is not enough. To avoid comparing noncomparable data requires sensitivity and, as in the example, cultural knowledge that few people have.

Inference of Faulty Cause–Effect Relationships.   Although a simple correlation does not prove a cause–effect relationship, people often infer a causal relationship when two things happen simultaneously or sequentially. The sun rises after the rooster crows, but the rooster does not make the sun rise. The rainfall in Ohio correlates with the number of letters in each month, but spelling does not cause the rainfall. Statistical relationships may be absolutely meaningless (rooster and sunrise). Intelligent observation and common sense are necessary in the study of cause–effect relationships.

Conviction That Conclusions Are Essential.   Suppose that, after working hard on a report, you find out that you cannot draw any conclusions. You believe that the study should be repeated on a wider scale and over a longer time period. To report that you cannot draw any conclusions or make any recommendations, however, seems like failure. After all, management is expecting a report to decide about inventory control, a new marketing plan, or new pricing strategies, for example.

Circumstances may have changed since you received the assignment. Perhaps new legislation was passed or there was an important court ruling on affirmative action. Unless you incorporate that information, your report is meaningless. If the report is due tomorrow, you obviously need an extension on the deadline. To turn your report in as if nothing had happened in the meantime would be dishonest and useless. As an extreme example, suppose you were about to finish a feasibility study for expanding your business into Panama when Noriega was ousted. No matter how good your analysis, you would have needed to reconsider your conclusions.

Skimpy Analyses.   By the time you are ready to analyze the data, you are thoroughly familiar with the topic. The facts may appear clear and logical to you. However, the reader is not familiar with the details. To report that the reasons for the failure of a new product are obvious is not helpful to the person who asked you to do the study. You must present and explain the reasons and give the supporting evidence in an orderly manner. By insisting that the reasons are self-explanatory you may lose the goodwill of the reader who is not familiar with the topic.

Unquestioned Reliance on Authorities.   "If a reputable journal has printed it, it must be right" is an example of the belief that authorities are infallible. Even though journal articles are carefully selected, you should read them critically and with an open mind. Even noted economists cannot agree on how the deficit can be cured or what the economy will be like a year or even six months in the future. Read what they have to say, evaluate and interpret the data against your company's background and needs, and then decide. Think clearly and question authority. Had the Wright brothers listened to authoritative opinion, they would not have learned to fly.

Oversimplification.   Decision making would be easy if it were based on the simplistic statement that a decision is either right or wrong, that there is no in-between. Unfortunately, the either–or position does not allow for pulling the best from a number of positions and creating a new position. Interpreting data involves weighing factors and drawing conclusions. Statistical evidence that a new training program would be more successful at motivating employees than the old one, for example, must be weighed against other factors such as cost, mobility of employees, disruption at the workplace, and space requirements before a decision is made to implement the new program.

Guidelines.   You must know the problems and fallacies of analysis in order to guard against them. The following guidelines may help you in this endeavor.

1. Keep the presentation and the interpretation of the data separate. Collect all your data before you begin a formal analysis. If you start the analysis after you have evaluated only half of your sample, you may fix certain conclusions in your mind and, as a result, leave out facts that will not agree with your first impression. On the other hand, the research process is not completely linear; you do many things at the same time. You may even reconsider your problem statement at some point in the report preparation.
2. Separate facts from opinion. A disciplined researcher is not emotional or prejudiced. Hearsay does not constitute a fact unless you verify it. You cannot rely on the company grapevine to decide on the performance of a new employee. On the other hand, the grapevine may provide the incentive to do some checking.
3. Approach your analysis in an orderly fashion. Just as you planned the methodology for collecting data, you should organize your findings according to breakdowns of your problem statement. This means you have to connect your interpretation to the problem statement. Keeping the problem in mind will help you to sort the relevant from the irrelevant information. It will help you to pick out the major points so that you will not become lost in trivia and meaningless detail.
4. Figure out your weaknesses, your gripes, and your emotional convictions. You may even want to put them on a sheet of paper and keep them handy so that you can check as you analyze your data.
5. Play Devil's advocate and examine the data from all angles.

PERFORMING ANALYSIS

Let us assume you are in charge of inspecting fast-food restaurants for a national chain. Looking over the inspection reports for recent months, you find that the restaurant in Prairie City has had poor marks several times. You

Exhibit 14.1   Data on Restaurant Inspection

Time	Service	Food	Waiting Time in Minutes
10:00 a.m.	Excellent	OK	1
10:30 a.m.	Excellent	OK	2
11:00 a.m.	OK	Poor	5
11:30 a.m.	OK	Poor	7
12:00 noon	Poor	Good	9
12:30 p.m.	Very poor	Excellent	10
1:00 p.m.	Poor	Excellent	7
1:30 p.m.	Good	OK	6
2:00 p.m.	Excellent	Poor	5
3:00 p.m.	Excellent	Poor	5½
4:30 p.m.	Excellent	Poor	4
5:00 p.m.	Good	OK	4
5:30 p.m.	Good	OK	4
6:00 p.m.	OK	Poor	6
6:30 p.m.	Poor	Excellent	7
7:00 p.m.	Poor	Excellent	8
7:30 p.m.	Poor	Good	6
8:00 p.m.	Excellent	Poor	4
9:00 p.m.	Excellent	Poor	3
10:00 p.m.	Poor	Poor	2

decide to have a special inspection. Your company has three types of inspections: the spot check, two times in one day; the intermediate inspection, five times in two days; the in-depth inspection, twenty times over a four-day period.

Several people inspect the Prairie City restaurant, and you organize their observations as shown in Exhibit 14.1. Because previous reports indicated problems in quality, waiting time (company standard is five minutes), and service, the special inspection has concentrated on those areas.

After you have organized the data, you must analyze it. Some people, when confronted with a lot of information in text or table form, are overwhelmed by the detail and start verbalizing the table. In the restaurant example, verbalizing could take the following form:

> At ten o'clock service was excellent, the food was OK, and waiting time was one minute. At 10:30 a.m. service was excellent, food was OK, waiting time was two minutes. . . .

This is not analysis of the data. Analysis should clarify information and not simply repeat it.

At the beginning of the analysis you have to determine categories for grouping the data. The way you group the data will depend partially on the problem you want to solve. The restaurant data falls into two patterns, off-hour and rush hour. The rush hour can be further divided into two time segments:

	Service	Food	Waiting Time
Off-Hours	Excellent	OK to poor	Within or slightly over standard
First Half of Rush Hour	Good to Excellent	OK	Over standard
Second Half of Rush Hour	Poor	Excellent	Far over standard

Your analysis based on this grouping of the data might be:

> The data suggests three distinct patterns: (1) off-hours, (2) first half of busy hours, and (3) second half of busy hours.
>
> During slow times the food is poor; service is excellent; waiting time exceeds the standard only slightly.
>
> During the first segment of the rush hour service is good; food is acceptable; waiting time begins to increase.
>
> During the second segment of the rush hour service deteriorates; the food is excellent; waiting time exceeds the standard by up to five minutes.

This sample analysis emphasizes the grouping of data into off-hours and two segments of rush hours. Service, food quality, and waiting time are discussed under each. An alternative would be to use service, food quality, and waiting time as the major groupings. The analysis might then read:

> Service, food quality, and waiting time are influenced by customer traffic. Service is excellent during off-hours; it deteriorates throughout the busy times. Food quality is poor during off-hours but improves as busy time progresses. Waiting time is within the standard only during off-hours. During busy hours waiting time always exceeds the standard. It is longest during peak times.

After you have analyzed your data, you must summarize your findings. If you write a complete analytical report, you must also draw conclusions and make recommendations.

DRAWING CONCLUSIONS

Conclusion
The conclusion establishes the meaning of the data in terms of the problem.

Drawing **conclusions** is a logical step after interpreting the data. Relevant conclusions are based on objective data analysis. In the final report the conclusions may come at the beginning. The actual sequence of the presentation will depend on the purpose of the report, the reader–writer relationship, and the opinions of the reader. If the requester of the report did not ask for conclusions and recommendations, the writer should not include them, of course.

Conclusions must come from the analysis, which seems obvious. Yet, reading some reports, you may wonder how the writer reached the conclusions. They do not seem to be supported by the data or the interpretation.

In the restaurant example, after you have analyzed the data and determined the patterns, you have to figure out what the patterns mean. You can draw conclusions related to the food, the service, and the length of waiting time during the three time periods. Because you are familiar with fast-food chains, you might draw the following conclusions based on the findings:

1. The food is poor or mediocre during off-hours and at the beginning of mealtimes because the cooks prepared too much. It has been waiting under warming lights.
2. The Prairie City restaurant does not follow company standards of quality. The cook keeps prepared food too long.
3. During busy times, the food that has been prepared ahead is used up. The fresh food is excellent. The staff is capable of serving quality food.
4. The time standard set by the company is met only during off-hours. The Prairie City restaurant is incapable of meeting demand at peak periods because it has too few employees. The company standards are unrealistic.
5. Service at the beginning of rush hours and during off-times is excellent when workers are rested and friendly. During rush periods the problems include the small number of employees, the layout of the counters, and the need for training in customer relations.

Some conclusions would not make sense. Based on the data you have, you cannot conclude that the noise from the traffic outside affects the courtesy of the employees. You cannot conclude that the French fries would be better if the potatoes were fresh rather than frozen. Without further investigation you could not conclude that the employees are purposely rude.

In summary, the conclusions must relate to the data. A strong background in the business is helpful. If you have worked in a fast-food chain, for example, you may better understand the problems. On the other hand, your experience might prevent you from seeing things you did not experience while working as a cook or a cashier.

You should present your conclusions in an orderly fashion and support each one with data. If your analysis was orderly and concentrated on major points, this task will be relatively easy.

You must draw conclusions based on the importance of the data. One rude cashier does not justify the conclusion that employees at that restaurant are inconsiderate and rude. Isolated instances and observations must be seen in perspective. In drawing conclusions, these guidelines will be helpful.

1. Conclusions must follow logically from the analysis.
2. Conclusions cannot introduce new material.
3. Conclusions must relate to the problem.
4. Several analysis points may lead to the same conclusions; one analysis point may lead to several conclusions.
5. Conclusions must be objective.

MAKING RECOMMENDATIONS

Recommendations
Recommendations are specific suggestions for solving the problem.

Just as the conclusions logically follow the analysis, so do the **recommendations** logically grow out of the conclusions. You cannot make recommendations unless you have drawn conclusions. If you do not draw conclusions about waiting time, you cannot make recommendations for solving the problem.

In the conclusions the report writer determines what the facts mean in view of the problem. In the recommendations the writer makes specific suggestions on how to solve the problem. The following examples illustrate the differences between conclusions and recommendations:

Conclusion:	*The test results show that the students were not sufficiently prepared for the test.*
Recommendation:	*Instructors should schedule a review session before each test.*
Conclusion:	*Sales dropped because of poor quality control.*
Recommendation:	*The company should hire a quality-control inspector.*
Conclusion:	*The secretaries seem to be overworked.*
Recommendation:	*The company should study workflow and workload to determine possible solutions.*

In these examples, additional recommendations might be made to solve the problem. When making recommendations, the report writer must determine whether they make sense in terms of the environment.

Recommendations must be specific. The simple statement that something has to be done is meaningless because it provides no specific guidance for action.

Sometimes writers are tempted to hedge. They do not want to commit themselves by saying, "Based on the conclusions, I recommend. . . ." or "A careful consideration of the conclusions suggests that the problem can be solved if the following recommendations are implemented." They are afraid of being direct. Because they fear blame if the recommendations do not solve the problem, they hide behind conditional clauses such as:

1. Maybe the company might want to consider . . .
2. Perhaps it would be helpful to . . .
3. Under certain circumstances it might perhaps be advantageous . . .

These are not recommendations. They do not direct the reader to take action. Furthermore, all of the vague words—*might, perhaps,* and *maybe*—utterly confuse the reader. If the writer concludes that no definite recommendations can be made based on the data, she should say so *clearly*.

Not every conclusion warrants a separate recommendation. Several conclusions might be combined. Sometimes several problems can be corrected with one recommendation. On the other hand, one conclusion may lead to several recommendations.

To return to the restaurant example, some logical recommendations can be based on the conclusions:

1. Survey how many hamburgers are served each day between 10:00 a.m. and 11:00 a.m., between 11:00 a.m. and noon, and between noon and 1:00 p.m. (The time span has to coincide with the busy hours and off-hours).
2. Revise the volume of preparation based on the sales records.

3. Compare the waiting time with other restaurants in the chain. If the others have similar problems, the time standard needs to be reexamined and possibly revised. If others have no problem, then examine reasons for the problem at Prairie City. (Of course, if you already know that the others meet the standard, you must change the recommendation.)
4. Train employees in courtesy.
5. Examine shift schedules with the goal of bringing in fresh employees at the middle of the busy hours in order to improve the service.

All of these recommendations come out of the conclusions. They are direct and in command form: *survey, revise, compare, train, examine.* The writer does not hedge. The reader knows exactly what is recommended and what is expected.

To make recommendations more effective, you should follow these guidelines:

1. Give the recommendation in a declarative statement.
2. Avoid words like *perhaps* and *maybe.*
3. Itemize your recommendations. This procedure is not absolutely necessary, but it will help the reader. It may also help you in reevaluating your recommendations.
4. Put each recommendation in a separate sentence. If you have several recommendations in one sentence, the reader may miss one.

Some writers combine conclusions and recommendations at the end of the report. Unless they are lengthy and detailed, this practice is acceptable; however, the novice writer may confuse the two. In short reports writers may draw conclusions as they go along, taking care to make a distinction between conclusions and recommendations in their minds. If conclusions are drawn at the end of every point in the analysis, only the recommendations would appear at the end of the report.

IMPROVING ANALYTICAL SKILLS

Many approaches are possible in learning how to analyze, draw conclusions, and make recommendations. One is to learn analysis by careful evaluation of other writers' reports. This involves examining how a good writer succeeds and how a poor writer fails.

As you look at a report, you can analyze the organization and ask whether it makes sense. You can examine the method, analysis, presentation, headings, summary, conclusions, and recommendations. You may have to read the report or article several times, and you may have to think about it. Then you will be able to determine whether you agree that it was the best way to present the data and the most effective analysis possible.

In effect, you will critically analyze the material by first abstracting the facts and then answering these questions:

1. Is the problem statement clear?
2. What are the strong and weak points of the methodology?
   a. How old is the data?

    b. Were the statistical tools appropriate?

    c. What sampling techniques were used?

3. Does the author accomplish in the report or article what was intended? For example, if the author at the beginning promises an answer to a certain question, you should check for the answer. If the author promises to examine four major points, you should check for the four points. You also must determine whether those four points are the most important ones.

4. Does the discussion relate to the problem or does it go off on tangents?

5. Is the discussion objective? (Check the discussion against the interpretation guidelines.)

6. Do the conclusions logically follow the discussion?

7. Are the recommendations clear, and are they a logical outcome of the conclusions?

An evaluation of the analysis of another writer's work should help you to improve your own analytical skills. Analysis takes practice and experience yet in many ways is a natural process. When you read a newspaper article on a controversial topic, you probably evaluate the arguments as you go along. By the end of the article you either agree or disagree.

Often your conclusion is based on emotional approval or disapproval rather than on a rational analysis of the data, however. In many cases the supporting data in newspaper articles may be weak. The difference between this type of analysis and research analysis is scientific orientation. In research analysis you weigh the data carefully, disregarding personal feelings. You do not draw conclusions without support or proof. You have a definite methodology for objective analysis.

SUMMARY OF LEARNING OBJECTIVES

To be familiar with analysis aids.

An awareness of the history of the problem, an understanding of personal biases, consultation with others, a critical viewpoint, and a sound understanding of research tools can help the writer overcome common analysis problems.

To become aware of problems in analyzing data.

Some of the more frequent problems in analyzing material are differing views of reality, a craving for the sensational, the temptation to make value judgments, the comparison of noncomparable data, an inability to distinguish the important from the unimportant, and confusion about cause–effect relationships.

To analyze data.

The writer groups the data and establishes patterns in order to examine the problem in detail. When analyzing, the writer must have the problem and the purpose of the report clearly in mind.

To draw conclusions.

Conclusions must be based on the analysis. They must be clear and concise. The conclusions cannot introduce new material.

To make recommendations.

Recommendations must be specific. Often they are itemized.

Although conclusions and recommendations can be combined, usually the best practice is to keep them separate. Conclusions are based on the facts and the analysis of the facts. Recommendations, on the other hand, are more subjective. They are based, to some extent at least, on the opinions of the writer.

To learn to analyze well takes time. Sometimes it helps to examine the analysis of material in reports and articles written by others.

KEY TERMS

Analysis   Recommendations
Conclusion

QUESTIONS AND DISCUSSION POINTS

1. Discuss the differences between analysis, conclusions, and recommendations.
2. What are some of the basic fallacies in analyzing data?
3. How can you improve your analytical skills?
4. What is the purpose of analysis?
5. Discuss the importance of grouping data before analysis.
6. Discuss the wording of recommendations.

EXERCISES

1. Read an article in your major field and write a critical analysis.
2. Analyze the organization and presentation of data in a newspaper article.
3. Select several tables in journals and newspapers. After you analyze them, compare your analysis with that of the author of the article.
4. You work in Prairie City for a real estate agency owned by Andrew Wood. Prairie City is growing as a result of attracting a major automobile assembly plant, but Andrew Wood knows that ultimately the housing market will be affected by national trends. He, therefore, asked you to collect information on home buyers in Prairie City and the nation as a whole. You have assembled the data in the accompanying table.

    Write a memo report. Present the information, analyze it, and draw conclusions about the situation in Prairie City as it compares with the nation and other metropolitan areas. Even though a decision on the expansion of the real estate agency will depend on many additional factors, such as competition and available funds, make recommendations based on your conclusion.

Prairie City Metro Area Home Buyer Profile

The following statistics on McLean County house buyers were gleaned from mortgage surveys done by the U.S. League of Savings Institutions. Last year's Prairie City metro profile is compared with those for small metro areas nationwide, North Central states, and the nation.

	Prairie City			Small Metros	North Central	National
	1983	**1985**	**1987**	**1987**	**1987**	**1987**
Traits						
Median age	31.1	33.1	32.8	36.2	35.1	37.0
Unmarried	15.0%	30.4%	27.7%	22.6%	24.3%	26.0
1 and 2-person house	51.0%	55.4%	42.5%	46.1%	48.3%	45.8%
2nd income important†	70.1%	62.9%	72.7%	54.6%	58.5%	54.5%
First time buyers	21.6%	38.6%	39.6%	30.9%	37.0%	35.1%
Condo buyers	6.0%	2.2%	1.6%	7.6%	6.8%	13.5%
New houses	19.0%	12.4%	18.4%	23.8%	20.5%	24.8%
25-year-plus houses	41.0%	48.3%	37.2%	28.2%	40.6%	30.0%
Medium house (sq. ft.)	1,283	1,576	1,430	1,574	1,525	NA*
Annual Household Income						
Under $24,999	17.0%	19.8%	15.5%	16.0%	15.0%	NA
$25,000–$34,999	26.0%	27.5%	24.1%	21.9%	22.6%	NA
$35,000–$44,999	35.0%	23.1%	21.7%	20.6%	22.7%	NA
$45,000–55,999	22.0%	29.7%	17.0%	16.2%	15.5%	NA
Over $55,000	NA	NA	21.7%	25.3%	24.2%	NA
Median income	$36,006	$35,448	$38,328	$40,200	$40,200	$45,996
Purchase Price						
Under $50,000	44.0%	41.3%	21.5%	22.7%	24.4%	NA
$50,000–$89,999	40.0%	42.4%	50.6%	40.8%	42.6%	NA
$90,000–$119,999	12.0%	6.6%	14.9%	15.2%	14.6%	NA
$120,000–$139,999	4.0%	9.7%	8.8%	8.0%	7.1%	NA
Over $140,000	NA	NA	4.2%	13.3%	11.3%	NA
Median price	$54,000	$55,900	$78,000	$75,500	$73,971	$95,000
Monthly Housing Expenses						
Less than $600	39.0%	45.7%	33.7%	46.1%	46.3%	NA
$601–$900	48.0%	33.7%	41.3%	29.2%	31.4%	NA
More than $900	13.0%	20.0%	25.0%	24.7%	22.3%	NA

(*continued*)

	Prairie City			Small Metros 1987	North Central 1987	National 1987
	1983	1985	1987			
Median Monthly						
Total	$682	$668	$726	$684	$671	$822
Mortgage	496	481	489	482	461	601
Real estate tax	71	71	97	77	90	96
Utilities	100	100	120	100	100	100
Hazard insurance	15	16	20	25	20	25
Downpayment						
10% or less	34.0%	34.8%	31.0%	21.2%	15.6%	NA
20% or more	29.0%	32.6%	29.1%	46.5%	50.8%	NA
Median paid	$8,403	$7,550	$12,700	$15,000	$15,000	NA

* Not available.

† Percentage of households with two adults in which income contributed by a second earner accounted for 10 percent or more of total household income.

MARKET WATCH/MAGAZINE ADVERTISING

MAGAZINE AD revenue in the first quarter of 1989 rose about 10% from the year before to $1.45 billion. Growth in the number of ad pages was more sluggish, however, at 2.6%.

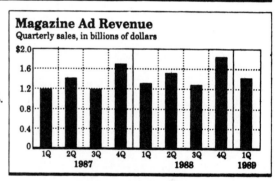

Magazine Ad Revenue
Quarterly sales, in billions of dollars

Top 10 magazines in advertising pages

	AD PAGES IN 1st QUARTER 1989	CHANGE FROM 1988 1st QUARTER
TV Guide	893.00	-11.1%
Business Week	891.66	8.2
People Weekly	804.10	7.9
Vogue	774.51	-7.5
Bride's	737.34	4.6
Sports Illustrated	704.18	-7.3
Forbes	628.44	4.3
New York	624.48	0.4
Fortune	622.44	-1.1
Modern Bride	611.81	11.4

Top 10 advertising categories in revenue

	1st QUARTER 1989 (in millions)	CHANGE FROM 1988 1st QUARTER
Automotive	$217.2	2.1%
Direct response	148.2	11.6
Toiletries and cosmetics	125.4	9.9
Business services	110.0	17.8
Food	103.3	17.9
Tobacco	100.0	35.4
Travel	94.7	19.5
Apparel	87.5	12.2
Computers	56.4	9.0
Retail	36.9	15.1

Source: Leading National Advertisers, Publishers Information Bureau

Source: *The Wall Street Journal*, 1989.

5. Part of your job in marketing research for a national women's magazine is to evaluate trends in print advertising. You have assembled the information in the table at the bottom of page 318. Analyze the data. Draw conclusions about the changes observed and the implications for your magazine.

6. Gail Harmony's company allows employees to take two 15-minute breaks, one mid-morning and one mid-afternoon. Aware that many people in her department take extended breaks, Gail has observed half of her workers for the past few weeks. Her notes show that 80 percent of those she observed go to the cafeteria for break. On the average, they come back about 12 minutes late. The people who remain in the office return to their desks within the allotted time. The problem is that the cafeteria is on another floor from the office, which has no coffee area.

   Office workers are paid $400 a week. As Gail observed, the company pays many of them for time during which they do not work. She believes that if a beverage and snack machine were available in the office, people would probably stay in the office for break and be back at work on time. She has determined the following:

- Two vending machines would cost about $2,500. The beverage machine would dispense coffee, hot water, tea, and soft drinks. The snack machine would offer candy bars, cookies, and an assortment of chips and nuts.
- The seller of the machines also stocks and maintains them. Gail's company would not incur any expense beyond the initial purchase price.
- The office has enough unused space to accommodate the machines.

Gail has written the following memo based on her research.

TO: Vice-President of Administrative Affairs

FROM: Gail Harmony

SUBJECT: Coffee Breaks

DATE: October 15, 19XX

Office Workers Take Extended Breaks

The office workers in my department are taking long breaks to get to the coffee shop downstairs. Elevators are crowded, and a number of other departments have breaks at the same time. Of the 50 people I observed, 40 came back an average of 12 minutes late from their breaks. As the following calculation shows, this costs the company a lot of money.

Wasted time per worker/week: 30 minutes × 5 = 150 min or 2.5 hrs.
Wasted time for office: 2.5 hrs × 40 = 100 hrs.
Cost of wasted time/week: 100 × $10/hr. = $1,000
My office pays $1,000 per week for which it gets no work in return.

Possible Solution

Since most people leave the office to get something to drink during break, people might stay in the office if coffee, tea, and soft drinks were available in the office.

The company can have a beverage machine and a snack machine installed for $2,500. There is enough space to accommodate the machines. The firm that sells the machines maintains them and stocks them. After the initial investment, our firm would not incur any additional cost.

The calculation assumes that all employees would be back from break on time. That may be somewhat idealistic. A number of employees may still want to go to the cafeteria to get away from the office and to meet some friends from other departments. However, even if only half the people who currently leave now stay in the office for breaks, the machines will still be worth it.

Recommendation

We might want to think about getting a vending machine to solve the problem.

Critique Gail's report, comparing her analysis, conclusions, and recommendations with the facts as stated. Rewrite the report.

Additional Problems for analysis of data can be found in the "Cases" section at the end of the book.

PRESENTATION OF
BUSINESS REPORTS

■

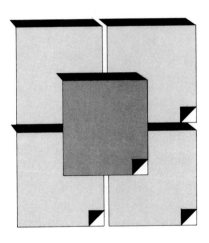

■

VISUAL AIDS

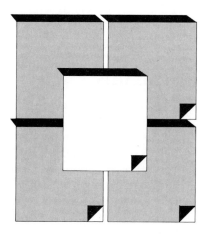

Learning Objectives

- To understand the purpose of visual aids.
- To understand the underlying principles of tables and figures.
- To design effective and appropriate tables and figures.
- To understand the role of computer graphics in report writing.

Sometimes you may organize the results of statistical analysis into tables and graphs and then analyze the data further. At other times you may want to do an in-depth analysis of the information and then present the results in a table or graph. Or you may simultaneously analyze the findings and prepare visual aids.

A visual presentation of the material can help you analyze your material and, as a result, write a convincing and effective report. The visual presentation will also help the reader to understand the report.

THE PURPOSE OF VISUAL AIDS

When designing visual aids, you will follow many of the planning steps discussed in Chapter 7. Without a clear understanding of the problem, the purpose of the report, or the needs of the potential reader, you would find it difficult to create effective visual material.

For example, a line graph showing an upward sales trend might provide enough information if used in a public-relations report for customers. If your task is to forecast sales, however, you would find such a graph totally inadequate. You would need a detailed table that gives sales by product, month, and geographic area. In addition, you would need figures to compare this month's sales with those in the same month of the previous year. You might also include graphs to show, at a quick glance, the trends in sales.

As a first step, you will need to determine whether the visual aid is a supplement to the text or whether the visual presentation *is* the report. That decision will shape the composition and entire appearance of the report. Assume, for example, that you are in the business of repairing appliances and heating and cooling systems. Over the past few years an increasing number of customers have complained about the cost of having a repairman come to the house to fix the air conditioning, the refrigerator, or the furnace. They argue that the repairman charges too much for the time it takes him to repair the appliance. Many customers believe that the money they pay goes directly into the pocket of the repairman or the owner as income. How can you tell your customers what your costs are? You might talk to them or write a memo, but most customers would not read a report justifying your price. Writing such a report would probably be a waste of effort.

You need something that conveys your message quickly. A number of businesses use the back of the payment receipt for the purpose. As illustrated in Exhibit 15.1, this type of report is actually a sequence of pictures illustrating the factors that contribute to the price. Anyone who looks at it has instant information on fringe benefits, taxes, and overhead costs. The report enables the customer to look at the price in perspective. Similar reports are frequently used in public-relations material because they make a complex point in a simplified way.

Used appropriately, the picture report can be effective, but it also has limitations. If you wanted to examine and, if necessary, redesign your firm's rate structure for repairs, you could not use a picture report. It simply would not give enough information to explain the new rates. In this case you would

Exhibit 15.1   **Picture Report**

use an in-depth report to examine expenses such as taxes, materials, wages, fringe benefits, office cost, building maintenance, and heating and cooling. You would give precise figures and an analysis of the figures. You would need to decide *how* to spread the overhead cost over all the services your firm provides. You would also have to consider the competition. Finally, you would present a detailed analysis of some of the most frequently performed repair services. Because presentation and analysis are the main aspects of this type of report, the tables would *supplement* the text and clarify the figures and cost items, but they would not replace it.

Both the picture report and the in-depth report deal with the firm's expenses and the charge to the customer, but the purpose of the two reports is not the same. The first illustrates the business expenses so that the customer understands and accepts the price; the second helps management to set and evaluate the prices charged to the customer. The different purposes determine the character of the reports and the role of the visuals in them.

TABLES

Tables are a systematic arrangement of data in rows and columns. A company presenting information on its income could provide that information in text form. In its annual report, for example, Dow Jones might have written:

In 1988 Dow Jones & Company had net earnings of $228,178 on total revenue of $1,603,110. Operating expenses amounted to $1,251,333.

However, the company did not present the information in sentence form but in a table (Exhibit 15.2). The information is easier to grasp in tabular form because the facts are categorized and arranged systematically. In addition, the table makes comparison of several years easy.

Exhibit 15.2

Tabular Organization of Income Information

CONSOLIDATED STATEMENTS OF INCOME

Dow Jones & Company, Inc.
For the years ended December 31. 1988. 1987 and 1986

(in thousands except per share amounts)	1988	1987	1986
REVENUES:			
Advertising	$ 685,931	$ 703,780	$ 678,247
Circulation	287,217	283,916	264,350
Information services and other	629,962	326,747	192,270
Total revenues	1,603,110	1,314,443	1,134,867
EXPENSES:			
News, production and delivery	445,510	351,828	287,656
Selling, administrative and general	437,087	356,247	312,778
Newsprint	139,432	134,301	119,277
Second class postage and alternate delivery	89,095	86,322	85,394
Depreciation and amortization (Note 1)	140,209	89,646	66,132
Operating expenses	1,251,333	1,018,344	871,237
Operating income	351,777	296,099	263,630
OTHER INCOME (DEDUCTIONS):			
Investment income	8,984	5,203	5,240
Interest expense	(28,597)	(16,514)	(8,592)
Equity in earnings of associated companies (Note 4)	5,276	35,687	21,368
Gain on disposition of investments (Notes 2 & 3)	106,495	42,208	49,426
Other, net	5,210	1,810	251
Income before income taxes and minority interest (Note 7)	449,145	364,493	331,323
Income taxes (Note 7)	182,080	151,194	147,961
Income before minority interest	267,065	213,299	183,362
Minority interest	38,887	10,281	
NET INCOME	$ 228,178	$ 203,018	$ 183,362
PER SHARE (Note 12):			
Net income	$2.35	$2.10	$1.89
Cash dividends	$ .68	$ .64	$ .553

The accompanying notes are an integral part of the financial statements.
Source: Dow Jones, *Annual Report,* 1988.

Exhibit 15.3

Ruled Table

Table 4

Would you please send the following items:

Item	Order Number	Color	Quantity	Price/ Unit	Total Price
Cotton	103/254	white	1 Bolt	$ 50.00	$ 50.00
Linen	253/689	red	2 Bolts	200.00	400.00
Silk	587/052	blue	1 Bolt	600.00	600.00
Wool	932/853	green	3 Bolts	400.00	1,200.00
Total					$2,250.00

In its simplest form a table can be part of the text. It may even be part of a sentence:

> We would like to order
> 1 bolt of linen #333/256 white at $10.00/yard,
> 1 bolt of Georgette #438/714 blue at $13.55/yard,
> 2 bolts of cotton #452/436 green at $5.35/yard.

Ruled Table
Headings are set off with horizontal lines.

Boxed Table
The boxed table uses horizontal and vertical lines to separate data.

In Exhibit 15.3 the writer believed it would be advantageous to use column heads, row titles, and rules. The result is a **ruled table**, which enables the reader to immediately separate the descriptors from the table data. The table might have a separate title and number, but this one is simple enough that it could also be incorporated in the text.

As a table becomes more complex, the need for setting it off from the text increases. The writer can add vertical lines to separate columns and create a **boxed table** as in Exhibit 15.4. The writer can also put a frame around the

Exhibit 15.4

Boxed Table

**Total Sales of Clover Department Stores, 1980–1990
(millions of U.S. dollars)**

Year	A	B	C	D	E	Total
1980	12	8	10	20	10	60
1981	12	10	9	20	14	65
1982	15	13	13	24	15	80
1983	18	14	16	25	17	90
1984	21	17	16	26	20	100
1985	25	23	22	35	25	130
1986	27	24	23	35	26	135
1987	28	26	25	36	25	140
1988	28	27	25	38	27	145
1989	30	31	27	42	30	160
1990	32	34	34	50	40	190

Branches — Spanner Head
Stubs
Stub Head
Column Heads

entire table including the title, source notes, and footnotes. This results in a framed or fully boxed table, as in Exhibit 15.5.

Labels added to Exhibit 15.4 identify the various parts of a table. The row titles are called stubs. The stub head identifies the stubs. In this particular table the stubs are years. Each column has a title or column head. The spanner further identifies the column heads. In this table the spanner head tells the reader that the column heads represent branches of Clover Department Stores.

Entries can also be separated by horizontal rules; however, rules should be used in tables only if they are functional. Look at the stock quotations in *The Wall Street Journal* and imagine that horizontal and vertical rules separated all the entries. They would create confusion rather than clarity.

Usually the column heads are at the top and the stubs are at the left margin of the table. In wide tables the writer may repeat the stubs on the right side of the table to facilitate reading. If columns are long, the column heads may be repeated at the bottom of the table. The decision will be influenced by the nature of the data.

In the stock quotations in *The Wall Street Journal* (Exhibit 15.6) the stubs are actually in the center of the entries. The stubs, in this case company names, separate the long-term price from the current price. Because the print is small and the rows are very close together, this arrangement makes it easier to read across the line.

The decision as to which information to put in the columns and which in the rows is not always obvious. If you want to design a table that shows the sales figures of Clover Department Stores by product line for each branch, for example, you can treat the branches either as stubs or as column heads. Exhibit 15.7 illustrates both possibilities.

Exhibit 15.5   **Fully Boxed Table**

Table 5
Breakdown of Sales by Product Line for Clover Department Stores, 1980–1990 (Millions of U.S. Dollars)

Year	Clothing	Appliances	Furniture	Total
1980	30	20	10	60
1981	30	20	15	65
1982	35	25	20	80
1983	37	30	27	94
1984	42	33	25	100
1985	53	42	35	130
1986	55	43	37	135
1987	58	45	37	140
1988	60	46	39	145
1989	63	55	42	160
1990	75	64	51	190

Exhibit 15.6 — Table Arrangement in *The Wall Street Journal* Stock Quotations

Stubs   Column Heads

THE WALL STREET JOURNAL TUESDAY, AUGUST 1, 1989 **C3**

NEW YORK STOCK EXCHANGE COMPOSITE TRANSACTIONS

Quotations as of 4:30 p.m. Eastern Time
Monday, July 31, 1989

Source: New York Stock Exchange Composite Transactions. (1989, August 1). *The Wall Street Journal*, p. C3.

Your decision on whether to use a descriptor as a stub head or a column head will often be based on mechanical considerations. Assume, for example, that you want to provide income statistics for ten different countries over the past five years. You could use the names of the countries either as stub heads or column heads; however, they have different lengths, and some may be too long to fit on one line if used as column heads. Years, on the other hand, will easily fit in columns, and the columns will be the same width. Therefore, arranging the table with countries as stub heads and years as column heads makes more sense.

You must also decide the order in which to present the information. Countries, for example, are usually presented in alphabetical order. You could, however, arrange them from highest to lowest income, group them by geographical area or political orientation, or divide them into developed and developing countries. The arrangement will depend on what you want to emphasize in your report.

At times you may not have complete information. In the example, you might not have income information for all ten countries for all five years. You must indicate the missing data by entering *n.a.* for *not available* or a dash in place of the amount. You cannot use a zero, which would indicate that the country had no income in a particular year.

In many tables you may have numbers representing dollar amounts, acres, bushels, pounds, or gallons. Because the table would be crowded if you repeated the unit of measurement beside every number, you can omit it except with the first number in the column. The dollar columns in Exhibit 15.3 are an example. When all data in the table is in the same unit of measurement, you can indicate this in a table subtitle, as in Exhibits 15.4 and 15.5. Spanner heads may be used, as in Exhibit 15.4, to avoid repeating the same word or words in several column heads.

Exhibit 15.7

Stubs and Column Placement of Data

Table 8
Breakdown of Sales Figures by Product Line for Each Branch of Clover Department Stores, 1989 (Millions of U.S. Dollars)

Branch	Clothing	Appliances	Furniture	Total
A	15 (50%)	10 (33%)	5 (17%)	30 (100%)
B	12 (38%)	15 (48%)	4 (12%)	31 (100%)
C	12 (44%)	10 (37%)	5 (19%)	27 (100%)
D	20 (48%)	15 (36%)	7 (16%)	42 (100%)
E	16 (53%)	8 (27%)	6 (20%)	30 (100%)

Table 8
Breakdown of Sales Figures by Product Line for Each Branch of Clover Department Stores, 1989 (Millions of U.S. Dollars)

Product	Branch				
	A	B	C	D	E
Appliances	10 (33%)	15 (48%)	10 (37%)	15 (36%)	8 (27%)
Clothing	15 (50%)	12 (38%)	12 (44%)	20 (48%)	16 (53%)
Furniture	5 (17%)	4 (12%)	5 (19%)	7 (16%)	6 (20%)
Total	30 (100%)	31 (100%)	27 (100%)	42 (100%)	30 (100%)

FIGURES

Figures provide overall information and impressions. In that sense, figures and tables complement each other. A report writer, for example, may present data in a table and also highlight the trends in a figure. Tables provide the reader with exact information, whereas figures concentrate on the visual impact of trends. At a glance the reader knows whether sales have increased or decreased, whether stock prices have gone up or down. The reader also gains some impression of the magnitude of the increase or decrease. Some of the most frequently used figures in business reports are line graphs, bar graphs, and pie charts.

Line Graphs

In line graphs the dependent variable is *always* shown on the *Y*-axis (vertical), and the independent variable is *always* shown on the *X*-axis (horizontal). If you want to show sales over a ten-year period, sales are the dependent variable, and the years are the independent variable; therefore, sales are shown on the *Y*-axis and the years on the *X*-axis.

The *Y*-axis must start at 0; the *X*-axis need not. If the values you plot on the *Y*-axis are high numbers, starting at 0 can be cumbersome and detract from the effectiveness of the graph. In that case you can cut the *Y*-axis. Three ways of accomplishing this are shown in Exhibit 15.8. If you decide to cut the *Y*-axis, you must follow two basic rules:

1. All lines must be on the same side of the cut. You cannot have one line above and one line below the cut.
2. No line may cross the cut.

You must also pay attention to the scale you use for the axes. The difficulty is to determine what a *correct scale* is. Most people agree that an incorrect scale distorts the data but do not agree on a correct scale. The examples in Exhibit 15.9 show how the same data can give a different visual impression if the scale is changed.

A general guideline for scale is that the space formed by drawing a vertical line from the first value on the *X*-axis and a horizontal line from the first value of the *Y*-axis should approximate a square. However, the marked intervals on the axes could be changed so that there is still visual manipulation of the data even though the first marked interval on the *X*-axis and the *Y*-axis form a square (Exhibit 15.9). In a distorted graph the figures are correct. The writer does not manipulate the data. The distortion is visual.

The problem is that most people will remember the slope of the line rather than the numbers on the axes. If a line to show increases in union wages is almost vertical, people will remember the slope rather than the exact numbers. If you design several graphs for comparison purposes, you must use the same scale for each graph in order to avoid distortion. If you compare wage

---

Exhibit 15.8   **Cutting the *Y*-Axis**

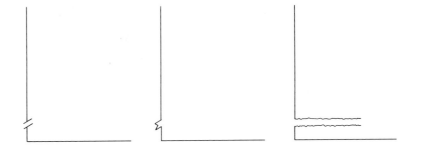

Exhibit 15.9 Scales of Coordinates and Visual Impact

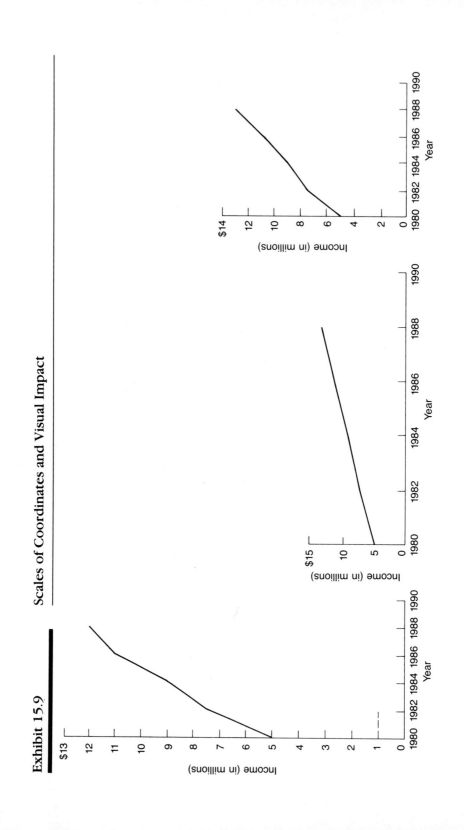

increases for various groups over the past ten years, for example, and you want to show the information in separate graphs, you must use the same scales for wages and for years in all of the graphs. You have an ethical duty to represent data fairly in visual aids.

Simple Line Graph. To show a change of sales figures over ten years for Clover Department Stores, you might use a simple line graph like the one in Exhibit 15.10. This and other graphs for Clover Department Stores are based on data presented in Exhibits 15.4, 15.5, and 15.7.

Multiple-Line Graph. Comparing data requires a graph with more than one line. If you want to compare the sales figures for Branches A, C, and D of Clover Department Stores, you can use a multiple-line graph, like the one in Exhibit 15.11. So that the lines are easy to distinguish, you can assign a different color

Exhibit 15.10   **Simple Line Graph**

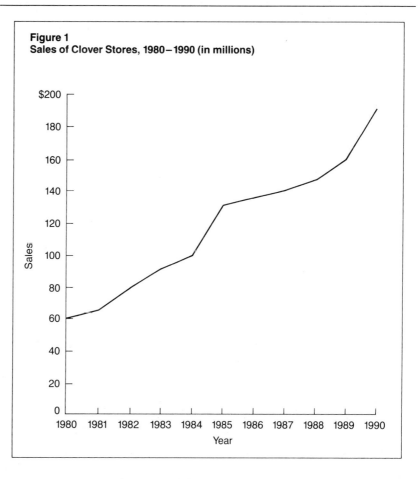

Figure 1
Sales of Clover Stores, 1980–1990 (in millions)

Exhibit 15.11   **Multiple Line Graph**

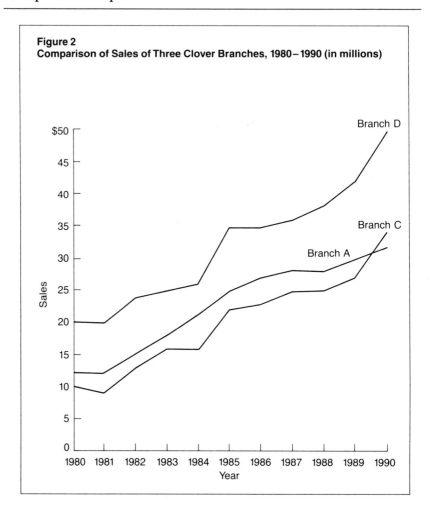

Figure 2
Comparison of Sales of Three Clover Branches, 1980–1990 (in millions)

Branch D

Branch C

Branch A

Legend
The legend provides the key to colors or patterns in the visual aid.

or pattern to each one. You can use a **legend** to identify the various lines, or you can label the lines directly on the graph. Users of a multiple-line graph will read every value from a point on the line they want to examine to the *X*-axis. For example, the sales figures for 1988 were as follows: Branch A, $28 million; Branch C, $25 million; and Branch D, $38 million.

A multiple-line graph with three lines is easy to read, especially if the lines are not too close together. More than four or five lines can have a negative influence on readability because the graph may appear too crowded. The exact limit depends on the data. If the lines are spread out, a multiple-line graph with five lines may be easy to read. If the lines are close together, the graph may appear crowded with four lines.

Exhibit 15.12   **Subdivided Line Graph**

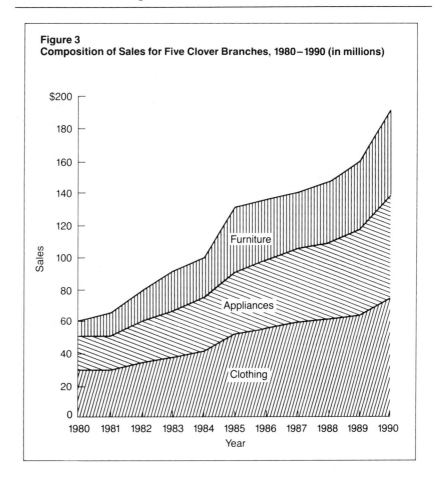

Figure 3
Composition of Sales for Five Clover Branches, 1980–1990 (in millions)

Subdivided Line Graph.   The subdivided line graph is also called a segmented or component line graph. It emphasizes the composition of data. For
example, Clover Department Stores have three major product groups: appliances, furniture, and clothes. The sales in these three areas over 11 years can
be presented in a subdivided line graph like the one in Exhibit 15.12.

Total sales are represented by the top line. Each individual product group is
represented by the area between the two lines framing the top and bottom of
the area. These areas are also called *bands*. The reader gains an impression of
the sales volume in each group, but, except for the band closest to the *X*-axis,
the exact values are difficult to determine. For example, in order to get the
value for 1988 for the second band, appliances, the reader would need to do
some arithmetic. This would involve reading the figure for 1988 at the top of

the appliance line and subtracting from it the value for 1988 clothing sales ($106 million less $60 million, or $46 million).

When trying to determine whether sales in a group have increased or decreased, looking at the shape of the curve is not enough. The curve on either side of the band may go up, and sales may still have declined. The important factor is the width of the band. If the band widens, then sales have increased; if the band narrows, sales have decreased. The subdivided line graph emphasizes the total and gives some impression of the magnitude of the individual components. You may decide to use both a multiple and a subdivided line graph to present data.

Bar Graphs

All of the bars in a bar graph must be the same width; differences are expressed only in the length of the bar. Some of the principles for constructing line graphs also apply to bar graphs. The axes must be labeled, and the intervals on the axes must be even. The bar graph can also be cut, and the same rules apply as for line graphs. If the axis is cut, all bars must be cut. Exhibit 15.13 illustrates what happens if they are not. Unlike line graphs, the depen-

Exhibit 15.13   **Visual Manipulation of Data**

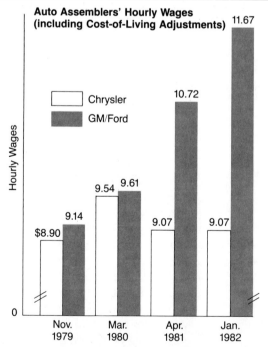

dent variable in bar graphs can be shown on either the horizontal or the vertical axis.

As you look at the wage figures for workers of the three auto manufacturers in Exhibit 15.13, the first impression is that the workers at GM and Ford earn more than twice as much as the workers at Chrysler. This visual impression is what most readers will remember. Only after examining the bar graph more carefully do you notice that the Y-axis is cut. The bars are not cut, however, and this omission leads to a misrepresentation of the data even though the wage figures are written on every bar. The visual impact is clearly misleading.

Simple Bar Graph.   If you want to show the sales figures for five branches of Clover Department Stores for 1989, the best way to present this data visually is in a simple bar chart, as shown in Exhibit 15.14. Here the sales figures are indicated on the Y-axis, and the five stores are on the X-axis. The result is a

Vertical Bar Graph
The bars sit on the X-axis.

vertical bar graph. In a vertical bar graph, the bars sit on the X-axis; that is, the dependent variable (sales) is on the Y-axis and the independent variable

Exhibit 15.14   **Simple Bar Graph**

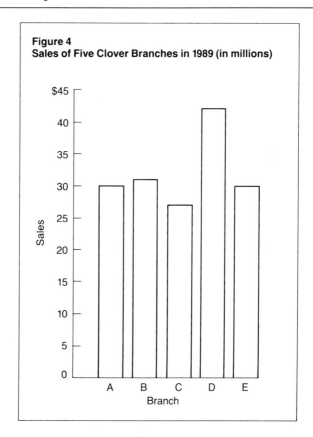

Figure 4
Sales of Five Clover Branches in 1989 (in millions)

Horizontal Bar Graph
The bars sit on the Y-axis.

(branches) is on the X-axis. You could change the graph to a **horizontal bar graph** by putting sales figures on the X-axis and the branches on the Y-axis. In this case, as illustrated in Exhibit 15.15, the dependent variable is on the X-axis and the independent variable on the Y-axis.

Some experts suggest that quantities should always be presented in a vertical bar graph, whereas distances are best shown in a horizontal bar graph. If you examine bar graphs in annual reports, newspapers, and scholarly business journals, however, you will find that this distinction does not always hold true. While it is true that many people do use horizontal graphs for distances and vertical graphs for quantities, distances and quantity are not necessarily the deciding factors.

Often the decision is based instead on the mechanics of page layout and available space. If you must compare five stores, you can easily put that comparison in a vertical bar graph with sales figures on the Y-axis. If you compare 20 stores, the vertical bar graph is not practical because of the difficulty of fitting 20 names on one line. You could type the names of the stores at a slant or vertically, but they would be difficult to read. A horizontal bar graph with the names of the stores to the left of the Y-axis is the best arrangement.

Exhibit 15.15   **Horizontal Bar Graph**

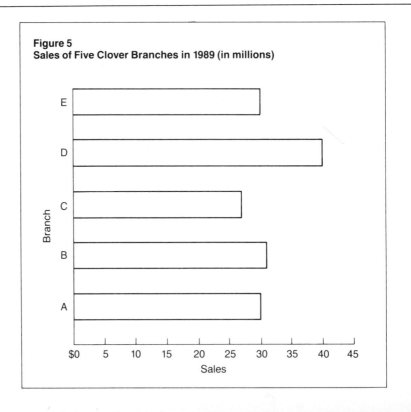

Figure 5
Sales of Five Clover Branches in 1989 (in millions)

Histogram. The histogram, illustrated in Exhibit 15.16, is a special type of simple bar graph. In a histogram the intervals between values are the same—in other words, a continuum, with no space between the bars. Age, weight, and income can be presented in a histogram.

You may wonder why the data, which is continuous, is not represented in a line graph. The age groups in the exhibit cover the same time intervals, and no age group is left out. The bars show how many people are in each bracket; however, the histogram does not show how many people are at each point in the bracket. If the brackets are small, the histogram approaches the continuum of a line graph. If the brackets are large, on the other hand, the data should be presented in a histogram.

Multiple-Bar Graph. To show a comparison of data, you can use a multiple-bar graph. For example, a comparison of the five branches of Clover Department Stores in the sales of clothes, appliances, and furniture is expressed in Exhibit 15.17. From the graph the reader can easily obtain figures for individual product sales but not the total sales figure. For that, the sales for clothes, appliances, and furniture must be added. To make comparisons easier, you

Exhibit 15.16 Histogram

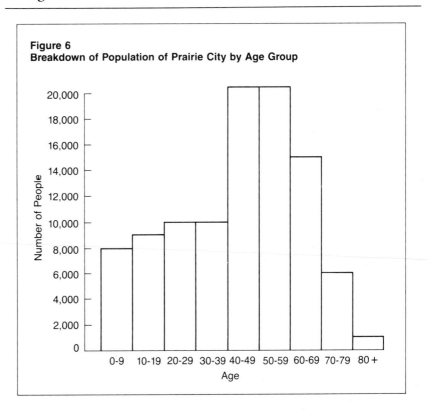

Figure 6
Breakdown of Population of Prairie City by Age Group

Exhibit 15.17   **Multiple Bar Graph**

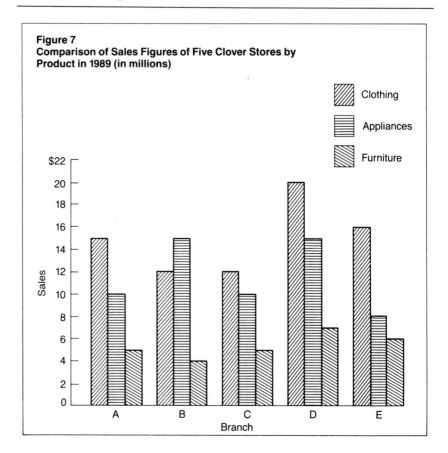

Figure 7
Comparison of Sales Figures of Five Clover Stores by
Product in 1989 (in millions)

should either crosshatch (use a graphic pattern) or color the bars and provide
a legend. At a glance the reader will then see which branch was highest in
furniture sales, which in clothing sales, and which in appliance sales. No rules
exist for determining how many parts each segment should have, but more
than three variables for one branch would crowd the graph and make reading
difficult.

Subdivided Bar Graph. The subdivided bar graph is also called a segmented
or component bar graph. The data used in Exhibit 15.7 are presented as a
subdivided bar graph in Exhibit 15.18. Each bar is the same size as in the
simple bar graph, but this time the bar is subdivided into sales components:
clothes, appliances, and furniture. The emphasis in the subdivided bar graph is
on the total. The reader gets some idea of the magnitude of the components
but, for exact sales figures, must make some arithmetic calculations. The writer
can insert the numbers into the bar segments to help the reader only if the bars
are large enough.

Exhibit 15.18   **Subdivided Bar Graph**

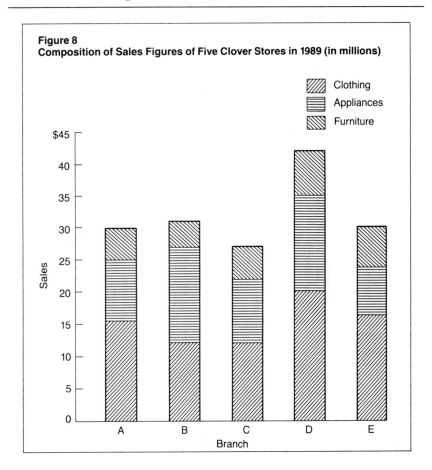

Figure 8
Composition of Sales Figures of Five Clover Stores in 1989 (in millions)

To decide between a multiple-bar graph and a subdivided bar graph, the writer must know whether to emphasize components or totals. In some cases the decision may be to present the data in both forms.

A special type of subdivided bar graph uses percentages rather than absolute figures. In Exhibit 15.19 all bars have the same length representing 100 percent. The various parts represent for example, appliance sales in Store A as a percentage of total sales in Store A and appliance sales in Store B as a percentage of total sales in Store B. The reader must keep in mind that a larger percentage figure does not necessarily represent a larger absolute figure.

To compare the several kinds of bar graphs, visualize the treatment of 1989 clothing sales for two Clover branches. Branch E sold $16 million and Branch D sold $20 million. In a multiple-bar graph, the bar for Branch E is shorter than for Branch D. In the subdivided bar graph showing absolute sales dollars, the clothing segment for Branch E is also shorter than for Branch D. In terms of

Exhibit 15.19   **Subdivided Bar Graph Based on Percentages**

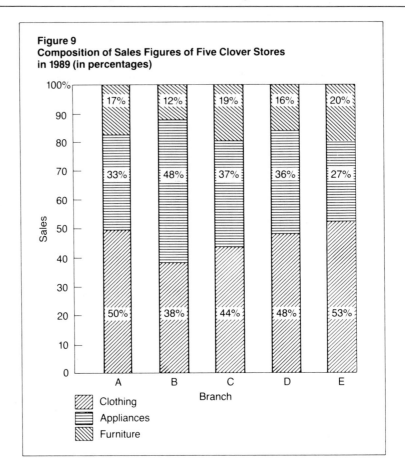

Figure 9
Composition of Sales Figures of Five Clover Stores
in 1989 (in percentages)

percentages, however, $16 million represents 53 percent of the total sales of Branch E, whereas $20 million represents only 48 percent of total sales of Branch D. In the subdivided bar graph showing percentages, therefore, the clothing segment for Branch E is larger than for Branch D.

The writer must tell the reader whether the report is about percentages or absolute figures, and the reader must take care in order to understand it. When either figure by itself might be misleading, the report should include both percentages and absolute figures. For example, conservatives argue that military spending has plummeted, whereas liberals argue that military spending is skyrocketing. Who is right? Both are. As a percentage of total budget, military spending has decreased; the absolute budget for the military has increased.

Advocates for either side usually do not point out the difference; they simply choose the argument that supports their point of view. The public, in the meantime, does not understand and may decide that both sides are lying. A business-report writer must ensure that the reader understands both the material and the context.

Bilateral Bar Graph. Bilateral bar graphs show both negative and positive values. The bars can be either vertical or horizontal. In the vertical bar graph the negative values are below the X-axis. In the horizontal bar graph the negative values are to the left of the Y-axis. Companies often show gains and losses in a bilateral bar graph, as in Exhibit 15.20. Clear labels are necessary for the positive and negative values.

Pictogram

The pictogram is related most closely to the bar graph. Instead of a bar, the pictogram uses an illustration of the product or item. Barrels might be used to represent crude oil production, houses to represent housing starts, or people to represent population figures. Exhibit 15.21, for example, shows the immigration figures for the United States between 1950 and 1980.

Pictograms must be constructed carefully because they can easily mislead the reader. One basic rule is that all the pictures must be the same size. Quantity is represented by the number of pictures, not by the size of the pictures. If automobile production has doubled since last year, for example, there should be twice as many cars representing this year's production. It would be unacceptable to keep the same number of cars and double their size. Changes in size would be misleading, because the reader would have difficulty making precise visual distinctions between the sizes of items.

Pie Charts

Pie charts are frequently used to show how a typical family spends each dollar of income or how a company spends or uses one dollar of revenue. The reason for using the pie graph is that it represents 100 percent. Because the dollar contains 100 cents, each cent equals one percent. The reader can have some understanding of how money is spent without converting percentages into absolute figures. Absolute or raw figures can be used in a pie chart, but the best practice is to show the percentages also. Each segment in the pie should be labeled and the percentages should be placed next to the descriptor. Clover Department Stores could represent the breakdown by product in 1990 in a pie chart like the one in Exhibit 15.22.

A pie chart with four to seven or eight segments is most effective. Too many segments may make it difficult to read. Coloring or cross-hatching can set off the various segments.

Exhibit 15.20   **Bilateral Bar Graph**

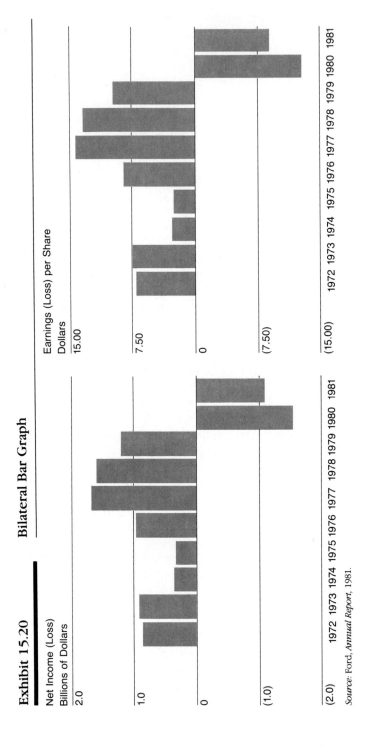

Net Income (Loss)
Billions of Dollars

2.0

1.0

0

(1.0)

(2.0)

1972 1973 1974 1975 1976 1977 1978 1979 1980 1981

Earnings (Loss) per Share
Dollars

15.00

7.50

0

(7.50)

(15.00)

1972 1973 1974 1975 1976 1977 1978 1979 1980 1981

Source: Ford, *Annual Report*, 1981.

Exhibit 15.21　　　　　**Pictogram**

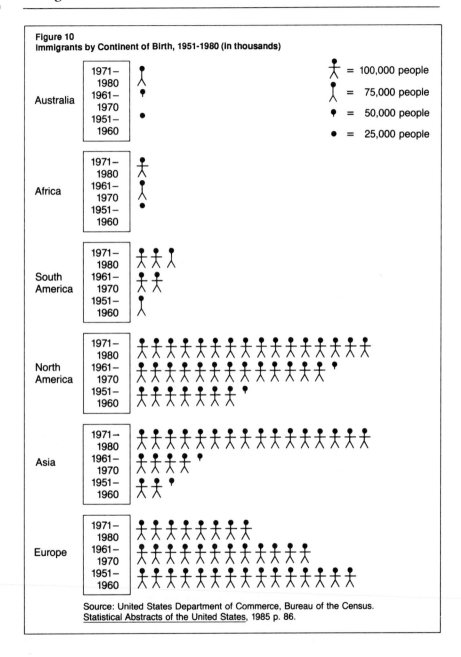

Figure 10
Immigrants by Continent of Birth, 1951-1980 (in thousands)

Source: United States Department of Commerce, Bureau of the Census.
Statistical Abstracts of the United States, 1985 p. 86.

Exhibit 15.22

Pie Chart

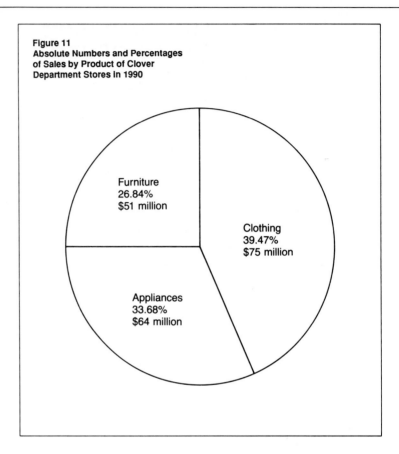

Figure 11
Absolute Numbers and Percentages
of Sales by Product of Clover
Department Stores In 1990

Furniture
26.84%
$51 million

Clothing
39.47%
$75 million

Appliances
33.68%
$64 million

Statistical Maps

Statistical maps are useful for illustrating sales territories, the location of branches in other countries, or production by geographic area. They are a combination of visual aids, as you can see in Exhibit 15.23. The most frequent combinations are:

- Geographic map and bar graph
- Geographic map and pictogram
- Geographic map and pie chart
- Geographic map and cross-hatching or color shading

The map in Exhibit 15.23 identifies temperature zones for one day in the United States. It also indicates weather fronts and precipitation.

Exhibit 15.23   Statistical Map

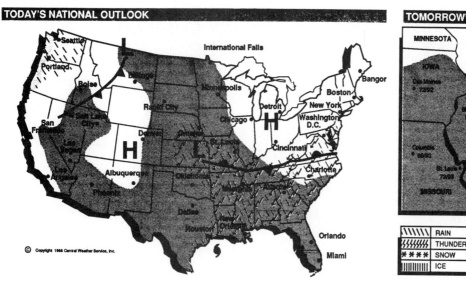

Diagrams

Diagrams are used frequently in technical descriptions. Because descriptions of a product or process tend to be abstract, an illustration can help the reader to understand the text better. Diagrams can show how to put a bicycle together, how to assemble toys, or how to repair a vacuum cleaner, as in Exhibit 15.24. They are used to show the electric circuits in a building. The diagram is a simplified presentation of a complex system.

Flowcharts

Flowcharts show processes. The workflow in an office or on an assembly line can be illustrated with the help of a flowchart. Because flowcharts show sequential steps, they can help to detect weak links in a process.

Flowcharts can be sophisticated and use specialized geometric symbols to classify the steps in a process. An oval usually stands for beginning and end, a diamond signifies a decision point, and the rectangle represents a major activity. Exhibit 15.25 illustrates the process for making investments. At the diamond, the investor must decide whether to go ahead with the investment. If the decision is to invest, the investor will initiate the steps necessary to purchase the stocks, bonds, or real estate. If the decision is *no*, the investor will go back to the start.

Exhibit 15.24   **Diagram for Vacuum Cleaner**

REPAIR PARTS FOR VACUUM CLEANER

The parts listed on these pages are only those parts which we feel the average person may want to replace himself.

If you need other parts or service, call your local store or catalog sales office. Give them the *Model Number:* 116_ _ _ _ _. The number is found on the bottom of each unit. They will have a complete listing of all replacement parts for your vacuum cleaner.

PARTS FOR POWER-MATE® ATTACHMENT

(THE POWER-MATE HAS ITS OWN MODEL NUMBER.)

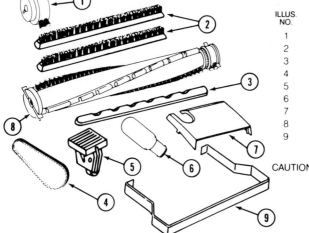

ILLUS. NO.	PART NO.	DESCRIPTION
1	742509	End Brush
2	742030	Brush Beater (2)
3	742029	Bar Beater
4	742024	Belt (Cogged)
5	742763	Foot Pedal Pad
6	596181	Bulb, Light (15 Watt)
7	743063	Bulb Housing
8	742036	Bearing and Housing Assembly
9	742767	Bumper

CAUTION: Use the part number on all orders (not illustration number).

A flowchart can also identify how much time each step takes. One form of the flowchart is PERT, which is used in complicated planning processes. The planner determines how much time each step will take under the most favorable, the least favorable, and the most likely circumstances. Using this data the planner can determine how long a project will take from start to completion. The project depicted in Exhibit 15.26 takes nine and a half weeks.

A PERT chart identifies tasks that can be done simultaneously and tasks that must be done sequentially. Even though roofers can work while electricians install the wiring, for example, the wiring and the roof must be completed before plasterboard can be installed.

Exhibit 15.25   **Flowchart**

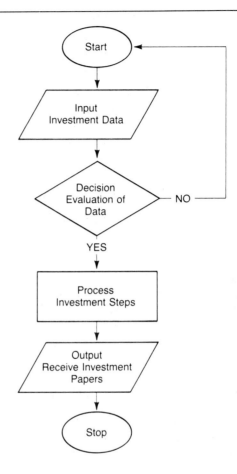

Exhibit 15.26   **PERT Chart**

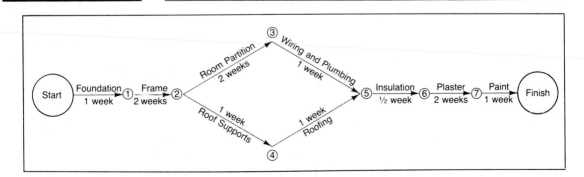

CONSTRUCTION OF VISUAL AIDS

Placement

If the material presented in the visual aid is necessary to the understanding of the report, it should be in the report proper. If the visual aid merely supplements the text, it can be placed in an appendix. The placement of a visual aid may also be influenced by the number of references made to it. Assume that a report contains a long, complex table important to an understanding of the text. Further assume that the text refers to the table several times. The writer must decide whether the table should be placed closest to the first reference, somewhere in the middle of the text, or in an appendix. If the writer chooses to place it closest to the first reference, the reader will need to locate it again when later references occur. Because the search may be annoying, the reader might be best served if the table is in an appendix.

Size

In general, the size of visual aids should not exceed the margins of the written text. A visual aid that extends into the margins distracts readers by breaking the visual pattern. Specifically, the size of a graphic is determined by the amount of data presented. Although a single-line graph might fit easily onto a quarter of a page, a multiple-line graph may require more space. The reason is that, with several lines to show, a writer might need to use a larger scale and to include a legend to explain the meaning of the various lines and colors.

If a table has too many columns to fit within the margins, the writer can turn the paper horizontally in order to fit the table on it, as illustrated in Exhibit 15.27. The table will be more difficult to read, of course, and some readers may not even look at it. As an alternative, the writer can also extend the page by pasting a sheet of paper to it and creating a foldout page. This is extra work, but the table will be easier to read if treated as a foldout.

Numbering

Visual aids are numbered. The numbers permit the writer to refer to them in the text by number rather than the more cumbersome description or title. Most report writers use separate numbering systems for tables and figures. A report can therefore have Table 1, Figure 1, Table 2, Figure 2, Table 3, Figure 3. Some writers label all visual aids as exhibits. This book is an example.

Traditionally, tables were given Roman numerals, and figures were given Arabic numbers. Today many report writers use Arabic numbers for all visual aids.

A report with several chapters identifies not only the number of the table and figure but also the chapter in which they are located. Table 1.2 refers to the second table in Chapter 1, for example, and Figure 5.3 is the third figure in Chapter 5.

Titles

Every visual aid should have a descriptive title so that the reader immediately understands the focus. The title follows the number, either on the same line or the following line. You should strive for consistency in the placement of titles. The following list and also Exhibit 15.28 illustrate the possibilities:

1. All table titles above the tables
2. All figure titles above the figures
3. All table titles below the tables
4. All figure titles below the figures
5. Titles for figures and tables sometimes alongside the table or figure

In older reports you may find that the table title is in all capital letters above the table, whereas the title for figures is in capital and lowercase letters below the figure. If you adopt this traditional practice, you must be consistent throughout the report.

Traditional: (always above the table)
TABLE 1
1985–1990 SALES FOR BRANCHES OF CLOVER DEPARTMENT STORES IN CHICAGO

(always below the figure)
Figure 1
1985–1990 Sales for Branches of Clover Department Stores in Chicago

Modern: (either above, below, or alongside the table)
Table 1
1985–1990 Sales for Branches of Clover Department Stores in Chicago

(either above, below, or alongside the figure)
Figure 1
1985–1990 Sales for Branches of Clover Department Stores in Chicago

Titles must be clear and descriptive. When appropriate, they should answer the questions who, what, where, when, why, and how. Of course, not every title needs to answer all of these questions.The title in the example for title placement answers the following: when (1985–1990), what (sales comparisons), and where (Chicago).

Source Notes

If the visual aid presents material drawn from a source other than your own primary research, you should credit that source in a **source note** placed immediately below it.

Source Note
The source note credits the secondary source of data.

Footnotes

Footnotes to visual aids must be distinguished from footnotes to the text, which identify the source of material used in the text. Footnotes to tables and figures are clarifying comments. The report writer uses them to explain a

Footnote
The footnote in a visual aid is an explanatory note.

Exhibit 15.27 Side Placement of Visual Aid

Maintenance Costs for Subcompact Cars

Car (Engine)	PM Costs to 45,000 Miles	Water Pump	Alternator	2 Front Brake Pads	Starter	Carburetor (Fuel Injectors)[1]	Fuel Pump (Fuel Injection Pump)[1]	Catalytic Converter	Lower Ball Joints	Transmission (FWD Cars)[2]	Relative Maintenance Costs[3]
Chevrolet Chevette (L4)	$366	$63	$156	$50	$157	$176	$39	$201	$68	$1044	Medium
Datsun 210 (L4)	358	47	241	24	160	235	36	333	73	784•	Medium
Datsun 310 (L4T)	356	35	240	22	106	214	48	335	63	(808)•	Medium
Datsun 510 (L4)	350	99	287	23	202	229	42	334	73	715•	Medium
Dodge Colt (L4T)	216	62	143	42	155	157	42	200	50	(1288)•	Medium
Fiat Strada (L4)*	315	72	283	42	126	(139)	(68)	243	170	(1016)•	Medium
Ford Escort (L4T)	115	98	145	82	95	204	39	308	153	(823)•	Medium
Honda Accord (L4T)	347	38	164	24	206	310	58	144	126	(623)•	Low
Honda Civic (L4T)	325	37	142	25	157	270	42	144	126	(586)•	Low
Honda Prelude (L4T)	385	41	170	38	206	310	56	144	138	(634)•	Low
Mazda GLC (L4)	236	73	204	40	174	272	36	645	44	993	High
Mercury Lynx (L4T)	115	98	145	82	95	204	39	308	153	(823)•	Medium
Plymouth Champ (L4T)	216	62	143	42	155	157	42	200	50	(1288)•	Medium
Renault Le Car (L4)	412	137	224	43	170	315	51	269	86	(915)•	High
Subaru DL 1600 (HO4)	472	65	184	38	250	291	82	117	68	(884)•	Medium
Toyota Corolla (L4)	311	107	171	26	169	262	39	262	171	756•	Medium
Toyota Tercel (L4)	374	83	181	27	171	242	36	124	137	414•	Low
Volkswagen Jetta (L4T)	333	121	203	31	227	(94)	(137)	215	63	(1110)•	High
Volkswagen Rabbit (L4T)	333	121	203	31	227	(94)	(100)	215	63	(1110)•	Medium
VW Rabbit Diesel (L4T)	179	126	203	31	329	(123)	(371)	▲	63	(1110)•	High
Average Vehicle Maintenance Cost	306	79	187	38	167	241 (113)	45 (169)	250	97	743 (934)	

• Manual transmission, all others are automatic.
* At the time of printing, only 1980 data was available. While some cost difference for 1981 models can be expected, they should not be significant.
▲ Cars with diesel engines do not have catalytic converters.
[1] Because diesel and gas cars with fuel injectors do not have carburetors or fuel pumps, the cost of fuel injectors and fuel injection pumps is given. These are noted by parentheses in the carburetor and fuel pump column.
[2] For front wheel drive cars, the entire transaxle assembly kit is usually replaced. This includes the transmission and the differential. FWD cars are noted by parentheses in the transmission column.
[3] This column gives you an idea of the relative cost of repairing each car based on the nine repairs listed in the chart, although many of the repairs are typical, there are currently no data available about exactly what will fail or how often. This column should only be used to compare the relative maintenance costs of the cars you are considering buying.

Due to stricter emissions requirements, cars sold in California may have different maintenance costs for some items.

Source: U.S. Department of Transportation. (1981). The Car Book. Washington, D.C.: U.S. Government Printing Office.

Exhibit 15.28   **Placement of Titles**

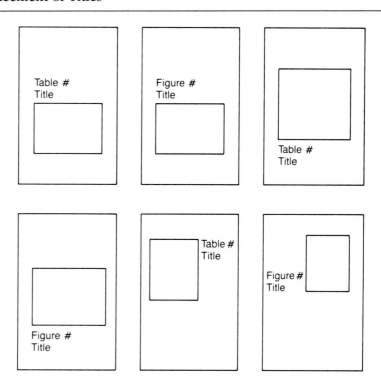

specific point in the visual aid or when data is missing in the visual aid. If, for example, in a table depicting income figures for several countries not all figures are available, the writer may explain the omission in a footnote.

Footnotes for visual aids are indicated by symbols such as asterisks, daggers, double daggers, crosses, and lowercase letters, but rarely with Arabic numbers. Numbers might be confused with text footnote numbers or with numerical data in the table or figure itself.

Footnotes can precede or follow the source note. In Exhibit 15.29, it precedes.

COMPUTER GRAPHICS

Computer Graphics
Computer graphics are visual aids generated by a computer.

A number of magazine and television commercials proclaim the power of **computer graphics.** Invariably, in the commercials the team with effective computer graphics gets the contract. The commercials claim that computer graphics will put you ahead of everyone else and give you an advantage in the corporate climb. Indeed, computer graphics have had a tremendous impact on corporate report writing and presentations. A recent study found that graphics get the desired message across 50 percent more effectively in 30 percent less time.

Exhibit 15.29

Placement of Footnotes in Exhibits

**Estimated Quarterly Gross State Product by Industry Division
Seasonally Adjusted at Annual Rates (Millions of U.S. Dollars)**

	1985[P]			
	I	**II**	**III**	**IV**
GROSS STATE PRODUCT	$187,556	$187,928		
GSP in Constant 1972 Dollars	(81,877)	(81,513)		
Private Nonfarm	167,270	168,994		
Mining	1,853	2,057		
Contract Construction	6,934	7,880		
Manufacturing	42,703	42,120		
Durable Goods	24,247	23,868		
Nondurable Goods	18,456	18,252		
Wholesale & Retail Trade	31,138	31,468		
Finance, Insurance and Real Estate	37,032	37,181		
Transportation	6,958	7,004		
Communication and Utilities	11,283	11,196		
Services	29,369	30,088		
Government	15,190	15,442		
Agriculture	5,096	3,492		

[P]—preliminary
Source: Illinois Department of Commerce and Community Affairs.

Computer graphics is one of the most rapidly expanding areas in computer science. Research in the fields of perceptual and cognitive psychology as well as computer and information science have helped in developing programs for both the highly talented designer and the novice. Large companies often have departments that specialize in designing and producing visual material. Using their services may take considerable time, however. If you can make your own visual aids, you can have the graph or picture you want when you need it. For small businesses, which usually do not have special design people, computer graphics offer the opportunity to enhance reports with effective visual aids.

Computer graphics allow you to enhance the visual aids you want to use in your report. The computer also allows you to compare possible visual presentations. Traditionally, you would type the text part of the report and leave space for visual presentations. You then would decide which type of visual—line graph, bar graph, or pie chart, for example—would present the data best. Next you would draw the figure and paste it in the report. The page would then be reproduced to visually integrate the visual aid into the text. Now a computer can do the cut-and-paste work for you.

If you must prepare the figures manually, you usually will not draw several in order to compare them for effectiveness because making visual aids is time consuming and tedious. With the help of the computer, however, you can experiment. After producing several possible illustrations, you can choose the one that is clearest and best highlights the important points.

Almost 200 different graphics packages are on the market today catering to all levels of expertise and talent. Some of the most popular are the following:

- *Harvard Graphics®*
- *Chart-Master®*
- *Microsoft Chart®*
- *BPS Business Graphics®*
- *Graphwriter®*
- *35 mm Express®*
- *VP Planner®*

- *Freelance Plus®*
- *Graphics Gallery®*
- *Lotus Graphwriter II®*
- *Energraphics®*
- *PC Illustrator®*
- *IBM Graphic Assistant®*

The novice may want to choose a package that requires few and simple steps; however, with such a package the user has limited options to adapt the package to personal needs. To add more variables, manipulate default values, change scales, and adapt the package to special situations, the user must have a sophisticated package. Such a package, of course, will require a more in-depth knowledge of computers and programming principles.

For the printing of visual aids, you can use dot matrix, ink-jet plotters, electrostatic plotters, or microfilm recorders. Some programs allow you to print the visual directly from the screen; some programs will print the visual only after it has been stored. The quality of the computer graph depends on the resolution of the computer and the printer. The higher the resolution, the better the quality will be.

The screen is made up of hundreds of horizontal and vertical lines that consist of dots, or pixels. As the number of pixels increases, the clarity of the picture improves. A typical American television screen has about 250 rows and 500 columns, or about 125,000 pixels. In the future, the screen will consist of about 4,000 rows by 4,000 columns, or 16 million pixels. This high resolution allows for almost photographic sharpness.

Spreadsheets

A spreadsheet is one of two basic types of graphics packages. It answers the question, "What if?" It helps the manager in forecasting, planning alternatives, analyzing trends, graphing results, and producing reports for decision making.

Assume, for example, that the manager of Hossbach Toys wanted to determine what would happen to net income if 1989 revenues were to go either up or down in 1990. Exhibit 15.30 shows revenues for 1989 at $1,000,000. Column C shows the dollar figures for expenses. In column E you can see the relationship between expenses and revenues. Except for rent, which is a fixed amount, all expenses are a percentage of revenues. Salaries, for example, are 25 percent of revenues. Net income for 1989 was $285,000.

If revenues increased to $1,750,000, income would be $510,000. Because the manager had entered the formula for the relationship between revenues and expenses in the spreadsheet, it automatically calculated the 1990 amounts for various expenses and net income (see Exhibit 15.31). On the other hand, as

Exhibit 15.30

Spreadsheet Calculation of Income

	A	B	C	D	E	F	G	H
1								
2			1989 INCOME STATEMENT FOR HOSSBACH TOYS					
3								
4								
5	Revenues				$1,000,000			
6								
7	Expenses							
8	Salaries		$250,000		@SUM(e5*.25)			
9	Rent		$15,000		$15,000			
10	Supplies		$200,000		@SUM(e5*.20)			
11	Advertising		$150,000		@SUM(e5*.15)			
12	Utilities		$100,000		@sum(e5*.10)			
13								
14	Total expenses		$715,000		@SUM(c8.C12)			
15								
16					————			
17	Income before taxes				$285,000	@SUM(e5-c14)		
18								
19								
20								

forecasted in Exhibit 15.32, Hossback Toys would lose $7,500 if revenues dropped to $25,000.

The spreadsheet also has the capability of creating graphs based on the information in the spreadsheet. The manager simply lets the computer know the type of graph he wants. In Exhibit 15.33, for example, income and expenses are shown in a pie chart. In that year, rent was 1.5 percent of revenue.

Exhibit 15.31

Income Calculation with Varying Revenue

	A	B	C	D	E	F	G	H
1								
2		PROJECTED 1990 INCOME STATEMENT FOR HOSSBACH TOYS						
3			(if revenue is $1,750,000)					
4								
5	Revenues				$1,750,000			
6								
7	Expenses							
8	Salaries		$437,500		@SUM(e5*.25)			
9	Rent		$15,000		$15,000			
10	Supplies		$350,000		@SUM(e5*.20)			
11	Advertising		$262,000		@SUM(e5*.15)			
12	Utilities		$175,000		@SUM(e5*.10)			
13								
14	Total expenses		$1,240,000		@SUM(c7.c12)			
15								
16					————			
17	Income before taxes				$510,000	@SUM(e5-c14)		
18								
19								
20								

30-Aug-89 11:05 AM

Exhibit 15.32   **Income Projection with Varying Revenue**

PROJECTED 1990 INCOME STATEMENT FOR HOSSBACH TOYS
(if revenue is $25,000)

Revenues		$25,000
Expenses		
Salaries	$6,250	@SUM(e5*.25)
Rent	$15,000	$15,000
Supplies	$5,000	@SUM(e5*.20)
Advertising	$3,750	@SUM(e5*.15)
Utilities	$2,500	@SUM(e5*.10)
Total expenses	$32,500	@SUM(c7*c12)
Loss	$7,500	@SUM(e5-c14)

Because rent is a fixed amount, the percentage will change as revenue changes. If revenue goes up, rent as percentage of revenue will decrease, and, as a result, income before taxes will increase as a percentage of revenue. In Exhibit 15.34, income and expenses for 1989 are shown in a bar graph.

The graphic ability of spreadsheets is limited to bar graphs, line graphs, and pie charts. Spreadsheets will not produce flowcharts and diagrams. Other graphics packages are necessary for that type of visual presentation.

Designated Graphics Packages

Designated graphics packages provide more options and, in many cases, better quality visuals than spreadsheets. The opportunities are almost unlim-

Exhibit 15.33   **Income and Expenses for Hossbach Toys**

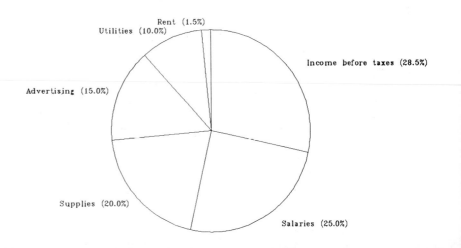

INCOME AND EXPENSES FOR HOSSBACH TOYS

1989

Exhibit 15.34   Income and Expenses for Hossbach Toys

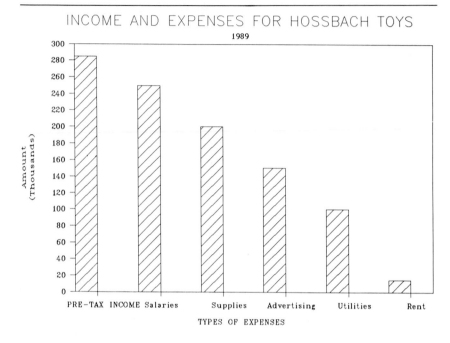

ited. With the help of a computer you can draw two- and three-dimensional images. You can use the computer for flowcharts, block diagrams, product design, and space planning. Special programs have been designed for drawing and technical designs. Engineers in automobile design, for example, can draw three-dimensional models of their car designs with the help of a computer.

The chart in Exhibit 15.35 was created with a designated graphics package.

Exhibit 15.35   PERT Chart Created with Designated Graphics Package

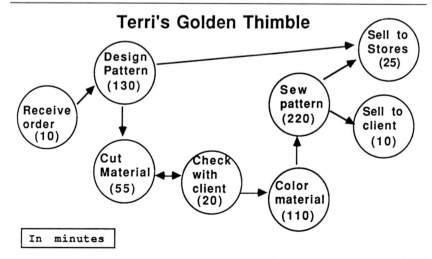

It illustrates the three production options available to the owner of Terri's Golden Thimble. She can design a pattern and sell it to a store; she can sew the pattern and sell it to a store; she can sew the pattern and sell it to an individual client. The chart shows how much time each option requires. Based on the time, she can determine the cost of each option.

Most graphics packages allow the user to pull data in from spreadsheets, eliminating the tedious step of reentering data. The selection of a particular package will depend on the ease and frequency of use. Some of the features that the report writer may want to look for in a graphics package are the following:

- Import data from spreadsheets.
- Create a variety of graphs. At a minimum, the graphics package should create bar and line graphs, pie charts, flowcharts, and organizational charts.
- Output to a film recorder or slide maker. This feature allows the user to make slides directly from the computer; it is particularly important if the material is to be presented orally.
- Add symbols from a business image library. For example, you may want to use barrels to illustrate oil production, cars to show automobile sales, and houses to show housing starts.
- Display the graph or chart on the screen for editing and proofing purposes.

Integrated Software Packages

When the first microcomputers appeared, the combining of word processing, spreadsheet, and graphic functions was not possible. The writer could not move freely back and forth between word processing and spreadsheet. To use a spreadsheet in a report, the writer had to abandon the word-processing package. To use the information created with a word-processing package, the writer had to abandon the spreadsheet.

Integrated Software
Integrated software combines the functions of several programs such as word processing, spreadsheets, and graphics.

Today, many **integrated software** packages allow an easy switch from spreadsheet to database, to graphics, to word processing. The writer can copy information from one application to another. For example, numbers from a spreadsheet can go into a report in the word processor, and addresses in the database can be copied into a letter.

Desktop Publishing
Desktop publishing uses microcomputer-based hardware and software to produce reader-ready documents.

The integration of various functions is one of the basic principles underlying **desktop publishing.** With the help of desktop publishing you can create professional-looking magazines, financial reports, brochures, and newsletters. Some of the most popular desktop publishing packages are *Legend®, The Office Publisher®, PageMaker®,* and *Ventura Publisher®.*

A Word of Caution

The impact of visual aids is powerful; therefore, the report writer must make certain that the information is correct. Further, because it is so easy to produce visuals and they are so attractive, the writer may be reluctant to choose between them. Too many visual aids can confuse the reader and take away from the importance of the message. That the data can be presented in a table, bar graph, line graph, and pie chart does not mean all should be used or all are equally good. The conscientious report writer will carefully evaluate the options. The choice will depend on the purpose of the report. The computer can help you to do a better job, but it is a tool that you must manage carefully.

TEXT DISCUSSION OF VISUAL AIDS

Visual aids clarify the text. To be certain that the reader will make the best use of them, the writer should direct the reader to each visual aid at the most appropriate time. The writer's introduction should tell the reader what the visual aid does. A clear introduction might be, "As the following table illustrates, the sales figures have shown a steady increase during the past five years." It gives more information than "The following table shows the sales figures."

Ideally the writer introduces the visual aid, presents the visual aid, and then discusses it. In the final layout of the report, however, this arrangement is often not possible. For example, the introduction may fall so near the bottom of a page that it cannot be completed in the space that remains. In that case the writer places the table at the top of the next page and then continues the discussion below it. At other times, the remaining space on the page dictates that the entire discussion precede the table or figure. The report writer should not divide a table and present it on two different pages.

For a simple table or graph, a one-sentence discussion may be enough. More detailed tables and figures require more detailed discussion. To say that the data in the table is self-explanatory is not enough. The writer must summarize the information, point out trends, compare data, and in any way possible facilitate the reading of the report. She must be careful to relate the data in the visual aid to the problem and the purpose of the report.

The following example is a discussion of Exhibit 15.21 in this chapter.

As the exhibit illustrates, immigration patterns changed substantially during the three decades beginning with the 1950s. Immigration shifted from Europe to Asia and North America, mostly Mexico. While the number of European immigrants was reduced nearly by half, the number of immigrants from North America doubled. From Asia eight times more immigrants came to the United States in the 1970s than in the 1950s. Immigration from Africa, Australia, and South America remained fairly stable for the three decades.

The immigration trend has definite implications for the United States. More people are coming from developing countries. In addition, they come from different cultural and racial backgrounds. Some of the results of the changing pattern can already be seen in the changing racial and religious mix of the population.

The trend has implications for educational programs, value structures, and expectations.

In the analysis of a visual aid, the writer must summarize the information and point out trends. The task of the writer is to facilitate the understanding of the reader. Unfortunately, too many report writers do not explain visual information effectively. As a result, even though they may be technically superb, graphs in many cases do not have the power and effect that a good interpretation would lend.

The following "analysis" of the pictogram presented in Exhibit 15.21 illustrates a poor example.

> Between 1951 and 1960, 1.5 million people immigrated from Europe. In the following decade the immigration from Europe was 1.2 million people. Between 1971 and 1980, immigration had dropped to only 800,000.
>
> In contrast, immigration from Asia was about 250,000 between 1951 and 1960. For the following decade immigration from Asia reached 450,000 people. For the years 1971 to 1980, immigration from Asia jumped to 1.6 million. . . .

In this "analysis" the writer simply repeats the information of the pictogram and fails to point out trends or implications of the trend. Phrases such as "immigration had dropped to only . . ." or "immigration jumped to . . ." do not make up for the lack of interpretation.

SUMMARY OF LEARNING OBJECTIVES

To understand the purpose of visual aids.

Visual aids are tools; they are not an end in themselves. Their purpose is to highlight, to summarize, to show patterns and trends, and to facilitate the understanding of complex processes and situations.

To understand the underlying principles of tables and figures.

The report writer must know the basic principles of designing visual aids so data is not misrepresented. In the line graph the Y-axis is always the dependent variable, and the X-axis the independent variable. The Y-axis must start with zero. In the bar graph the dependent variable can be on either the X-axis or the Y-axis. Practical considerations often influence the decision.

The writer must pay special attention to the scale of the axes. Designing effective and correctly scaled visual aids involves an awareness of business ethics.

In tables the stubs and columns can be switched. The decision is based on the appearance of the finished table.

To design effective and appropriate tables and figures.

Visual aids must be titled and numbered. They should be introduced and discussed in the text. Visual aids must be clear and easy to read to fulfill their purpose.

Tables are systematic arrangements of data in rows and columns. Tables present quantitative information.

Figure is an overall term that includes all visual aids except tables. Line graphs show trends and patterns over time. Bar graphs are effective for comparisons at a particular point in time. Pie charts illustrate the composition of a whole. Pictograms combine pictures and bar graphs. The statistical map is a combination of maps and line graphs, bar graphs, or pie charts. Other visual aids frequently used in business reports are the diagram, the organizational chart, and the flowchart. More and more businesses use the computer to design graphs.

To understand the role of computer graphics in report writing.

Computer graphics make it easy to convert numeric data into graphs. The report writer can compare several visual presentations of the same data and then choose the most effective one for the report.

Spreadsheets allow the writer to produce appropriate tables and graphs to enhance the meaning of the report. Spreadsheets are helpful in examining options as conditions change. Integrated software combines the functions of several programs such as word processing, spreadsheet, and database.

Designated graphics packages allow the report writer to present pictograms, flowcharts, maps, and diagrams in addition to line graphs, bar charts, and pie charts.

KEY TERMS

Ruled Table	Source Note
Boxed Table	Footnote
Legend	Computer Graphics
Vertical Bar Graph	Integrated Software
Horizontal Bar Graph	Desktop Publishing

QUESTIONS AND DISCUSSION POINTS

1. What are some of the problems of scaling data in a line graph?
2. Why must the bars in a bar graph be the same width?
3. When do you use a subdivided and when a multiple-line graph?
4. Discuss the ethical problems inherent in designing visual aids.
5. Name the major parts of a table.
6. Examine the visual aids in several annual reports and evaluate them. How effective are they?

7. Discuss the most appropriate location of visual aids in a report.
8. Examine the visual aids in your local newspaper or student paper. Are the figures mechanically correct? What is the visual impact?

EXERCISES

1. Design a PERT chart for the course work in your major.
2. Present the following data visually. What types of graphs are possible? Justify your choices.

Per Capita Consumption of Major Food Commodities (in kilograms)

Commodity	United States	France	West Germany	Soviet Union
Beef	46.9	18.5	21.5	11.0
Pork	33.3	9.9	50.3	23.5
Poultry	27.7	17.2	9.6	6.0
Fresh Fruit	40.2	63.6	84.0	34.0
Sugar	38.0	15.0	35.6	42.2
Cheese	8.0	18.2	13.9	n.a.

Source: United States Department of Commerce, Bureau of the Census (1985). *Statistical Abstracts of the United States.* p. 848.

3. Design appropriate graphs for presenting the data in the following table. Discuss your choices.

Veterans' Benefits—Expenditures by Programs (in millions of dollars)

Program	1978	1979	1980	1981	1982	1983
Compensation and Pension	9,630	10,540	11,257	12,492	13,348	13,881
Education	3,337	2,800	2,383	2,333	2,001	1,676
Medical Services	5,684	6,206	6,647	7,199	8,009	8,722

Source: United States Department of Commerce, Bureau of the Census (1985). *Statistical Abstracts of the United States.* p. 349.

4. Present the following information visually. Justify the type of visual aid you choose. Summarize and analyze the information.

House and Condo Sales in McLean County, 1980–1989

Year	Second Quarter	Full Year	Volume	Average Price
1989	558		$43,317,881	$72,895
1988	521	1,859	$39,915,220	$76,613
1987	597	2,046	$44,321,785	$74,241
1986	678	2,186	$45,335,490	$66,866
1985	439	1,603	$27,815,185	$63,360
1984	375	1,301	$23,361,643	$62,297
1983	433	1,323	$26,445,275	$61,074
1982	268	957	$16,225,197	$60,562
1981	448	1,200	$21,161,927	$60,629
1980	292	1,210	$16,380,475	$56,098

5. Present the data in the following table as a graph. Name all of the acceptable types of graphs you might use. Choose the one that will present the information most effectively. Justify your choice. Summarize and analyze the information.

Unemployment Rate Percentages for Selected Illinois Counties and Metropolitan Areas, April–May 1989

County	May	April	City	May	April
Champaign	3.8%	3.8%	Twin Cities	4.75%	4.63%
DeWitt	7.6	6.9	Champaign	3.8	3.8
Ford	6.4	6.7	Chicago	6.1	5.7
Iroquois	5.7	6.0	Decatur	7.1	7.0
LaSalle	9.2	9.3	East St. Louis	11.5	12.3
Livingston	5.4	5.8	Joliet	6.6	6.3
Logan	7.0	6.0	Kankakee	7.7	8.0
McLean	4.75	4.63	Peoria	5.7	5.6
Mason	7.5	6.7	Rockford	5.7	5.9
Piatt	6.0	6.0	Springfield	4.6	4.5
Tazewell	6.1	6.0	Tri-Cities	6.0	5.9
Woodford	4.3	4.1			

6. The following table presents so much information that you will not be able to use it all in a single graph. Prepare at least three graphs using the data. Justify the types of graphs you choose. Explain the information your visual presentations highlight.

The Superpower Contenders Compared

	United States	Soviet Union	Japan	European Community	China
Population (in millions)	243.8	284.0	122.0	323.6	1,074.0
Gross National Product (in billions of 1987 U.S. dollars[a])	$4,436.1	$2,375.0	$1,607.7	$3,782.0	$293.5
Per capita GNP (1987 U.S. dollars[a])	$18,200	$8,360	$13,180	$11,690	$270
GNP Growth Rate					
1966–1970 (annual average)	2.8%	5.1%	11.0%	4.6%	N.A.
1971–1975 (annual average)	2.3%	3.1%	4.3%	3.0%	5.5%
1976–1980 (annual average)	3.3%	2.2%	5.0%	3.0%	6.1%
1981–1985 (annual average)	3.0%	1.8%	3.9%	1.5%	9.2%
1987	2.9%	0.5%	4.2%	2.9%	9.4%
Inflation (change in consumer prices)	3.7%	−0.9%	0.1%	3.1%	9.2%
Total Labor Force (in millions)	121.6	154.8	60.3	143.0	512.8
Agricultural	3.4	33.9	4.6	11.9	313.1
Nonagricultural	118.2	120.9	55.7	131.1	199.7
Unemployment Rate	6.1%	N.A.	2.8%	11.0%	N.A.
Foreign Trade					
Exports (in millions of U.S. dollars)	$250.4	$107.7	$231.2	$953.5[b]	$44.9
Imports (in millions of U.S. dollars)	$424.1	$96.0	$150.8	$955.1[b]	$40.2
Balance (in millions of U.S. dollars)	−$173.7	$11.7	$80.4	−$1.6	$4.7
Energy					
Consumption (in bbl. of oil equiv. per capita)	55.6	37.3	22.7	24.4	4.8
Oil Reserves (in billions of barrels)	33.4	59.0	0.1	7.6	18.4
Oil Production (in millions of bbl. a day)	9.9	12.7	Negligible	3.1	2.7
Natural Gas Reserves (in trillions of cu. ft.)	186.7	1,450.0	1.0	112.9	30.7
Coal Reserves (in billions of metric tons)	263.8	244.7	1.0	90.5	170.0

(continued)

The Superpower Contenders Compared (*continued*)

	United States	Soviet Union	Japan	European Community	China
Agriculture					
Grain Production (in kilograms per capita)	1,150	740	130	480	402
Meat Production (in kilograms per capita)	109	65	31	82	18
Military					
Active Armed Forces	2,163,200	5,096,000	245,000	2,483,400	3,200,000
Ready Reserves	1,637,900	6,217,000	46,000	4,565,800	1,200,000
Defense Expenditures Share of GNP	6.5%	15%–25%	1.6%	3.3%	4%–5%
Living Standard					
Life Expectancy (years)	75	69	78	76	68
Automobiles (registrations per thousand)	570	42	235	347	Negligible

Note: The data presented—with few exceptions—is for 1987.
a Data was converted at U.S. purchasing power equivalents.
b Data includes trade between European Community members.
Source: Compiled from *CIA Handbook of Economic Statistics 1988; International Institute for Strategic Studies; The Military Balance 1988–89; British Petroleum Statistical Review of World Energy;* and *OECD Economic Outlook,* December 1988; published in The 90s & beyond: the U.S. stands to retain its global leadership. (1989, January 23). *The Wall Street Journal,* p. A8.

7. Summarize and analyze the information in the bar graph. What are the trends?

U.S. Advertising Expenditures by Category
(In billions of dollars)

Source: The Wall Street Journal, September 23, 1989.

8. Prepare a graphic presentation of the information in the table. Justify the type of graph you choose. Summarize and analyze the information in the table.

Cable Television's Growing Reach

As cable becomes widespread ...

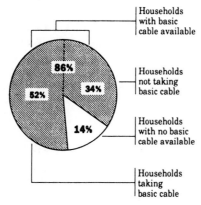

Households with basic cable available

86%

52%

34%

Households not taking basic cable

14%

Households with no basic cable available

Households taking basic cable

Source: Paul Kagan Associates, Inc., Cable TV Investor
Source: The Wall Street Journal, August 10, 1989.

Users pay more for the service

	AVERAGE MONTHLY PRICE OF BASIC CABLE (In dollars)	CABLE REVENUE FROM BASIC SERVICES (In millions of dollars)
1980	$7.85	$1,648.5
1981	8.14	2,100.1
1982	8.46	2,678.6
1983	8.76	3,101.0
1984	9.20	3,632.2
1985	10.25	4,366.5
1986	11.09	5,083.7
1987	13.27	6,552.7
1988	14.40	7,724.7

CHAPTER
16

PRESENTING
THE LONG
FORMAL REPORT

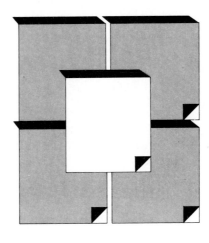

Learning Objectives

- To understand the role of the preliminary pages, the body of the report, and the supplementary parts.
- To present an attractive and effective long report.

Most long formal reports are special reports intended to help management in solving special problems and in making major decisions. The long report is the result of detailed work. It reveals to management how well you can organize your time, how up-to-date your research tools are, and how well you can analyze information, draw conclusions, and make recommendations.

All of your planning, research, analysis, and organization were preparation for synthesizing the material into a long report. The examples in this chapter and the sample report in the chapter appendix will guide you in writing your long report.

PARTS OF THE REPORT

The discussion of the parts will follow the order in which they will appear in the final report, although you will not necessarily write them in this order. In fact, you will write the report itself before you write most of the preliminary pages and supplementary parts. A long formal report may include all of the following:

Preliminary Pages
Preliminary pages are at the beginning of the report.

Body of the Report
The body of the report is the actual report.

Supplementary Parts
Supplementary parts support the report. They are helpful but not necessary for understanding the report.

Preliminary Pages
  Cover
  Title Fly
  Title Page
  Letter of Authorization
  Letter of Acceptance
  Letter of Transmittal
  Acknowledgments
  Table of Contents
  Table of Illustrations
  Executive Summary

Body of the Report
  Introduction
  Findings and Analysis
  Conclusions and Recommendations

Supplementary Parts
  Appendix
  Bibliography
  Index

The length and the formality of the report will determine which parts to include. Formal and long reports may have all of them. Medium-length and short formal reports, which tend to be less formal, will have only some. Exhibit 16.1 illustrates the parts of typical long, medium, and short formal reports.

Exhibit 16.1   **Parts Included in Typical Formal Reports**

Long Report	Medium Report	Short Report
Cover	Cover	
Title Fly		
Title Page	Title Page	Title Page
Letter of Authorization		
Letter of Acceptance		
Letter of Transmittal	Letter of Transmittal	Letter of Transmittal
Acknowledgments		
Table of Contents	Table of Contents	Table of Contents
Table of Illustrations		
Executive Summary	Executive Summary	
Body of Report	Body of Report	Body of Report
Appendix	Appendix	Appendix
Bibliography	Bibliography	Bibliography
Index		

Preliminary Pages

The first pages of a report are called preliminary pages, preliminary parts, or prefatory pages because they precede the body of the report. They provide background information and give guidance to the reader.

Cover.   The cover usually carries the title of the report. Depending on company policy, the cover may also carry the name of the writer. All important reports should have covers to set them off from less important documents and also to protect them. Your company may use a company cover and standard binding. If you can decide on the cover to use, choose one that is durable. Many people may read your report, and you want it to look as good when the tenth person receives it as when the first one reads it.

Title Fly.   The title fly, which may be included in very long formal reports, carries only the title of the report. In order to reduce the number of pages, the writer can easily omit this page.

Title Page.   The title should be concise (a maximum of 10 words) but descriptive, giving the purpose and subject of the report. As a guide to title content, reread your purpose and problem statements. Check that your title tells what, why, how, when, and where. If the title runs over to a second line, break the line at a logical place, center each line, and leave a double space between them.

The title page carries the title of the report, the name and title of the receiver, the name and location of the receiver's business, the name and title of the writer, and the date. It may also have the name and location of the writer's business. Exhibit 16.2 illustrates the title page of a formal report.

Exhibit 16.2

Title Page

AN EXAMINATION OF COMPUTER SCANNERS

FOR KREISNER FOODS

Prepared for
Ralph Kreisner
President
Kreisner Foods
240 College Avenue
Springdale, Colorado
73598

Prepared by
Paul Meere
Staff Analyst

Blooming Grove, Illinois
November 15, 19XX

Source: Reprinted by permission of Paul Meere.

Letter of Authorization.   The letter or memo of authorization is the original request for the report and may be included to provide justification for the particular report project. The letter of authorization may be particularly useful if the report is to be kept for future reference.

As illustrated in Exhibit 16.3, the letter of authorization makes clear what the final report should cover. This letter also indicates that Paul Meere was asked to write the report because of his knowledge of scanner systems. As guidance to the writer, it explains why the report is requested, when and how it will be used, and when the report is needed.

Letter of Acceptance.   In the letter or memo of acceptance the writer accepts the task of writing the report. Few writers include it in the final report. If the letter of acceptance also summarizes the writer's understanding of the assignment, it gives the requester an opportunity to clear up any misunderstandings. In the example in Exhibit 16.4 Paul Meere accepts the assignment, promises to complete the report on time, and mentions the topics the final report will cover.

Letter of Transmittal.   The letter of transmittal typically is part of the preliminary pages. However, it can be sent as a cover letter instead. An outside consultant, for example, might not want to have the letter distributed to all potential readers but rather sent only to the immediate recipient.

If the report goes to people within the company, the letter of transmittal may be replaced with a memo of transmittal. The information is the same as in the letter.

Regardless of whether the letter or memo is loose or is part of the report, it is typed in regular business format. A letter has all the standard parts of a business letter: return address, date, inside address, salutation, body, complimentary close, and signature block. It is single-spaced even if the report is double-spaced.

The letter or memo of transmittal begins with a sentence similar to these:

> The attached report evaluates possible sites for Company A's new plant.
>
> Following is the report that you requested on September 15, 19XX.

The letter states the problem or purpose of the report and may also include its scope and limitations. How much of that information is included will depend on the formality of the report.

The letter of transmittal may include acknowledgments if the report has no separate section for them. In shorter and less formal reports, the letter might even contain a summary of the findings of the report. The short letter of transmittal in Exhibit 16.5 transmits the report but does not summarize it because the report has a separate summary at the end of the preliminary pages. The letter in Exhibit 16.6, on the other hand, provides a summary of the findings, conclusions, and recommendations; therefore, a separate summary in the preliminary pages is not necessary.

If additional work is necessary to solve the problem, the writer may want to mention that in the letter. It is possible that time and budget constraints did not

Exhibit 16.3   **Letter of Authorization**

KREISNER FOODS
240 College Avenue
Springdale, CO 73598
(309) 438-7144

January 15, 19XX

Mr. Paul Meere, Staff Analyst
Kreisner Foods
1215 N. Main St.
Blooming Grove, IL 61761

Dear Mr. Meere:

Based on the December meeting of Kreisner managers, Kreisner Foods is considering installing scanners in its stores. You impressed me with your detailed knowledge of scanner systems, and I would like you to prepare a report on the feasibility of scanners for Kreisner Foods.

The report should cover information on the impact of the scanners on store operations, reactions of customers to the scanners, and the cost of a scanning system.

So that the report can be distributed before the April meeting, my office will need the report by March 25.

Please let me know if you have any questions.

Sincerely,

Ralph Kreisner

Ralph Kreisner, President

rw

Source: Reprinted by permission of Paul Meere.

Exhibit 16.4   **Letter of Acceptance**

KREISNER FOODS
1215 N. Main Street
Blooming Grove, IL 61761
(312) 555-6321

February 5, 19XX

Mr. Ralph Kreisner, President
Kreisner Foods
240 College Ave.
Springdale, CO 73598

Dear Mr. Kreisner:

I gladly accept the assignment to prepare a report on scanners in Kreisner supermarkets. Because I have been collecting material on scanners for the last few
months, I will have no difficulty completing the report by March 25.

I will examine the impact of scanners on such store operations as inventory control and shelving. To examine consumer reactions I plan to interview consumers
and checkout clerks. Obtaining figures on the cost of installing a scanning
system will be no problem. The possible savings for Kreisner will be more complicated to determine, but possible savings can be estimated based on the
experiences of other stores.

I am excited about the project and believe that the results will be helpful in
deciding whether Kreisner could benefit from the installation of scanning devices.

Sincerely,

Paul Meere

Paul Meere
Staff Analyst

jp

Source: Reprinted by permission of Paul Meere.

Exhibit 16.5   **Letter of Transmittal (no Summary)**

KREISNER FOODS
1215 N. Main Street
Blooming Grove, IL 61761
(312) 555-6321

March 15, 19XX

Mr. Ralph Kreisner, President
Kreisner Foods
240 College Ave.
Springdale, CO 73598

Dear Mr. Kreisner:

Here is the report you requested concerning the feasibility of introducing computer scanning devices into Kreisner supermarkets.

Based on the research presented in the report, I recommend that you go ahead with installing a CSD system. The scanners would save the company money and help with inventory control.

Sincerely,

Paul Meere

Paul Meere
Staff Analyst

jp

Source: Reprinted by permission of Paul Meere.

Exhibit 16.6　　　　　# Letter of Transmittal (with Summary)

KREISNER FOODS
1215 N. Main Street
Blooming Grove, IL 61761
(312) 555-6321

March 15, 19XX

Mr. Ralph Kreisner, President
Kreisner Foods
240 College Ave.
Springdale, CO 73598

Dear Mr. Kreisner:

Here is the report you requested concerning the feasibility of introducing
computer scanning devices into Kreisner supermarkets.

The impact of the scanners on the following aspects of operations was evaluated in
detail: inventory control, marketing strategy, costs, customer satisfaction, and
employee efficiency. The results are encouraging. With the exception of customer
satisfaction all aspects are expected to be influenced positively.

Consumer reaction is mixed. Some prefer the new systems because they provide a
detailed receipt, but others object to scanners because they make comparison of
prices very difficult. However, stores that have introduced the system have had
few complaints from consumers.

The system could save each store about $174,200 annually after the second year in
operation.

Based on the research, I recommend that Kreisner Foods introduce computer scanners
into its supermarkets.

Sincerely,

Paul Meere

Paul Meere
Staff Analyst

jp

Source: Reprinted by permission of Paul Meere.

allow for a complete investigation. It is also possible that new developments in the economy, the competition, or the organization of the firm would necessitate an update of the report within a certain time period.

The letter should end positively. The writer, if an outside consultant, may express appreciation for the opportunity to prepare the report and an interest in future assignments from the client.

Acknowledgments.   Writers sometimes receive valuable help in the form of interviews, data, or verification of information. Acknowledging that help in the report is appropriate. The note of acknowledgment can be presented under a separate heading in the report or in the letter of transmittal.

Table of Contents.   The table of contents is completed after the report is typed and the page numbers are known. All headings and subheadings in the report must appear in the table of contents, worded and capitalized exactly the same as they are in the report. The level of headings, that is, their degree of importance, should be apparent from their placement on the contents page. You may therefore either include the numbers and letters designating degree of importance, as shown in Exhibit 16.7, or you may omit them. Except for the executive summary or synopsis, preliminary pages do not appear in the table of contents.

The words *Contents* or *Table of Contents* appear at the top of the page in capital letters. The list of headings and subheadings may be single-spaced or double-spaced, depending on whether you are trying to fit a long table of contents onto a single page. Even if it is single-spaced, you may want to leave extra space between major sections. To make the page easier to read, you may use rows of periods, called *leaders*, between each heading and the corresponding page number.

Table of Illustrations.   A table of illustrations is used only if the report has more than four illustrations or if the writer wants to call special attention to the illustrations.The layout is the same as for the table of contents. Illustrations are listed in order of appearance in the report. As shown in Exhibit 16.8, the table gives illustration numbers, titles, and page numbers. If you have numbered figures and tables in two separate series, you may list them separately on the illustrations page.

Executive Summary.   The executive summary or synopsis is a summary of the entire report. It emphasizes the results or findings but also briefly states the scope, problem, method, and background. In many companies, the executive summary may not exceed one single-spaced page, regardless of the length of the report. After reading the executive summary, the reader should have a clear understanding of the report content.

The summary may be written in deductive or inductive order. In deductive order it begins with the conclusions and recommendations, followed by a summary of the introduction, and finally by a summary of the findings and analysis. The executive summary in Exhibit 16.9 is arranged deductively. The

Exhibit 16.7 Table of Contents (with Heading Levels Designated)

TABLE OF CONTENTS

Exhibit 16.8

Table of Illustrations

TABLE OF ILLUSTRATIONS

Exhibit 16.9   **Executive Summary**

EXECUTIVE SUMMARY

Kreisner Foods should install computer scanning devices in all of its stores.

Studying the feasibility of installing the scanners involved the evaluation of the following factors: marketing strategy, inventory control, customer satisfaction, employee efficiency, and cost and savings of the system.

In marketing the scanners are invaluable for pricing and advertising strategies. Scanners help in the allocation of shelf space. They also assist management in relocating items and rearranging merchandise by brands and sizes.

Consumer reaction to the scanners is mixed. Some consumers prefer the detailed receipts provided by the system, but others complain that individual items are not priced. They argue that comparison shopping is difficult without individual pricing. However, stores that use scanners have not suffered a loss of customers. It seems that consumers will get used to the new system without any major problems.

The scanners help eliminate pricing errors that occur if prices are stamped on items manually. Discounting and couponing can be used more effectively and efficiently with the help of the scanners.

Inventory control is simplified, and manual counting of goods is almost completely eliminated.

Savings should amount to about 1 percent of sales. With sales of $20 million, a store could realize savings of $200,000. Considering leasing and maintenance costs of $25,000 per year, net savings of $175,000 can be expected.

Kreisner Foods would definitely benefit from installing computer scanners.

Source: Reprinted by permission of Paul Meere.

writer gives the recommendation at the beginning. The reader is told how the data was collected. The summary of the findings highlights three areas of investigation: impact on store operations, reactions of consumers, and cost.

Body of the Report

The report must have headings to guide the reader. If you center the major headings, the degrees of importance can be differentiated as follows:

FIRST-DEGREE HEADING

Usually the title of the report is the first-degree heading. It is typed in capital letters and underlined.

SECOND-DEGREE HEADING

Chapter titles in the long report are typed as second-degree headings. They are typed in capital letters but are not underlined.

Third-Degree Heading

This heading uses upper- and lowercase letters. It is underlined.

Fourth-Degree Heading

The fourth-degree heading uses upper- and lowercase letters. It is not underlined.

Fifth-Degree Heading

This heading is on the left margin. It uses upper- and lowercase letters.

Sixth-Degree Heading

It is typed the same way as the fifth-degree heading, but it is not underlined.

Seventh-Degree Heading. This heading becomes part of the paragraph. It is no longer set off in a separate line.

If you block the entire report, including the headings, the levels will appear as follows:

FIRST-DEGREE HEADING

SECOND-DEGREE HEADING

Third-Degree Heading

Fourth-Degree Heading

Fifth-Degree Heading: This is part of the paragraph.

When deciding how to set up the headings in your report, remember that:

1. Centered headings are more important than headings on the margin.
2. Capitalized headings are more important than lowercase headings.
3. Underlined headings are more important than headings that are not underlined.

Introduction.   The introduction serves as an orientation for the reader. The major parts of the introduction are background, problem and purpose, scope, method, limitations, and, where applicable, time and budget information. All those parts were discussed in detail in Chapter 7.

The introduction is the revised report plan. It contains all the information that was in the research plan with the exception of the tentative outline and the bibliography. The tentative outline for the report becomes the table of contents, and the bibliography appears at the end of the report. Another difference between the report plan and the introduction to the final report is that they are written in a different tense. The research plan is written in future tense because the writer plans to do certain things. In the report itself the writer has done all those things; therefore, the introduction is written either in present or past tense.

Writers sometimes feel that the introductory material is unnecessary because the reader probably has the information already. At this point, however, the writer has to understand that she is more thoroughly familiar with all aspects of the problem than the person who requested the report. The introduction refreshes the memory of the reader who is knowledgeable about the problem; it serves as orientation for the reader who is not.

A report is seldom read by only one person. Even if the requester knows all of the background details, other readers may not. If the report is to be kept for future reference, the detailed introduction is absolutely necessary. In the future new employees who are not familiar with the situation may need to consult the report.

Findings and Analysis.   The presentation of the findings and the analysis is the heart of the report and forms the basis for the conclusions and recommendations. The material is divided into chapters, and the chapters are again divided into subparts. Clear organization and logic are necessary to make the presentation effective. Chapters 9 through 15 of this book are devoted to secondary and primary research, the analysis of data with the help of statistics, and the presentation of the data with the help of visual aids. Their object was to prepare you to present your findings and analysis in the written report.

Conclusions and Recommendations.   Conclusions and recommendations must be stated clearly and concisely. No new facts should be introduced at this point. Conclusions and recommendations are based on the presentation and analysis of the facts. For a detailed discussion of how to draw conclusions and make recommendations, you should check Chapter 14. The recommendation report has both conclusions and recommendations. Some analytical reports have conclusions but no recommendations. The writer may combine conclusions and recommendations or present them in separate sections. Informational reports, of course, have neither; they have only a summary.

Supplementary Parts

Appendix.   In the appendix you present supplementary material that is useful but not absolutely necessary for understanding the report. You may want to put copies of questionnaires or working papers in the appendix (Exhibit 16.10). Detailed statistical information may also be included.

Bibliography.   The bibliography lists all the secondary sources that you used in writing the report and the interviews you conducted. Some writers include only sources cited in the report body; others include those they used as background but did not cite. In most cases, a bibliography listing only material cited is sufficient. This type of bibliography is also called *references.*

For a detailed discussion on the compilation of a bibliography check Chapter 10.

Index.   An index is a listing of all the key words in the report with the page numbers on which they occur. Business reports seldom use an index because of the time required to put together a good and functional index. Most reports depend on the clarity of the table of contents instead.

PHYSICAL PRESENTATION

Appearance

A neat report indicates that you care about your work, just as a sloppy report with errors and poor page layout indicates that the work was not important to you. The report communicates to management how seriously you take your work. Because you are responsible for the work that goes out under your name, you should carefully proofread reports typed by your secretary or a secretary in the word-processing center. If it has your name on it, it is your report; you—not your secretary— will be blamed or praised for it.

Many companies tell the writer what paper to use for a particular purpose. The more formal and official the report, the higher quality the paper should be. The most important reports are on 20- or 16-pound bond paper.

If the report is to be bound on the left, the writer must leave about half an inch additional space on the typed page to allow for the binding. Otherwise, the left, right, and top margins should all be the same, usually about one inch in a double-spaced report. The bottom margin is somewhat larger, about an inch and a half. The bottom margin may vary slightly because visual aids, for example, may end above or below the normal margin. For the first page of the report body and for pages that start with major headings, the top margin is usually two inches rather than one inch. This treatment is called a *dropped head.* A frequently used page layout for business reports is illustrated in Exhibit 16.11. Special reports may require special layouts.

Page Numbering

Page numbers may appear at top center, top right, or bottom center. Which ever pattern is chosen, the placement must be consistent. The traditional placement pattern uses Arabic numbers at the top of the page for the report

Exhibit 16.10   **Appendix**

APPENDIX

<u>Manager Interview Questions</u>

1. What brand of optical scanners does this store use?

2. How long have the scanners been in the store?

3. How do the scanners aid in this store's labor productivity?

4. How do the scanners help in terms of operating costs?

5. How does the system aid in inventory control?

6. Does this store use the system data for shelf-space allocation?

7. Does the information from the system help you make better decisions?

8. Do consumers complain about item price removal in your store?

9. Please describe any disadvantages you see with the system.

10. Do you believe that most stores will adopt scanning systems? If so, why?

Exhibit 16.11   **Page Layout and Numbering**

AN EXAMINATION OF COMPUTER SCANNERS

FOR KREISNER FOODS

ORIENTATION TO THE PROBLEM

Background of Computer Scanners

Many supermarkets have already installed computer scanning devices (CSDs). As of May of this year, more than 40 percent of all supermarkets used CSDs. It is estimated that more than 10,000 stores will be using scanner systems by the end of the year. The scanners are designed to reduce errors in inventory records, the waiting time in checkout lines, and pricing errors.

The CSDs utilize the Universal Product Code (UPC) to read information from packaged goods. The UPC represents the product code, the manufacturer, and the associated price and product class. The UPC has been in existence since 1973. Most products in the Kreisner supermarkets carry the code, but so far Kreisner's does not take advantage of the system.

The use of the CSDs is easy. The clerk simply slides the coded item over the scanner's eye. The eye is a laser beam that reads the code and enters the information into the computer. The clerk does not need to enter any information manually except in cases where the code is not clearly marked on the product. These products typically include produce, fresh meat, and fish.

CSDs can be used to generate data on advertising response rates and merchandising success rates.

Problem

How can computer scanning devices help Kreisner Foods to stay competitive?

Source: Reprinted by permission of Paul Meere.

Exhibit 16.11   **Page Layout and Numbering (*continued*)**

2

Scope of the Study

In order to determine how Kreisner Foods can benefit from computer scanning devices, the report will examine the impact of scanners on productivity, inventory control, and marketing strategy at Kreisner Foods.

Once the possible savings in those areas have been determined, it will be possible to calculate the time required to recapture the initial investment. A cost-benefit analysis will help decide how profitable the scanners will be for Kreisner Foods.

Limitations

Because Kreisner has not used scanners in the past, no data on the impact of scanners at Kreisner was available. Some of Kreisner's competitors have been using scanners for some time, but their data, of course, is not available to Kreisner. A telephone survey of consumers in the area helped to establish the attitudes of consumers toward scanners; however, such a survey faces some serious limitations.

Methodology

Two hundred consumers in Central Illinois were interviewed by telephone. The respondents were divided into two groups: consumers who had been exposed to scanners and those who had not. Out of the sample, 150 consumers were familiar with scanners. The questionnaire used a Likert-type scale for responses.

The survey was conducted during the first week of March between 6:00 p.m. and 8:00 p.m. by four college students who had had a marketing research class. Before they called consumers, they received instruction in telephone etiquette and the purpose of the interview. The students then conducted several practice interviews.

body. They may be either centered or flush with the right margin. A double-space separates the page number from the text. On pages with a dropped head, the number is at the bottom, separated by a double-space from the text.

The preliminary pages are numbered with lowercase Roman numerals. All pages are counted in the report, but the number does not appear on all of them. If you look at the beginning of this book, you will find that the first few pages are not numbered. In a formal report the first page that normally carries a number is the table of contents. The preliminary pages may be numbered at the bottom or in the upper right-hand corner. As in the body of the report, however, pages with dropped heads should have page numbers at the bottom. This would include the first page of both the table of contents and of the executive summary.

Most word processing packages automatically place page numbers at the bottom of a page, and many businesses use the default values for page numbers and margins. It is usually very easy to change the default values and put page numbers wherever your boss wants them. For class purposes, you should check with your instructor for special requirements.

Indentation

If you single-space and block your report, you double-space between paragraphs. If you double-space the report, you should indent paragraph beginnings. Blocking a double-spaced report would require triple spacing between paragraphs to make clear where paragraphs begin. There is no definite rule by how many spaces a paragraph has to be indented. It is important, however, that you are consistent. Most report writers indent between four and ten spaces.

SUMMARY OF LEARNING OBJECTIVES

To understand the role of the preliminary pages, the body of the report, and the supplementary parts.

This chapter presented the parts of the most complete type of analytical report. Not all parts are necessary for each report. The decision as to which ones to include will depend on the nature of the topic, the purpose of the report, and the reader.

A formal report has three major sections: the preliminary pages, the body of the report, and the supplementary parts. The preliminary pages provide background information on the report. The reader can see who requested the report, why the report was written, and how much time and money were available for putting the report together. The preliminary pages put the report in perspective so that the reader can understand it better. In formal reports, an executive summary or a synopsis is included in the preliminary pages.

Preliminary pages are unnumbered except for the table of contents and the executive summary, which carry Roman numerals. The report proper carries Arabic numbers.

The body of the report may be arranged inductively or deductively. The inductive order leads up to the conclusion and recommendation, whereas the deductive order gives the conclusion and recommendation at the beginning of the report.

The supplementary parts usually consist of the appendix and the bibliography. Copies of questionnaires or detailed statistical information are often presented in an appendix.

To present an attractive and effective long report.

The specific format and page layout will depend on conventions in any given company and considerations for the use of the report. The writer must use good judgment and discretion in the choice of the final format of the report.

KEY TERMS

Preliminary Pages	Supplementary Parts
Body of the Report	

QUESTIONS AND DISCUSSION POINTS

1. What is the purpose of the preliminary pages, the body of the report, and the supplementary parts?
2. Discuss the role of the letter of transmittal. What information can appropriately be included?
3. Discuss the system for numbering pages in the formal report.
4. Discuss the advantages and disadvantages of a deductive or inductive arrangement of the report.
5. Discuss the role of the introduction in relation to the report planning process.
6. Discuss the role and format of the executive summary or synopsis.
7. Obtain a long business report and discuss its format.
8. Discuss the role of the appendix.
9. Discuss the role of the index.
10. Your company builds brakes for automobiles. Business is going well and management is considering purchasing a factory building to expand production. You are asked to write a report to examine the potential of the building for your company. You are also to recommend whether or not to purchase the building. What parts should your final report have? Would you arrange the report inductively or deductively? What supplementary parts might the report have?

EXERCISES

Go to the "Cases" section at the end of the book for suggestions for long reports.

A Sample Long Formal Report

DEVELOPING A NEWSLETTER FOR THE

PRAIRIE CITY PUBLIC LIBRARY

Prepared for
Peter Kroft
Director
Prairie City Public Library

Prepared by
Krysta Long
Graphics/Marketing Associate
Prairie City Public Library

Prairie City, Illinois
June 21, 19xx

PRAIRIE CITY PUBLIC LIBRARY

205 E. Olive Street
Prairie City, Illinois 61701

June 21, 19xx

Mr. Peter Kroft, Director
Prairie City Public Library
205 E. Olive Street
Prairie City, IL 61701

Dear Mr. Kroft:

The attached report outlines the development of a newsletter for the Prairie City Public Library. Specifically, the report addresses the purpose, goals, and objectives of the newsletter. It also identifies the target audience, the editorial content, a possible format, and publication schedule. Estimated staff time and production costs are examined also.

I look forward to editing this newsletter which offers an exciting opportunity to market the Prairie City Public Library in the community.

Sincerely,

Krysta Long

Krysta Long
Graphics/Marketing Associate

TABLE OF CONTENTS

EXECUTIVE SUMMARY

The proposed newsletter will be one facet of the Prairie City Public Library's print promotion plan which currently includes the following: brochures for extension services, adult services, children's room, a general welcome brochure, a monthly calendar of events, flyers for all programs, and the bookmobile schedules.

The primary purpose of the newsletter will be to increase the community's awareness of the library's value. Its objective will be to entertain, educate, and remind library users of the variety of information and services available to the community. The proposed newsletter is intended to supplement rather than duplicate other library publications.

It will be most cost effective to target the letter to a large audience; therefore, the library newsletter will be designed for city residents of all ages. The primary target group is the 14,000 cardholders of the Prairie City Public Library. Copies of the newsletter will be available in the library. The newsletter will also be distributed by mail to Friends of the Library, newcomers to the community, library staff, and the city council of Prairie City.

The recommended format for the newsletter is 8 1/2" x 14" folded in half to create four pages. It will be produced in-house on white vellum text with black ink. The staff for the newsletter will determine the name and banner of the newsletter. The cost for the intended production run of 5,000 copies per issue will be $258.10. This cost does not include the 40 to 50 hours the staff will spend on the project.

For maximum effectiveness, a bi-monthly publication schedule is recommended.

DEVELOPING A NEWSLETTER FOR THE

PRAIRIE CITY PUBLIC LIBRARY

ORIENTATION TO THE PROBLEM

Every library needs to work to maintain a visible profile in its community. Visibility is crucial in providing effective service and attracting adequate funding. By effectively communicating the library's message to the community, the library can increase the perceived value of the library. The newsletter will be an important tool in promoting the library.

Background

In May 1988, Prairie City Public Library created a full-time graphics and marketing position. The purpose of this position is to create materials which effectively communicate the library's message to the community. In September 1988, the library received grant moneys from the Library Services and Construction Act (LSCA) to conduct a direct mail campaign. Part of the $38,000 grant was used to establish an in-house printing operation. As a result, Prairie City Public Library now has the capability to produce a variety of promotional materials in-house.

Prairie City Public Library currently produces a variety of print materials. Brochures for extension services, adult services, children's room, and circulation are available. A general welcome brochure is being revised and will be available later this summer. Bookmarks listing the phone numbers for Dial-a-Story and the schedule for story times at Eastland Mall have improved participation in these programs. The graphics/marketing area publishes a monthly calendar of events and a six-month bookmobile schedule. Prairie City Public Library also issues news releases for all programs and services.

1

2

Description of the Problem

Through a newsletter Prairie City Public Library is trying to increase its visibility in the community. The library tried a newsletter once before, but the effort failed. The previous newsletter, <u>Whirlwords</u>, was started in March 1983. It had a publication life of seven issues: March 1983, July/August 1983, October/November 1983, Spring 1984, Fall 1984, and Spring 1985. Time constraints were the major factor forcing <u>Whirlwords</u> to cease publication. The regular staff was expected to publish the newsletter in addition to performing the regular tasks. In the long run the workload was too heavy, and the time between publications increased. Establishing a realistic publication schedule and a manageable format will be crucial to the success of the newsletter.

The editor of the newsletter must be careful that the newsletter does not duplicate existing publications. It is also necessary to identify the target audience. So far, seven potential audiences have been identified. All share a common interest in the library; however, each has a varying level of interest. To make the newsletter cost effective, the largest audience will be targeted as the primary audience.

Scope of the Report

This report concentrates on the identification of the target audience, examination of features, and schedule and costs of production of the newsletter. It does not address the specific title and banner head of the newsletter.

Limitations

Limitations of staff, problems of workload, concerns about cost and in-house production capabilities will have an impact on the type of newsletter that can realistically be produced.

Methodology

Telephone interviews with two editors of library newsletters were helpful in assessing cost factors and time implications. A survey of secondary sources provided information on typical content, format, and publication schedules for library newsletters. The mission statement of the Prairie City Public Library helped to ensure that the newsletter will match the goals and objectives of the library.

IDENTIFICATION OF TARGET AUDIENCE

To build a loyal audience, the newsletter must meet the interests and needs of the target audience. Articles and other information must be useful and meaningful to the readers.

The Primary Target Audience

Library users are the primary target audience for the newsletter. Prairie City Public Library has 11,614 adult and 2,990 juvenile library cardholders. This group is interested in the library's programs, services, and materials. A newsletter will provide them with regular information and encourage them to be active users.

In a recent study (Novelli, 1988) library users were found to be parents of young children from two-income households with slightly higher incomes than non-users. Users had a wide variety of interests and more active social lives than non-users. Novelli also found that with 90 percent of the users being high school graduates and 30 percent being college graduates, users were better educated than non-users. Madden (1979) found that library users are active people. They like to take vacations, discuss stocks and bonds, and take an active interest in politics. Based on these studies, it becomes apparent that libraries are an important part of the lives of active people.

Prairie City is the headquarters of two insurance companies and two universities. The city's educational level and income are well above average for the state. Furthermore, the city is growing, and a newsletter would help to attract more members.

Newcomers to the community are an important target group because they represent potential library users. Experience shows that new residents are receptive to information from the library. A newsletter delivered by the welcome wagon to the newcomers will further encourage interest in and use of the library. According to U.S. census data, the Prairie City area posted the largest percentage increase in population in Illinois between 1980 and 1987. Projected growth for Prairie City between 1987 and 1992 is 4.2 percent. This means that the population will grow from 55,000 people to 57,310. If the percentage of residents using the library remains the same, the number of cardholders will increase from 14,604 to 15,217 people.

4

The Secondary Target Audiences

Another important target group is the city council. The newsletter should strengthen the image of the library and attract increased support. A special cover letter to the city council will further highlight important issues and developments at the library.

Other groups receiving the newsletter will be the library staff and their families, members of the library board, Friends of Prairie City Public Library, and managers of city departments. The cardholders will, however, present the largest single group of people who will be used as the target audience of the newsletter.

FEATURES OF THE NEWSLETTER

Image

The newsletter will provide a friendly and open image. It will present the library staff as helpful and competent. To be successful, the newsletter must instill in the readers the desire to come to the library. The library must come across as providing an important service for people of the community.

Content

The newsletter will keep the 14,614 cardholders informed about events and developments at the library. The newsletter will provide some stories, more in-depth information, and interviews after an event has taken place. All announcements of upcoming events will still be made through flyers and press releases.

The first page of the newsletter will have a feature article. Inside pages will have a children's corner, library news, an editorial by the director of the library, and information on new books. The back page will contain an article on a specific library service, library hours, and information required for bulk mailings.

Format

The recommended format for the newsletter is 8 1/2" x 14" folded in half to create four pages. The use of white vellum paper will facilitate the use of color and provide the opportunity to incorporate photographs.

5

Although graphics are of less concern than content, it is important that the newsletter project a professional image, be readable, and have a design that enhances the content.   Details for the recommended design are presented in the following exhibit.

Exhibit 1:   Details for Suggested Design of Newsletter

Paper size	8 1/2" x 14"
Paper color	white
Texture	vellum text
Format	4 pages
	2 columns on each page
	self mailer - bottom third of back page contains return address and mailing permit
Typeface	Times Roman - copy
	Helvetica - headlines
	Bookman - special emphasis items
Ink Color	black
	second color optional
Nameplate	design still to be created

IMPLEMENTATION OF THE NEWSLETTER

Production Schedule

Publishing the newsletter on schedule, within budget, and within the established quality standards will require efficient use of time.   Because the newsletter will be a high priority during production time, the most manageable publication schedule would be a bi-monthly newsletter.

6

The newsletter, as described, will require approximately 40 to 50 hours to produce. This estimate is based on telephone interviews with two editors of library newsletters (Haddad, 1989; Richter, 1989). One of the newsletters is produced by one person in about 40 hours. The editor of the second newsletter indicated that it takes three people 50 hours to get the newsletter ready for printing. The second newsletter is printed commercially.

Developing, writing, and editing stories will take about 40 hours of staff time. The actual composition and printing of the newsletter will take about 10 to 15 hours. The use of existing mailing lists will help to keep the number of hours down. To ensure that every issue of the newsletter is published on time, every contributor will receive a copy of the timetable and publication schedule. Exhibit 2 illustrates the production timetable.

Production Costs

In-house production will help to keep production costs down. The library will need to print about 5,000 copies of the newsletter to reach all the target audiences. Based on the cost breakdown in Exhibit 3, the cost for one issue of the newsletter would be $258.10. The annual cost for a bi-monthly newsletter will be $1,548.60.

CONCLUSIONS AND RECOMMENDATIONS

Producing a newsletter offers an exciting opportunity to market the Prairie City Public Library to the community. The newsletter will keep readers informed of what is new at the library. It should increase interest in the library.

It is important that the newsletter be targeted to people who, based on research, are most likely to use the library. The growing community and the high level of education in the community provide good opportunities for increased library use.

The projected cost of the newsletter is within the budget of the library. In-house production will help to contain costs.

7

Exhibit 2: Timetable for Production

2 months before printing:	Prepare general outline of forthcoming issue
1 month before printing:	Meet with library director Contact staff for stories Prepare rough draft of stories
2 weeks before printing:	Collect all stories Prepare preliminary paste-up
1 week before printing:	Create final paste-up Print newsletter Fold newsletter Order mailing labels
1 day after printing:	Prepare bulk mailing Write cover letter for city council
2 days after printing:	Distribute the newsletter in the library and to council members Mail the newsletter

---

Exhibit 3: Production Cost per Issue

$104.10	Paper at $10.41/ream
100.00	Ink and supplies
50.00	Ink and supplies for second color for one page
4.00	Paper plate for 8 masters
————	
$258.10	Total cost/issue

8

The following recommendations should help to make the newsletter a success:

1. Publish the newsletter bi-monthly.

2. Carefully monitor production schedules.

3. Develop a style guide for all people working on the newsletter to ensure consistency.

4. Evaluate the success of the newsletter after six issues and make any necessary changes at that time.

9

REFERENCES

Haddad, B. (1989, June 5). Personal Interview.

Madden, M.J. (1979). Library user/non-user lifestyles. <u>American Libraries</u>, <u>10</u>, 78-81.

Novelli, D.P. (1988). Profile of the library user. <u>Library Imagination Paper</u>, <u>10</u>, 3.

Richter, R. (1989, May 31). Personal Interview.

17

ORAL REPORTS

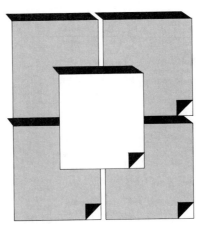

Learning Objectives

- To prepare a good oral presentation.
- To prepare effective visual aids.
- To evaluate strengths and weaknesses of a speaker.
- To deliver an informative speech.
- To analyze the audience and adapt the speech to the audience.
- To evaluate the presentation objectively.

Writing is only one way of communicating. In business you will not only write reports but will also present them orally. You may talk with one person, present your findings to a small group for discussion, or speak before a large audience. Oral reports can range from an informal exchange of ideas to a very formal presentation. This chapter will concentrate on the more formal oral reporting settings rather than on the informal one-on-one exchanges of ideas.

COMPARISON OF ORAL AND WRITTEN REPORTS

Like written reports, oral reports can be short or long, formal or informal, informational or analytical. Some of the basic characteristics are also the same. Good oral reports require planning, organization, and effective delivery.

Audience Analysis

The report writer, carefully analyzing the audience for the report, must answer these questions:

1. Who is the reader?
2. What are the needs of the reader?
3. How is the reader going to use the report?

The oral reporter conducts the same analysis but must be even more aware of the audience. A speaker analyzes the audience both during the planning of the speech and during the delivery. Unlike the reader of a report, the listener to an oral presentation provides immediate feedback, and the speaker must be able to adapt the speech on the basis of the feedback received.

The oral report must be instantly understandable because the audience cannot reread it. The reader of a written report can think about it, make notes, and compare it to other reports. The listener in oral reporting must keep up with the speaker; therefore, the speaker has to pay special attention to clarity and the use of examples.

Use of Visual Aids

Visual aids play an important role in written and oral reports. In both they clarify and emphasize data. Visual aids in oral reports, however, must be simple. They should concentrate on some key points rather than all of the details. At the beginning of a presentation the speaker may outline the topics he will discuss in a visual aid. Complex arguments and conclusions may be effectively summarized in a table that presents the most important points.

Nonverbal Communication

In written reports nonverbal communication is limited. In oral reporting, on the other hand, nonverbal communication influences the response of the audience and the delivery of the speech. The intonation of the speaker, the appearance of the speaker, the lighting, the gestures, and facial expressions all have an impact on the effectiveness of the oral report. The nonverbal aspects of oral communication will be discussed in detail later in this chapter.

PLANNING OF ORAL REPORTS

As you plan your oral report, you should answer the following questions:

1. What is the purpose of the oral report?
2. What is the occasion for the speech?
3. Under what conditions will you deliver the speech?
4. Who is the audience?
5. What visual aids will help you to make a good presentation?
6. What are your characteristics as a speaker?

What is the Purpose of the Oral Report?

You must determine whether you are to present information, analyze information, draw conclusions and make recommendations, or persuade the audience to a particular viewpoint. A good request for an oral report will tell you what is expected, but the request you receive may not be specific. If you have any doubts about what you are expected to do, you must ask. As an example, assume that you have written a 50-page evaluation of production costs in your plant. If you are asked to present the evaluation orally to a group of top managers, you must determine the **purpose of the oral report.** It might be one of the following:

Purpose of the Oral Report The purpose of the oral report may be different from that of the written report.

1. To give an overview of your findings
2. To give a summary of your recommendations on how to cut waste
3. To analyze the impact of inflation on production costs

As you begin your planning, you should write down the purpose of the oral presentation. If it will be based on a written report, you may also want to list the differences between the purpose of the written and the oral reports as in the following example:

Purpose of Written Report:
To analyze the reasons for the increase in production costs

Purpose of Oral Report:
To summarize the reasons for production cost increases to upper management

The writing of the purpose will guide you in your preparation of the oral report. You will not always write a formal report before making an oral presentation. If you are asked to give only an oral report, you still should write down a precise purpose statement. The purpose is related to the audience. If you talk about the subject to a group of production workers, for example, you may want to concentrate on their role in cutting costs. Presenting detailed findings and management's role in cutting costs might be useless and irrelevant.

In summary, the purpose of the oral and the written report can be identical, but it may also be different. The purpose of the speech is influenced by the audience, the situation, and the time you are given to deliver it. In ten minutes you could give only an overview of how to keep down production costs. In an hour you could go into detail.

What is the Occasion for the Speech?

Occasion for the Speech
The occasion influences the tone.

The **occasion for the speech** will influence the tone, the style of delivery, the examples you use, and the amount of detail you include. If you give an oral report to the same group under different circumstances, your report will be different. Assume that you talk to managers about the influence of the economy on company performance. For a dinner speech you use a somewhat lighter approach than for a workday session on policy formulation. The purpose of the dinner speech is not only to inform but also to entertain.

As an example, assume that you are a sales manager. In this position, you have available a great deal of information on sales figures, performance of individual salespeople, data on customers, and insight into the performance of the competition. When you make a presentation, you will adapt your information, presentation style, and tone to the occasion, the purpose of the speech, and the expectations of the audience.

For your Monday morning sales meetings, you will emphasize trends for the year and comparisons of individual people. You will give a motivational speech to inspire your team to go out and sell more. You want to praise, encourage, and inspire them to even better results.

When you give a report to upper management, however, you must determine what information they need. Do they want information only or an analysis and recommendations? Depending on the request, you might prepare transparencies with sales figures for several months or years. You might relate advertising expenditures to sales performance. You might use the performance of salespeople as the basis for a plea for better training.

In a staff meeting of managers from other departments, you may be asked to give a short informational presentation on sales performance. This data may be used to coordinate efforts of the various departments.

Under What Conditions Will You Deliver the Speech?

Conditions
The speaker must examine the physical environment for the speech.

The good speaker determines the answers to many questions during the planning stage. You need to know whether you will be one member of a panel, one of many speakers, or the only presenter. Will you speak in a large lecture hall or give your report in a small seminar room? What equipment will be available? Is there a projector, a blackboard, a podium? Must you bring your own projector, extension cords, and spare projector bulbs? You need to know whether you will stand on a stage removed from the audience or whether you will be on the same level. In small groups you may use different visual aids than in a large hall. If the audience will sit around a table, your delivery style will be different. The **conditions** under which you will deliver your speech will influence what you say and how you say it.

Who is the Audience?

Audience Analysis
Knowledge of the audience
helps in effective planning.

Audience analysis is essential. The speaker must know who the audience is. The occasion and the situation will serve as indicators, but the speaker should get as much information as possible about the audience, both as individuals and as a group. These are some questions you may want to ask:

1. How large is the audience?
2. How old is the audience? Are there notable age differences within the group?
3. What is the background of the audience?
4. Do the listeners have the same educational background?
5. Do the listeners have common work experiences?
6. What are the political beliefs of the audience? (This question may not be important for all reports.)
7. Does the audience hold certain beliefs about your topic?
8. Is the audience conservative or liberal?
9. What are the interests of the audience?
10. What does the audience expect?

The more you know about your audience, the better you will be able to adapt your oral report to the audience. If you know that your audience is suspicious of environmentalists and government regulation of industrial waste, for example, you will use a different approach for your report on the effects of industrial waste than if your audience is convinced that industrial waste is harmful and endorses legislation to deal with the problem. The substance of your report is the same, but your introduction, your examples, and your visual aids may be different. One audience has recognized the problem, whereas the other audience has to still be convinced that a problem exists.

What Visual Aids Will Help You Make a Good Presentation?

Visual Aids
Visual aids in speeches
have to be clear and
simple.

In oral reports, **visual aids** have different functions than in written reports. In oral reports they are often used to let the audience know what the speaker will emphasize. They are also used to summarize important facts and conclusions. In a written report the summary is in paragraph form, but a speaker may find that a verbal summary is not clear enough. The speaker may therefore decide to highlight the key points with a visual aid.

For example, the conclusions in Exhibit 17.1 concentrate on savings in three areas: elimination of credit cards, reduction of direct-dial calls, and reduction of long-distance calls. The reader of the report can think about these conclusions. In an oral report, however, the listener may have difficulty remembering all three areas. A summary like the one in Exhibit 17.2 can make the conclusions much clearer. The speaker can point to each conclusion as it is discussed.

The speaker may find that visual aids from a written report must be adapted for use in the oral presentation. Although they were effective in the written report, they may contain too much detail for an oral report. Exhibit 17.3 shows

Exhibit 17.1   Conclusions and Recommendations in Written Report

Conclusions and Recommendations

The Illinois Valley Library System has successfully controlled telephone
costs during the last three years; however, with rising costs additional efforts
are needed. At the same time we must continue to provide quality service to
member libraries. The analysis suggests the following:

Elimination of credit cards would save $683 annually.
Reduction in direct-dial calls would save $514 annually.
Reduction in length of calls would save $514 annually.

In addition, a special committee should examine alternative telephone
systems for the library so that we can increase our service to member libraries
and stay within the limits of our budget.

a detailed income statement for Walgreens for three years. The speaker who
wants to show the company's performance during the past year should simplify the information and highlight only major points, as Exhibit 17.4 does.

You can present your visual aids in many different ways. You may choose
flipcharts, blackboards, opaque projectors, overhead projectors, slide projectors, or handouts. Your choice will depend on the availability of material,
the size of the audience, the formality of the situation, your artistic ability, and
your handwriting.

Which visual aid you choose will also depend on the type of presentation
and the emphasis you want to set. As in the written report, visuals are intended
to facilitate understanding and the retaining of information. They are not

Exhibit 17.2   Conclusions and Recommendations in Oral Report

ELIMINATE CREDIT CARDS	$ 683.00
REDUCE DIRECT CALLS	514.00
REDUCE LENGTH OF CALLS	514.00
SAVINGS	$1,711.00

Exhibit 17.3   Visual Aid in Written Report

Eleven-Year Summary of Selected Financial Data (1)

Walgreen Co. and Subsidiaries
(Dollars in Thousands, except per share data)

	Fiscal Year	1985	1984	1983
Net Sales	Drugstores	$3,028,034	$2,614,265	$2,238,217
	Food Services	122,322	119,411	112,815
	Other Sales	11,579	10,949	9,582
	Total Net Sales	3,161,935	2,744,625	2,360,614
Costs and Deductions	Cost of sales	2,192,367	1,900,703	1,637,133
	Selling, occupancy and administration	791,697	691,139	601,623
	Other expense (income)	4,171	2,800	1,309
		2,988,235	2,594,642	2,240,065
Earnings	Earnings from U.S. operations before income taxes	173,700	149,983	120,549
	Income taxes	79,531	69,340	53,873
	Earnings from U.S. operations	94,169	80,643	66,676
	Equity in net earnings of Mexican operations	—	1,205	3,113
	Gain on sale of equity investments in Mexican operations, net of income taxes	—	3,598	—
	Net Earnings	$ 94,169	$ 85,446	$ 69,789
Net Earnings per Share(2)	Assuming full dilution	$ 1.53	$ 1.39	$ 1.13
	Assuming no dilution	1.53	1.39	1.14
Per Share(2)	Dividends Declared	$ .44	$ .36	$ .30
	Shareholders' Equity	7.83	6.76	5.74
Long-Term Obligations	Debt	$ 44,336	$ 24,472	$ 24,821
	Capital Leases	27,604	28,725	29,142
Assets and Equity	Total Assets	$ 961,938	$ 840,803	$ 718,022
	Shareholders' Equity	$ 480,974	$ 414,618	$ 351,705
	Return on Average Shareholders' Equity	21.0%	22.3%	21.4%

(1) Excludes the operations of the Globe Discount Department Store Division discontinued in fiscal 1978.
(2) Per share data have been adjusted for two-for-one stock splits in 1985, 1983 and 1982.

Source: Walgreen Co. and Subsidiaries, *Annual Report,* 1985.

important in themselves. The test of effectiveness is not how many good slides or transparencies you have prepared but whether they have enhanced the understanding of the audience. Ten transparencies are not necessarily better than one.

Exhibit 17.4   Visual Aid in Oral Report

Walgreens' 1985 Performance (Thousands of Dollars, Except per Share Data)

Net Sales	3,161,935
Costs	2,988,235
Earnings before Taxes	173,700
Net Earnings	94,169
Net Earnings per Share	$1.53
Return on Equity	21%

Flipcharts.   Using a flipchart, you can create visual aids as you speak. You will need a supply of colored pens as well as the flipchart itself, which is cumbersome to transport. Your handwriting must be neat, of course, and your creativity sufficient to make meaningful drawings on the spot. The result is usually less neat and not as attractive as other forms of visual aids.

Flipcharts are most effective in small groups during genuine discussions. For a formal presentation, the visual aids should be prepared ahead of time. Because the flipchart is small, people sitting in the back of a large room might not be able to see the illustrations.

Blackboards.   The blackboard has many of the same characteristics as the flipchart. The speaker can create visual aids on the spot. A drawback is that the speaker, while writing on the board, turns his back to the audience. If the audience is large, the viewers in the back of the room may not be able to see the visual aid. The speaker who counts on using a blackboard must make sure that a blackboard, colored chalk, and an eraser will be available.

Opaque Projectors.   The advantage of the opaque projector is that no special transparencies need to be prepared because it projects printed material. By moving the projector, the presenter can adjust the size of the projection. An opaque projector requires a dark room; as a result, the speaker has no eye contact with the audience. Opaque projectors are large, and few convention centers or hotels have them.

Overhead Projectors.   The overhead projector, which projects transparencies, is probably the most widely used machine for showing visual aids. The visual aid can be produced ahead of time. It will be neat and can be multicolored. With the help of a thermofax machine the visual aid can be transferred from a written report to a transparency.

The writing on the transparency must be large enough so that people at the back of the room can easily read it. As a general rule, typing is too small. If you do not have access to a typewriter or computer with large fonts, enlarge regular typing on a specialized copier before you run it through the thermofax machine.

If you have generated graphs with a computer graphics package, you can easily transfer the graph to a transparency. Before you use the graphs from a written report, however, evaluate them to determine whether they are appropriate for an oral report. You may want to change the amount of information or change the emphasis.

An advantage of the overhead projector is that you can use overlays. By placing one transparency over another, you can show developments over time. By using a special pen, you can also make notations on the visual aid as you talk. The overhead projector combines the advantages of the flipchart and the opaque projector.

By moving the machine, you can adapt the size of the projection to the size of the room. When you are talking to an audience about a transparency, you should face the audience and not the screen. Stand by the projector only if you do not block someone's view. While you explain a transparency, point with a pen or pointer to each area as you discuss it and keep eye contact with the audience.

Most businesses, convention centers, and hotels have overhead projectors. Still, before making the decision to use transparencies, you should check to see whether the necessary equipment will be there for your use.

Slide Projectors.   A slide presentation can be very effective. The slides can be prepared professionally and can be used many times. Some speakers combine slides with taped music and a recorded script. Slide presentations can be creative and of high quality, but the production of slides is more costly than the production of transparencies. Unless you will use the slides a number of times, the expense may not be justifiable. In addition, because the lights must be turned off when you show slides, you will lose eye contact with the audience. You will need to weigh the advantages and disadvantages of slide presentations carefully.

Handouts.   The handout is useful because listeners can follow the material on the handout while you explain it. The disadvantage is that the audience may get ahead of you and concentrate on the handout rather than on your presentation. Some speakers, to overcome this problem, give handouts at the end of the oral report. The result is that the audience does not have the material available when it would be most useful. In general, if you do not use any other visual aids and if the presentation is rather technical, you should give the handouts at the beginning of the presentation.

What Are Your Characteristics as a Speaker?

In order to give a good speech, you should know your strengths and weaknesses as a speaker. You should also know what helps you give a good speech and what makes you nervous. In the examination of your characteristics you can draw on your evaluation of past performances. The better your evaluation was then, the better your preparation can be. You may want to pay particular attention to timing, use of examples, nervousness, and actual preparation or practice of a speech.

Timing
The speaker has to consider the length of the entire speech and of the parts.

Timing.   Do you have difficulty staying within a given time limit? If you are asked to speak for ten minutes, are you still talking after 30 minutes? **Timing** difficulties can be caused by lack of organization and preparation. If you have ten minutes, you should practice your speech to see whether you can deliver it in ten minutes. You must determine the essential points so that you will not spend too much time on unimportant details. With experience you will develop a better sense for timing, but in the beginning practice may be the only way to find out how well you manage your time.

Timing is also an element of delivery style. A speaker who delivers an entire speech without a change in tempo will be boring. A speaker should slow down to explain difficult material and perhaps speed up at a climax. After an important point a speaker may pause for reflection. The speed of delivery must match the content.

Use of Examples.   Some speakers can think of example after example, whereas others are hard pressed to think of one. If you notice that the audience is puzzled, you may need more examples to make your point. In the middle of a speech, however, you will not have time to search your mind for examples; you must have them ready. Chances are that with experience this aspect of speaking will become easier for you, but in the beginning you should prepare more examples than you think you will use. You should write down the key points of all the examples and have them ready.

Nervousness.   People react differently to nervousness. Some people sweat, some tremble, some suffer from a dry throat. You know how nervousness affects you, and you should prepare accordingly. If you may need a glass of ice water, request it. Even if you do not drink it, simply having the water available may help. If you have a tendency to sweat, you may want to wear lightweight clothing. In most cases nervousness decreases once the speaker has started the presentation. The most important factor in overcoming nervousness is the confidence that comes from knowing your material and being thoroughly prepared.

Preparation of Your Speech.   Most speakers speak from cards. Some write out their complete speeches verbatim, and some memorize them.

Note Cards
Note cards have to be readable and contain key words.

Note Cards.   Unless you have a complete speech ready (perhaps as a previously written report), writing one out may be too time consuming. **Note cards** will give you the key words and the outline of your speech. With the notes your speech will be well organized, and you will not need to carry a stack of paper with you. An audience that sees 50 pages of material may worry about the length of your speech. Note cards are less conspicuous.

Note cards do not hold a lot of information. They do not give you the exact formulation for every idea. Some speakers, worried that note cards are not detailed enough, begin to write complete sentences on every card. That practice destroys the concept of the note card by tempting the speaker to look at the cards too often. If you use note cards, you should write only key words and quotations on them. The quotations should be marked so that you can find them easily.

Entire Speech on Paper
If the entire speech is on paper, the speaker may be tempted to read and, as a result, lose eye contact.

Complete Written Report.   The biggest advantage of having the **entire speech on paper** is that you know everything is there. Because you cannot forget anything, you may relax more. The biggest problem is that you may concentrate on your paper and forget the audience in front of you. It is tempting to read the speech if it is in front of you. But when you read, you will not look at the audience and may lose control. Without eye contact you may miss important feedback.

In some situations a business person must read a speech or large portions of a speech because of technical details, possible litigation, and briefings. The following guidelines may help you if you must read your presentation:

1. Have the entire speech printed in large print.
2. Read the speech ahead of time and know the material thoroughly.
3. Highlight key points and use them as guides through the presentation.
4. If at all possible, have the podium high enough so that you do not have to lean down and forward to read your speech.
5. Establish eye contact.
6. Work on timing and intonation. Many read speeches are ineffective because the speaker does not vary the speed of delivery and has a monotonous intonation.

Memorized Speech Memorized speeches are delivered in a monotonous voice.

Memorized Speech.   In most business settings, speaking without notes is not effective. The speaker must provide precise numbers and facts, and memorizing them is pointless. Moreover, **memorized speeches** have a tendency to sound monotonous and boring. The speaker may mentally concentrate on a perfect recitation rather than on an effective delivery of the speech. The speaker who loses his concentration may forget the rest of the speech. As in the case of a read speech, the establishment of contact with the audience is difficult.

You must determine which approach works best for you. Your past experience will help you to prepare. If you know that you will be tempted to read a complete report, you should not take the complete report with you. If you know that you are nervous about the opening and transitions, you may want to prepare those parts more carefully and practice them more often than other parts of your speech.

Extemporaneous Speech.   Although an extemporaneous speech appears spontaneous, it is, in fact, very carefully prepared. To deliver an extemporaneous speech well requires confidence. The speaker typically has no note cards. He seems to miraculously find the right words. Beginning speakers should not try to deliver a speech extemporaneously.

Impromptu Speech.   The impromptu speech is delivered on the spur of the moment. For example, a manager may be in a meeting with other managers. The discussion may turn to training programs, and he may give an impromptu speech on the feedback he has received about motivational training at one of the subsidiaries. The manager did not have time to prepare his remarks in advance. He has to organize his ideas fast and decide what is most important. Most impromptu speeches take place in smaller groups.

Practice Practicing a speech builds confidence.

Practice of Your Speech.   If you feel childish practicing a speech, it may help you to know that many speakers **practice** in front of a mirror. They time their speeches and practice the precise wording of key elements. They may even practice the nonverbal elements of their speeches. Once you are in the business world, you will not have time to practice every speech, but in the beginning you may benefit by practicing the actual delivery.

Rather than memorize the introduction, key points, and important transitions verbatim, you may be better off to practice those sections several times. Each time you may vary the wording slightly, and that is good. This way you do not concentrate on the exact wording, which you might forget during delivery. Good and meaningful practice can help you to relax by building your confidence.

Your practice should be as realistic as possible. If you will give your speech standing behind a podium, practice standing behind a podium. If you are to speak to a smaller group sitting around a conference table, practice sitting at a conference table. You should time your speech and be aware that most speakers speed up when they deliver their speech to an audience.

DELIVERY OF ORAL REPORTS

During the delivery of your speech you will repeat the same evaluation process that was part of your preparation. You must examine the situation, your style, and the audience.

Situation Analysis

If you have given any speeches at all, you know that the situation, in spite of careful preparation, may not always be what you expected. The room may be smaller or larger than you anticipated. Perhaps you were one of two scheduled speakers, but the second speaker did not arrive. Perhaps you anticipated a small group and audience participation instead of 100 people and a podium.

In any case, you must adapt your delivery to the new situation. Obviously you cannot prepare for all eventualities, but you should make some contingency plans in case something goes wrong or differs from your expectations. In your preparation you might want to think about how you would change your presentation for a large or a small group.

Self-Analysis

The analysis of your delivery goes hand in hand with the audience analysis discussed in the next section. Already aware of your strengths and weaknesses, during the delivery you must be aware of your presentation. You can only analyze your presentation, however, if you are thoroughly familiar with the material you are presenting. As a report presenter you must give a speech that is informative, factually correct, well organized, and interesting. At the same time, you must be aware of style of delivery, because the effectiveness of a speech depends on more than content and organization.

Self-Confidence
A confident speaker
presents a positive image to
the audience.

Confidence.   The more you speak, the more **self-confidence** you will develop. Beginning speakers often are nervous because they are not sure how well they will do. They may be worried about the topic, their delivery, and the audience reception. Although preparation is important for all speakers, the beginning speaker, who often is nervous and unsure of himself, must know the topic inside out. If the delivery is not perfect, at least the content will be organized. Of course, even experienced speakers are not all relaxed. Many suffer stage fright before large audiences.

What can you do to overcome the fear and apprehension? Most important is to realize that nervousness is not all bad. In fact, you may not want to eliminate all of your anxiety. You simply want to get rid of the excess and the crippling fear. Some anxiety can be beneficial in starting your adrenalin to flow; it readies you for the speech. In a completely relaxed state you might give a thorough talk but probably not an inspiring or exciting one. You must realize the difference between being scared and simply being nervous in anticipation.

If you are truly afraid of speaking to groups, the following suggestions may help you overcome your fear:

1. **Be positive.** The worst thing you can do is to "psyche yourself out" by telling yourself that your speech will most definitely be a failure. Instead, contemplate the positive aspects. You know the material and have practiced your speech. Your transparencies are clear and well designed. You have every reason to be confident. Concentrating on your preparation may help you to forget your fear.
2. **Be excited about your speech.** Enthusiasm can build your confidence. After all, you are talking about something that is of interest to you and of importance to the audience.
3. **Think of the audience as an ally rather than an enemy.** The audience is there to get information. In a weekly sales meeting, for example, the salespeople want to know how to improve their performance. They want encouragement. They need your suggestions.

   At a convention, delegates will come to hear you because you have researched a particular topic that they are interested in. They want to learn how they can apply your findings or how your research relates to their work. They are there because they need you.

   Most audiences are friendly. They show goodwill and want the speaker to succeed. People are willing to listen, and they are not there to see you fail.
4. **Look at your audience.** The audience is not one big mass. It consists of individuals. Picture how they might use your information.
5. **Be confident of your ability.** You have a message to deliver and, in order for that message to reach your audience, you adapt to that audience just as you adapt to friends and colleagues. The basics of good communication remain the same for a more formal talk.

Sincerity.   You must believe in what you say, and you must be sincere in your delivery. The audience will detect quickly if you yourself do not have confidence in your findings. As an example, assume you are speaking on business ethics. In your speech you examine ways of improving the ethical conduct of business people. If your voice, your examples, and your nonverbal signals tell the audience that you yourself think the whole subject is blown out of proportion and that no problem exists, you are not sincere. The audience will detect your attitude and react to it. In any case, the audience will not learn much about how to improve ethical conduct. **Sincerity** cannot be faked.

Sincerity
Sincerity has to be genuine to be convincing.

Friendliness.   As a speaker, you want to be friendly rather than aloof. A smile as you approach the podium, the establishment of eye contact as you address the audience, and nonthreatening gestures as you speak tell the audience that you are friendly. Like sincerity, friendliness must be real. The audience will respond to a friendly speaker.

Nonverbal Communication

Although the most important part of a speech is its content, the success of a speech is not determined by content alone. The content may be factual and well organized, and yet the audience may be confused and puzzled because of distracting or inappropriate **nonverbal signals.** On the other hand, a speech may be judged excellent because the speaker used effective gestures and facial expressions to highlight key points. Nonverbal communication is not an adjunct to a presentation; it is an integral part. Appearance, gestures, posture, facial expressions, and eye contact are elements of nonverbal communication.

Nonverbal Signals
Nonverbal signals must support the words.

Appearance.   Your **appearance** will reflect confidence or lack of confidence, sincerity or lack of sincerity. You may argue that your appearance has nothing to do with the content of your speech, which the audience should judge on its own merit. You may be right, but that is seldom what happens. Inappropriate clothing will draw attention to itself. If you want the audience to concentrate on your speech, you must dress to support what you say by underlining your friendliness, sincerity, self-confidence, and your authority.

Appearance
The speaker must plan her appearance to fit the occasion and the purpose for the speech.

If you are a male in upper management, you will wear a conservative business suit for most of your presentations. If you speak to workers as the boss, the business suit is appropriate. If, on the other hand, you want to talk to workers as a manager who seeks their cooperation and suggestions, the suit may be too intimidating. You may decide to wear slacks and a shirt. If you visit an oil rig or a farm, you may wear overalls or jeans.

Your attire will also depend on what you want to communicate. Do you want to project an image of authority, friendliness, or technical competence? And what is the purpose of your speech? The two must be combined. For example, a few years ago coal miners were on strike. In a television report the miners first voiced their grievances, and then the chief executive spoke. The CEO did not sit behind his executive desk in a dark business suit. He talked in the yard with a mine shaft as a backdrop. He wore slacks and a flannel shirt and a hard hat. Clearly, the company wanted to project an image of management concern and understanding.

John T. Molloy, a clothing consultant, described appropriate and successful dress for men and women in his book, *The Woman's Dress for Success Book* (1977). He advocated business suits in basic colors and conservative tailoring. While some business people accept this advice, others find such recommendations too narrow and stifling. Women face an additional problem when choosing business dress. For centuries women have been the target of the fashion industry. Women's clothing is generally more colorful, stylish, and trendy than men's. And women may ask why they should wear suits and boring colors just because they have advanced to management ranks.

The issue is not what is most comfortable but what is most effective in communicating. A woman speaking to an audience on fashion merchandising and style will wear something different from the woman who presents her recommendations for the purchase of a new computer system to upper management. This may not be fair, but the two speeches have different audiences and functions. If the woman recommending computers is wearing the latest styles with flashy colors and gaudy costume jewelry, her recommendations might not be taken seriously. Although her recommendations may be excellent, the perception of her as insincere and unbusinesslike may influence their reception.

If you prepare for a television presentation, the producers may tell you which colors and styles are most appropriate. Some colors are better for television than others. You will need to get expert advice.

Gestures

Gestures must be in harmony with the words.

Gestures.   Confidence, apprehension, or nervousness can be indicated by **gestures.** The experts do not always agree on what specific gestures mean. Much depends on content and circumstances. Gestures, nevertheless, are important in effective communications. A speaker who stands behind the podium with arms straight down does not look relaxed. A speaker who grasps the podium with white-knuckled hands does not inspire confidence. A speaker who taps his note cards throughout the speech will appear nervous although the habit can also indicate a lack of concentration. Hand movements that support what you say, on the other hand, will help the audience understand your speech better. Taking a few steps can underscore a point you are making.

Gestures are culture related. Americans are more restrained in their gestures than people from Latin America, Southern Europe, or the Middle East. Northern Europeans and the Japanese, on the other hand, are more reserved than Americans. The degree of gesturing and arm movements will be influenced by a careful audience analysis.

During a formal speech, walking could be perceived as informal and inappropriate. In a less formal setting the speaker may walk, for example, from the podium to the overhead projector to point out specific data on the transparency.

Posture.   The speaker must be relaxed and comfortable without slouching. Posture not only will communicate to the audience, but it also will influence the speaker's self-perception. Because posture is a personal trait, absolute rules are difficult to set. Good posture proclaims confidence. Slumped shoulders can mean insecurity. Those are general statements, however, that do not always hold.

Posture is a component of the entire image the speaker presents. Posture can underscore the speaker's words but can also negate them. Good posture will help the speaker with a delivery of the presentation because it facilitates breathing. Many excellent speakers take instruction in posture and breathing so that they do not become tired during a long speech.

Facial Expressions.   Facial expressions, more than any of the other nonverbal components, show sincerity. Because the audience looks mostly at the speaker's face, the speaker must be aware of facial expressions. They can underline or contradict words and give away the true feelings of the speaker. They can show friendliness and respect or disdain for the audience. Facial expressions also must be synchronized with the content of the speech. A broad smile is not appropriate when discussing the harmful effects of pollution.

Eye Contact
Eye contact provides feedback to the speaker and helps in audience adaptation.

Eye Contact.   Part of facial expression is **eye contact,** one of the most powerful tools for holding an audience's attention. Eye contact also signals to the speaker how the audience feels and reacts. Is the audience becoming bored? Is the audience agreeing or disagreeing? Does the audience understand? The feedback is crucial in adjusting the delivery of the speech. Long before the audience begins to fidget, the speaker can determine restlessness through eye contact. A good speaker will adapt his speech, change his voice, or shorten the speech to keep the audience's interest.

To elicit feedback, you must look at the audience. This means that you look at people; you do not simply glance. You look directly at individuals in all parts of the room. If you look at people, they will feel personally addressed, and they will respond personally.

Question-and-Answer Sessions

At the end of many speeches the audience is given the opportunity to ask questions. Listeners may ask for clarification of remarks in the speech. They may want to know more about the method for data collection. Some may ask about related topics that were not specifically addressed in the speech. As the speaker, you must be prepared to answer questions. You should reflect beforehand on the types of questions the audience might ask and bring supporting material, such as statistics. If you do not know the answer to a question, you should say so. The audience will not expect you to have every detail committed to memory.

Most audiences are friendly, but occasionally you may face a hostile audience or hostile individuals in an audience. If you have delivered a speech on your company's advertising, you expect questions related to advertising. If your company has been in the news because of pollution problems, however, someone may ask you about those problems even though pollution is not your area. If the pollution problem was "big news," you should have anticipated that someone might ask. You should be familiar with your company's position and be able to make a brief statement. You can also point out that you simply are not familiar enough with that area to talk about it. You can suggest the name of a person to contact for more detailed information.

Whatever you do, you should avoid being pulled into an argument. When only a few hostile persons are in the audience, the rest of the audience often comes to the speaker's aid by asking friendly and topic-related questions. During question-and-answer periods you can show how well you know your area and how well you can handle pressure.

Audience Analysis

Responsibilities of the Speaker. Even though you carefully analyzed your audience before the presentation, you must also analyze the audience during your presentation so that you can adapt your speech. Based on feedback—from eye contact, for example—you may need to delete or add examples, provide additional background information, or cut part of the background. You may want to emphasize some points more than others. In any case, you must respond to the audience.

You must make it easy for the audience to listen. This means you have to get their attention at the beginning and hold it throughout your speech. The following guidelines will help you to keep the interest of listeners:

1. Tell the audience at the beginning what you are going to talk about. Give the necessary background information. Describe exactly what you will cover.
2. Lead the audience through your presentation. Let them know where you are. If you have finished point three and are ready to start point four, say so. Summarize complicated or long parts so that the audience can remember the important points.
3. Summarize the speech at the end. You may want to itemize the crucial points in order to emphasize them.

Communication is a two-way process in which the audience is actively involved and has obligations and responsibilities. All of you will not only be speakers but also listeners. Let us examine some of the aspects of a good and responsible audience.

Responsibilities of the Audience. The following guidelines will help you to become a better member of an audience:

1. Come prepared. If you know the topic ahead of time, think about it. If you are expected to read material related to the presentation, you must prepare. The speaker will base her presentation on the assumption that you have read the material.
2. Provide feedback. You play an active role. Even good speakers have difficulty giving a good presentation if the audience does not participate. Theater people can testify to that. An excellent performance can fall flat

if the audience does not become involved, that is, if the audience does not respond, applaud, or react in some manner. Actors need feedback. Many actors find it difficult to act without an audience. A speaker is in the same situation as the actor. As a member of the audience, you are essential to the success of the presentation.

3. Be attentive. Your posture, facial expressions, and attitudes should tell the speaker that you are listening actively. In most business settings you are not there to be entertained but to obtain information. You spend your time and the company's money to listen to that speech. You have an obligation to learn all you can.

Listening

Effective listening requires concentration and an open mind.

Listening is not always easy. Experts say that the brain can process up to 500 words a minute but that a speaker can deliver only about 250 words per minute. That allows you plenty of time to daydream. While your mind wanders, you may miss important points, and you may have difficulty picking up the train of thought. A good speaker takes those occurrences into account and will organize the speech accordingly. The speaker can give summaries, itemize points, and give clear objectives for every section; however, the task of communicating is shared with the audience. Good listening requires determination and discipline. The suggestions below can help you to become an effective listener:

1. Limit distractions.
2. Look at the speaker. Looking at the speaker rather than staring into space will help you to follow the speech.
3. Avoid being critical of the delivery of the speech, that is, the voice, the appearance, or the nonverbal skills of the speaker. Control your emotions.
4. Concentrate on the content of the speech. What does the speaker say? What is the central theme?
5. Listen for ideas and patterns of reasoning.
6. Imagine that you must summarize the speech for someone else several hours after you have heard it.
7. Listen actively rather than passively. Summarize material and points in your mind as you listen.
8. Be open minded. Do not make up your mind beforehand that the topic is boring.

EVALUATION OF ORAL REPORTS

Evaluation

The evaluation of the speech must be thorough and systematic to be of any use in the future.

Part of every presentation is an **evaluation** of your strengths and weaknesses. You must be honest with yourself as you go through that process. Glossing over problems will not improve your skills as a speaker. You must determine what went particularly well and what went less well, and you will also want to find out the reasons. A checklist like the one in Exhibit 17.5 might be a good place to write down the main points in your evaluation. You can use this feedback in preparing for your next presentation.

Exhibit 17.5   **Form for Speech Evaluation**

	Good	Average	Weak	Comments
1. Organization				
2. Summary				
3. Transitions				
4. Examples				
5. Visual aids				
6. Eye contact				
7. Ability to adapt to audience				
8. Confidence of speaker				
9. Nervousness				
10. Effectiveness of preparation				
11. Effective adaptation to time constraints				
12. Summary of material				
13. Overall evaluation of speech				

ADAPTATION TO GROUP SIZE AND SETTING

A presentation to a large group requires different skills, techniques, and preparation than a presentation to a small group. The following points may help you in giving an effective speech to groups of different sizes and in different settings.

Large Groups

1. Your presentation to a large group must be more formal than to a small group.
2. You are removed from the audience; usually you will stand behind a podium, probably on a stage.
3. Your visual aids must be large enough so that people sitting in the back of the room can see them.
4. In a large group people may feel uncomfortable asking questions; therefore, you must sense whether people understand what you say. You must watch the audience closely for feedback.
5. You may ask the audience to hold questions until the end of your presentation.

Small Groups

1. A group of 20 to 40 people is relatively intimate. You may stand close to the audience. This provides you with better feedback, but the audience can also look more closely at you.

2. In a small group you may accept questions during your presentation, but you can also ask your audience to hold questions until the end.
3. Whether you invite an open discussion or maintain a more formal atmosphere will depend on the topic and the group. If you give a presentation to colleagues on a topic that has already been discussed at length, you might decide in favor of a dialogue. However, the danger with a dialogue or discussion is that you lose control of the presentation. The audience may jump ahead and bring up points that you prefer to bring up later. Unless everyone is well informed, the organization of the material may suffer with too much audience participation. The relationship between facts may be lost as a result.

Conference Setting

1. In a conference setting people usually sit around a table. The group is closed.
2. You may stand or sit for your presentation. Your decision will depend on the group and on the material. Some groups may resent it if you sit. Others may prefer that you sit so that the presentation is more personal.
3. If you have visual aids, you may need to stand.
4. In small conference groups, you must be aware of political currents. Your personal relationship with group members may influence the acceptance of your presentation.
5. The place on the agenda and the time allotted for your presentation are key factors in your presentation.
6. To save time, you may use handouts.
7. The conference setting is usually goal oriented. Your presentation will not be simply a general overview or a pep talk. In a conference setting you present specific issues about which many group members may be knowledgeable. You must therefore be able to support your presentation with data and facts.

SUMMARY OF LEARNING OBJECTIVES

To prepare a good oral presentation.

In the preparation you must determine the purpose and the situation of the speech. You must determine who the audience is and what visual aids to use. You must also evaluate your strengths and weaknesses as a speaker.

To prepare effective visual aids.

Many ways are available to present material visually. You may choose a slide projector, an opaque projector, an overhead projector, a flipchart, a blackboard, or a handout. Size of the audience, size of the room, and purpose of the presentation will influence the method of visual presentation.

To evaluate strengths and weaknesses of a speaker.

You must determine what makes you comfortable and what makes you nervous. Do you prefer note cards or the complete report? Do you read your speech or memorize it? Do you have a tendency to speak longer than you were asked to speak? Honest answers to these questions will help you prepare and deliver your speech.

To deliver an informative speech.

You should use audience feedback to adapt your speech to the audience. You must show confidence, friendliness, and sincerity.

To analyze the audience and adapt the speech to the audience.

Audience analysis is an ongoing process. You must read the nonverbal signals the audience sends you to adapt to your audience. Most audiences are friendly and show goodwill.

To evaluate the presentation objectively.

After you have given your speech, you must evaluate your performance and use the feedback to improve future speeches.

KEY TERMS

Purpose of the Oral Report
Occasion for the Speech
Conditions
Audience Analysis
Visual Aids
Timing
Note Cards
Entire Speech on Paper
Memorized Speech

Practice
Self-Confidence
Sincerity
Nonverbal Signals
Appearance
Gestures
Eye Contact
Listening
Evaluation

QUESTIONS AND DISCUSSION POINTS

1. What are the characteristics of a good oral presentation?
2. How can you overcome nervousness before and during a speech?
3. Discuss the role of nonverbal communication during a speech.
4. Discuss the role of appearance when giving a speech.
5. What role does the audience play during a speech?
6. What is the role of eye contact?
7. Discuss the three delivery styles—reading of a speech, reciting from memory, and using note cards.
8. Discuss the elements of good listening.

EXERCISES

1. Listen to a speech and try to write down the most important points afterward.
2. The next time you listen to a speech, evaluate the performance of the speaker.
3. You are the treasurer of a student club (your choice). Prepare a presentation for the Student Government Funding Board about funds needed for club activities for the coming year.
4. Prepare a five-minute speech for the Academic Senate of your university arguing that student evaluations of instructors should be made public.
5. Use the same situation as Exercise 4, but argue that the evaluations should remain confidential.
6. As president of a student organization, prepare the introduction of guest speaker.
7. Prepare a ten-minute speech on the importance of good communication skills in business. You will deliver the speech to graduating seniors, who are involved in job interviews.
8. As a personnel manager of a firm, you regularly select employees to recruit graduating seniors on college campuses. Prepare a ten-minute speech on the importance of screening candidates for effective communication skills.
9. Prepare a speech on career opportunities in your major.
10. Prepare a speech on the preparation of resumés and cover letters.
11. As a personnel manager, prepare a speech on the status of the progress of women in the workforce.
12. Identify a problem in an organization of which you are a member. Analyze the problem and identify a solution (or solutions) to the problem. Present your report to the board of directors.
13. You are a member of the board of Students for Academic Excellence, which has been asked to report to the College Council on the importance of academic standards. Prepare an oral report.
14. As a volunteer for the Red Cross (or an organization of your choice), prepare a speech to motivate people to contribute their services as volunteers or in other capacities, such as donating blood.

Reference

Molloy, John T. (1977). *The Woman's Dress for Success Book*. Chicago: Follett Publishing.

CASES

The cases are divided into two groups, those that do not require further research and those that do. Cases 1 to 14 provide all of the information necessary to write a report. You can add more detail, but you should not change the data provided. Cases 15 to 37 give only background information, along with a description of the audience of the report and the position of the writer. Assembling the necessary data to write the report will require secondary research, primary research, or both.

One word of caution: the case-writeups are not perfect; therefore, you should avoid copying the case verbatim for your report.

Case 1

BUSINESS ORGANIZATIONS AND MANAGEMENT

All business students at Central State University must take Business Organizations and Management. Last year Dr. Feldstein, a management professor, reorganized the course. Up to that point four sections of the course with 45 students each were taught every semester.

Now all 180 students meet in the same class once a week. During that time the professor lectures and introduces new material. Twice a week the class is broken up into lab sections of about 15 students. Lab managers, who are in charge of the lab sections, are undergraduate students with a minimum grade point average of 3.5. During the lab sessions the lecture material is discussed. The lab managers also must supervise group projects. For the purpose of the projects students are divided into groups of five students. The group projects provide some problems because not all students work equally hard.

You are a graduate assistant to Dr. Feldstein. Your job is to supervise the lab managers. Based on your discussions with the lab managers and with students who take the course, you are concerned about the effectiveness of the course organization.

You have formulated the following hypotheses and have decided to test them.

1. Lab material is repetitious and not challenging enough.
2. Lab section managers do not possess the necessary teaching skills to motivate students.
3. The written group report causes students to withdraw from lab activities.

You administer a questionnaire to two lab sections, one with 16 students, the other with 15 students. You have tabulated the results of the survey in the accompanying table. Now you must evaluate the responses. Analyze the material to determine whether the findings support the hypotheses. Write a report of the results for Dr. Feldstein.

RESPONSES TO QUESTIONNAIRE

Number of students in both sections	Percentage of students in both sections	Number of students in section 03	Percentage of students in section 03	Number of students in section 04	Percentage of students in section 04	
1. Which section are you in?						
		16				Section 03
				15		Section 04
2. What sex are you?						
16	52	9	56	7	47	Male
15	48	7	44	8	53	Female
3. What year are you in college?						
						Freshman
						Sophomore
23	74	10	63	13	87	Junior
7	23	5	31	2	13	Senior
1	3	1	6			Graduate
4. How would you rate the level of class participation in lab activities?						
7	22	4	25	3	20	Excellent participation
21	68	9	56	12	80	Good participation
3	10	3	19			Average participation
						Below-average participation
						Poor participation
5. How clear are the objectives and purpose of lab-experience material?						
5	16	1	6	4	27	Consistently clear
17	55	8	50	9	61	Generally clear
5	16	4	25	1	6	Inconsistently clear
4	13	3	19	1	6	Seldom clear
						Never clear
6. Does your lab manager create interest in the lab material?						
13	42	6	38	7	47	Stimulates interest to a high degree
13	42	8	50	5	33	Stimulates interest at times
5	16	2	12	3	20	Neither stimulates nor reduces interest
						Reduces interest
						Destroys interest
7. What is the level of the lab-experience material?						
3	10	2	13	1	7	Course material too easy, no challenge
11	35	6	37	5	33	Course material at right level, no challenge
14	45	5	31	9	60	Course material at right level, challenge exists
						Course material too difficult, too much of a challenge
3	10	3	19			Course material merely a repeat of material from other courses

Number of students in both sections	Percentage of students in both sections	Number of students in section 03	Percentage of students in section 03	Number of students in section 04	Percentage of students in section 04	
8. How enthusiastic is your lab manager?						
12	39	8	50	4	27	Highly enthusiastic
18	58	8	50	10	67	Generally enthusiastic
1	3			1	6	Occasionally enthusiastic
						Rarely enthusiastic
						Never enthusiastic
9. How would you rate the overall effectiveness of your lab instructor?						
13	42	7	44	6	40	Excellent
18	58	9	56	9	60	Good
						Fair
						Poor
						Very poor
10. Do you participate in group activities?						
21	68	11	69	10	67	I always participate.
5	16	3	19	2	13	I generally participate.
5	16	2	12	3	20	I occasionally participate.
						I almost never participate.
						I never participate.
11. Does written group work encourage you to participate in lab activities?						
1	3	1	6			It always encourages me to participate.
7	23	2	13	5	33	It encourages rather than discourages me to participate.
21	68	12	75	9	60	It does not affect my participation.
2	6	1	6	1	7	Written group work always discourages me from participating.
12. Have any of your previous classes discussed the material being presented in lab experiences?						
13	42	4	25	9	60	None of my previous classes covered this material.
8	26	4	25	4	26	One previous class covered this material.
5	16	3	19	2	14	Two previous classes covered this material.
2	6	2	12			Three previous classes covered this material.
3	10	3	19			Four or more previous classes covered this material.
13. Which areas, in your opinion, need the most change?						
1	3	1	6			Lab-manager preparation
3	10	1	6	2	13	Student participation
11	36	6	38	5	34	Lab material
14	45	8	50	6	40	Written group work
2	6	1	6	1	7	Do not know

Case 2   NUTRITION CONSULTANTS

Nancy Redgrave, the owner of Nutrition Consultants, is receiving an increasing number of requests for nutritional information on fast food. After the local papers ran several articles on the link between a high-fat, high-salt diet and heart disease and high blood pressure, people seem to be more concerned about what they eat. Furthermore, an article by the diet center Trim-Slim emphasized the fact that most Americans consume too many calories. Nancy Redgrave feels that it is time to have a systematic nutrition evaluation of fast foods to answer questions of clients. She asks you to collect the data on fast food in town and report the findings to her in a standard memo report.

You have assembled the material in the accompanying table.

Which Fast Food Entreés Are the Most Nutritious?

			Nutritional Factors			
Fast Food Entreés	Serving Size (oz.)	Calories (no.)	Fat (gm.)	Carbohydrates (gm.)	Total Sugars (gm.)	Sodium (mg.)
Hamburgers						
Burger King Whopper	9	660	41	49	9	1083
McDonald's Big Mac	7.5	591	33	46	6	963
Wendy's Old Fashioned	6.5	413	22	29	5	708
Hamburger Group Average	8	555	32	41	7	918
Fish						
Long John Silver's	7.5	483	27	27	0.1	1333
Arthur Treacher's Original	5.25	439	27	27	0.3	421
McDonald's Filet-O-Fish	4.5	383	18	38	3	613
Burger King Whaler	7	584	34	50	5	968
Fish Group Average	6	472	27	36	2	834
Chicken						
Kentucky Fried Chicken	6.75	405	21	16	0	728
Arthur Treacher's Original Chicken	5.5	409	23	25	0	580
Chicken Group Average	6	407	22	21	0	654
Pizza						
Pizza Hut Pizza Supreme[2]	7.75	506	15	64	6	1281

[1] Recommended daily allowance for an adult woman, as set by the National Academy of Sciences/National Research Council.
[2] One-half of a 15½-ounce 10-inch Pizza Supreme Thin and Crispy.
Source: Adapted from Fast-Food Chains. (1979, September). *Consumer Reports,* p. 509.

Case 3   ST. MARK CHURCH

The congregation of St. Mark faces a problem. The church was built in two phases. The first part was constructed during a time when asbestos was widely used; the new part does not have any asbestos. The asbestos in the older part is restricted to the ceilings in the basement under the fellowship hall. The four rooms in that area are used one hour a week for Sunday school classes for grades 1 to 4. The rooms are not used during the week.

As soon as the announcement was made that asbestos was in the ceilings, parents of the children who are affected became very concerned. The church had tests run that showed some particles in the air, but the particles were not identified as asbestos. The concern is that the ceilings might begin to disintegrate with age. An additional problem is that the results of the asbestos exposure in the Sunday school classes will not be known for many years.

Nutritional Factors

Percentage of RDA Requirements[1]

Protein (%)	Vitamin A (%)	Thiamine (%)	Riboflavin (%)	Vitamin B_6 (%)	Vitamin B_{12} (%)	Niacin (%)	Calcium (%)	Phosphorus (%)	Iron (%)	Average Total (%)
57	12	51	30	19	67	55	9	29	26	35.5
59	5	52	33	13	63	55	23	44	23	37.0
52	8	36	26	13	83	45	8	24	27	32.2
56	8	46	30	15	71	52	13	32	25	34.8
72	5	17	12	16	133	24	3	46	3	33.1
46	3	11	6	10	27	18	2	32	3	15.8
35	3	39	19	6	23	25	14	27	9	20.0
48	3	38	20	7	60	31	8	50	12	27.7
50	4	26	14	13	61	25	7	39	7	24.6
78	4	21	25	19	40	72	6	35	14	31.4
57	3	12	10	24	10	87	2	23	4	24.2
68	4	17	18	22	25	80	4	34	9	28.1
61	36	59	40	17	43	49	41	46	24	41.6

The church faces possible liability suits from parents and their children but also from workers who would be involved in removing the asbestos. The church has three options:

1. Do nothing. A number of people argue that one hour is not sufficient exposure to cause any harm. Research has examined only high-level exposure over long periods of time.
2. Encase the asbestos. In that process a material is sprayed over the ceiling to ensure that the asbestos will not flake off. That process would cost about $9,000. Any crack in the coating, however, would expose the asbestos again. A number of people insist on the removal of the asbestos.
3. Remove the asbestos. The removal would solve the problem, but this alternative is very costly. The church asked three firms for bids on the cost of the removal of the asbestos and the installation of new ceilings. The bids were as follows:

Firm A	$25,000
Firm B	$38,000
Firm C	$33,000

All three companies seem to be reputable.

Currently the church does not have the money to pay for Option 3. It would have to be raised through either bonds or special donations. Before this problem surfaced, the Finance Committee had decided to have a special fund drive for a sister congregation in Central America. During an earthquake the church of that congregation was badly damaged. The roof collapsed, and the furniture was destroyed. The congregation of that church has asked for support from St. Mark. The committee in charge of special projects at St. Mark feels that the congregation will be hard-pressed to finance both projects.

Write a report to the membership explaining the situation and making recommendations on what to do. The ultimate decision lies with the congregation.

Case 4   TOOLS INC.

Your company, Tools Inc., has plans to expand into Western Europe. Tools Inc. will face tough competition, but management thinks that with good planning Tools Inc. will be able to establish itself in the market. Tools Inc. specializes in tools for the do-it-yourself person. Over the past five years the do-it-yourself market has grown tremendously in Western Europe. Tools Inc. is considering manufacturing tools in Europe rather than just exporting them from the United States. Ron Houston, Vice President for Sales, has asked you to collect information on the cost of labor and inflation rates in selected countries. Of course, additional information will be necessary before any decision can be made, but Ron Houston believes that the information on labor costs and inflation can help in narrowing down the number of countries under consideration for production of your tools.

Organize the data you found and analyze your findings in a memo to Ron Houston.

Cost of Labor (U.S. dollars)

	Direct Cost per Hour	Indirect Cost per Hour
United States	$26.09	$10.36
Switzerland	20.18	9.89
West Germany	15.63	12.69
Netherlands	14.64	11.86
Belgium	14.38	11.14
Denmark	18.76	4.24
Italy	11.71	11.01
France	11.89	9.69
Austria	10.83	10.29
Great Britain	12.70	5.27

Rate of Inflation

United States	3.4%
Switzerland	3.0
West Germany	1.8
Netherlands	2.3
Belgium	4.6
Denmark	4.1
Italy	9.5
France	5.6
Austria	2.6
Great Britain	6.2

Case 5   ELECTRONIC INSTRUMENTS INC.

You are the public-relations manager for Electronic Instruments Inc. Your company has decided to expand production into Korea. Management feels that the expansion into Korea is the only way the company can stay competitive. Plans are to have production and routine assembly of basic components done in Korea. The finished components will then be shipped to the plant in Freemont, Iowa. Freemont has a population of 30,000. Currently the company employs 1,000 people. As a result of the move, 500 people will be laid off. The company hopes that the move will increase sales by 15 percent after the second year and profits by 20 percent after five years. The company also thinks that employment in Freemont will slightly rise as production in Korea expands. The jobs in Freemont will become more sophisticated. The move by Electronics Inc. will have an impact on the community.

It is your task to write a press release for the local paper, *The Freemont Star.* Keep in mind that you write as a company spokesperson.

Quarterly Summary Report of Job-Absence Rates: Sweet Grain Inc.

| | JUNE 30, 19XX | | | | | | SEPTEMBER 30, 19XX | | | | | |
| | Hourly | | Salaried | | Total | | Hourly | | Salaried | | Total | |
	1–4 Total	All Total	1–4 Total	All Total	1–4 Total	All Total	1–4 Total	All Total	1–4 Total	All Total	1–4 Total	All Total
Bedford	2.7%	2.7%	1.6%	8.4%	2.3%	4.8%	2.9%	2.9%	2.4%	6.9%	2.7%	4.3%
Clinton	4.3	7.0	1.3	2.2	3.7	6.1	4.8	7.4	1.2	1.9	4.1	6.4
Cleveland	3.0	5.3	1.1	1.7	2.6	4.4	2.9	4.9	1.2	1.8	2.5	4.1
Charleston	2.4	5.9	1.3	3.2	2.0	4.9	2.1	7.1	1.2	3.0	1.8	5.6
Dallas	4.1	7.7	1.1	2.0	3.0	5.7	4.3	7.5	1.0	1.9	3.0	5.4
Danville	2.1	3.4	1.1	1.2	1.9	2.9	2.2	3.7	1.0	1.2	2.0	3.1
Frankfort	3.3	5.0	2.3	5.3	2.9	5.1	3.6	5.8	1.8	3.8	2.9	5.0
Jackson	1.1	2.7	1.6	1.8	1.2	2.5	1.2	2.8	1.6	2.2	1.3	2.7
Lexington	1.2	1.5	2.1	2.4	1.5	1.8	1.2	1.6	1.9	2.2	1.4	1.8
Milford	3.3	6.3	1.3	3.0	2.8	5.4	3.4	6.7	1.4	3.0	2.9	5.6
Oakbrook	2.3	2.9	1.2	1.2	2.1	2.6	2.0	2.5	1.7	1.7	2.0	2.3
Winston	1.3	1.9	1.0	1.0	1.2	1.7	2.1	3.3	.8	.8	1.9	2.8
Rockford	2.9	5.0	2.1	3.4	2.7	4.7	2.9	5.3	1.9	3.1	2.7	4.8
Salem	2.9	5.6	1.5	2.4	2.6	4.9	2.8	5.7	1.3	2.3	2.4	4.8
Seattle	3.6	6.4	1.4	1.7	3.0	5.1	3.7	6.6	1.1	1.3	3.0	5.2
National Average* (B.N.A.)					1.8						1.8	

* The criteria of the Bureau of National Affairs (B.N.A.) for measuring job-absence averages is to count *only the first four days of any unscheduled* absences. Therefore, the B.N.A. national average should be compared *only* to "1–4 Total" rates in the total section for each quarterly period. (The "all total" rates reflect all absences.)

Case 6   SWEET GRAIN INC.

You work in the personnel department of Sweet Grain Inc. It is your job to regularly evaluate absentee rates at your various plants. The company has 15 plants across the United States. Every three months the plants send in absentee data for hourly and salaried employees. The company is concerned about unscheduled absences because they disrupt production and cost the company a considerable amount of money every year.

DECEMBER 31, 19XX						MARCH 31, 19XX					
Hourly		Salaried		Total		Hourly		Salaried		Total	
1–4 Total	All Total	1–4 Total	All Total	1–4 Total	All Total	1–4 Total	All Total	1–4 Total	All Total	1–4 Total	All Total
3.0%	3.0%	2.0%	5.4%	2.6%	3.9%	3.2%	3.2%	.4%	.4%	2.2%	2.2%
4.9	7.4	1.2	2.0	4.2	6.4	4.4	6.7	1.1	2.6	3.8	5.9
3.0	4.9	1.1	1.6	2.5	4.1	2.8	4.3	1.0	1.2	2.3	3.5
1.9	7.7	1.2	3.4	1.7	6.2	.7	6.5	.8	2.5	.7	5.2
4.4	7.0	1.3	2.0	3.2	5.0	1.6	2.3	1.1	7.7	1.4	4.4
2.2	3.7	1.0	1.2	2.0	3.1	2.3	2.3	1.4	1.4	2.1	2.7
3.3	5.0	1.8	3.8	2.9	4.6	3.3	5.1	1.6	1.6	2.8	4.0
1.1	2.7	1.6	2.3	1.2	2.6	1.0	2.4	1.6	1.9	1.1	2.3
1.2	1.8	1.8	2.6	1.4	2.0	.8	2.5	2.1	5.3	1.1	3.3
3.5	7.1	1.3	2.7	2.9	5.9	3.5	8.0	1.3	3.4	3.0	6.9
2.1	2.8	1.8	2.0	2.0	2.5	2.7	2.8	2.0	6.5	2.6	3.7
2.3	3.6	.7	.7	2.0	3.0	1.4	1.4	1.0	3.9	1.4	1.9
2.9	5.2	1.9	3.4	2.7	4.8	2.1	2.9	1.6	1.8	2.0	2.6
2.8	5.9	1.3	2.1	2.5	5.0	2.2	4.4	1.4	3.1	2.0	4.1
3.8	6.7	1.1	1.2	3.1	5.2	3.6	5.8	1.6	1.6	3.0	4.6
				1.9						N/A	

You have organized the data for the past four periods in the table entitled *Quarterly Summary Report of Job-Absence Rates* (see pages 432–433). Now you must evaluate the information and write a report to Frank McDonald, Vice President for Personnel.

Case 7   ANNA REED MUSEUM

You have just left a stormy meeting with the trustees of the Anna Reed Museum. Last spring the Friends of the Arts in your town approached you with a request to schedule an exhibit of the young avant-garde artist René Tremblay. The contacts with the artist were made, and he seemed to be excited about the possibility of showing his multimedia exhibit of man's environment in the past, the present, and the future. The past and future environment components were safe enough, but the present posed a problem. Mr. Tremblay was planning to include live members of a street gang in the exhibit. It took a lot of effort to convince him to drop that idea. But one problem remained. Mr. Tremblay has insisted on showing about 20 photographs of the city's worst tenements. The photographs include revolting scenes from the slums. Each photograph is carefully labeled with the name of the owner. Some of the owners are prominent business people in town. They have given much money to local charities and the arts. During the past year, in fact, they gave about

Green Thumb Inc., June 19XX

| Expense Classification | Current Month | | | |
	Plan	Actual	Actual Better (Worse) Plan	Better (Worse)
Salaried Payroll	$ 5,092	$ 5,463	$ (371)	(7.29)%
Illness–Accident	2,500	2,551	(51)	(2.04)
Income Security, Full	0	0	0	.00
Income Security, Partial	334	728	(394)	(117.96)
Miscellaneous Tools and Supplies	43	4	39	90.70
Sundry Expense	447	46	401	89.71
Workman's Comp Insurance	3,980	2,473	1,507	37.86
Workman's Comp Supplement	282	276	6	2.13
Employee Activity—Training	3,843	3,039	804	20.92
Personnel Telephone	34	43	(9)	(26.47)
Travel	668	74	594	88.92
Uniforms—Laundry	150	12	138	92.00
Fringe Benefits	2,053	2,036	17	.83
Total	19,426	16,745	2,681	13.80

$100,000 to help with the remodeling of the museum. Without their generous help the museum would not have been able to finance the needed structural work.

You have talked to the artist, but he insists that the names are an integral part of his work and that any attempt to influence him to leave off the names infringes on his right as an artist. He has made it clear that he will not change his mind. The board of trustees, on the other hand, argues that the exhibit will alienate museum goers, not to mention the business leaders. The trustees are worried about a libel suit. They want the exhibit canceled.

You must decide what to do . Will you go on with the exhibit or will you cancel it? You are torn because you can see the viewpoints of both sides. In an effort to be as objective as possible, you draw up lists for and against each side. If you decide to hold the exhibit, write to the trustees explaining your decision. If you decide to cancel the exhibit, write to the artist explaining your decision. In order to avoid similar problems in the future, draw up guidelines.

Case 8   GREEN THUMB INC.

You have just received the figures for last month's manufacturing personnel expenses. As production manager of Green Thumb Inc. you must analyze and summarize the information in a report to Ross Klinger, your supervisor. You are aware that the organization of the information in a table does not have the same impact as a graph. You, therefore, decide also to present the data in a graph.

	Year-to-Date		
Plan	Actual	Actual Better (Worse) Plan	Better (Worse)
$ 61,104	$ 64,086	$ (2,982)	(4.88)%
30,000	36,462	(6,462)	(21.54)
0	0	0	.00
4,000	5,456	(1,456)	(36.40)
500	521	(21)	(4.20)
6,350	2,390	3,960	62.36
47,760	39,781	7,979	16.71
3,386	1,548	1,838	54.28
27,900	21,609	6,291	22.55
400	393	7	1.75
5,000	2,362	2,638	52.76
1,800	1,851	(51)	(2.83)
23,636	23,817	(181)	(.77)
211,836	200,276	11,560	5.46

Case 9   GAHR GLASS INC.

As EEO officer it is your job to regularly analyze the composition of the workforce at Gahr Glass Inc. Since you were hired five years ago, you have actively tried to recruit women and minorities. Your company is committed to affirmative action, but in spite of all your efforts you have not been very successful. You have just assembled the data for the quarterly status report, potential promotions, and applications received. You are ready to analyze the information and examine the possibilities of hiring more women for management positions. Address your report to Robert Galyen, President of Gahr Glass Inc.

Gahr Glass Inc.
Period Ending August 31, 19XX
Quarterly Status Report

| | All Employees | | | Minority Employees | | | |
| | | | | Male | | | |
EEO-1 Job Category	Total	Male	Female	B	A/A	A/I	S/A
Officials and Managers	9	9					
Salaried Foremen	9	7	2				
Professionals	4	3	1				
Technicians	10	4	6				
Sales Works	2	2					
Office and Clerical	9	2	7				
Craftsmen (skilled)	67	65	2			1	
Operatives (semiskilled)	36	27	9				
Laborers (unskilled)	122	48	74		1		
Service Workers	4	3	1				
Total	272	170	102		1	1	

B—Black.
A/A—Asian American.
A/I—American Indian.
S/A—Spanish American.

Case 10 DILUTED OIL COMPANY

As a junior executive in charge of site selection for the Diluted Oil Company, you must select one of three sites that have been recommended for a new service station in Utopia, California. You have collected the following information:

Hill Avenue and 37th Street: This is a commercial area. The lot is 150 × 100 feet. It is a corner location. The lot costs $25,000. Traffic count per day is 4,200 cars. Distance from the nearest company station is 3.1 miles.

311 Belmont Street: This is a commercial area. Lot size is 200 × 100 feet. It is a noncorner location. It costs $24,000. Traffic count is 9,000 per day. Distance from the nearest company station is 3.9 miles.

Avenue at Independence Street: This is a commercial area. The lot size is 150 × 150 feet. It is a corner location, and the site costs $30,000. Traffic count per day is 6,000 cars. The distance from the nearest company station is 2.1 miles.

Minority Employees				Job Openings to Fill Through:		Female		
Female					New	Current	Available	
B	A/A	A/I	S/A	Recalls	Hires	(%)	(%)	Goals
							12.6	1
						22.2	14.8	
						25.0	62.7	1
						60.0	25.3	
							8.2	
	1					77.8	70.9	
						3.0	14.9	2
						25.0	24.7	
1				3		60.7	40.5	
						25.0	69.0	1
1	1					37.5	43.0	5

Gahr Glass Inc.
Current Employee Profile

EEO-1 Category	Current Period Data as of September 1, 19XX										
	All Employees			Minority Employees							
				Male				Female			
	Total	M	F	B	A/A	A/I	S/A	B	A/A	A/I	S/A
Officials and Managers	9	9									
Salaried Foremen	9	7	2								
Professionals	4	3	1								
Technicians	10	4	6								
Sales Workers	2	2									
Office and Clerical	9	2	7						1		
Craftsmen (skilled)	67	65	2			1					
Operatives (semiskilled)	36	27	9								
Laborers (unskilled)	122	48	74		1			1			
Service Workers	4	3	1								
Total	272	170	102		1	1		1	1		

All of these sites have relatively the same amount of competition in the immediate area. Each has a competitive station within five blocks. Your task is to analyze the data and rank the sites. Present your analysis and recommendation in a memorandum report to Dennis Maine. Use deductive organization and include an appropriate table.

Case 11   TEXAS BIG TIME OIL EQUIPMENT COMPANY

As assistant to the personnel director of international affairs at Texas Big Time Oil Equipment Company, write a memo to the director evaluating and ranking the three finalists for an opening in Nigeria. Twenty people applied for the job.

Timetable Period from September 1, 19XX to February 28, 19XX							
Percentage		**Job Openings**					
		* Anticipated Vacancies	To Be Filled by:				
M	**F**		**Recalls**	**Transfer**	**Promotions**	**New Hires**	**Total**
100							
78	22	1			1		1
75	25	1			1		1
40	60	1			1		1
100							
22	78	2			2		2
97	3	2			2		2
75	25	3			3		3
39	61	3	3				3
75	25						
62	38	13	3		10		13

* In the absence of other bona fide criteria, the preceding year's record of activity should be used.

After examination of the resumés and references, three are left for the final selection process.

Nigeria, the largest country in Africa, has many tribes. There are 84 million people who speak 250 different dialects. English is the language of business and commerce and the basis for communication between the tribes.

Job Description: Texas Big Time Oil Equipment Company looks for a Director of Sales in Nigeria. The major business for the company comes from government contracts. The Director of Sales will have to deal with government officials at many different levels and at many stages of negotiations. The person hired for the job will be in charge of making initial contacts. The director will have public-relations responsibilities to develop a positive company image. Social contacts and interactions will be important. The company is looking for someone with international experience, preferably in sales.

Gahr Glass Inc.
Applicant Flow Summary

Job Categories	Total Applicant Flow		
	Total Applicants	Total Male	Total Female
Officials and Managers	5	5	
Professionals			
Technicians			
Sales Workers			
Office and Clerical	15		15
Craftsmen (skilled)	2	2	
Operatives (semiskilled)			
Laborers (unskilled)	208*	150	58
Service Workers			
Total	230	157	73

* Includes applications for temporary summer positions.

The finalists are Mohamed Aljanabi, Susan Gessler, and Okie Johnson.

Mohamed Aljanabi is from Kenya. He is married and 30 years old. He has four years of experience in the United States and Kenya selling agricultural equipment on established routes. He speaks French and English. His references say that he gets along well with people. He is a hard worker along established lines.

Susan Gessler is from the United States. She is 32 years old, is single, and has an M.B.A. She has worked for six years for U.S. banks on international loans. She has frequently dealt with government officials from Africa. Susan Gessler speaks English, French, and some Arabic. Her references say that she is very ambitious. She works hard and expects her subordinates to work hard as well. She is fair and well respected.

Okie Johnson is from the United States. He is 40 years old, is married, and has two teenaged children. He has a B.S. He worked for 10 years as a petroleum engineer in Texas. He was in Saudi Arabia for two months eight years ago. He has no sales experience. His references say that he is congenial and easygoing. He gets along well with people.

Minority-Group Applicant Flow										
Male				Female				Percentage		
B	A/A	A/I	S/A	B	A/A	A/I	S/A	Minority	Female
			1					20	
									100
1	1		1					1.4	27.9
1	1		2					1.7	31.7

Case 12   METROLINE (A)

Your business, Metroline, has decided to centralize all word-processing activities into a word-processing center. Ten secretaries will work in the center. Some of these secretaries have been with the company for many years, and they are not very excited about the change.

The center will have ten word processors, three microcomputers, four printers, and two copying machines. One of the copying machines has the capability to enlarge or reduce documents. Managers have three options in submitting their work. They can submit a handwritten or typed copy, they can submit a tape, or they can dictate their material over the phone.

The company needs someone to supervise the center. The supervisor will report to the vice president of personnel. You are looking for someone who can develop guidelines and procedures for the center. The person must be familiar with modern office equipment. In addition the supervisor must have managerial and supervisory skills. The supervisor will have to coordinate and schedule the work for each secretary.

It is your task to write a job description for the position.

Case 13   METROLINE (B)

Assume you have written the job description requested in Case 12. You received a number of applications and have selected three finalists. Analyze the credentials of the three finalists and rank them in order of preference. Send your report to Caleb Woodyard, Vice President of Personnel. Following are qualifications of the finalists.

> Joanne Right: She is 22 years old and married with two children. She graduated with an office administration major from Central University. She has a GPA of 3.7. During her last year she had an internship in office administration with a large company. Mrs. Right is familiar with modern office equipment. Her recommendations say she is organized, hard working, and well liked.

> Anne Hanson: Anne Hanson is 30 years old and single. She attended two years of college, where she took mostly secretarial courses. She has worked as a secretary for ten years, the last five at Metroline. For the last three years she has used a word processor. She is a conscientious worker. References say she is easygoing and gets along well with coworkers. She is an excellent typist and secretary.

> Robert Green: Mr. Green is 26 years old. He has a degree in management and has gone through a management-training program for an office-equipment firm. He did very well in his training program. Mr. Green is an excellent programmer. References say that he has good technical skills. He is hard working, and people respect him.

Case 14   PROFESSOR HINSBERGER

You are Professor Hinsberger's assistant. Professor Hinsberger teaches business communication. This semester he decided to give all his students a writing-apprehension test at the beginning of the semester. The test was developed by Daly and Miller. Scores for the test range from 26 (low writing apprehension) to 130 (high apprehension). The test asks students to indicate whether they strongly agree, agree, are uncertain, disagree, or strongly disagree with statements about writing. Some examples of these statements are "I avoid writing," "I look forward to writing," and "I am afraid of writing when I know I will be evaluated."

Professor Hinsberger hopes that the results will help him in adapting the course material to the specific needs of the students.

You have supervised the test for two classes and calculated the scores for each student. You have arranged the data in the accompanying table. Now you are ready to evaluate the findings. Present the results and your analysis in a memo to Dr. Hinsberger.

Results of Writing Apprehension Test

Scores	Section 1		Section 2		Total	
	F	M	F	M	F	M
52	1				1	
55				1		1
56	1				1	
57		1	1	1	1	2
58				1		1
59	1	1	1	2	2	3
61		1		1		2
64				1		1
66	1		1		2	
68		2	1	1	1	3
69	2				2	
71				1		1
73				1		1
74		1				1
75	1				1	
76	1	1		1	1	2
78		1				1
79				1		1
81		1	1		1	1
82	1	2			1	2
84		1				1
85		1				1
86				2		2
89			2		2	
91		1				1
94				1		1

Case 15   SECURITY SYSTEMS

Mr. Roberts is the owner of an established jewelry store in Rock City. His store is located in the downtown area. Even though a shopping mall was built on the outskirts of town three years ago, the downtown area has continued to do well. At this point Mr. Roberts does not intend to move the store to the mall. Many of his customers work downtown. There is plenty of parking for shoppers.

During the past six months, three stores in the area were robbed, one during the day, two at night. In all three cases the robbers were apprehended. Mr. Roberts is beginning to be concerned and would like to investigate up-to-date security systems to prevent break-ins.

Mr. Roberts has contacted you for information on security systems that are appropriate for smaller retail establishments. He wants information about cost, ease of installation and operation, and legal ramifications. Prepare a report with your analysis and recommendations and direct it to Mr. Roberts.

Case 16   PREVENTION OF SHOPLIFTING

Eileen Ni, the manager of Mede's Department Store, has called a meeting to discuss last year's sales and profits. Although profits have increased, she is very concerned about shoplifting. Last year shoplifting amounted to about 5 percent of sales. However, this figure includes only thefts by people who were caught. Ms. Ni estimates that the actual figure may be 10 percent of sales. She bases her estimate on talks with managers from other stores and information published in the press.

Mede's has not upgraded its theft prevention program in several years, and Ms. Ni thinks it is time to explore new approaches to prevent shoplifting. In the meeting she asks you to examine the latest developments in preventing shoplifting. She is particularly interested in getting information on types of programs and devices, costs, complexity of equipment, and legal and ethical ramifications. She wants your report in three weeks.

Case 17   PARKING ON CAMPUS

You are the assistant to the Director of Parking Services. Everyone complains about parking. Students argue they should have the same rights as faculty. Faculty want more reserved spaces closer to the buildings where they have their offices. Write a report assessing the situation on your campus. Examine possible alternatives for improvement and make your recommendations. Direct your report to the Director of Parking.

Case 18   FITNESS TRENDS

Malinda Ringer is convinced that there is money in the fitness business. With everyone exercising and counting calories, she thinks a fitness studio would be very profitable. When she discusses her idea with friends, they caution that the fitness craze is over and that she might lose money going into this type of business now. Malinda comes to you, a small business consultant, for advice.

Prepare a report for Malinda in which you examine trends in the fitness industry. Analyze the opportunities for future growth and direction of the industry.

Case 19   COMMUNITY DEVELOPMENT

You are working for the Board of Realtors in your town. Every year the board prepares a profile of the community and analyzes the impact of changes in the community on construction and housing. Your boss has asked you to put together this year's report.

Address the growth in the community, family demographics, business developments, and the patterns of real estate sales during the past year. Close your report with an outlook for the housing market in your city.

Case 20   ACCOUNTING-FIRM ADVERTISEMENT

Advertising by accounting firms has been legal for several years, but many of them still shy away from it. At Garret & Morgan, the senior Mr. Morgan retired last month. His son, also a member of the firm, believes that advertising could help to bring in more business. He has contacted you for guidance in making a decision.

Prepare a report in which you examine the status of advertising by account-ants. Present legal and ethical ramifications. Also, research the percentage of accounting firms that advertise and how effective their advertising is. Finally, make recommendations on whether Garret & Morgan should advertise.

Case 21   ACCOUNTING SOCIETY

Prepare a report for the Accounting Society at your university about beginning jobs in accounting with large accounting firms. Cover aspects such as salary, hours, fringe benefits, and promotion.

Case 22   NATIONAL CEREAL INC.

Your company, National Cereal Inc., is headquartered in Chicago. The com-pany has plants in Memphis, Tennessee; Marion, Ohio; Rockford, Illinois; and Jackson, Mississippi. Currently the company is considering building or acquir-ing a plant in Dallas, Phoenix, Seattle, or Philadelphia. In order to make a good decision Clayton Shriver, who is in charge of the project, has asked you to prepare a report comparing the four cities in the following areas: unem-ployment, cost of living, unionization, transportation, cultural activities, schools, and quality of life. Direct your report to Clayton Shriver.

Case 23   WOMEN IN BUSINESS

You are the president of Women in Business in your community. Your group is quite concerned about the image of women in print advertising. You have decided to examine the issue in more detail and prepare a report to be sent to major advertising firms and corporations. You will select advertisements from at least five magazines published during the past year and compare them with ads from five years ago.

Case 24   INTERNATIONAL ADVERTISING

You work for an advertising company that designs ads for the international market. International advertising is a sensitive area, and it is important that you understand the culture in which you market a product. Religion, values, and traditions influence what is acceptable and not acceptable. Your boss has asked you to examine the image of women in advertisements in several countries. (You will find copies of international magazines and newspapers in your library.) Select ads from at least three different foreign magazines and compare the way women are portrayed in the ads.

Case 25   LINDGREEN INSURANCE

You work for Lindgreen Insurance. Lindgreen Insurance employs 3,000 people at headquarters. It has branch offices in every state. A number of the corporate employees have requested that the company implement a daycare center for the children of the employees. Management is aware that daycare is a problem in town. There are not enough places, and the quality of care varies. Charles Geigner, Vice President of Personnel, has asked you to examine the possibilities of corporate daycare and feasible alternatives. You should examine aspects of cost, space, stockholder reaction, branch-office reaction, and impact on employee satisfaction.

Case 26   QUALITY CIRCLES

Your company produces parts for automobiles. A few months ago your boss, manager in charge of production, visited similar companies in Japan. He came back all excited about quality circles, and he would like to implement quality circles in your plant. He has asked you to research the topic in more detail before he approaches upper management with the idea. In your report you should examine quality circles in view of Japanese culture. You should address the changes that would have to be made to use quality circles successfully in the United States.

Case 27   # SUCCESSFUL WOMEN

Over half of all women are in the workforce. Some people argue that women have made rapid progress in advancement, while others maintain there has been very little progress. Research the progress of women into managerial and executive positions. Develop a profile of successful women and make recommendations to women business majors on how to prepare for climbing the corporate ladder.

Case 28   # CAFETERIA-FOOD STUDY (A)

For one week, record the food served in the cafeteria of your dorm. Document variety, overall quality, freshness, temperature, and appearance. Assemble your findings in a table and discuss them. Present your results and recommendations for improvement to the cafeteria manager.

Case 29   # CAFETERIA-FOOD STUDY (B)

The President for Student Affairs has received a number of complaints about the food in the cafeteria, and he has asked you to research the problem. Prepare a questionnaire to evaluate attitudes of students about cafeteria food. Address issues of waiting time, variety of food, temperature, freshness, and quality of service. Because you want to know whether there are differences in the opinions of women and men, freshmen and seniors, you will need to ask for selected personal demographics. Prepare a report to be sent to the cafeteria manager.

Case 30   # WORLD BANK

You are an employee of the World Bank. During the past few years many developing countries have run into problems with repaying the loans they took from private banks and the International Monetary Fund. The inability to pay the loans back as scheduled is threatening the stability of banks in industrialized countries. In addition, some countries with outstanding loans have threatened to stop payment completely. You are asked to prepare a report on the loan status of selected countries (your choice). You should examine where the money was borrowed and how it was used. You will also have to analyze the countries' past record of paying back debts, the attitude of the countries toward the debts, and the outlook for the future. Write your report to the President of the World Bank.

Case 31   CLUBS ON CAMPUS

Incoming freshmen are confused by the variety of extracurricular activities in your Business College. You remember that it took you quite some time to become familiar with the variety of clubs. Now that you are on the committee representing all the clubs in the college, you have decided to do something about the problem. You will prepare a pamphlet for all incoming freshmen. The pamphlet will have the following information on each club:

- Name of club
- Purpose of the club
- Names of officers
- Dues
- Frequency of meetings
- Sample program titles for previous year

Case 32   KISSINGER AND THOMPSON

Kissinger and Thompson is a very successful law firm. During the past ten years the office has grown tremendously, and the number of clients has doubled. The firm started out with two secretaries. As time went on, two more were hired. Lynn Hayes has been in the office for ten years. She works hard, but she is not open to changes. She likes her typewriter and manual files and considers computers and word processors a waste of money. Jackie Meldahl has been with the firm for five years, Rose Parkins for three years, and Sue Johnsen for one year. Only Sue has been exposed to modern office technology. At a professional seminar Mr. Kissinger talked to a number of colleagues and friends, all of whom are into computers. The presenter in one session emphasized the importance of hiring an office manager so that lawyers can concentrate on their legal work rather than on administrative details. The partners discussed the matter and decided to hire Sarah Grady as office manager. Sarah is an office-administration graduate. She had hoped to manage a modern office, but she thought things over and decided to accept the challenge of modernizing Kissinger and Thompson. She would be able to select equipment and design the entire office.

Imagine you are Sarah. After you have thoroughly familiarized yourself with current procedures, you decide to write an equipment proposal for approval by the partners. You would like to get micros for correspondence, accounting, and filing. You will also need a copying machine. You will have to evaluate appropriate software and hardware for cost and usefulness in a law firm. Address your proposal to the partners.

Case 33   BRADY INVESTMENTS

You are an investment consultant with Brady Investments. One of the many sources you use in making investment decisions is annual reports. In the past you have found that many of your clients barely look at the financial information in the annual reports. Particularly, older clients tend to read the letter to the stockholders and the graphs. You have decided to examine how well this material reflects the financial performance of the company. You will examine at least four annual reports, two of companies that were profitable last year and two from companies that had losses. Analyze the letter to stockholders and the visual aids in view of the financial performance. How did the companies present bad news and good news? What was the focal point of the letter to the stockholders? Address the report to John Brady, the president of Brady Investments. You believe that the information will be useful for all investment consultants.

Case 34   SAVINGS AND LOAN ASSOCIATION

For many years home buyers would get a fixed-rate mortgage when purchasing a home. The mortgage used to be for 30 years. As inflation increased and interest rates rose, mortgage rates changed. Homeowners now face a variety of options. They can take mortgages with variable interest rates, increasing interest rates, fixed rates, and several others. You work for a savings and loan association and are in charge of the department for mortgages. Because there are so many options and the whole area is very confusing, you think it is important for all loan officers to be familiar with the options home buyers have. Write a report discussing the available options and evaluate the advantages and disadvantages of each.

Case 35   BUSINESS CLIMATES OVERSEAS

Your company is considering going international. Before any detailed discussion, the president has asked you to prepare a report on the business climate in the foreign country. She wants you to examine the areas of government regulation of business, management practices, marketing strategies, transportation, and value structures as they influence your product.

Some suggestions for products and countries:

1. Cosmetics Unlimited is considering entering the Middle East.
2. Pleasure Burger is considering entering Italy.
3. Cornchunks is considering introducing its breakfast cereal in France.
4. Hotplate Company is considering entering the Japanese market with household appliances.
5. Tractor Company is considering entering India with agricultural machines.
6. Oklahoma Oil is considering entering China with its petroleum-extraction equipment.

Case 36   GUNNING FOG INDEX

Your grandmother just bought a new car, a Mercedes. She wants to make certain that she gets the appropriate insurance policy for the car. Because you studied business communication and finance in college, she asks you to examine the policy with her. As you read the policy, you become very frustrated. The insurance jargon is difficult to understand, and the small print is almost impossible to read. After you have struggled through, you decide to write to the insurance company.

You determine the readability level of the policy. You examine two random samples and calculate the Gunning Fog Index. Of course, you are aware that other factors than the ones the index measures influence the readability also. You evaluate layout, print, etc. Tell the insurance firm what you found, and make recommendations for improvement. (You can do the same with policies for health insurance, home insurance, or any other policy.)

Case 37   SAMPLE INVESTMENT PORTFOLIOS

You work for an investment firm. You supervise investment counselors who have been recently hired. From experience you know that new counselors can be overwhelmed by the number of combinations and portfolio options in investments. You have talked to your boss about putting together sample portfolios that could be used as guides by the new people. Your boss thinks the idea is very good, and he encourages you to go ahead.

You know that personal preferences and risk attitudes influence investment decisions. In the initial interview with a client the counselor can establish a profile of the client concerning risk and investment goals. Once the profile is established, the counselor can refer to the sample portfolio. You are convinced that sample portfolios would be a great help.

Develop three sample portfolios (each for $200,000). In your report you must explain how to use the samples. They are guidelines rather than investment blueprints. And they do have to be updated regularly. In your report you must address various types of investment possibilities, return on equity, purchasing price, and tax implications. Distribute your report to the people you supervise and to your boss.

INDEX